SINGING THROUGH FIRE

SINGING THROUGH FIRE

A Memoir

FINDING SURPRISING JOY IN
LIFE'S DARKEST TRIALS

Lara Silverman, J.D.

Isaiah 4320 Press
SORROWFUL BUT REJOICING

SINGING THROUGH FIRE

Copyright © 2025 by Lara Silverman. All rights reserved.

No part of this book may be reproduced, stored in a retrieval system, or transmitted in any form or by any means—electronic, mechanical, photocopying, recording, or otherwise—without the prior written permission of the author, except for brief quotations used in reviews or scholarly works. This is a work of nonfiction, but some names and identifying details have been changed to protect the privacy of individuals and institutions. Any resemblance to actual persons, living or dead, or entities, is purely coincidental.

Published by
Isaiah 4320 Press

Paperback ISBN: 979-8-218-71499-4
E-book ISBN: 979-8-218-71500-7

Cover design and interior formatting by DAMONZA
Photographs provided by Lara Silverman. All rights reserved.
Printed in the United States of America
First Edition, 2025

Unless otherwise noted, all Scripture quotations are taken from the Holy Bible, New International Version®, NIV®. Copyright ©1973, 1978, 1984, 2011 by Biblica, Inc.™ Used by permission. All rights reserved worldwide.

Scripture quotations marked NLT are taken from the Holy Bible, New Living Translation. Copyright ©1996, 2004, 2015 by Tyndale House Foundation. Used by permission of Tyndale House Publishers, Inc., Carol Stream, Illinois 60188. All rights reserved.

Scripture quotations marked NKJV are taken from the New King James Version®. Copyright © 1982 by Thomas Nelson, Inc. Used by permission. All rights reserved.

Scripture quotations marked KJV are from the Holy Bible, King James Version, which is in the public domain.

For rights and permissions, please contact larapalanjian@gmail.com.

For Gracy,
who never stopped burning the midnight oil

"If just one more life is saved because of my suffering, I am happy to go through it again."

- Matthew John S.,
2016 Sermon in Fond Doux, Haiti

Contents

Author's Introduction................................ xi
Prologue.. 1

Act One *5*

1: Everything Going As Planned...................... 6
2: The Word With "Sin" In It....................... 15
3: The Dream Job.................................. 21
4: Down The Toilet................................ 25
5: The Bed.. 33
6: The Promise.................................... 44
7: The White Coat Musical......................... 49
8: Kid Gloves Off................................. 57
9: Matthew John................................... 62
10: Deeper Still.................................. 71
11: The Jaw & Jericho............................. 79
12: Poodles Have It Better........................ 87
13: Wait, What?................................... 91
14: The Dream..................................... 95

Act Two *103*

15: The Cross-examination........................ 104
16: Not Funny.................................... 115
17: The Bag of Basic Blessings................... 128
18: My Funny Valentine........................... 138
19: Jekyll & Hyde................................ 148
20: The Rainbow.................................. 153
21: The Plot Thickens............................ 156
22: On the Brink................................. 160
23: The Philippians 1 Dilemma.................... 164
24: On the Cheek................................. 168

25: The 19 Day Ban 178
26: Lion Number Two Needs A Haircut 184
27: Joy In Grief 188
28: From Test to Testimony 191
29: Victorian Fantasies........................ 197
30: Finally!.................................. 208
31: The Box in a Box 216
32: God's Wild Ride........................... 227
33: Sick High Glamor 236
34: Streams In the Desert 242
35: The Meltdown.............................. 249
36: If Just One More Life Is Saved 255
37: How Great Thou Art 265
38: Miracle of Miracles!...................... 270

Act Three.................................279
   39: Rejoice! 280
   40: The Love Story Goes Marital 291
   41: Honeymoon's Over 301
   42: The Caged Bird Sings Indeed 310
   43: Marie & Louis 317
   44: The Wardrobe 325
   45: The Silverman Show..................... 332
   46: Jazz & Joy 339
   47: The Night Before Christmas............. 350
   48: Stayin' Alive.......................... 354
   49: Can't Get a Break 360
   50: A Musical Love Story................... 370
   51: The Days Are Evil 377
   52: Normal 383
   53: Hope 391
   54: Hi, Doc?............................... 395
   55: The "H" Word........................... 399

Act Four *407*
    56: The Fruit of the Vine 408
    57: Don't Let Death Scare You. 416
    58: Because He Lives 422
    59: Kingdom Economics: Sorrow In, Joy Out 429
    60: Glory 436
    61: Empty 440
    62: God Always Writes the Best Stories 449
    63: The Email. 455
    64: The Story Is Not Over 462

Epilogue. 476
Appendix One: Pictures 478
Appendix Two: Sermon Collections 495
Acknowledgments 496
About the Author. 497

Author's Introduction

A wise gentleman once said to me, "God always writes the best stories." Let me tell you one now.

I wrote this memoir for one reason only. In August 2024, I felt an inner prompting from God to share the true story of two Christians navigating faith in the face of suffering. What you find in these pages is the unvarnished truth—honest and raw—because I value authenticity as deeply as I delight in playing pretend on stage. I'm an actor, after all, and that's why I structured this memoir in four acts—to help you better understand the unfolding drama of this eight-year journey. Sarcasm fuels me, and comedy sustains me. You've been warned. (Please know I wield both without any intent to offend.)

I confess that while writing, I felt sharply hypocritical at times, considering the long stretches when I wrestled with great anger. I ask for your grace as you journey with me through the tension of faith and doubt that shaped this real-life story.

Similarly, some of the spiritual experiences shared in these pages may seem exceptionally strange. I simply ask that you read with an open heart, allowing space for mystery and remembering that God often works in ways we don't expect. For readers outside the Christian faith, this memoir offers a meaningful glimpse into how Christians wrestle with the concept of suffering. Please note that the names of certain people and institutions have been changed.

Just one more word before the story begins. If you've grieved the loss of anything—be it a loved one, or any tender or towering dream such as your health, career, love, or the simple desire to be happy; if you've known the ache of chronic pain, the sting of loneliness, or the quiet fear of death; if you've grieved the seeming futility of any kind of emotional or physical pain as you move through the highs and lows of singleness, marriage, or life in general—*then I believe there is a nugget of truth and hope for you somewhere in these pages.*

May God use this work for His glory and purposes, whatever they may be.

Lara Silverman, J.D.

Prologue

February 10, 2023

What do you do if you fall in love right before you die?
I don't know.
I *do* know that when misery strikes, its timing is often impeccable.

Indeed, today, it strikes with the precision of a scalpel.

"But you can't die now. Everything is about to change next month."

The words claw their way out of me.

Raw. Desperate. Comically futile.

Yet they taste like ash—bitter, burning.

I lie flat on my back in bed, blinking back tears, staring at the blank ceiling of my dimly lit bedroom. My mind is a freight train, barreling through thoughts I can't control.

He sits across from me in the corner like a shadow, his back stiff against his chair. He silently meditates, his left hand resting on his chest, his eyes fixed to the floor as though the weight of his own thoughts might anchor him there.

The silence feels like an accusation. Heavy. Suffocating.

We're just one month away from the biggest day of our lives, but hope is now a cruel illusion—like a key that fits but refuses to turn.

Minutes pass.

Finally, he speaks.

"I know."

Two words.

Flat. Resigned. Final.

Silence again. The kind that stretches wide. The kind reserved for elevators after someone sneezes, but no one says "bless you."

I finally shift my gaze from the ceiling and look directly at him.

And then I see it—a single tear slipping down his left cheek. His empty gaze meets mine, communicating a vast, endless void he's lost in.

"I don't know why I'm not a match for this last clinical trial," he says. "I was so close. But it's too late now."

He pauses.

Then—"I can't fight with a dead end."

His words land between us like a deflated balloon—useless, lifeless, yet refusing to disappear.

A respectable person might let this moment breathe.

I, regrettably, am not that person.

Before I know it, a dam breaks within me. "Well, either you're going to die or I'm going to die. Fantastic."

The sarcasm rolls off my tongue like cheap wine, bitter and unsatisfying. *Lara, reel it in*, I tell myself. *Take a deep breath.*

I inhale sharply, then try again, softer. "What are we going to do now?"

He shifts uncomfortably in his chair, tugging at the tubes tangled with the chemo pump around his chest, adjusting them out of habit.

"I don't know."

I try again, as if pleading for an answer I'll never get. "My whole life I thought God wants to bless us, not torture us. What am I missing? That's not too much to ask of a loving God, right? God created logic and reason. He should play by His own rules, shouldn't He?"

Silence.

Thirty seconds later, he exhales hard. "A lot of times, we just can't understand what God is doing on this side of eternity. His ways and thoughts are higher than our ways, right?"

I don't answer.

I don't want to.

"But," he adds, "when we do get to see cool glimpses of His redemption on this side, those stories help us trust Him in situations where we don't get an explanation here." His voice is now steady, firm. As if he's trying to convince me. Himself. Both of us.

It's no use. The cold weight of doubt presses into me. *Don't cry.*

My voice wavers, and a tear escapes down my cheek. "So, you honestly still believe God has a purpose for all this? This makes about as much sense as a 2 A.M. infomercial."

He doesn't answer. Instead, he does something absurd.

Something indecent under the circumstances.

Something downright irritating.

He *smiles*.

"Listen," he says, his tone now carrying something dangerously close to a faint optimism. "We just might make it. You never know."

He straightens in his chair, the tension in his shoulders easing slightly. There's a flicker of something new in his eyes—resolve, faith. Maybe just sheer audacity.

"I mean, God can do more than we ask or imagine. I know He can."

Is that—was that a smirk on his face?

Honesty compels me. "There's just one thing I can't understand."

He raises an eyebrow, waiting.

"If God is good, why can't He just...*be* good?"

He exhales long and slow, pats his legs, and stands abruptly. He grabs his scraggly, navy hat off the bed and angles it on his head—with the air of a man who just sold sand in the desert and left with a profit.

"Just wait and see, Lara."

He walks to the door and grabs the handle.

Then—he stops.

"Look," he says, turning back with some hesitation. "I may not know what's going to happen tomorrow...or even next month."

He looks down at the ground a second, almost lost in thought, then lifts his gaze and looks me straight in the eyes.

"But I do know one thing—God always writes the best stories."

Act One

"I hold the world but as...a stage where every man must play a part, and mine a sad one."

— Antonio, Act 1, Scene 1, The Merchant of Venice, William Shakespeare

"Dear friends, do not be surprised at the fiery ordeal that has come on you to test you, as though something strange were happening to you. But rejoice inasmuch as you participate in the sufferings of Christ, so that you may be overjoyed when His glory is revealed."

— 1 Peter 4:12-13

1

Everything Going As Planned

October 2017, three months before the storm

Oh, that delectably sweet feeling when your dreams start lining up like loyal little ducks—blissfully unaware they have a choice.

I reread the last paragraph on Janet's desktop.

Three more times.

Eyes glued to her screen as if my gaze alone could perfect the words.

It's 9 P.M., and Janet and I are the only ones left on the twelfth floor. She's my legal secretary at "Stereotypical White Shoe Big Law Firm" in San Francisco, and we're filing a consequential legal brief online in the big *Claricaran* intellectual property case. It's my last week on the job, and I'm getting things tied up in pretty bows before I go.

"Please put an extra space after the citation in footnote five. It's missing one."

"You got it." Janet knows the drill. This isn't our first rodeo.

"Okay, we're ready. Hit file, Janet!"

Ten seconds later, I hug Janet like I'm accepting an Oscar, bowing dramatically and announcing in a fake British accent,

"I'd like to thank my secretary Janet, my overpriced law degree, the inventor of espresso shots, and of course, the unsung hero: my ergonomic chair."

Then I cackle.

Near maniacally.

Janet giggles. "I'll miss you, Lara. Congrats on the new gig. But please, don't do that evil laugh thing again. Terrifies me every time." (I played an insane woman named "Mad Margaret" in a British operetta years ago, and liked the role maybe a little too much. Insanity can be a useful tactic—on occasion.)

The hollow echo of my black heels clicks against the floor as I walk back to my office through the dark hallway past empty offices. *That's a wrap. I've got to catch the next metro.*

I clean my disheveled desk, pull on my dressy black suit jacket over my blue satin blouse, grab my briefcase, and skip out of the shiny office doors. I cruise down the elevator and step outside the Embarcadero Building into the city's hustle and bustle. There's a signature, hurried "Lara bounce" in my step as I tap into the city's palpable energy and head to my favorite corner shop.

I love this feeling. The honking cabs, the smell of chestnuts from the corner vendor, the crisp autumn air mingling with the salty breeze from the bay. Fall has always been my favorite season.

Would my humble Armenian immigrant parents—who used to run a little "mom and pop" pharmacy—have ever imagined that their daughter would be a high-powered lawyer with her own secretary in her late twenties? With an ocean view office? Jetting around the country speaking at legal conventions? And actually loving it—stress and all? *Thank you, Lord Jesus, for granting me my career dreams.*

I've wanted to be a lawyer since kindergarten—when obnoxious little Lara, armed with apparently too much confidence and a box of Crayolas, drew herself in a black judicial robe like some kind of toddler Judge Judy. The other kids were drawing astronauts and princesses, but there I was, ready to argue over nap time regulations.

As I step into the corner coffee shop now, the rich aroma of cinnamon and the sharp bite of burned espresso immediately envelop my senses. I order my usual—a pumpkin spice latte and artisan chocolate bar—and rush toward the metro.

A few minutes later, the metro train hums beneath me, the rhythmic clatter of steel-on-steel filling the near-empty car. A teenager slouches in the corner, hood pulled low, head bobbing to the bass line leaking from his earbuds. Across from me, a businessman types furiously. As I sip my latte, letting the warmth seep into my hands, the inevitable question creeps in—*Are these late nights really worth it?*

Absolutely.

Why?

I genuinely love the thrill of channeling my energy into something meaningful.

A well-argued debate? I'm in.

A legal brief honed to perfection? Sign me up.

Acting on stage? Pure adrenaline.

Whatever the arena, I love turning passion into performance and power. Don't we all?

Let me rewind a bit. The moment five-year-old "me" learned that stickers were a gateway drug to achievement, I started chasing gold stars.

Type A. Perfectionist. Control freak. For better or worse—and probably for the worse.

Exhibit A: crying and questioning the reason for my existence at age ten after my two-second church solo—because my voice allegedly didn't "sound good." I guess my wobbly soprano wasn't exactly giving Mariah Carey.

Exhibit B: crying for days after being named "Salutatorian" in high school, because second place? A Shakespearean tragedy to my seventeen-year-old mercilessly self-critical self. *Not good enough.*

By the end of college, my relationship with "success" was still borderline pathological. When Stanford Law rejected me despite my sweat-earned 3.99 grade point average, my mature inner monologue at the time: *I'll show you bimbos.* I marched into UCLA Law, spent the year revenge-studying, ranked first place in the first year class, and promptly reapplied to Stanford Law to prove my point. You know, to join the other "bimbos." (Others seek therapy for inner turmoil. I, apparently, seek vengeance.)

Stanford accepted me—which made sense to me. *That's how life works, Lara,* I thought at the time. *Work hard and God will ultimately bless you. God blesses those He loves. Worth comes from success.* Proverbs 13:4 says, "A sluggard's appetite is never filled, but the desires of the diligent are fully satisfied."

Clearly, I had a "healthy" relationship with success back then. I'm no psychotherapist and don't know where this drive came from—only that it was there.

Now?

I plead the fifth.

As the metro murmurs through a tunnel, I take a bite of my chocolate bar while my fingers absently trace the Armenian cross at my neck—the one my mother fastened around my neck at graduation. It's more than jewelry. It's history.

Perhaps what nags me subconsciously is the belief that my maternal grandfather—a hardworking Christian reverend who miraculously escaped the Armenian Genocide—didn't do all that so grandkid number eight would be a slacker.

Let me tell you something about Armenians. There aren't many of us. We're a people born in sorrow. The first nation to embrace Christianity, yet cursed by geography. Over the centuries, we've been trampled by empires—the Byzantines, Persians, Russians, Turks. And during World War I, the Ottoman Turks tried to erase us entirely. The Armenian Genocide.

That's why we stick together. Success, to us, isn't just about achievement. It's redemption. It's not just generic old-world propriety that fuels our need to marry Armenian, thrive in our careers, and build strong families. It's something deeper, stitched into our blood. We don't want to just survive. We want to thrive—because our ancestors were supposed to vanish. My existence is a miracle if you consider how the Turks spared my dad's great-grandfather's family as well, because they wanted to utilize their rare skill in horse saddle-making—a trade too useful to erase.

And then there are my parents. They fled a war in Lebanon and sacrificed everything so I could have the so-called "good life" in America. They're surprisingly "chill" for Armenian parents, but the unspoken lesson has always been clear nonetheless: earthly blessings—*i.e.*, the "perfect" Armenian life—equals happiness. Work hard, marry well, raise babies, grill kebab on Sundays after church, honor your Armenian past, then die.

That's the formula for joy. I'm all in.

The train finally screeches into Millbrae station, and I step out onto the platform into the still night air, the cold biting through my suit jacket.

10:30 P.M. and not a soul in sight.

My heartbeat quickens as I dart several blocks to my car, knowing my mom Grace is up waiting, worried sick. But this is corporate life. (I've been living at home in the suburbs with the folks for the last eight years. I'm lucky enough to love my retired parents' company.)

Thirty minutes later, I'm home and sprinting through the garage door into the family room. "Mom, I'm officially done with all my cases. Four days left!"

Mom ties her night robe, hugs me tight, and kisses my left eye—her signature, tender way to say everything without a word. She looks at me with those deep brown, almond-shaped eyes, thin lips, and button nose, framed by soft, wavy brown hair.

"Proud of you. But remember to rest. If you know how." She rolls her eyes, flashes a playful smile, and heads to sleep.

I rush to my bedroom, slip into my cozy koala pajamas,

and dive into bed. Nothing screams "peak adulthood" like fuzzy marsupials.

Then, a silent prayer—*Thank you Lord Jesus, for all Your blessings and this new job. I know You'll help me thrive there. I love You. Amen.*

The prayer rolls off my tongue the way it has for years since that sweet old lady in Sunday School introduced me to Jesus and I accepted Him as my Savior—me and four other sugar-high seven year olds. So far, that Jesus guy had been good to me: a wonderful childhood, loving parents, my favorite mint chip ice cream on the regular, the occasional band-aid, and a sweet older sister named Sevan who was smart enough not to cross me. Who wouldn't want eternal life like that?

And even up through today, faith has always felt somewhat like a simple transaction. If Jesus loves you, He'll ultimately bless you. He just will. That's been the evidence so far, anyway.

Oh, except God's one *big* indiscretion with Aunt Jackie. You know, the one my family shoves down, denies, and never discusses.

The memory randomly seeps into my head now, like cold air through a cracked window, as I pull the covers up to my chin.

Aunt Jackie was a brilliant chemist.

Loving.

Faithful.

Kind.

But cancer didn't care.

Neither did God, I told myself, standing at her gravesite eight years ago at age twenty-one, fists clenched, shivering in a stiff black dress, and digging my heels into the damp, unsteady grass, just like my faith. *Why are we all acting as if everything is okay and God has been fair and kind?*

Justice has always driven me. The need to balance scales. To call out the unfair. It's why I chose law. But Aunt Jackie's premature death at age fifty-four?

Not fair.

I press my face into my pillow now, exhaling hard. *Don't think about this.*

When Aunt Jackie died, my faith cracked—like a glass dropped onto concrete. The pieces were still there, but they would never fit the same way again. But punishing God ultimately felt easier than trying to understand why the good suffer. So, for six months, I waged silent rebellion against Jesus. No prayers, no church. No God to worship equals no one to get angry at.

Right?

Wrong.

I couldn't sustain it. I felt like something deep within me had broken. I *knew* God was real, as Jesus had revealed Himself to me through His Word in small but tangible ways up to that point. So one day, my sister's question—"Are you gonna ignore God forever, Lars?"—stuck with me like a piece of gum on a hot sidewalk. (FYI: "Lars" is the affectionate nickname my family uses to manipulate me when they need to pacify me.) I went to church grudgingly that Sunday. As I sat in the pews, these words during Pastor Nerses' sermon shook me: "Is there someone here today who has quit on God? God is saying 'Don't give up on Me.'"

Coincidental timing, or Providence? I instantly knew the Holy Spirit was speaking directly to me, and I turned back to God in faith right there and then. I devoured theological books exploring reasons why God allows suffering, coming to some tentative "insights" that temporarily pacified me. I even joined a "Bible Study Fellowship" class when my friend Lisa and Auntie Nanor separately suggested it the same day out of the blue. (Again, chance or Jesus wooing me?)

During the next few years, my faith really grew. I almost don't recognize myself now at age twenty-nine compared to who I was at twenty-one. I've found Jesus to be a deeply personal God, one who doesn't love me from a distance but wants an intimate relationship with me.

But.

All that notwithstanding.

The bare bones truth is I've never "forgiven" Him for taking Aunt Jackie.

And I fancy I never will. *Where is Aunt Jackie, really?* It's one thing to read about Heaven in the Bible, but can we actually understand what it means that Heaven is a place of permanent joy and bliss?

Nor have I ever *really* trusted God again. My trust looks more like, "Trust, but keep one eye open."

I know what God is capable of, folks. That whole "surrender to His will" thing? That's for the Bible's "greats." Think Job from the Old Testament—the poster child for trusting God amidst suffering.

Me? A lawyer trained to skeptically evaluate evidence and reach rational conclusions. Rational Conclusion No. 1 after Aunt Jackie's death: God cannot be trusted. It's one thing to believe Jesus died for my sins. It's another to trust that He is *good* even when He allows intense suffering.

But I admit. I'm still curious. God tested that Job dude up the wazoo, allowing evil forces to kill all of Job's children, wealth, and health, yet Job still had the gumption to praise God in that famous line—"Though [God] slay me, yet will I hope in Him[.]" Job 13:15. Was Job unhinged? What am I missing? Are there actually any persuasive reasons justifying God's allowance of unimaginable suffering without explaining Himself, giving and then stripping everything from us? Answers that would help me trust His goodness again? Or trust Him period?

Regardless, tonight, as I lie in this bed, I'm clinging tight to a belief I've etched in stone—*God won't ever dare to defy me or my family again.*

I let out a breath that deflates my entire body.

No, no. Everything's going according to plan. I'm about to start my dream job. You'll help me, right Lord? This milestone will give me so much purpose and joy.

And I'm really hoping this Saturday night surprises me...

Sure, God will give me "average" suffering here and there to keep me "humble" like everyone else. But deep down I know God wants *Lara* to thrive, based on His past blessings. That's how you assess a case: evidence.

Plus.

After God's felony crime concerning Aunt Jackie, I gave Him a plea deal years ago. (My courtroom, my rules.) I told Him I'm willing to suffer and still remain a believer, so long as He comes through for me each time in the end.

It was a reasonable deal.

And God is going to keep His end of the deal.

2

The Word With "Sin" In It

The next Saturday night

I glance at my watch and shift in my seat, pretending to look tired. *I can't fake laugh one more time.*

"Well, it was truly wonderful meeting you, Ara," I say, sipping the last of my cinnamon spice tea in this downtown vintage coffee shop. *Wonderful? Why are you always overly nice when trying to escape?* "I better get going. Getting late." (It's only 8 p.m.) "But thanks so much for treating me."

An arrogant Armenian investment banker with borderline average good looks sits across from me, coffee in hand, somehow deluded that we've been on the same wavelength the last two hours. Judge Lana Santin—my former boss—connected me to her friend who knew this guy. Judge Santin and I have a running gag that she'll stop at nothing to find me a suitable Armenian Christian man.

Ara smiles, giving off a weird combination of nerves and undeserving cockiness. "You're gonna go out with me again, right? Next Friday?" He leans in confidently, like a man who's just crushed a job interview.

Except I'm HR, and he's not getting the position. *Is he really this dense? I thought MBAs have emotional intelligence? Has he not sensed our lack of chemistry? Am I a bad actress? A good actress?*

"Oh...um..." I smile awkwardly. "I'll let you know."

I know full well I will go home and text him: "You're great, but..." (Something vague about how I'm busy saving stray cats.)

It's a script I know by heart.

And that's why last year, at age twenty-eight, I finally took legal action. I formally charged God with criminal negligence for failure to gift me a husband (the one other black dot on God's "*Lara-curated* rap sheet.")

I was patient in my mid-twenties, but as the years drag on, I've started resenting Jesus a tad bit for this "single" status. What genius came up with that dumb word anyway? It even has the word "sin" in it.

The interplay between divine blessing and human desire has always mystified me. I've read testimonies of Christian women who remained permanently single despite desiring marriage, testifying that they surrendered to God's will because He "knew what's best." *This mentality makes zero sense to me. What am I missing? Lord, humble me.* (FYI: One of my exceedingly admirable traits is that I'm stubborn. I take "no" for an answer the same way a cat takes "get off the counter"—as a mild suggestion I plan to ignore.)

God made the world order this way—Adam *and* Eve—but for some of His children, it's "sorry, this isn't best"? Matthew 7:11 even says, "[H]ow much more will your Father in Heaven give good gifts to those who ask Him!" *So why do You withhold from some Christians, Lord? I'm asking genuinely.*

Again, can God really be trusted? I've never understood the Bible's proclamation that God's "ways" are "higher than [our] ways[.]" Isaiah 55:9. *That's the point, Lara. You won't get it. He's the God of the universe and you are an ant.* Pride, anyone?

But let's get real. In my gloriously self-righteous worldview, no hard-working Christian Armenian girl should be "single" at age twenty-nine. Am I right? If God giving Armenians the double whammy of big noses and short height is His misdemeanor, failing to deliver Lara a suitable Armenian Christian man by age twenty-five is His felony.

Why the two conditions, you ask? Armenian. Godly.

Godly: because I love God and hold devout evangelical beliefs. I don't want to be unequally yoked with an unbelieving egg. (Get it? 2 Corinthians 6:14.)

Armenian: I was raised to seek this. My parents took Sevan and me to our Armenian church in San Francisco every Sunday so we'd soak up Armenian culture and the Bible. *Ah*, Calvary Armenian Congregational Church, the place where Mom's dad, Grandpa Sadakian, was honored as a notable reverend from the old country, thereby crowning me one of ten celebrated "torn-eegs," *a.k.a.*, grandkids.

I learned the game fast—be charming, respectful, and strategic around the adults talking to Mommy so as to maximize my chances of finding a gorgeous Armenian Christian dude to marry by age twenty. I worked the crowd like a tiny politician, kissing cheeks and making promises—"Vote Lara for Most Eligible Torneeg!" I also devoured the dusty copy of "How to Win Friends and Influence People" on Grandpa's bookshelf, coaching myself to be tactful. But unless "tactful" means eternally unattached, I think I missed a chapter.

Bottom line—with this narrowed pool, I'm fishing in a shot glass. I haven't gotten beyond a (third) date with a guy between the ages of twenty-one and thirty-five for a decade now. I've vetoed every Godly but non-Armenian Tom, Dick, and Harry in the Bay Area out of the gate, worried they won't understand the cultural angle, and I've vetoed every Armenian Vartan, Armen, and Haig because they didn't love Jesus.

Regardless, this is why I'm here tonight—donning a last-season ruffled purple skirt with my dark brown curls cascading over my shoulders—saying hello and goodbye to this week's date: Ara.

If love is about getting your "checklist," Ara ain't checking any boxes.

We finally exit the coffee shop, and I initiate the obligatory awkward hug.

"Bye."

"Bye."

He walks away in the direction of Union Square. *So long, Ara.*

If God can part the Red Sea, why doesn't He part me from these tragic dates? I certainly haven't been able to pull a simultaneously sexy and Godly Armenian man out of thin air myself.

But God can.

So what's the hold up? *Is there a glitch in the Husband Deliverables department up there? Would a bribe help? I've got cash.*

I order an Uber ride to get out of the city. *Oooh, it's chilly out, and dark.*

As I wait, I consider—isn't dating inefficient and like a never-ending bad community theater show? Over-rehearsed lines, forced chemistry, dressing the part.

Look, I love acting and singing. They're my jam. My favorite way to communicate profound themes through creative expression. My parents channeled my energy as a kid into musical theater and I had an oddly eccentric pull toward the weirdest, most outlandish characters, leading to a hilariously bizarre résumé of roles the last twenty years. *E.g.*, evil stepsister, deranged psychopath, British con artist, dumb Shakespearean spinster. Who wants to play boring little Cinderella anyway? *Cue*: maniacal evil stepsister laugh. You scared yet?

But "modern dating" is a musical I would very much like *not* to be cast in. Alas, I'm stuck in the lead role for now, and I've never waited so desperately for a curtain call.

Thank God my Uber is finally here. I step in, kick off my heels, and ask once more—God's sovereignty aside, maybe I'm still single because of my "impossibly high standards"? If that's the problem, we simply can't budge there. My husband is to be (a) *very* smart,

(b) *very* Godly, (c) *very* kind, and (d) *very* good-looking. *Very* funny and *very* talented are cherries on top but can be negotiated with Jesus. My prayer life sounds a lot like a business deal lately. "Lord, I can let go of the six-pack abs if You throw in an extra dose of Godliness. Final offer."

An hour later, I'm perched on Sevan's couch, shoveling a spoonful of delightful mint chip ice cream into my mouth, the cool, creamy mint melting on my tongue. Sevan is a teacher with a warm smile and thoughtful hazel eyes that soften even my hardest moments. We're sisters, but we ruthlessly hate each other's professions.

"Don't worry, Lars," she teases. "God will punish you by making you marry a teacher."

"Why don't we just move to Salzburg to be nuns at this point? We both love *The Sound of Music*."

"Even Maria pinned down the Captain, Lars." *Touché.*

After shoveling in another spoonful, I smile inside the moment I remember. *God's got a plan. Keep trusting.*

That's right. I've got a little basket that I'm confidently putting all my heart-shaped eggs in lately. I was praying for a husband one night a few months ago, and I opened my *Daily Streams* app on my phone. It's a Christian devotional I use to get daily Christian inspiration along with my Bible reading. The message of the day explained that the rainbow symbol sometimes acts as a sign of God's promise to a believer on something his or her heart desires. It made me cry because it felt like the Holy Spirit was encouraging me. (Christians believe in a triune God—one divine being in three persons: God the Father, Jesus the Son, and the Holy Spirit.)

About an hour later, my Christian friend randomly texted me a rainbow emoji, writing, "I'm praying for you and believe God has a husband for you!" Coincidence?

The next day, a card arrived in the mail from my other friend in the UK. She had mailed it two weeks ago, and it had a big rainbow on it. She wrote, "God can give His children specific promises.

I'm praying that it's His will to bring you a husband." Rainbow. Promise. What were the chances?

I was convinced the timing of these messages wasn't a coincidence. Jesus was telling me He *will* gift me marriage. Since that day, I've clung to that promise, doubts notwithstanding. I even wrote it down in my sacred (and super sparkly) *God is Good* evidence journal—yes, my detailed record of every time God speaks to me. Did you expect anything less? I'm a lawyer; I collect evidence, people.

So God's likely got the goods.

But when's the delivery?

Do I need to sue for divine delay?

3

The Dream Job

January 2018, three months later

"I'm Lara. Nice to see you again."

I give the attorney next to me a wide smile and a firm handshake—firm enough to assert confidence, but not so firm that I'd get sued for battery.

Goal: make an amazing first impression.

I'm donning "law and order chic" today—a white silky blouse and a fancy black suit jacket and skirt set tailored precisely to my measurements. I just bought it in Hong Kong during my mini "in between jobs" vacation.

As I sit down in the black conference room chair behind me, I notice the walls are lined with dark wood paneling polished to a sheen, creating a sense of gravitas. In one corner, a large American flag stands proudly. The floor is covered with a plush, deep burgundy carpet that adds warmth to the otherwise austere atmosphere.

The Criminal Division Chief, Alyssa, begins speaking with a blend of professorial authority and eager enthusiasm.

"Welcome Jared, Lara, and George! I hope you three settled

in last week. For orientation today, we're refreshing the Federal Rules of Criminal Procedure. Then it's off to your new caseload."

As Alyssa talks, I can barely focus, because I'm preoccupied with one simple fact.

I've made it.

I'm a thirty-year-old brand new federal criminal prosecutor, or "Assistant United States Attorney." It's my second week on the job in downtown San Francisco. To say I'm stoked would be like saying a squirrel is *kind of* into nuts.

This is one of the most sought-after roles in the legal world, and I'm deeply grateful because God prepared me for *this* moment my entire life. Middle school speech contests, college mock trial competitions, stints at the District Attorney's office and the U.S. Department of Justice, trial work at the law firm. One of my favorite verses has always been Isaiah 1:17—"Learn to do right; seek justice... Take up the cause of the fatherless; plead the case of the widow." Now, I finally have the opportunity to be a trial lawyer fighting for criminal justice day in, day out.

This isn't just a job. It's my calling.

Drug lords? Gangs?

Bring on the Al Capones of the world, baby. I'm one of three lucky new hires out of thousands of applicants, who now has the privilege of saying these coveted words in a federal court of law—"Good morning, Your Honor. My name is Lara and I represent the United States of America." After law school, I landed prestigious jobs with two federal judges to increase my chances of landing this specific position later. The plan—I'll do ten years as a prosecutor, then some smart President will appoint me to serve as a federal judge for life—*if only I work hard enough.*

Today, I'm one step closer to the promised land.

Ten minutes later, Alyssa is still talking but I'm doing an internal panic check.

Abdominal pain. Sweaty palms. Intense ear pain. A headache that feels like a construction crew is jack-hammering inside my skull. *Hold it together, Lara. Focus. What's wrong with you? Do you have the flu?*

Minutes pass.

Nothing changes.

Pain seems to intensify.

I shift in my seat. Sweat dampens the back of my neck under my tight hair bun, and my body is involuntarily swaying in an ironic effort to steady itself. The room feels too warm, and yet my fingers are ice cold, clutching the edge of the conference table. My thoughts are foggy, my vision is oddly blurry, and I can't focus on Alyssa's voice. *Something's off. Very off.*

Alyssa's voice drifts in and out. She's saying something about Criminal Rule No. 16 when—

BOOM, the world flashes white in my vision. *What on...*

Alyssa pauses, eyeing me as I hobble up in an effort to stand. "Lara, are you okay?"

"I'm sorry, Alyssa. Can I please go to the bathroom?"

She furrows her brow with concern. "Of course."

I wobble to the bathroom, holding onto walls to keep myself steady and avoiding eye contact with anyone at all costs.

In seconds, I'm sitting on an uncomfortable toilet seat with the toilet lid down, hunched over with my hand on my chin, a vision of pure confidence.

I gulp down my water bottle, wondering if dehydration is the issue.

No change.

I sit a little while longer. *I can't believe this is happening. What am I missing in the orientation room? Why do I feel so off? They didn't tell me in law school that the real courtroom drama happens in a bathroom stall.*

I guilt myself for another ten minutes, shaming my body that it's a complete failure. (In "Laranomics," self-compassion and rest are for the weak, and feelings are for defense attorneys.) *Why are the fluorescent lights attacking my eyeballs? Do I have sunglasses?*

Oh, great idea—just throw on some aviators and channel your inner undercover agent. That'll earn you credibility real fast in court.

And then it happens again—

BOOM, something explodes in my left ear, and my vision flashes white again. But this time, I see another lightning flash out of the corner of my right eye and the bathroom door starts waving back and forth in my vision, as if it's about to take flight. *What on earth?*

I clutch the bathroom door, trying not to lose it. *Gross.*

I'm holding onto everything—my dignity, my balance, my very sanity. In seconds, I pull the toilet seat up, lurch forward, and out comes the beautiful croissant I ate this morning. My newly tailored Hong Kong suit now has the distinct aroma and feel of regret and partially digested pastry. *Fantastic.* Nothing screams "future judge" like *eau de vomit. This cannot be happening.*

I force myself to regroup, giving myself a psychological pep talk. *Look, God has always protected and blessed you because He loves His children. You'll get better. Just drag your caboose in there and handle this.*

A few minutes later, I walk out of the bathroom like a disgraced pageant queen and saunter back into the conference room. All eyes turn to me as I walk straight to Alyssa and state the unthinkable in Laranomics.

"Sorry Alyssa, I think I need to take a taxi home. I don't feel right, and I think I might have the flu…or something."

"Of course."

I stuff my newly minted Department of Justice badge into my briefcase, slap my black coat on, and wobble out of the federal building, holding onto walls when necessary. *Perfect. I'm debuting my new legal career with the impression of a drunken flamingo. This better heal fast, whatever it is.*

If I have to limp into my first court trial like this, the only thing I'll be prosecuting is my dignity.

4

Down The Toilet

October 2018, ten months later

"Help!"

"Hang on Lars, I'm coming," Pops yells back, as I count the milliseconds until he sprints over to my bedroom. Mom's not home so my dad Vayel (whom I call "Pops") is holding the fort. He rushes in.

"Pops! Something strange is happening. I'm not just dizzy anymore. The outside world is…rotating 360." I grab him with my right hand while clutching my bedroom dresser with my left. *Did I accidentally sign up for the 360-degree version of Disneyland's teacup ride?*

"What do you mean?" he insists, confused.

"Hang on, let me steady myself," I mumble, feeling like I'm about to pass out from just trying to stay upright.

It's now ten months into this dumb illness. Last January, after three weeks convincing myself I had the "flu," I realized I was up against a much more formidable enemy. The U.S. Attorney's Office graciously put me on a temporary sick leave and told me to take all the time I need to heal from this "thing."

The timing could not have been worse. I had been healthy as a horse for the first thirty years of my life.

Enter stage left, the crew of doctors. *Ah, yes, the doctors.*

Countless specialists gave me a laundry list of diagnoses and we've been chasing pertinent treatments since. I say "we" because this illness has literally been a family affair. That's how our family rolls. The different docs each gave their own pet theory on how this "thing" started living rent-free in my brain.

One doc said I have "vestibular migraines" because airplane travel, my fever in Hong Kong, and my low Vitamin D levels all apparently conspired to mess with my inner ears. He said the flashes of lightning and world shaking/blurring are migraine episodes where my brain fails to understand the faulty signals from the ear and thus doesn't know how to process where yours truly is in space. I had never even heard of the "vestibular system," which is a sensory system in the inner ear that controls balance and spatial perception. It's made up of semicircular canals and otolith organs. Who knew our tiny ears could cause so much havoc when gone rogue?

Another doctor said *no, no,* this is "migrainous vertigo," a related chronic condition that makes you dizzy nonstop and is treated with certain drugs and "vestibular" training. People with this kind of vertigo experience a false sensation that either *they* are spinning or moving, or that *the world* around them is spinning, or both.

Another doc said *no, no,* this is "BPPV," a vertigo condition that gets triggered episodically when ear crystals randomly dislodge out of your ear, causing your vision to experience hard 360-degree spins of the world around you, without prior notice.

Yet another doc said I was born with a rare ear condition called "SSCD," and lucky for me, on both sides, because my CAT scans revealed small holes in *both* of my inner ears. Apparently, when these holes expand due to aging, the ears start giving faulty signals to the brain, causing a host of strange vertigo symptoms.

The diagnoses continued—"functional neurological disorder" associated with migraine headaches. *Doesn't sound right?*; *mal de debarquement* syndrome causing persistent motion sensations like swaying and rocking. *Hmm*; vestibular neuritis that shouldn't last long if I'm lucky. *Am I?*; cervicogenic dizziness thanks to my two previous car accidents; and vestibular paroxysmia from an artery compressing an inner ear nerve.

You get the picture.

It felt like they were pulling diagnoses out of a Scrabble bag. I'm no doctor, but some diagnoses sounded right, some didn't. To me, it was all noise. All I've cared about: *what do I have to do to get back to work.*

But that hasn't been in the cards.

Chasing treatments has been like playing medical whack-a-mole, without winning any rounds. Standard protocol drug treatments, vestibular testing, diets of all kinds for migraine and vestibular conditions, rapid weight gain and weight loss due to said diets, vitamin therapies and supplements of all flavors, MRIs, CAT scans, you name it, I've tried it. My body feels like it's undergoing rapid fire military testing.

Our official family motto—"No treatment left behind." We're all reading research articles on vertigo nonstop. Mom and I have been keeping track of every single thing I eat and every single symptom in a comprehensive "migraine" diary. The "coffee alternatives" I'm trying at present taste deliciously like...dirt.

And then, there's the ER. I'm a regular, due in part to severe episodes and in part to the side effects of countless "not so benign" medical drugs I'm popping. *E.g.*, costochondritis stabbing chest spasms that one drug triggered. (Super fun.) I overheard one ER nurse say one time, "There's that chick with the fluffy hair again." *Yeah, that's me.* Big, unruly brown curls, thin lips, and almond shaped brown eyes, living her best life in the ER (in those sophisticated koala pajamas).

I'm proud of how emotionally resilient I've been though, and I feel like I'm growing spiritually at least. I'm shocked, actually, that I haven't been bitter. Every time a treatment fails, I'm reminded my worth must be in God, not work (*hmm*); God is sovereign and knows the right timing. Things of this nature. As Martin Luther wrote, suffering is like fast-track seminary school. It imprints God's truths on our hearts because we are forced to live them in practice.

Inspirational self-talk every morning: "Jesus was willing to die for me. That means He'll heal me eventually, and I'll be back in that courtroom in *His* timing. Sure, He doesn't heal everyone but if I do my part, He'll chip in. Always has."

Due to my condition, I've been isolated at home, but my Christian friends have kept my spiritual muscles up with compassionate texts like, "Keep going, God has good plans for you in this job," "God's not going to waste your law degree," "Delays are not denials." So I know God won't abandon me. He brought me this far in my legal career.

The problem—I'm running out of time now. We're back to fall. But instead of sporting a cute pumpkin clad scarf and gallivanting through a pumpkin patch with that gorgeous Christian husband I was promised, Pops is holding me up as I lean against my dresser.

I'm currently trying my ninth experimental drug: the dreaded birth control pill. Apparently, stopping female hormones stops migraines. For me? Triggered sixty days of bleeding. Because that's exactly what my life needed—two months of playing the lead role in a horror movie called *The Never-Ending Period*. I guess the "pill" finally pushed my symptoms over the edge.

"Listen Pops," I groan, "the outside world is like turning... almost like it's about to tip upside down." Apparently *today* is when the world really starts spinning—literally and figuratively.

"Oh my gosh. It's turning full circle again! I can't stay up anymore; help me lie down on my bed. Help me, Lord Jesus!"

Luckily, Pops and I are very close. He's an adorably petite man—five-foot-four, bald head, a few silver curls dangling at the back, and intelligent blue eyes hiding behind black-rimmed glasses. We've been in the trenches together like this before. Like that one glorious bonding session when I called him from theater camp in ninth grade, asking him to help me pass a "more painful than it should be" trapped gas episode via phone at 1 A.M. (Mom was in Fresno at a women's convention.) This is how Armenian families roll. Or, maybe just us.

"Just fart, Lars, fart! Pass the gas! You can do it!" Pops yelled into the phone. At least that was funny.

Today, not so much.

As Pops helps me onto my bed, I blurt, "I told that neurologist this pill was making my symptoms worse, but she didn't believe me!"

"Don't worry," Pops replies. "I'm sure it will calm down." *Sure Pops.* He's been declaring I'll get better, but after months of treatment, we both know he's just moonlighting as a motivational speaker. "Your ears are just playing musical chairs with your brain, Lars. Stay strong." *Great, let me know when they pick a winner.*

I stay on my bed all day and all night, opening my eyes once every fifteen minutes to see if the outside world is still spinning in full circles.

It is.

The next day, we stop the birth control pill, but the damage is done. I try to sit up but can't stay seated upright for more than ten minutes before my blood pressure drops. I can only walk around the house twice before I start feeling faint from the turning sensation. It feels like I'm on a boat in a storm, without any control over where I'm going. I lie on my bed all day assessing the situation and my options.

My health literally just got worse. Unbelievable. I had *just* strengthened the connection between my ear and brain through nine months of intensive vestibular ear therapy—*i.e.*, ear, eye, and brain exercises that train the ears and brain to coordinate on processing motion in space again.

Imagine walking in a straight line making yourself *dizzier* with rapid left and right eye movements in order to make your brain feel better in the *long run*. That's how the therapy works. It's CrossFit for your eyeballs and ears except instead of getting ripped, you just get dizzier at first. It had helped to reduce about fifteen percent of the dizziness. *Did the drugs ruin all that rehabilitation work? What's happening in my brain now?*

And what am I going to tell the U.S. Attorney's Office? They need to know by the end of next week if I'm returning or not because they can't extend my leave further. I've been praying desperately for last-minute answers and healing.

Nothing.

What do I do Lord? If I quit, will I ever get hired as a prosecutor again?

Around 3 p.m., my cell phone rings on my nightstand. Sevan.

"Lars, did you by chance read the *Daily Streams* devotional app today?"

"No." *Maybe it has a nugget of truth that might encourage me?* I cautiously open up the app on my phone, and the devotion of the day glares back at me:

> Do not rely solely on your own understanding. Sometimes, what God does in the end may seem to contradict His original plan. In those moments, your role is simple: listen, trust, and obey Him—even when it feels irrational. God will bring everything together in the end, but at first, His path might look like He's willing to lose. So when you recognize His voice, don't get caught up in outcomes. Obey—even if you're walking blindly. When God seems to make no sense, He is weaving something beautiful.

My heart immediately starts beating in a complicated rhythm. *You've got to be kidding me.* Did Jesus literally just tell me to quit my dream job? The one I prayed for years to get? The one He opened the door to? This doesn't make any sense. *Is this a joke, Lord?*

I now have a pit in my stomach. You might know the kind—when you *know* that the Holy Spirit wants you to do something you don't want to do.

If God *is* weaving something beautiful here, is He going for an abstract piece? Because this feels more like an ugly Picasso. *Do I cry or shout?*

Sevan senses my irritation over the phone but cautiously suggests, "We've been praying, and maybe this is your answer? I know, it's so tough."

I hang up and lie on my bed in silence, waffling between shock and confusion.

At 8 A.M. the next morning, I open my eyes and feel the world turning pirouettes around me. *Nothing's changing. This is so terrifying and uncomfortable.* My body is stiff and my head is encased in a heavy fog. I pull the blanket tight around me, burying myself to escape what I have to do.

Okay, Lord, I can't believe You're making me do this. Have Thine own way, Lord. I will submit. I love You. Keep it together, Lara. People are dying of hunger all over the world. Perspective and maturity. It's just a job, right?

I slowly push myself up, clasping onto the headboard, and move briskly to my desk, knowing I likely only have minutes before I will feel extremely faint and need to lie back down. I sit at my desk and steady myself, bracing against a sharp turn of the world around me. I open up my email, and type the following words:

> Hi Alyssa,
>
> *I regret to inform you that my condition has deteriorated*

despite pursuing countless treatments. I have no choice but to resign permanently. I am beyond grateful for your understanding this entire year, and I hope you know how thankful I am that the office took a chance on me.

With deep gratitude,

Lara

I pause and proofread it.

I hit "send."

I sit still for a minute, feeling its finality, like the last page of a book I don't want to finish.

My lifelong dream to be a criminal prosecutor is now officially down the toilet. Thrown out faster than a bad piece of evidence.

God opened the door to this job only to slam it shut.

I thought God's plan for me was to fight crime, not gravity? Turns out God really cannot be trusted.

The worst part: I never got the chance to say those coveted words in federal court—"Good morning, Your Honor. My name is Lara and I represent the United States of America."

5

The Bed

The following year is a blur, literally and metaphorically.
Day in, day out: identical.
Goal: stay sane.

I lie here on my back in bed, my mind drafting a mental itinerary for Paris and traveling there in my imagination. *Ah, Paris. So magical.* Never been, but, by golly, I'm living there in my mind right now. I can almost touch the cobblestone streets, the glittering lights, the sidewalk cafés.

Rome? Went last Thursday.

Prague? Yesterday.

London? Next week.

Who needs British Airways? I may not have a passport stamp, but I've got a first-class imagination—and no baggage fees, layovers, or jet lag.

Just bed sheets.

Sometimes I imagine cross-examining my doctors, exacting retribution with every well-aimed word. *Redemption at its height*.

Forty minutes later, boredom strikes, and my mind retreats from Paris' seductive allure to the cruel reality of being tethered to this bed.

What's the point? I'm not really in Paris. At least my imagination beats staring at every stray mark on this master bedroom ceiling. I've memorized every blemish—left, right, front, back. Art is art.

I think back over the past year—this unrelenting odyssey that began after I quit the job. Confused and disillusioned thoughts back then: "I just lost my dream job and any semblance of 'control' over this illness. Does Jesus do this to others to test them too? Give them their dream then take it away right after? I even asked God to open the door only if it was His will. I thought God had good plans for me? What on earth does Jeremiah 29:11 mean? "'For I know the plans I have for you,' declares the Lord, 'plans to prosper you and not to harm you, plans to give you hope and a future.'"

But I knew something in my perspective needed to change, or I was going to have a mental breakdown. So somehow, that disillusionment led to a kind of reluctant surrender to God's mysterious agenda—"He'll have me working again in no time. God rewards tenacity. Keep trusting. He must have some reason for this detour. Thank God I read all those books on Christian suffering years ago. God was preparing me so I would have the proper framework to deal with this."

But that was just the beginning.

Since then, every attempt to sit upright has been a literal battle. For months, I could only get off my bed a handful of times per day—just enough to stagger to the bathroom, vomit, suffer bouts of diarrhea, or shuffle into the living room and lie down there.

This "big" celebratory event involved me sitting up in slow motion and steadying myself to gain balance, while Mom played my human crash pad behind me just in case. I would then lie immediately back down to cope with the intensified spinning symptoms resulting from that very short upright walk in space. I would then wait two hours for my brain to calm back *down* to its normal baseline level of chronic spinning.

Each time I sat up for just ten minutes to gulp down food, it felt so good to actually move my joints, but I was promptly punished with a tsunami of even more ocean waves in my brain, forcing me to lie back down *right after*. Fast forward a few months and my physical condition deteriorated even more so as the illness rapidly worsened, thanks to just that minimal amount of daily upright walking.

Where I am today: my brain processes the world—in a nonstop chronic fashion—as if my body is a boat that is bobbing up and down in either full circles or big turbulent waves. Simultaneously, I visually see the walls and ground moving up and down, left and right, *nonstop*, whether I'm lying down or sitting up, though it gets sharply worse when sitting upright and/or walking. Imagine being dropped into a bizarre horror/sci-fi movie. That's the sensation. My initial sheer terror has morphed into a sort of weary moment to moment acceptance of these exceedingly painful sensations.

Things have gotten so bad now that the minute I sit up slowly at any angle—even fifteen degrees—the neurons in my brain start firing and inform my vestibular system that an even greater "attack" is on the rise, leading to an even harder spinning sensation. Thus, my parents hand me food to eat while I'm lying down, and I've stopped walking around the house completely. I have no choice: I get up just to go to the bathroom and come right back, only three to four times a day.

Put simply, I'm near completely bedridden.

I prefer to call it "bedridden chic."

Move over, Paris Fashion Week—here comes the fall/winter "horizontal Lara couture" collection! *Ugh. I need to file a malpractice claim against my brain for breach of contract.*

My parents have been exiled from sleeping in this master bedroom so we can spend time together in this larger bedroom all day as I lie down. Pops joked last week, "Grace, our golden retirement years aren't even brass."

As I lie here under this plain gray comforter, I scan this sparse functional master bedroom—a small dresser, a modest beige rug guarding the hardwood floor, and a single brown chair that doubles as Mom's pajama perch. The room is a silent testament to Mom's meticulous nature, holding only what matters to her most.

At this point, it's me.

The sound of people walking outside the open window suddenly rouses me from my thoughts, slicing through the relentless hum of my spinning brain. *Man, I'm so jealous they're walking. Why is God doing this to me? Does God love me? I know He does. It's okay, Lara, wait. Patience is Godliness.*

My daily existence has crystallized into endless hours on this bed—replaying memories, planning my next "move," and begging God for direction. Mom, Pops, and I strategize constantly on what drug to try next, even if a doctor has not recommended it. We're a motley crew—Pops, an ex-pharmacist with a pragmatic cynicism; Mom, an ex-nurse with stubborn hope; me, a lawyer who thrives on argument and order.

And we're kind of…failing. Despite racking up bills consulting every West and East Coast vertigo expert out there. Even a renowned British vertigo guru in the UK who suggested four classes of new drugs. We've probably been given twelve different diagnoses, but no results from their individualized treatments. We must have the wrong diagnoses? The UK expert said he had not seen such a severe case. *Hooray!*

The nightstand beside my bed overflows with pill bottles. But if the drugs are supposed to help, they've clearly missed the memo. Each new drug is like a contestant on a bad romantic reality show—"Will this one finally be *the one?*"

The cycle for months has been: take pill A. Doesn't work, makes symptoms worse. Take pill B. Doesn't work, makes symptoms worse. Repeat.

Owww. My head suddenly shakes rapidly left and right. *Oh, there must be a big car passing by.* In a cruel twist, the drugs have decided to audition for the role of "villain" by adding new symptoms to the mix. This month, an epileptic medication has put my hypersensitive "migraine brain" into overdrive, causing a neurological "head shake" where my head whiplashes left and right involuntarily in response to certain electric stimuli like cars. We have no clue why. The flavor of the month last month was a "pressure cooker" sensation, which I can only describe as someone squeezing your brain out of your head.

And don't start me on the so-called "anti-depressant" class, one of the three main drug classes doctors give "migraine brains" to pacify them. Vertigo conditions are under-researched, perhaps because vertigo is a silent neurological disease that no one can see. So the status quo is that doctors throw the kitchen sink of drugs meant for *other* illnesses at you. Blood pressure drugs, epilepsy, anti-depressants, etc. But these supposedly "benign" anti-depressant drugs are anything but.

My first "SSRI" gave me severe neuropathy and numbness in my limbs, and spiraled me into a three-minute involuntary, hysterical fit of manic laughter because my serotonin levels apparently shot up too high. (I wasn't acting that time.) Suffice to say we got off that drug immediately. *Is this what trauma feels like? Maybe I can use all this to prep for future acting roles. Think redemption.*

Apparently some people are way more sensitive to drug side effects, and I'm a lucky winner. No matter what drug I try, my body can't tolerate it. *E.g.*, the blood pressure medication which dragged me down to a perilous 82 over 55 mmHg. *Woo, that was fun!* Especially while trying to walk again last month—which I've tried around the house countless times now (out of pure desperation) since I completely stopped walking but for bathroom trips. But every time I force myself to sit up and walk for a sustained period, I get faint, my blood pressure drops, and the spinning gets sharply worse. My brain is simply unable to process where I am in space, penalizing me every time I try to move an inch.

To make matters worse, most of the drugs come with a side effect of "vertigo" themselves. *Brilliant.* My body and the meds are playing poker, and I'm the one losing all my chips. *Ah, the irony.* Every drug prescribed to help me ends up magnifying my torment. I'm trapped on a sinking boat in a storm, and each new medication is a heavy anchor pulling me further into despair. And each drug gives me withdrawal symptoms, taking months to get completely out of my system once I stop.

Bottom line—if I take the drugs, my condition gets worse, but if I don't take drugs, nothing is changing. A classic catch-22. I feel like that poor bleeding woman in the New Testament who "had suffered a great deal under the care of many doctors and had spent all she had, yet instead of getting better she grew worse." Mark 5:26.

Mom, Pops, and I are constantly adjusting to a new kind of more depressing "normal." If "adjust" means we are each secretly in despair. *Lord, You really should consider better PR. The whole "allowing us to suffer" thing isn't exactly a crowd-pleaser. If I unknowingly signed a sanctification contract, can I renegotiate a softer clause on affliction?*

Luckily, we have countless prayer warriors encouraging us via phone. Church ladies, friends, family, and the dream team I call Mom's four "Golden Girls," *a.k.a.*, my aunts Rosalie, Arax, and Nanor, and our dear friend Astrid.

In a moment of desperate prayer, I start a conference room meeting with Jesus now: "Lord, are You working against me? Why did You let me take the last four drugs that sent me spiraling, even though I asked for wisdom before taking them? The genetic testing done by private doctor No. 4 showed that my body cannot tolerate certain classes of drugs, but we got this information only *after* I had already experimented on my own body. Isn't Your 'good timing' off sometimes?"

Great. Now I'm wrestling with the God of the universe—kind of like that Biblical Job character. Lost my job. Lost my health. Am I unknowingly auditioning for the "Book of Job Part 2: A modern musical"? *Pff, I'm no Job. I love the Lord too, but I'm about as humble as a toddler in a Batman cape. And I've got things to do. Like standing up.* My earthly dad would heal me in a heartbeat if he could. So why won't my Heavenly Father do the same?

The atheist approach fascinates me. No higher being to debate with. No divine plan to wrestle in suffering. Just resignation. But that sounds awful. How can one live without believing one has a purpose beyond this trivially short life? Each to his own, but I'd be depressed. "Yay! I can't wait to just be dust in the ground when I die!"

And, while atheists argue that if a loving God existed, He would prevent evil, that raises a deeper question. How do we even know something is evil unless there's an objective standard of good? When someone says "this is wrong," they're appealing to a moral law. But moral laws require a moral lawgiver. If everything is just random atoms and evolution, where does the idea of "ought" even come from? No one needs a degree in philosophy to know murder is evil and love is good. That moral compass—it's not just a social construct. It feels deeper than that, like it came from somewhere—or *someone.*

God.

Nor does the atheist worldview add any insight by claiming all suffering is ultimately meaningless. If that were true, we wouldn't recoil so much at the idea of it. Suffering, rather, alerts us to the fact that there must be a meaningful, moral order to the universe, but something has gone gravely wrong.

Consider the paradox. The world brims with breathtaking beauty and goodness. A cascading waterfall, a snow-capped mountain, an enchanting symphony—each infused with logic and undeniable order. And yet, alongside this grandeur, there exists unbearable chaos, cruelty, and suffering that defies reason. Christianity doesn't dismiss this contradiction; it confronts it. It tells us that a benevolent Creator designed this world in perfect harmony, embedding within us a moral compass and deep longing to reflect His beauty and glory.

But the order fractured when humanity chose sin and destruction over devotion to God. Suffering, then, is not without cause. It's the bitter consequence of a world that has fallen from its intended perfection. *But why does God—the One who breathed life into all that is good—allow this extreme extent of suffering? Shouldn't there be limits? Is there even a purpose to all of my misery?*

"Look at me, all posh and proper," I blurt out now in a British accent, channeling *My Fair Lady* vibes. Distraction of the week—pretending I'm on Broadway in my bedroom. My rendition is so good, even my pillow applauds.

Performing once represented my fantastical world of creativity. Now, every note is a desperate bid for survival and serotonin boosts. Perhaps my brain is just seeking a subconscious reminder of God's goodness to me when I played *Eliza* in *My Fair Lady* years ago. Performing has always felt transcendent to me. A way I connect with God, the ultimate Artist and Creator.

Yet just as I launch into a thrilling rendition of *The Sound of Mattress*, Pops strides in, Bible in hand. *Good, I need a show tune sabbatical.*

I recruited Pops recently to be my professional Bible reader. (The poor lad had no choice.) His nightly readings have become our ritual—a mix of theological debate, giggles, and shared sorrow. We have a great thirst given all the spiritual questions we have about suffering. He's never had a thirst for studying the Word. *Looks like this pain has brought one beautiful answer to my prayer years back to grow his faith.*

When we got mutually pissy one time about how Adam and Eve landed us in this mess with their original sin, Pops sneered, "I definitely wouldn't have eaten that apple...unless it was a Fuji." Then there was the time Pops confused Old Testament concubines with porcupines. I'm hardly an expert, so I let it slide.

As his voice fills the room reading Scripture, my mind drifts like a leaf caught in a slow-moving current until a single word strikes me, like a truth I've been avoiding.

Surrender.

Every instinct in me wants nothing to do with *that* framework anymore. Not only am I relying on others for my every need, but the frustration of not being able to cure my own illness has been unbearable. Forget career and health. I've lost myself. I was such a bubbly kid, spreading joy as a desperate means to express my bigger than life personality. Dancing in my underwear to Chopin at 10 P.M. to avoid being put to bed. Tap dancing for Mom's trapped guests. Joy always came naturally to me, and I chronically wanted more of it. And nothing to the exclusion of it.

But look at me now.

Smaller than life.

Motionless.

Flat on a bed.

Suddenly, Pops recites, "Blessed are those who mourn."

"Pops," I interject, "can I just say the Christian elephant in the room? What's the meaning of all this Beatitudes stuff? Aren't these theological puzzles better left to a Lincoln debate among angels? How are those who mourn blessed? That's not what I see at funerals."

He furrows his eyebrows. "Christianity does seem upside down sometimes, Lars."

Honestly, it is. Nonbelievers assume Christianity is all about conservative and rigid rules, when at its core, it's just about a humble Middle Eastern man who claimed to be God incarnate, loved us so much that He took the bullet for us, and then proved He wasn't bluffing by rising from the dead, just like he said he would. (Thus flipping the world's logic on its head.) If that's not the ultimate "liberal" love story—sacrificial love without asking us to pay anything in return—I don't know what is. So either it's the biggest hoax in history—which it can't be, because I've experienced Jesus firsthand—or there really is a loving God who allows all this agony for reasons we can't see. *But can I just get a small glimpse into those reasons, please?*

Pops shifts uneasily in his chair. *Just try to make Pops laugh. It'll help you both.* Joking about everything is our latest "new normal." Our only form of survival to hide our emotional pain.

I deadpan, "Pops, why did Jesus ride into Jerusalem on a donkey? I would have chosen a swanky golden chariot." Pops belts out his signature infectious laugh that reverberates at 1,000 decibels in any setting. *Mission accomplished.*

Mom's voice cuts in from the living room, sharp and insistent. "Lara, maybe you have Ménière's disease? This article says it can be hard to diagnose."

She might as well be awarded an M.D. at this point. Her tenacious eyeballs are almost bleeding from reading research blogs late into the night.

Pops cocks an eyebrow telepathically communicating—*I'm exhausted and have no clue, what do we tell her?*

I eye back—*I doubt that diagnosis is right*—then yell to Mom: "Don't think so, Mom. My symptoms don't have that presentation."

Pops shrugs his shoulders and lets out a dispirited yawn. *Man, I want to make him proud like I used to.*

Goal: If I conquer this, I'll make my parents proud and go on to pursue that "perfect Armenian life" my parents deserve to see me nestle into. I might even prove to myself that I *can* trust God. That Jesus *is* faithful.

If I fail, I'll have no worth (*duh*), my brain will be wasted (so much for any humility angle) and I'll be a miserable chronically ill person who misses out on the joys of life, including marrying Mr. Hot Genius Armenian Christian.

In the meantime, there is one thing I *do* have control over—making Pops laugh.

I start belting out *Brush Up Your Shakespeare* from *Kiss Me, Kate* like I'm waiting for my audition call, except my only audience is my nightstand and Pops.

Maybe I should write a memoir at this point, titled, *Sing Anyway: The Chronicles of a Bedridden Believer.*

Pops' thunderous laugh fills the room, softening the edge of our shared despair. "You need a good acting role to channel all your pent-up energy, Lars."

I roll my eyes. "Yeah, right. Calling all agencies seeking bedridden talent! Special skills: dramatic monologues, blanket choreography, and award-winning eye rolls."

6
The Promise

Bedridden 9 months

It's midnight.

I'm lying in bed (as always) flat on my back in the dark, feeling the room turn in meaningless circles. *Why couldn't this disease be episodic, not chronic?*

Life goals: heal faster than Amazon Prime.

God subpoenaed my comfort, and I haven't seen it since. *Can't we settle out of court, Lord? I'll tithe extra and never skip Leviticus again.* I'm tired of being on hold with Heaven's customer service line—"Your miracle is important to us, please stay on the line."

Ugh. At least God has proven to me that He is in fact "close to the brokenhearted." Psalm 34:18.

Lately, Jesus' presence feels...uniquely close. Never felt it quite like this when I was healthy. It's like He's whispering to me through countless little coincidences that keep popping up, and at just the right moment. Not all coincidences are from God, obviously, and God speaks to each Christian differently. But thematic patterns—whether repeated Bible verses from different sources, counsel, or providential circumstances—have always been a major way the Holy Spirit speaks to me. Now, God has been showing off His divine timing to encourage me that He's walking with me through this pain. Job 36:15 states that God "speaks to [sufferers] in their affliction." Turns out this promise really *is* true.

Take, for instance, my three-day hospitalization at Bayside Health two months ago, when I got nothing but blank stares from neurologists and two excruciatingly loud MRI "spa sessions." (Think spinning around in circles while an electrical machine pounds into your brain.) Sevan sent me a sermon her friend had texted her that weekend, which happened to be about how many Biblical figures went through terrible trials but "courageously trusted that they would 'see the goodness of the Lord in the land of the living,'" as promised in Psalm 27:13. The pastor's words felt like a timely encouraging nudge from Jesus to keep trusting.

Or take a few weeks ago, when I cried to Mom, "My boat is sinking." I meant it metaphorically and literally, because my body and brain feel like they're navigating violent ocean waves nonstop. Mom opened my third daily devotional app on my phone a few hours later. (I've got four Christian apps and we use each randomly on and off.) Lo and behold the message of the day was the story of Jesus' disciples struggling on a boat in a raging storm, when Jesus instructed them to have more faith in His sovereignty and loving care. The devotional emphasized that Christians can persevere in their own severe storms because "Jesus is in the boat and won't let the boat *sink*."

Coincidence? The next day, Mom read my second devotional app's daily verse and it was Psalm 69:1-2: "Save me, O God, for the waters have come up to my neck...I have come into the deep waters..." Again, coincidence? Or Jesus comforting me that He understands my emotions and what I'm going through?

A third example—some months ago when my health declined to the point where I couldn't even sit up to eat anymore, I cried to Pops in an emotionally charged moment that I felt like a *prisoner*. Later that night, Pops read my *Daily Streams* daily devotional which was about the Apostle Paul's courageous attitude in prison, and how "in desperate situations God is training and changing us."

So, I guess God's prepping me for something? I still don't get why I need this *kind* of training though. I never understood why God allowed Joseph in the Old Testament to suffer years in a dungeon before his eventual government job. Yeah, yeah, Prime Minister, but still. The training seemed to have no correlation to Joseph's future position, other than forcing him to trust God in dire circumstances. *I guess that's enough? Faith, Lara. Humility. Some things we just can't understand.*

And then a few nights ago, right after yet another drug trial failed, Pops read me a Christian article and the first line struck me—"Has Jesus lead you down a bunch of dead ends? Keep trusting." That felt like another little wink from God, telling me I'm on the right track to permanent healing.

All of these encouragements have given me hope. What else can these things mean? *I will completely heal.*

Even stranger, God has given me explicit warnings multiple times right before something frightening was about to happen. For example, one morning, Joshua 1:9 randomly popped into my mind and resonated with my spirit—"Have I not commanded you? Be strong and courageous. Do not be afraid; do not be discouraged, for the Lord your God will be with you wherever you go." An hour later at breakfast, Mom read one of our daily devotional verses: Joshua 1:9.

I knew right then that the Holy Spirit was warning me not to be afraid of something ahead. I already knew God gives inaudible promptings in our hearts through His "still small voice" (1 Kings 19:12) (KJV), but I didn't know He specifically warns us of upcoming danger! So His warning terrified me at first. *Why do I need to be brave, Lord?*

Sure enough, two days later, a faint twitch appeared in my leg, but within hours, it escalated into relentless spasms—jagged, merciless, as if a hot knife were slicing straight into my leg muscles.

Every two minutes, the pain struck with violent precision, seizing my body and tearing a raw, involuntary scream from my throat. "Lord, help me! Lord, help me!" I howled into the night with Mom and Pops at my side, my voice ragged with desperation, almost taking an ER trip.

After five hours of agony, we traced the culprit—the latest medication was wreaking even greater havoc on my nervous system. We stopped it immediately. Still, a strange kind of gratitude settled in. *Thank you, Lord, for telling me in advance that You would be with me.* Apparently, sometimes God gives His children heads up like this right before they walk through great suffering, because He wants to reassure us that He's still in control. In Acts 20:23, the Apostle Paul himself writes that "in every city the Holy Spirit warns me that prison and hardships are facing me."

Argh, my back. Lying here, it feels like cardboard, stiff and unyielding. I want to move so badly—just stretch or turn to my side to fall asleep that way. But I can't. Turning my head left or right is a *no-go*, or else my ear crystals will pop out of place again, and the world will spin violently harder. Mom will have to administer another "Epley treatment maneuver" on me (where a nurse rapidly spins your head into a new position to shift your ear crystals, while you scream into a rollercoaster sensation.) It won't work, and we won't know why. *Sigh.*

Nothing works.

For now, I'm stuck in an eternal game of *don't move off your back*, and the stakes are my sanity.

Ten minutes later, as I'm about to fall asleep, I hear an inaudible voice in my heart. Something quiet but clear:

"I AM COMING."

Lord, is that You? I think I just heard from the Holy Spirit! He just told me He is coming...to help me?!

I gather my wits and immediately pray—"Lord, if that was

You, will You please give me a 'fleece sign' like You gave Gideon? To confirm? I believe You're telling me You're 'coming' to help me, and I just have to wait!"

The next morning, Mom reads me the *Daily Streams* app devotion of the day, and I gasp as Mom reads the words: "Are you waiting by chance on the Lord's *coming*? Trust His voice and eternal plans, and He will walk with you through the mighty sea."

Are you kidding me? This cannot be a coincidence. Jesus just gave me the confirmation I asked for—next day delivery! He's "coming." Finally.

My heart swells with a hope I haven't felt in a long time. I now know that if I wait, He'll heal me in the end, in His timing.

Maybe I really can trust God? I can't wait until You come to heal me, Lord. Maybe He'll put His hand on the next drug I'm trying?

Come Jesus, come!

When will the miracle be?

Can I get priority shipping?

7

The White Coat Musical

14 *months*

"Stay strong, Lars!" Mom shouts. "See you at Dumford Hospital!"

Two paramedics carry me out on a gurney toward the ambulance on our driveway, each thud of their boots echoing down the wooden steps of our front staircase. The uneven stretcher digs into my bones with every jolt, like it's trying to make a point.

Recently, I've been pushing myself desperately to sit upright and walk *again* for short stints wearing a heart monitor. But after two weeks, I'm now experiencing sharply enhanced spinning, pain, and sharp drops in blood pressure.

When trying again earlier today, I actually fainted, and Mom and Pops called for an ambulance during the few seconds I was out. When I came to, they helped me slam right back into bed, but we figured it's best to head to a hospital anyway. We've been discussing this option for months, and it's our last realistic chance for help. I've been hospitalized before, without success. But Dumford Hospital, a preeminent research institution, should certainly hold the key. God promised me He's "coming" to end my suffering. *Deliver me now, Lord.*

Since that "promise" from God five months ago to "come" for me, I've felt empowered. I even forced Mom to make me a vision board of everything I will do once I heal. Forget judge. If I run for Congress, I'll win on the sympathy vote alone. "Vote for me...I've been through enough!"

Paramedic No. 3 shifts my attention now: "Can you tell me what you're feeling?" He slaps a blood pressure cuff on my arm as the stretcher moves into the cold ambulance. I repeat what I've said to some 62 doctors to date—"I probably have migrainous vertigo, vestibular migraines, dislodging ear crystals, and two structural holes in both ears which cannot be repaired surgically but which cause me nonstop vertigo, and electrical and nerve pain in my body and brain. There's something wrong in the physical, neurological connection between my ears and my brain, and part of this disease remains undiagnosed because the treatments haven't worked." *At least I can still talk coherently.*

Before I know it, the ambulance is moving.

Fast.

This ain't gonna be pretty. Lord, please sustain my brain. I'm so scared. The motion of a car is akin to the motion that my brain can't process when I walk.

But a million times faster.

Fuel to the fire.

I decide to cope with the only logical coping mechanism. I channel my inner *Maria* and mentally belt *I Have Confidence* from *The Sound of Music*, all while death-gripping my gurney like it's a lifeboat for me and my hideous koala pajamas (still going strong).

I lie in a narrow, stiff bed, coddled like a flat piece of overcooked toast.

Location: Dumford ER, three hours after arrival. A sterile space with a small window, bathed in the cold, fluorescent glow of overhead lights. Air thick with the faint tang of antiseptic and stale coffee. An ugly IV pole next to my bed.

Status: My brain feels like exploding electrical fireworks. Every sound hits like scratching on a wall. *Oh, the superpowers of a hypersensitive migraine brain.* The steady, sharp beep of a heart monitor punctuates the air behind the curtain in front of me.

I brave to open my eyes. Everything turns in gigantic circles at 200 miles per hour, thanks to the duration and speed of the ride. *Oh my gosh. I can't keep my eyes open.*

Mom sits tense on a plastic clinical chair, its dull gray legs scraping against the floor with her slightest movement.

Thoughts on my mental conveyor belt:

> *Thank God Mom's always at my side*
> *The light in this room is super bright*
> *I need a hat to cover my face*
> *I'm no therapist, but that ambulance ride*
> *had trauma written all over it*
> *Beep, beep, beep. I hate hospital sounds*
> *These people better be smarter than the Bayside doctors*
> *Why is this room so ugly?*
> *What did you expect, the Ritz?*
> *Close your eyes, it hurts*

Knock knock. The door creaks open and in comes a doctor wearing thick glasses and an unbuttoned white coat, with her sleeves rolled up. After a curt "Hi," she checks my tongue and ears with a probe-like object, makes some niceties about how she's an Ear, Nose, and Throat doctor who will review my files, fake smiles, and leaves. I'm a lawyer trained to read witnesses. I know a fake smile when I see one.

Six and a half hours later, we find out from a nurse that this vertigo "expert" recommended I be sent right back home with just some "meclizine" and orders to consult my Ear, Nose, and Throat doctor back at Bayside.

What? Why would I be here after being bedridden for fourteen months if my Bayside doctor knew what to do? Mom and I beg the ER team to hospitalize me and try experimental testing, *anything*.

Hours later, at 1:30 A.M., they reluctantly agree, and only because a friend of mine at Dumford Medical School has a connection to one of the ER doctors. *Is this how the medical system works?* If they don't understand a certain illness, they just send you home? If I'd investigated criminal cases the way these doctors investigate diagnoses, I'd be charged with malpractice.

Before they transport me to my hospital room on a gurney, Mom kisses my left eye, triggering an intense sense of nostalgia. "I'm sure they know what they're doing now. We finally got here, and God will answer."

In this tender moment, it dawns on me that there's only one way we're both getting out of this sane: humor. I decide that *this* is going to be a musical. And sure enough, the next morning at 7 A.M., it starts.

One by one, fifteen "white coats" start taking turns marching in like a badly choreographed Broadway show. Each one "sings" some trivial questions about my symptoms, peers down at ambiguous looking charts, purports to care with pretty lousy acting, and leaves after stating some canned lines about possible vestibular therapy options to try "at home." Next white coat in, repeat. Except each white coat somehow manages to know or care less than the last.

It feels like an awful chorus number (with tap dancing) that never ends. *Are these people even discussing anything together? I'm no doctor, but have they even reviewed my history?*

Two days in, I start naming the "characters" based on their "compassion" and/or "helpfulness" levels.

That's when "Couldn't Care Less" Doctor No. 7—apparently

the secondary lead with Einstein's hairstyle—strolls in. An older guy with deep lines etched into his forehead, he barely glances at me before mumbling impatiently, "How would you best describe your condition? Have you tried vestibular therapy?" After scribbling down my response, he says curtly, "Well, whatever this is, at least you're able to explain it. So it hasn't affected your mental capacities."

Then, he delivers the zinger at the end of Act One—"Vertigo is hard to treat. Treatment is hit or miss sometimes. You must be depressed given your condition." *Okay, Sherlock. Why don't you try being strapped to a bed. I'm doing pretty good singing show tunes; let's see how you'd handle it.*

The cycle continues—doctors, nurses, specialists—each one offering a fragment, a theory, a half-formed diagnosis, without any new solutions. Some truly kind. Others not so much. The clock on the wall ticks steadily, but no one knows precisely what is wrong and why the typical vestibular therapies are not working on my brain after two years.

Thus, I start trying novel prayer tactics. "Lord, let's talk economics. Keeping me in this endless pit of misery lacks efficiency. We can get much more spiritual output by putting me back in the workforce. I'll witness to all the nonbelievers at work. See the math here? Didn't Abraham talk numbers with You in Genesis 18?"

At one point, the nurses shoot some drugs in my veins to see what might work to tame the hyperactivity in my brain. The drugs enhance my pain almost instantaneously. *Agony.*

Finally, on the fourth day, at 9 P.M., "Gives Off Villainous Vibes" Doctor No. 15 sings the closing number that steals the show: "We don't have any further options. Your case is a medical mystery neurologically in terms of its severity, and you've already tried the other thirty-four drugs we would try on you. It's probably the holes in your ears like Bayside concluded, but research on vertigo is underdeveloped. We're discharging you."

My cheeks immediately heat up and my heart pounds. *Isn't this a research institution? Aren't you going to consult your East Coast colleagues? Did you even review my genetic testing to check for other rare diseases?* Have you read the latest vertigo literature from Germany, which Pops texted Mom last night? Can't you see how debilitating this is on my functionality? I can't even lift my head off of one pillow without spinning harder. Isn't there anything you can suggest that we haven't tried? Analogies to treatment solutions for other neurological diseases?

I present a version of these arguments, but it's no use.

"I'm referring you to our outpatient ear clinic. Seven month wait for an appointment."

Mom's jaw clenches. "Seven months? But we can't even get her back here in a car because of the motion! We've even applied to medical mystery shows asking them to take on her case. No one's gotten back to me. We have no options left!"

"There's nothing more we can do. Given that she can't sit up, we set up an ambulance to take her back home tonight. I wish you well."

If words could land like a pile of bricks, these would pile high.

He leaves and the door slams shut behind him. I couldn't have scripted a more perfect "villain takes the final bow" ending if I tried.

I feel so dehumanized. I wish I were dumb. Things would be easier to accept. At least I wouldn't be fighting. Maybe I am dumb and that's why I don't know how to heal. Ugh. How on earth am I going to survive the car ride back?

Second hospitalization: FAIL.

A drop of water rolls down my chin.

Another one.

Is that a raindrop? It's sprinkling! Oh, that feels delightful on my skin after a year of being cooped up in a bedroom.

Two youngish looking paramedics carry me in the pitch dark on a stretcher from the ambulance on our driveway to the top of our front stairs.

Welcome back home to my regularly scheduled programming—Bed, Koala Pajamas, and Frustration. *Isn't rock bottom where You start handing out miracles, Lord? Or did I miss the sign-up sheet?*

Pops directs "traffic" as the paramedics slowly maneuver their way (and me) into the master bedroom. Once in, Kind Paramedic No. 1 slowly lifts my body in its entirety off of the stretcher like he's Prince Charming swinging Cinderella—except without the poetic feelings. Kind Paramedic No. 2 simultaneously holds my head parallel to the floor so that I need not sit up.

They slowly place me down into my old friend, the master bed.

"Ow!" I blurt out. *Ugh. Another brain zap.*

No. 2 shifts, startled.

Because of the forty-minute car ride both ways, I'm experiencing harder electrical currents in my brain and new brain "zaps" all over my body. Each zap feels like electricity coursing through my nerves. The docs said these *may* be a sign of an overstimulated nervous system which stemmed from progressing migraines which stemmed from motion sensitivity which stemmed from who knows what. Two years and two hospitalizations in, we still have no concrete diagnosis.

"Ow! Oh my gosh. Sorry to scare you."

"Don't be sorry," No. 1 whispers. "Actually, hey, can we pray for you?"

"Oh, you guys are Christian?" I ask.

"Yeah."

"Thanks so much. We're desperate."

No. 1 clasps my hand, and after a short but genuine prayer, he turns to Mom. "I'll keep praying for your daughter. One of my favorite verses is that God comforts us in all our troubles, so that we can comfort others in their pain too. Good luck."

"Thank you so much," Mom responds, a tear slipping down her cheeks. *Exhaustion or hope?*

If these guys offer a "Pray Now, Miracle Later" plan, I'm officially switching my insurance to paramedics.

8
Kid Gloves Off

18 months

I wake up to sunlight filtering through the window.

The endless buzzing sound of tinnitus immediately rings in my ears, like I'm living in a broken karaoke machine. My back is so rigid from not moving, it could double as a board for a Monopoly game.

My tricky relationship with the master bedroom bed, however, is evolving. It's a long-term commitment now, longer than most Hollywood marriages. If this bed really were my husband though, we'd be in couples counseling. The spark's gone, the support is questionable, and it's gaslighting me into thinking it's my fault.

I dare to open my eyes for half a second and watch the room swinging back and forth like a carnival ride. I close and beg, pounding my right fist on the bed. *Please heal me. When are You coming? You promised me You are coming!*

Such is the daily pleading ritual.

Morning.

Afternoon.

Evening.

Rinse and repeat.

Sense of self and purpose in the world: shattered.

Imaginary banner on the wall of this bedroom: demoralized.

Goal: remain a Christian.

No real treatment options left. What now? This is all happening because you asked God seven years ago to grow your faith, Lara. Way to go. No good deed goes unpunished. Now I'm in spiritual maturity "suffering boot-camp."

Symptoms: worse to worser. Yes, I just invented a new word. It's therapeutic.

Just when we thought things couldn't get any worse, I now have to keep my eyes shut 24/7 because the spinning of the outside world is too much for my system to tolerate after those two grueling back-to-back thirty-mile car rides. I'm now trying to "habituate" my eyesight *back* by opening them seven times a day, one minute each. The negative psychological effect this has had on my morale is almost impossible to describe in words.

Second, I can't even get up to go to the bathroom anymore, which was the *one* aspect of mobility I had throughout the day before Dumford. *Poof. Gone.* I pushed my brain too much with the walking attempts, car rides, and all the drugs.

"I'll bring your food in five minutes," Mom yells from the kitchen.

God bless her. She's now my full-time nurse, taking care of all my needs, including showering *on a bed*. Visualize luxury spa package—minus the luxury and spa.

No.

Dignity.

Left.

My dignity and I have parted ways…but not amicably.

And forget show tunes—my brain is now tap-dancing toward insanity.

Mom comes in with a plate of bland oatmeal my brain can tolerate. She takes out a notebook, jotting down my symptoms and the food I'm eating. Diary number seven. *What's the point?* Then, she's off to Costco.

I lie here alone, mentally reciting my losses in an obligatory "pity" inventory, like I'm preparing for the Saddest Awards Show. And the winner for Most Pathetic Life Situation goes to...Lara!

I'm thirty-two years old
I lost my career and dream job
I lost my health
My ears are on fire and my brain is a battlefield
I have nerve pain all over my body
I'm an invalid on a bed
I can't open my eyes
I can't take care of myself
It's spring outside, but what does it matter?
I haven't seen my friends in two years
This is prison
Scratch that, it's psychological torture
Still "single." Gosh, I hate that word
I need a show tune, but I'm tired of Les Miserables
At least staring at my inner eyeballs is better than watching that ugly ceiling
Does God want every Christian to suffer this much, or just me?

The evidence stacks high in the courtroom of my mind—nonstop searing pain, unanswered prayer—screaming in unison like a hostile witness: "God is not good." The only thing that comforts me is shouting accusations at God. I do so promptly. *Kid gloves are off, Lord.*

God, I knew You would let me down, just like Aunt Jackie. God promised me He was "coming." What could that have meant but to help me? Did I hear Him wrong? Did He lie? God doesn't lie. Maybe health is not God's plan for me after all? Would He actually want to give me a lifelong chronic illness? Why did God take me to Dumford if that wasn't the answer and He knew the car rides would make me astronomically worse? Is this a test of never-ending hoops to see if I will remain faithful?

God, You dangled my dreams in front of me and betrayed more than my body. You opened the door to my dream career only to slam it shut. Is my legal career really over now? It doesn't look like I'm going to be sitting up anytime soon, let alone presenting opening arguments. What was the point of it all? I could have gotten straight C's and this bed wouldn't care! Was God dangling that rainbow promise way back when to give me a spouse too? How am I going to meet, let alone marry, a guy while strapped to a bed? I believe in miracles, but unless he's an EMT or a mattress salesman, I'm out of luck.

God, why do You want me to suffer so greatly? I won't ever work as a lawyer again, just heal me! Is that what You want? Isn't divine help and healing the point of having a faithful and loving God? Why do You keep closing all doors? What is the point of praying for direction? Do You even love me?

After all my ranting and raving, I'm upset.

With myself.

Man, look at me. I used to have such strong faith and love for Jesus. My spiritual backsliding is causing me emotional pain in and of itself. Please forgive me, Lord. Does suffering disillusion everyone? Was it just that my faith was never tested? Like *really* tested?

At least I'm in good company. Examples of Biblical figures wrestling with God abound:

Jacob (Genesis 32:22-32), who literally wrestled with God and was renamed Israel, meaning "he struggles with God";

Moses (Exodus 3-4), who argued with God about his calling, feeling inadequate to lead Israel out of Egypt;

Jeremiah (Jeremiah 20:7-9), who complained that God had deceived him and lamented his prophetic calling;

Habakkuk (Book of Habakkuk), who questioned God's justice and timing, asking why evil always seemed to prevail.

I know struggling with God is part of faith. That's how I bounced back after Aunt Jackie, to deeper trust and transformation. Could it be that my faith will eventually grow stronger, despite—and maybe even through—all my intense anger and disillusionment?

How did that Job guy handle his heartbreak?

God said Job was so "blameless and upright" that there was "no one on earth like him." Job 1:8. That must be why Job did what so few of us could—he worshiped God right after his initial, unimaginable suffering hit (including the tragic deaths of all ten of his children at once). But as his affliction lingered on, including when Satan inflicted painful sores all over his own body, his patience eventually cracked.

He started pleading with God, protesting, and questioning God's justice. After all, he'd been faithful, so why had God let his life fall apart? Job didn't mince words in his prayers: "The arrows of the Almighty are in me, my spirit drinks in their poison; God's terrors are marshaled against me." Job 6:4. Job also lamented, "[Y]ou toss me about in the roar of the storm." Job 30:22. *This guy is so relatable. I'm being tossed about in literal ocean waves too.*

Job even accused God of abandonment at one point: "Why do You hide your face and consider me Your enemy?" Job 13:24. *Wow. I can't believe God put these verses in the Bible. Thank you, Lord, for letting us air our deepest, darkest emotions to You.*

Maybe I really should write my own modern-day book of Job at this point.

Working title—*Why???*

9

Matthew John

22 months

"I don't get why the Bible says we must 'rejoice in suffering' and 'count it all joy.' This is so counterintuitive. Am I supposed to be a masochist?"

One new thing in our routine is that Matt—a five-foot-ten half Armenian, half Jewish guy with boyish looks from my church—calls on the dot once every two months to check in. He reached out to Mom eight months ago when we got back from Dumford, because she's handling my phone calls now.

Matt is this really sweet engineering nerd four years older than me. He can best be summed up in two words that rarely describe the same person—brilliant and meek. I frankly don't want to talk to anyone else, mostly because the electrical signals from phone calls enhance my pain, but also because he's really helpful. He encourages me to keep trusting God, and compassionately answers my tough theological questions. Kind of like my spiritual Google.

Today, he's listening closely. "I totally get it," he consoles in his deep voice. "I know it's almost impossible for you to view this as 'joy' right now. God wants us to authentically grieve our losses. But we can persevere with hope because God's doin' a million good things through all this, even if we can't see 'em. Just think of all your friends you'll witness to about God's sustainin' grace if you get out of this thing and say, 'Hey, Jesus walked with me the whole way.'"

I know he's right. Ugh. Thank God he can't see me wearing these hideous hippo print pajamas. (I've upgraded.)

So far, Matt has impressed upon me that while humans recoil from suffering, God doesn't. In Exodus 4:11, God even admits, "Who makes [humans] deaf or mute? Who gives them sight or makes them blind? Is it not I, the Lord?" Other such verses abound, *e.g.*, Isaiah 45:7—"I bring prosperity and create disaster; I, the Lord, do all these things." While this idea is incredibly shocking and hard to swallow, the Bible makes clear that we "suffer according to God's will[.]" 1 Peter 4:19.

But there's a critical nuance here. God (paradoxically) allows and wills suffering in His sovereign power—*despite hating it*. Due to "His unfailing love," God "does not willingly bring affliction or grief to anyone." Lamentations 3:32-33. Matt explains that God permits suffering only when He plans to accomplish some eternal (and greater) *good* purpose through that evil. One that will make it all worth it in eternity when we see His final plans coming together.

As Romans 8:28 promises, "in all things God works for the good of those who love Him, who have been called according to His purpose." While not all things are "good," Matt says that God *uses* all things—even the worst things—for a good redemptive purpose.

Flagship example—"[I]t was [God's] will to crush [Jesus] and cause Him to suffer" on the cross (Isaiah 53:10), but only because that tremendous evil would redeem mankind by paying the penalty for mankind's sin. God also allowed "a messenger of Satan" to "torment" the Apostle Paul with a chronic affliction (a "thorn in [his] flesh") to teach him to rely on God's all-sufficient strength and grace. 2 Corinthians 12:7-9. Thus, while the Bible portrays

Satan as the instigator of many illnesses (Luke 13:16), God allows Satan this limited power for God's mysterious and redemptive *good* purposes.

The "good" God pursues isn't always earthly either—it's the eternal things, the stuff we don't yet fully see now, but will in Heaven. As Paul writes in 1 Corinthians 13:12, "Now I know in part; then I shall know fully[.]" This means, Matt says, that we must recklessly trust God's goodness, even if certain earthly outcomes are completely contrary to what we'd think a loving God would do.

I definitely don't have *that* kind of faith. It sort of feels like a non-responsive cop-out to the problem of evil: "We won't understand until Heaven." But Matt tells me such trust cannot come from human reasoning, but must be spiritually discerned through pure faith. *Lord, please give me this faith. Change me.*

Matt comforts me that my illness isn't punishment either. Many believers face crippling illness with no direct link to personal sin. When asked why a certain man was born blind, Jesus answered, "Neither this man nor his parents sinned…but this happened so that the works of God might be displayed in him." John 9:3.

Today, Matt clears his throat and adds, "Lara, don't forget all the reasons God allows us to go through seasons of suffering." He outlines them in detail:

We learn to humbly trust His purposes and realize we're not in control, but are dependent on God for life, breath, and everything else.

We bear spiritual fruit by testifying to nonbelievers about God's sustaining power and grace even in suffering, thus pointing the world to Christ's suffering and the gospel.

The genuineness of our faith is tested and refined, thereby showcasing God's worth and glory to the world and shaping our character into the likeness of Christ.

We experience greater intimacy with Jesus by obediently suffering God's will like He did. Because Jesus Himself knows what it's like to suffer, He draws near and "empathize[s] with our weaknesses[.]" Hebrews 4:15. This is unique to Christianity and makes all the difference in suffering.

Suffering reminds us we are "foreigners and exiles" on this earth (1 Peter 2:11) and shifts our focus to eternal things rather than the temporary pleasures of this world, thus creating real and lasting hope.

Twenty minutes later, as Matt finishes praying for me, I'm feeling lighter. Matt debates theology like it's the spiritual Olympics. He vaults over my doubts, backflips through verses, and sticks the landing every time. It helps me mature spiritually.

"Look," Matt reassures now, "let's let God use you where you are right now. In the meantime, I'm prayin' for miraculous help." I like how he makes me feel like he's walking through this suffering with me—"*Let's* let God use you."

I don't know why Matt wants to spend this time counseling me. Goodness of his heart? Some divine responsibility to check in on poor, unfortunate souls? But these calls are my lifeline, and strong evidence of God's love for me right now—even amidst my anger. Here's a mere acquaintance with wisdom who wants to show me he cares intimately about my pain.

"Thanks much, Matt. Talk to you soon."

"Sure thing." *I like how he always replies with that. "Sure thing." Reassuring.*

Matt and I were never close like this before. He grew up in the Bay Area, left for school, then moved back in 2014 when he started as faculty teaching Clinical Laboratory Science in San Francisco State University's Medical Diagnostics program. I didn't get to know him until 2017, when we were stuck alone together in a car for six hours on our way to a weekend Armenian Christian camp called "**Camp Arev**" in Los Angeles.

First impressions then—he seemed a little…shy. Maybe even a little awkward around me. I disarmed him by asking one million questions and it worked to put him at ease. We had a really great time intellectually the whole ride, laughing about topics as diverse as physics and Broadway.

I quickly learned Matt was remarkably well balanced for an engineer; he liked discussing politics and law, and had innovative ideas on countless topics. He clearly had a sharp disdain for rambling lawyers and politicians. They were the butt of many of his jokes, after which he would chuckle with this kind of "engineer-type" giggle. Almost like his brain calculated the perfect amount of sound waves needed to express his mischievous joy.

We talked theology nonstop because it fired us both up. I asked him every question under the sun about the intersection of science and faith, and parts of the Bible that made no sense to me. Nothing seemed to be outside the scope of his knowledge. I quickly realized Matt's mind was a high-speed train, and I was lucky to be hanging onto the caboose.

I came to other conclusions on that trip, the first being that this guy was simply unique. No other word for it, really. He had this chipper, nerdy walk thing going on with a youthful bounce that exuded cheerfulness in each step. And to this day, he still has that boy-next-door charm, mixed with "somewhat robotic and stoic professor." There's an innocence to him that's something refreshing.

Nor does he fit the mold of your typical nerd. His "onion" has far more complex layers. For one thing, he's quite literally a genius—and I'm talking scary smart. In camp circles he's known as the science and theology genius. He has undergraduate, master's, and PhD degrees in Chemical and Biomolecular Engineering from UCLA, where he pioneered a new area of research in PET imaging for the detection of pancreatic cancer.

Yet despite this, Matt gives himself absolutely zero airs of importance. His rare, humble energy puts you at ease the minute you start talking with him, and it's unclear how he accomplishes this feat given that his body language simultaneously screams "I'm shy" the minute you meet him.

Matt is also unabashedly unique in that he has zero—if not

negative—interest in worldly things. He enjoys debating philosophy and politics, but only for the momentary sport of it. He's just genuinely unimpressed by the world. A modern-day Paul? Here's a guy who's made breakthroughs in cancer research and could probably build a rocket in his free time, and he doesn't even bat an eye when you talk about fame or fortune. His middle name is John to boot, so his name "Matthew John" screams "disciple" all over it. He's the kind of guy who probably has an Excel sheet titled *Things to Pray For* with pivot tables. If salvation were an algorithm, Matt would've optimized it by now.

I mean, the guy doesn't even idolize food—in stark contrast to yours truly. Three hours into the car ride, he pulled out a four-inch sad-looking PB&J sandwich and a tiny water bottle. That sandwich looked so sad I wanted to lay hands on it and pray for healing. I, in turn, busted out a gourmet foot-long Lunardi's Italian sandwich with all the trimmings (think feta cheese, specialty pickles), a large cookie, a Snickers bar, and a Pepsi.

Feeling awkward—and gluttonous—I improvised. "You want half?"

"Sure, thanks."

Luckily, I'm an actress and acted like I wanted to share it.

I didn't.

Matt's lack of worldly interest also extends—for better or worse—to his, shall I say, quirky and somewhat unpredictable fashion sense. At church, he characteristically sports tucked in shirts, colorful ties screaming '80s, and his phone attached to his hip like a pager on a '90s dad. But on random occasions, he looks pretty darn chic. *Who is picking this guy's outfits?*

And then, there's his celebrated navy leather hat covering his bald head—an Indiana Jones number that never quite matches anything he wears. He always stands near the church entrance door wearing it, holding his Bible up to his chest and beaming his characteristic, infectious smile. The kids at church affectionately call him "Matt in the Hat."

What Matt's body language and demeanor proclaim to the world: *I don't care what you and your pop culture think of me, I'm only interested in one thing—making disciples.* During his PhD years, he taught Sunday school at our sister church in Los Angeles, where he was on the Board of Christian Education and led an after-school tutoring program.

He moved back to the Bay Area with the specific goal of growing my church's youth group, so now he volunteers his time as our unpaid youth pastor, teaching Sunday School lessons and driving the whole load of kids to **Camp Arev** every summer and winter in his van. He has served as a counselor there for about fifteen years, without missing a single season. He's known for doing funky science explosions and chemical reactions for the kids, with a spiritual lesson always lurking in the background.

One more thing—Matt has somewhat of a reputation. For suffering. He's the unfortunate guy in Armenian evangelical circles who had to fight Stage 4 non-Hodgkin's lymphoma at age fourteen, facing tumors all over his young body. But he beat it after a year of chemo treatments and painful surgeries. Today, Matt is considered a walking miracle in our church circles.

But instead of chasing glory and the treasures of this world, he uses that brush with death to keep his eyes on God. It's inspiring. Matt often preaches from the pulpit as a lay member about his cancer, including how he later *thanked* God for his cancer because it made him a less selfish person and made him seek God for the first time. Today, he spends his summers doing missions work in Haiti, moonlighting as a part-time missionary.

The guy sounds like a caricature, doesn't he? Hand on my heart, it's the bare-bones truth. Matt's so saintlike that if he passed gas, even the church council would be shocked. Okay, maybe *that's* an exaggeration.

Matt does appear to have one critical flaw though—an unabashed hatred of stuffy church banquets. You know, the kind where the main event isn't charity or breaking bread, but an unholy desire to dress up and fan our own egos. Matt's disdain, combined with his no-nonsense, somewhat terse speaking style, got him into trouble once when he scolded the church council that "if fundraising were really the goal, we'd all be better off clocking in at McDonald's for a week instead of charging hundreds per banquet ticket just to feed ourselves instead of the homeless." Matt recounted that story to me in that 2017 car ride, giggling with pride.

At the end of that trip, we stayed acquaintances. He's the kind of guy I wouldn't recklessly flirt with because I'd feel guilty playing fast and loose with his pure heart, and he reverted to being painfully shy around me anyway. Sometimes, when I saw him glancing at me during coffee hour, he'd flash me his signature smile, take off his celebrated hat and tip it, then place it right back on—with all the respectful courtesy of a British gent.

I couldn't help but wonder if maybe the scars of his childhood cancer ran deeper than the physical, etching a quiet insecurity somehow? He did tell me on that trip: "We all walk around with scars—some you can see, some you can't. Mine are on my body. Chronic back pain and a jagged scar runnin' down my back from a brutal infection, both from the cancer. And a smaller one on my chest where the chemo port used to be. For the longest time, I wouldn't go near a beach. Too self-conscious to peel off my shirt."

Perhaps that fear of being seen, of being truly known with all his scars and trauma, made rejection from women feel inevitable to him before he even tried? As a lawyer, I used to love analyzing people, but he was a tough case to crack.

Fast forward a few years and now each of Matt's telephone calls is a breath of fresh air in this stale bedroom. A rare gem of intellectual stimulation chatting with a PhD. My only connection to a world that still makes sense. Matt's suffered big time, so he gets it, and he's a trustworthy guy.

Oddly enough, though, our dynamic has changed. The guy who was once very shy, robotic, and reserved in 2017 now speaks with a boldness I haven't heard before. He's the same guy, but somehow…more? I on the other hand, feel emotionally naked and vulnerable. Something has changed and I can't put my finger on it. Whatever it is, Matt's deep, reassuring voice, unassuming yet wise, is a balm on my weary soul.

When I get off this bed, I'm going to hug that engineer so tight, he'll wish he had a PB&J sandwich as a shield.

10

Deeper Still

26 months

"Thank you, Doctor Barich, for considering my case," I dictate to Mom in bed *with my eyes closed*—the norm 24/7 now. "We anxiously await your response."

Another day, another desperate letter to "vertigo expert" No. 567.

It's almost dinner time, one year into the COVID-19 pandemic, and Mom, Pops, and I are thrilled everyone else is stuck inside too. Back to another Christmas season. "Tis the season to be weary, Fa-la-la-la-la, la-la-la-la!" *Whatever, at least Sevan promised to bring me ten gifts just for me to open on this bed.*

If you'd told me a few years ago that I'd spend every consecutive Christmas lying flat as a pancake while my parents fed me soup like I was a toddler, I would've laughed. Now, I laugh to keep from crying.

I open my eyes briefly and see Mom—at the foot of the bed—looking ironically serious in her zebra print pajamas, furiously scribbling down my letter. Not that I'm looking any hotter sporting the same hippo print pajamas morning, noon and night. Changing outfits feels like hosting a fashion show lately, considering how rare it is. All because I can't lift my head even a centimeter off my pillow without a corresponding tsunami of more symptoms.

"That should do it," Mom sighs. "I'll tell your father to type it up."

As she starts toward the door, emotion grips me and the words vomit out. "Mom, I can't do this anymore. Been lying here with my eyes closed without moving for one whole year. Tried thirty-six drugs, hospitalized twice."

Mom gives me a wry look that shouts—*Don't ask me, I'm overdue for an emotional oil change myself*. As my full-time nurse for a year now, not to mention my full-time health care advocate, she's burdened with a third 24/7 job—worrying about her daughter.

Even supportive phone calls from her four Golden Girls haven't been enough to keep her chin up. Mom has been begging God, but her faith is waning. She hides her grief with sarcasm, joking yesterday, "No one ask me anything; I'll start shouting." She's been my rock this whole way, a vision of miraculous strength and grace, but now I see some cracks.

Since Dumford a year ago, we've tried every therapy known to man. We gave up on drugs and started trying more novel "therapies," *e.g.*, nervous system stimulating devices, occupational therapists, homeopaths, herbalists, osteopathy. *Willing to come to our home for a fee? Come on over.*

But no matter what I try, no dice. To pacify ourselves, we strategize every day like we're running a Fortune 500 company, except our sole product is confusion. We go to sleep and wake up the next day, only to repeat the same dead-end conversation. Pops jokes nowadays that "Mom's hanging by a thread, and the rest of us are hanging onto her skirt."

The height of our therapy "Renaissance"?

Perhaps the hypnotist. But the only thing he put into a trance was my bank account.

Perhaps the "healer" from Hollywood—a lawyer friend

connected me—who charged us $150 to hum "fadalalala" at me over the phone while instructing Mom to "soak my feet in water" to "connect my energies." (Don't laugh—when desperate, you pay anyone.) Pops' take: "Next time holler Lars, and I'll hum for free."

Perhaps the "functional neurologist" who randomly ordered a pregnancy test, which I promptly refused—"Unless immaculate conception comes with vertigo, I think you're barking up the wrong uterus."

Perhaps lying on the bed with acupuncture needles sticking out of me, auditioning to play the porcupine in the master bedroom musical.

Perhaps the exceedingly bright nutritionist who suggested I'm losing weight because I'm probably anorexic. *Ah*, so I can't move and my body physically *can't* eat much due to severe nausea, so I'm *choosing* not to? Cool, can I also "choose" to be healthy again? I suppose my next 102-degree fever also means I just love being warm.

Perhaps the $1,083.67 bill we received for a seven-minute video consultation with Bayside's out-of-network vertigo experts who expertly concluded, "We can't help." Pops asked, "What's that extra 67 cents for? A participation trophy?"

In addition to the nonstop vertigo and electrical currents in my brain, new issues have popped up as a result of my immobility. Severe abdominal pain. Persistent nausea from the spinning sensation. Joint pain. Muscle spasms. Muscle atrophy. I've started working with a physical therapist who helps me exercise my limbs on a bed to keep my circulation going.

If we're on a journey, we're in the deep swamp now. I've been isolated without seeing my friends for three years. *But oh, to glance at just one other room in the house, or the outside world.*

Mom walks over to me now, with a firm but loving tone. "Lara, you have to sit up and try to walk again despite your brain spinning. If you don't you're going to die from lack of circulation, or a bed sore."

I open my eyes again for ten seconds, just long enough to look into her tired eyes and gray hair. Guilt gnaws at me. *She's stopped dying her hair. I have to get better somehow. For Mom.*

"Mom, I want to walk so badly. But you know what happens when I sit up, let alone walk. My brain is in a pattern where neuroplasticity has gone wrong; my brain has learned the wrong patterns, and I've tried one million ways to retrain it! There's got to be another winning therapy out there before I try walking again."

I slam my eyes shut again.

"We don't have a choice, Lara. If you don't move again, sooner or later you will die from a blood clot from lying still!" This time her desperation leaks through.

"I'm not going to die, Mom! God is protecting me. He promised to come for me. God keeps his promises."

Right on cue, Pops barges in with a dinner tray. "Grace, can I give her dinner?"

"Yes," she replies, walking out.

"Mom, you know you're my rock, right?"

"More like a puddle of play dough," she whines from a distance.

I open my eyes to find Pops sitting right by me, soup tray in his lap. Tonight's special: green pea soup. What I can tolerate. Not exactly the chef's kiss. More like the chef's "meh."

"Pops," I ask, "how long am I supposed to suffer?"

He sighs deeply. "You have to sit up and try to walk again, Lars. It's been one year since our last try."

He places a towel on my chest and starts feeding me with a big spoon, his heart undoubtedly breaking. His daughter is a prisoner in a cell made of flesh and bone. I still have all my motor skills, but it's easier for him to feed me when my eyes are closed, so that we don't spill.

"Pops, you know I tried that so many times and it just made me worse. That's why I ended up hospitalized at Dumford!"

He feeds me another spoon. "We don't have a choice."

Mom shouts from the living room. "Lars, Matt texted just now. He says 'This Christmas, don't give up hope. God came to save us. He's with you.' Anyway, oh, wow, there's a rainbow over the hill. Pretty. All the colors, Lars. Has it been drizzling?"

Hmm. Rainbows meant so much to me at one time. I better have Mom write this down for me, along with Matt's hopeful text. (Mom has been playing secretary whenever I need to dictate an encouragement from God in my award-winning "God Redeems Illness Journal.") *Wait...I feel something coming on.*

"Oh no! Pops... Wait...let it pass." An acutely harder spinning episode has come on. On top of the chronic vertigo and involuntary, neurological head shaking, my brain still takes random harder spins out of nowhere in response to certain external stimuli.

"Just let the symptoms take their course, Lars," Pops insists.

"They're taking course all right," I mutter.

We both wait a second...then simultaneously burst out laughing. *Ah, a welcome distraction during this hard spin. Just let the ocean waves pass over you.*

"Pops, just hold my hand for a minute to steady me. It'll pass soon."

Two minutes later, the episode is over. *Phew.*

After ten minutes, Pops boldly announces, "Just one more spoon."

"Too nauseous. Don't want any more. You said one more spoon four spoonfuls ago."

"I have my tricks."

We both chuckle again. It's Pops' job to make me laugh every night. He takes it seriously.

"Pops, tonight will you read to me from that online British travel blog?"

My parents have been satisfying my desperate need for intellectual stimulation lately by discussing anything and everything from British history to foreign affairs to macroeconomics to jungle animals to traveling to Scotland. I'm literally in a self-enrolled homeschooling program with my eyes closed.

Moreover, Pops has now finished reading me the entire Bible, along with a whopping 210 seven-page Bible Study Fellowship packets. That means we've essentially done a seven-year Bible course in two years. (I'm expecting an honorary seminary degree in the mail any day now, as I'm no doubt the most theologically astute bedridden person in North America.)

Through all this, we've grown spiritually together amidst our despair. It's hard to have hope, but in this desert of pain, Jesus has given me this deep comfort in His Word. As Psalm 119:92 states, "If Your law had not been my delight, I would have perished in my affliction." *Relatable, Lord.*

"I'm done eating," I say. "Please. No more." I open my eyes to see Pops furrow his eyebrows as he caves and puts the soup down. Then, he grabs my hand desperately. He's an emotional type, like me, who can't resist a wave of intense emotion.

"God put us here on this planet," he rambles. "Why can't He let us enjoy it?" He is half joking, half dead serious. The reality of his words cuts deep, leaving us both nervously fumbling in the awkward silence that follows. *Shove it down. Use sarcasm.*

"God has His timing, okay Pops? Let's stay strong. We're fighters. But listen, I have an important theological question for you. Why would a rational God create the porcupine? So ugly. Was He up there thinking, 'some spikes might look cool on this one'?"

Pops eases into another chuckle, blowing off some steam. "That's not important. What's important is figuring out which lucky lad you're gonna marry when you get off this bed. I want to shed my PSI status now!" (PSI—a term Pops and I coined when I was healthy—meaning "Parents Seeking In-laws" because their daughter is still single.) "And…I want to see you on stage asap."

My parents' heroic efforts to keep me smiling are Oscar-worthy, especially given that everything else has gone sideways recently. Forty-three mishaps and counting, including:

*A burglar is caught crossing our front
yard during a police chase
Two toilets break
Water heater fails
Toaster breaks
Two shutters break
Washing machine breaks
Pops lands in the ER after a soccer ball hit to the eye
Sevan lands in the ER twice for food poisoning
Mom burns her finger and makes two ER
trips for blood pressure scares
Two car batteries die
Theo, Sevan's Maltese dog, makes two midnight ER visits
A huge pumpkin in a rolling cart slams into
Mom's car in a Safeway parking lot*

Ah, the pumpkin ambush this family really needed.

I'm realizing more and more how the Bible's explicit teaching on suffering—what Matt keeps urging me to rest in—diametrically opposes our modern values of seeking pleasure and happiness above all. Acts 14:22 states, "We must go through many hardships to enter the Kingdom of God[.]" Jesus Himself warned about life's trials in John 16:33—"In this world you will have trouble. But take heart! I have overcome the world."

This means Christians are *promised* suffering. This exposes the absolute falsity of the supposed "health, wealth, and prosperity" gospel. Why are we even surprised? Our religious emblem is literally a cross. A symbol of torture. We are disciples of a suffering Savior. 2 Corinthians 1:5 even states that "we share abundantly in the sufferings of Christ[.]" The bottom line—Christianity requires costly perseverance if we are guaranteed suffering in the initial terms of the contract. But to any rational mind, eternal life after death (in Heaven) is beyond worth it.

Pops now instigates the next step in our nightly "routine." He brings a cup of water and my toothbrush, slapping a towel on my chest. I brush my teeth, swirl the water, and spit it out—all without lifting my head. *I deserve a medal for this.*

"I want you to stroke each and every chopper, Lars."

"Pops, your obsession with choppers is unsettling."

His thunderous laugh reverberates.

"What day is it again?" Mom shouts from the living room.

Pops chuckles, shouting back, "Today is Monday, tomorrow is Tuesday, the next day is Wednesday. What difference does it make? We're in the same boat."

I swoosh more water around then spit out, laughing so hard I almost choke.

"Yeah, but we're rowing with one oar and no map."

11

The Jaw & Jericho

29 months

"Just hold still as I stretch it out. This will hurt."

A dentist has joined the cast of characters in our master bedroom today.

It happens to be Mom's brother.

Uncle Albert.

For ninety days now, my entire jaw muscle has been frozen tight in a tense clamped position due to an unexplained neurological spasm.

Translation—my jaw is a prison, and I'm its unwilling inmate.

I can't open my mouth—not even a centimeter—which means I can't chew or eat. Muscle relaxants and other experiments haven't worked, so Mom has been pulverizing food into a fine puree using a blender and feeding it to me *through a straw.* That's three meals a day.

Liquidized and served.

Last ninety days.

We've been praying for a miracle.

I can't talk or sing, other than mumbling like I've got marbles in my mouth, because I can't open my jaw. On the bright side, all the top law firms are clamoring to hire me now. I'm an exceptionally skilled bedridden orator...who can't speak!

To top it off, I've had an intense stabbing sensation in my jaw on and off the last thirty days. It comes on suddenly, lasts about four minutes, then stops. I've lost twelve pounds and am only a few meals away from getting a VIP ticket to the ER for a feeding tube. My body is starving, and I've been humming *Food, Glorious Food* from the musical *Oliver!* to keep myself calm for weeks now. (This one's not a joke.)

But today, Mom and Pops have front row tickets to another Broadway special—*Chew On This: A Spectacular New Jaw-aching Musical*, featuring Lara, Uncle Albert, and "The Jaw."

"Okay, feel free to yell, Lars," Uncle Albert offers matter-of-factly while hovering over me, standing upright next to my bed. "It might release your tension...Okay, one, two, three..."

"Ow!" I scream, as Uncle Albert yanks my jaw around like he's twisting the lid off a stubborn pickle jar. Left, right, up, down in huge circular motions.

"Ow! Ow! Ayeee."

Oh.

My.

Gosh.

Interestingly, last week, God put the Book of Joshua on my heart one morning. Then, I kid you not—Pops walked in six hours later and suggested, "Let's read Joshua tonight, yeah?" *Did Pops read my mind or is this from God? I hadn't even told Mom.*

So Pops started reading. There, the city of Jericho was "tightly shut" with gates (Joshua 6:1) (NLT) but God promised to give Joshua and the Jews the city—even though it seemed impossible. I couldn't help but notice the parallels to our situation. My jaw, like Jericho, is "tightly shut." And it feels like this muscle spasm—or whatever it is—is an enemy too formidable to win. I asked God, *Are You promising me You will do for me what you promised*

Joshua, and open up this "city" (my jaw) so I can eat again? Please, Lord. This feels like You're trying to encourage me.

A few days after reading the Jericho story, Uncle Albert called Mom. "An idea just came to mind. Let's try it before she goes to the ER. Worth a shot."

So here we are.

Screaming.

"Ow!"

"Just keep yelling, almost done." Uncle Albert is one of those guys who would be calm defusing a bomb.

Pops chimes in as the encouragement gallery. "Yes, yell Lars, yell!"

"Owww!" *This is the longest thirty seconds of all time. Lord, help me tolerate this. My brain is shaking so hard. Actually...I feel Your strength getting me through this? Think Philippians.*

Earlier this morning, I woke up dreading what Uncle Albert was going to put me through. Mom read me the daily verse in my first devotional app and lo and behold it was Philippians 4:13—"I can do all things through Christ who strengthens me" (NKJV). *Good timing, Lord. And now, God's giving me courage to get through this.*

Seconds later, Uncle Albert slams my jaw back into place with his forceful but steady fist, like he's reattaching a loose door hinge. Supposedly this maneuver might snap my jaw back into alignment.

He wraps a tight circular headband from the crown of my head to the bottom of my jaw, pats me on the arm, and declares, "Keep that band on for seven days. No excuses."

Seven days? The *same* amount of time Joshua and his crew circled Jericho before the walls came down miraculously. Coincidence? *Will I have to do a full parade and play trumpets too, Lord? If You want theatrics, I'm all about it.*

"Keep me posted. Keep fighting, Lars," Uncle Albert chirps as he walks out. "Nanor is praying for you nonstop." Nanor is his wife, Mom's Golden Girl No. 2.

After seven days of looking like a poor soul who lost a bet with a chiropractor, parole day finally arrives. Mom is in my room with scissors, about to take the sacred band off my head. She nervously begins cutting and unwrapping the band.

First inch. Off.

Second inch. Off.

Third inch. Off.

Until seconds later…it's off.

This is it. Push your jaw down slowly to see if it will move. One…two…

My jaw suddenly drops open, as if someone just unlatched a cage.

"Oh, thank God! Mom—it's moving! Up and down! I can talk! Wait, let me try moving it left and right…Ooh that's a bit tight, but it's moving!"

Pops runs in, shouting, "We are free from dental Alcatraz?! Praise the Lord!"

Mom slaps a wet kiss on my left eye, as happy tears slip down her cheeks. "I can't believe it! Hallelujah! I am so *done* with that blender."

Two hours later, we're still in disbelief. *I can chew again. Wow.*

And you guessed it, Pops made me barbecue shrimp and I'm chowing down like it's my last meal on earth.

𝄞

Hours later, I'm alone in bed in the dark, listening to the wind rustle outside.

Wow. I can't believe You gave me a Jericho today, Lord. God's still in the business of last-minute saves.

Today's parallel to the Jericho story was uncanny. The Bible really *is* "alive and active" (Hebrews 4:12), speaking into our life situations, even prophetically sometimes! My jaw was "shut up" just like the city of Jericho, and just like God delivered the city into Joshua's hands after seven days of circling, God delivered my jaw from that awful spasm after seven days of wearing that headband. *Thank you, Lord! Have I learned any other valuable lessons about God's love the last few months?*

I know Psalm 34 is still true. God is *still* near to the brokenhearted.

Though God hasn't explained the *why*, He continues to show His care for me by giving me His intimate presence as Isaiah 41:10 promises—"So do not fear, for I am with you; do not be dismayed, for I am your God. I will strengthen you and help you; I will uphold you with my righteous right hand." He's still speaking to me and encouraging me in countless ways through what I now call "Holy Spirit Text Alerts."

For example, one month ago, my friend Rachael texted Mom to tell me that "God doesn't abandon His children," and later that night, Pops said the same exact phrase to me in Armenian, without knowing. Another friend texted Hebrews 1:14 this week, which says God's angels protect us, and later the same night Sevan randomly said, "Angels are protecting you, Lars, don't worry." Sevan was as shocked as I was when I told her my friend had just sent me that same message.

God even showed up on my birthday. That morning, I didn't mince words—"Lord, You've forsaken me on a bed for a second year!" Seven hours later, a surprise gift of fifty pink roses arrived on our doorstep. My church friend Toukhig had sent them, and she told us later she had no idea it was my birthday, but had been praying for months asking God when and how she should encourage me. It was unmistakable that God sent her gift specifically on my birthday out of 365 days to explicitly tell me that He "s[ees] my affliction and kn[ows] the anguish of my soul," as Psalm 31:7 promises.

Next, if Psalm 23 ever needs a defense witness, it might as well be me. For two years now, the Lord has literally "prepare[d] a table before me in the presence of my enemies." How else have I safely eaten 2,190 meals on a bed, lying on one pillow, with my head shaking involuntarily on and off, and the last year with my eyes closed? With all sorts of random throat and muscle spasms making it very dangerous to swallow? If this isn't "sustaining grace," I don't know what is.

A final example. One night, when I refused food due to severe nausea despite Pops' protestations, we pivoted to Bible study and stumbled upon Acts 27:34, where the Apostle Paul begged his fellow boat passengers, in a violent storm, to stop refusing food—"I urge you to take some food. You need it to survive." Pops gasped at the timing. "See, Lars? God is instructing you. I'm bringing the meal again." I complied and was able to keep it down entirely without vomiting. Coincidence?

So God really does speak into our situations and sustain us in the fire, even though His grace might not "feel" sufficient a lot of the time. I feel acute grief because I cannot open my eyes but for fifteen minutes a day at this point. But I'm learning we only need His grace and strength *one moment* at a time, which forces us to trust Him for the next moment.

This is the most difficult lesson I'm learning in this dire situation, and God even called me out on it. One morning, after I had just cried to Mom that God's grace wasn't enough, my daily devotional verse was 2 Corinthians 12:9—"My grace is sufficient for you, for My power is made perfect in weakness." *Touché, Lord.* He literally "perceive[d] my thoughts from afar" (Psalm 139:2), and gently reminded me to cling to the truth of His Word regardless of my feelings.

I move my legs around now to get some circulation as I keep reflecting.

Wait, am I starting to trust God again? Like really trust?

I know I've started to sacrifice my will to His as far as the job loss. Who cares about being a lawyer at this point; just heal me, Lord! Who needs law when I can give motivational speeches on surviving liquid diets?

On our last call, Matt emphasized that "kings are made in caves, not palaces," a reference to King David of the Old Testament who hid in caves for many years before becoming king. Matt said maybe God has some work for me later which He's training me for through all this suffering. Who knows?

Matt also encouraged me not to idolize careers by recounting one of his own tough career choices. "My first PhD advisor told me one day that I couldn't pursue my PhD anymore if God was still the priority in my life. I went up to the roof of the engineering building every mornin', askin' God what I should do, and God's answer was 'keep doin' what you're doin'.' I had to ask myself: if I come out of this lookin' like a fool and a failure, but God is glorified, would I be okay with that? I decided to keep goin' to church. Sure enough, that advisor kicked me out of the lab along with all my other lab mates, for other crazy reasons. But God provided another lab I transferred to, out of nowhere, to finish my PhD."

Matt is helping me see that everything on earth is accomplished by God's grace, for *His* glory. Isaiah 64:6 even says "all our righteous acts are like filthy rags" in God's eyes. Even our best works, secular or faith-based, are just tools in God's hands. *Maybe this means I still have some worth, even lying flat on this bed? Hmm. My identity is in Christ, right? Come on Lara, you know this.*

Lately, though, God has also impressed upon me the concept of "acceptance." I'm not exactly sure what He means, but I'm surrendering to this valley *for the time being* as we keep searching for treatments. *Ah, surrender.* That word doesn't sting so much anymore. I still have hope for my future—God promised me He's "coming," so He will heal me, just like he opened my jaw. "Acceptance" can't possibly mean God wants me to stay chronically ill permanently, right?

Especially considering that a few months ago—while shedding tears one morning—a massive gift box arrived just in time from Auntie Arax (Golden Girl No. 1) with a big cross inside. It was her fifth care package; God's been using her unwavering love as an extension of Jesus' own hands. When I told Sevan, she replied, "Oh! I literally prayed last night that God would give you a sign that He has blessings in store for you!" *This must mean I will heal completely?*

God is sending comfort with tracking numbers now?

Divine logistics at its finest.

12

Poodles Have It Better

32 months

"We have to wash your hair in the water bin after breakfast, Lara. Been four weeks. I refuse to let you get bed sores on your head."

Mom's words land like heavy, unyielding bricks on my chest. *I don't want to do this.*

Guilt overwhelms me as she marches into the room. I know her heart breaks seeing me in the same position day in, day out with my eyes closed. I have not moved an inch off this bed now for a year and a half, my whole existence compressed into the space between these sheets, with nothing but the flicker of my eyelids to show I'm still here.

We used to share such a beautiful life. Museums, shopping, coffee. *How long can we keep going like this? Lord, when do I try walking again? Will I ever walk again? Do I risk it all again? Will I faint into the ER again? But I'm spinning even when lying down anyway. What do I do?*

Mom brings in some towels and that wretched water bin, her movements mechanical, chipping away at her soul. I grunt, then open my eyes briefly. "Mom, I'm in so much pain. Can we please do it tomorrow?"

I know I shouldn't fight. My hair is so filthy, I'm pretty sure my pillow is filing for separation.

Sevan walks in, balancing a breakfast tray. She puts it down and flashes me a nervous but compassionate smile. She's visiting today.

"Wasn't it great when life was fun and joyful?" she deadpans, trying to get a laugh out of me or Mom. Or both. Ten seconds tick by in awkward silence.

"Okay, tough crowd," she sighs. "Lars, I know it's tough...but we have to wash it." When tensions are strained among the three musketeers, Sevan is the glue that holds us together. She doesn't live with us, and the distance gives her a chance to breathe and retain sanity. She knows her role full well and plays it.

I hate that she's right. I want to shout. Pushing for tomorrow is less about not wanting to face the pain today and more about asserting control over my own schedule and body. *I am an invalid. I depend on others.*

"Sevan, no. Please tell Mom we should do it tomorrow." I open my eyes and give her the look of death.

No dice.

She knows how to handle me—thirty-four years of big sister practice. "Just get through it, Lars, and then why don't you call that Matt guy today?"

An hour later, every head scratch by Mom's fingers sends mini electrical shock waves through my body because my brain doesn't exactly appreciate the extra stimulation and shaking.

Welcome to our mother-daughter "Bonding & Torture Water Spa," offering a motherly scalp massage...with a side of trauma. *I cannot believe thousands of women—heck, even poodles—are sitting in salon chairs right now taking it for granted.* (You know it's bad when you envy a poodle's grooming routine.)

As Mom finishes the hair wash, she carefully removes my head from the water bin and slobbers a gigantic kiss on my left eye, showcasing her temporary high from the satisfaction of finally being able to do *something* towards her daughter's health. "Get some rest, Hokees." (*Hokees*—the Armenian word for sweetheart.)

I love you, Mom. You take such good care of me. I'm sorry I resisted earlier; it's a symbolic fight for independence.

Pops shouts from the kitchen, "Look on the bright side, Lars. At least you still have hair. Mine left years ago."

Next thing I know Mom is lamenting to Pops in the kitchen, sounding close to tears. *Guess the high was short-lived.*

"Vayel, I can't do it anymore. I still can't believe Doctor Barich's office said he can't help us." *Is she serious? I guess Mom didn't even tell me so as not to upset me. Ugh.*

"I know," Pops murmurs.

"Why us? I just...nothing I do is..." Mom sighs. "And I'm so tired of finding doctors all over the world who can't even help us in the end!"

"Just hang in there, Grace; we only have God at this point."

Pops has clearly grown in his faith and is now upholding Mom's. *Lord, please sustain our faith. We're drowning.*

Hours later, Pops walks in, feebly cracking a joke. "You've been spinning your wheels for three years, Lars. When are we arriving?"

Silence.

Second attempted joke of the day: fail. *I refuse to smile today.*

"Mom says I'm supposed to call Matt for you. It might help change your mood." *Will it? I guess it's a good idea.*

Pops dials then hands me the phone.

Ring, ring.

"Hello?" Matt answers in a puzzled voice.

"Hi Matt, how are you? It's Lara."

"Oh, hey Lara. It's so good to hear your voice." *He always says that. Kind of sweet.* His words instantly feel like a lifeline. Something to hold on to.

"Thanks, Matt. Is this a good time? Sorry we didn't schedule in advance. Been two months since our last call."

"Of course."

Silence.

"Lara, actually. I know this might not be the best time but it's kind of funny you're callin' now. There's somethin' I haven't told anyone…and it just happened."

"Oh really? What is it?" *Is that a nervous tremor in his voice?*

Silence.

Too much of it.

"My doctor called me twenty minutes ago. Said my recent scan came back."

Scan?

Thicker silence.

"He said I have…"

He pauses again.

"I have…"

What's he waiting for?

13

Wait, What?

"I have cancer again."

Matt's words land like a death sentence.

Cancer?

I must not have heard him correctly.

"Wait, what?"

"My doc just told me I have gastrointestinal adenocarcinoma. Small intestinal cancer. Stage 4. Was havin' all sorts of abdominal pain the last few months and they thought it was just irritable bowel syndrome, but the scans now say otherwise. Been growin' silently I guess."

Cancer.

The weight of that word—and the truth it carries—crashes over me all at once. A word I've heard so many times since Aunt Jackie died yet never thought it would land in my life again. Not to someone I care about.

"I'm about to write up my farewell video for the youth group kids as a sort of goodbye in case this thing progresses fast."

I open my mouth to say something—anything—but the words don't come.

Finally, I blurt out, "Wait, what? This can't be right. Are you sure? This is so unfair!"

"Well, I just told God that if He wants me in Heaven soon, isn't there some other way like rammin' me into a tractor and bein' done with it in one split second?" He chuckles his characteristic Matt giggle—with intense nervousness mixed in.

Then, his tone shifts abruptly. "Sorry. Didn't want to alarm you, but you just called me, and I didn't know how else to say it."

"Matt, don't apologize for something you didn't choose!"

"I'm actually really glad you called because now I'm able to tell a friend rather than be alone right now." *Oh my gosh. This phone call is clearly God's timing.*

Silence.

"So..." he adds, "this kind of cancer is very painful. People die by starvin' to death because there comes a point where you basically can't eat."

I have no reason to question his assessment. The guy has a PhD in cancer diagnostics. "Oh my gosh, Matt. Hang on, hang on. Are the doctors sure? You're too young—and you already had cancer as a kid. Can they do another scan? How can God allow this?"

"All I know is that the sermon at church yesterday was about Joseph's story of suffering and how God redeemed that evil for good in the end. I actually just finished puttin' together a devotional video for the youth on that verse, Genesis 50:20."

"No way! Wait...wow. That's not a coincidence. Maybe this will be your time of suffering before God lifts you up into some cool calling for God's Kingdom, just like He did for Joseph! The church needs you Matt. All of your texts, prayers, and calls have kept me going these last few years. I can't do this without you!"

"Thanks, Lara. Glad I've been a help. I better go call my parents. I don't know how I'm gonna break the news. Maybe I'll write up a quick Facebook post askin' for prayers."

"Got it, of course."

"Talk to you soon."

Click.

I open my eyes and stare at the phone, questioning if the last few minutes was a dream.

My heart beats faster and my thoughts instantly spiral—"What is the purpose of life? I thought I was finally learning what it means to trust that God loves and sustains us amidst adversity. But Matt accepting a terminal illness at age thirty-seven? God, do You even care? If the purpose of life is to enjoy God's good blessings, then if Matt is dying young, that means God doesn't care to bless him? Lara, you know better. Then why is God taking him out of the game early?"

I immediately tell Mom and Pops, oscillating between shock and denial. A few hours later, Mom reads me Matt's new Facebook profile post:

> It's no coincidence that our church is studying the story of Joseph this week. God arranges timing sometimes to show He's still in control, even in difficult situations. I want to share that I just got diagnosed with gastrointestinal cancer. I don't know what the future holds, and I know this season will have a lot of hardships, but it can also be one marked with joy, peace, hope, and love. As we seek God, He will fill us with a greater portion of His Spirit, and He will empower us to do more things than we ever thought we could.
>
> Joseph's story is one of God turning tragedy into triumph. As a direct result of years of unjust suffering in prison, Joseph was finally appointed Egypt's prime minister, and saved many nations from famine. Genesis 50:20 says God thus allowed the evil of Joseph's suffering for God's good purpose—'the saving of many lives.' This story comforts us that God uses even the

most desperate situations to bring salvation to many. In this season, let's remember that our hardships are not the end. There's always a greater purpose being worked out by God.

Wow. How can one face a terminal diagnosis and still post Christian inspiration? Isn't he angry at God? Just one bit?
Cancer?

14

The Dream

38 months

"We'll be there in a minute, Hokees," Mom shouts with urgency.

Here we are.

Fourth December on a bed.

Six months of begging God not to take Matt.

Worse still, I've lost my strong confidence in God's rescue to "come" for *me* also.

It all started with a daily devotional Mom read aloud one morning which resonated with me for some reason—"God doesn't save us from all our storms. But He sustains us through them." *Doesn't save?*

That triggered this strange sense that God was implying He wasn't going to heal my illness after all. I fought the thought off at first, but as time passed, this nagging sense turned into an overwhelming conviction—*God's will is that I suffer with this chronic illness permanently, whatever that looks like.*

I've been begging Jesus day and night for clarity. No clear answer.

But didn't You give me a promise that You're "coming" to end my suffering, Lord? What could "I AM COMING" have meant, other than to heal me? Is there still hope? Am I supposed to just give up? That doesn't sound Biblical, does it? Do You actually call some people to *permanent* "acceptance" of debilitating chronic illnesses? You did call the Apostle Paul to that. Is that why You gave me the word "acceptance" a while back? *Oh no…*

I try to debate myself out of this weird new conviction, telling myself we all have "feelings" about God's plans that often turn out wrong. It's no use. Everywhere around me—Pops' Bible readings, devotionals, texts from friends—God gives me themes about putting my hope in my *ultimate* healing in Heaven. *Yeah, yeah, Lord, I know all about Heaven, but You are going to heal me in this life too, right?*

While it's normal for someone in a hopeless situation like mine to lose hope in God's power, this isn't that. I still believe in miracles. I've read too many testimonies of them. But it just feels like God is saying that's *not* His will for my life.

Meanwhile, my physical situation is somewhere past the combination of abysmal and dire. My formerly youthful body is unrecognizable, having deteriorated as a result of being entirely bedridden for two full years now, without sitting up *once*. And don't forget the year before that—"bedridden chic," *a.k.a.*, bedridden but with trips to the bathroom.

I've lost enough weight to be a walking anatomy lesson. No semblance of muscle or fat can be found on my eighty-eight pound malnourished body. (We weighed me on the bed last week, lying on a scale.) Atrophy is the polite word, but it feels more like a slow, painful disappearance. My frame is little more than a collection of sharp angles, each bone a visible promise of frailty. My skin, stretched taut across my ribcage, has a ghostly sheen. My legs, thin as twigs, lie limp below my waist, their veins and tendons standing out in stark color.

I'm practically a human reed. Think Skeletor's less intimidating niece.

My nausea, immobility, and migraine food restrictions have taken a toll. My iron and salt levels are at critically dangerous levels too, for the first time ever.

Family: past breaking point. But today, this family is on a mission.

Operation: "Get Lara Vertical."

"Okay Hokees, let's try again," Mom reassures, as she and Pops bust into my room. They take hold of my nonexistent back muscles, and start lifting me up, slowly. At a ten-degree angle. Every few seconds.

Three weeks ago, even despite my new conviction about God's will, I made a desperate decision. I didn't even know if God was calling me to it or not. It didn't matter. After two years of not moving left, right, up, or down, I forced my eyes open and sat up for the first time in two years. The world immediately turned upside down in my vision, followed by a nonstop sensation of severe turbulence (*i.e.*, think walls and ground shaking up and down, left and right, sharply more severe than the normal chronic level I experience when lying down). But it didn't matter anymore. *I will tolerate this sensation, agonizing or not.*

It wasn't about healing. I had zero confidence it would somehow "heal" my symptoms. But I no longer had a choice: *move or die*. It was a Christmas gift I gave to my family. To myself. I knew I *must* move again, whether I faint into the ER again or not. What did I have to lose? I had waited to find *any* therapy that would help and not aggravate my brain.

Nothing.

Today, I still have no choice—even though the last two weeks of sitting up has made the electrical pain, brain zaps, and spinning/shaking astronomically worse. So long as my blood pressure remains stable, I am committed this week to try walking just five steps each day. I've already tried it a few times.

As Mom and Pops lift me to a sitting position now, I feel like an overcooked spaghetti noodle flopping around in the air. Mom cautiously moves the twigs (legs) off the bed as Pop lifts me up off the bed with his arms under my shoulders.

"Hold me, Pops. Please. God will help me. Please, Lord!"

The act of standing, once instinctive, demands all the focus I can muster. I grip Pops like he's the only thing standing between me and falling into a black hole, and clutch onto my fashionable new walker. *Oh my gosh, the world is spinning even harder left and right like a wild rollercoaster. I must do this. I do not care anymore.*

Move or die.

As I take one step toward the door, my trembling legs bear the weight of years spent tethered to a bed.

Step two.

Stop.

One foot in front of the other.

Step three.

Stop.

My legs shake but my resolve is unshakable.

I am *actually* walking after two years. *I don't care if my brain has a seizure.*

After step five, Mom and Pops seat me in a wheelchair and we're rolling out of the master bedroom in style. Sort of.

Then, it spreads before me like a beautiful painting. *The living room!*

I feel like I'm stepping into a memory. *Oh, how the different objects and colors in this room are a feast for my senses.* The afternoon sunlight filters through the windows, casting golden streaks across the floor. I take in the scent of the air, a unique blend of lemongrass and coffee that had always lingered here. *I am alive!*

A few days back, the first time we did this, tears flowed. Mom couldn't believe my eyes were even open. Mom's joy was as overwhelming as winning the grand prize in a lifetime lottery—despite a lingering sadness that I haven't healed. *We're just forcing this.*

Mom and Pops help me out of the wheelchair and lay me on the couch.

The minute my head hits the pillow, I clench my teeth. *Just pretend you're on a plane.* Larger ocean waves, more severe shaking/turbulence, and electrical currents immediately flood through my brain.

Nausea.

Intense stabbing pains in my ears and brain.

Sensations of massive earthquakes crashing into my skull.

My job is the same as the last few days—lie here with my eyes closed for six hours, compensating for the wild tsunami we just instigated.

A few seconds in, reality sinks in.

Why am I doing this? If there is a way to heal, this isn't it. This isn't a real resurrection, and you know it. Am I going to go to the ER again in a few weeks? Wait, no, no. I don't care about my brain anymore. My body needs this. Move or die.

"Mom, can you put on Matt's recent Advent sermon at church? Might distract me."

She does, and Matt's calm, deep voice takes a stroll through my mind: "Going through cancer, I could get so focused on the pain and danger that I forget my eternal hope. I don't know everything the future holds, but Jesus promises a place in His eternal Kingdom for all who put their trust in Him, and there's nothing in this world that can take that away. So let's not forget this Christmas, no matter what challenges we face, the same power that raised Jesus from the dead is at work in us, and leads us into life everlasting." *This guy is something else. Facing death like a warrior. I want this kind of faith.*

Six hours later, I'm still lying here, getting ready for my big "trek" back to bed.

I can't believe I actually sat up for dinner for six minutes to scarf food down. And used my own utensils. With my eyes open. I am a human again. Bring it on, electrical zaps!

Mom and Pops slowly lift me up from the couch onto the walker.

First step.

Second step.

Third Step.

"Ow! Mom it's turning upside…" This isn't walking—it's a budget version of Space Mountain. Minus the fun.

"Almost there, keep going."

Two more steps and a wheelchair ride later, I'm back in the master bed.

"Good job, Hokees," Mom says, slobbering a kiss on my left eye with triumph. "I know how incredibly painful this is. We have no choice."

As fireworks explode in my brain, I instinctively pray—"I beg You Lord Jesus, help me sustain this pain. You've left me in a corner. I don't know if it's Your will that I try this again but I am. And what is this weird new sense I have that You won't heal me? What did You mean when You made your original promise to me: **'I AM COMING.'** Please, answer me. I love You."

Five days later, 7:30 am
I stand in a vast, endless expanse of white that wraps around me like a soft, glowing cocoon, shimmering brightly. No walls, no edges—just light, pure and endless. In my hands, I hold a white scroll—massive, weighty, glowing with an eerie brilliance of its own. My fingers feel the smooth parchment. I know, somehow, that it's meant for me. I don't know how I know, but I do.

And then, from somewhere deep within, my own voice rises as I read the scroll—soft at first, then stronger, chanting these words:

"MY CHILD IS CLIMBING THE LADDER. MY CHILD IS COMING TO THE REALIZATION THAT CHRIST IS COMING TO TAKE HER HOME."

The words pour from my mouth, steady, rhythmic. My voice is different here—richer, deeper. It echoes around me, bouncing off the nothingness, filling the space with something weighty, something Holy.

The scroll glows even brighter and heavier in my hands now, and the brightness around me starts pulsating gently. Then suddenly, the brightness swirls and folds in on itself, and I feel a gentle tug pulling me backward,

back down,

back—

I open my eyes and shift awake, with a sharp inhale.

I gasp.

My eyes adjust to the dim light filtering through the blinds of the master bedroom. No majestic whiteness, no scroll, no voice. Just me, normal Lara, and my old friend, the bed.

Oh.

My.

Gosh.

I just had a dream from...

Fifteen minutes later

"Matt, help me!"

"Oh, hey Lara!"

Matt's voice on the phone is the kind of casual when you're heading into work. Meanwhile, my skin is damp, my heart hammering. I'm alone in the bedroom.

"Glad you're callin' me, what a nice surprise, Lara. Was gonna call you in a couple weeks. Don't want to bother you too often."

"I'm sorry to call you so early, Matt. You're not gonna believe this. I don't know what to do...I..."

"No problem. I'm just in the lab with a few students. What's wrong?"

"I...I just had the strangest, most vivid ethereal dream!"

"What dream?"

"I woke up from it right now. It was unlike anything I've ever experienced and was super real and I instantly knew somehow that it was from the Lord."

"Oh... Okay? Well, what happened in it?"

Wait. I'm about to drop a theological bombshell on Matt, and I'm pretty sure he's going to think I'm either hallucinating...or a lunatic.

Or both.

Should I really tell him? This is all he needs in the middle of cancer.

My emotional side fights back. *It doesn't matter. I don't care if he thinks I'm a loony and reports me to the authorities.* I don't know where else to turn.

I take a deep breath and plunge in. "Matt, listen. God has finally revealed His will to me. In the dream, I saw a vision of myself in a big white expanse holding a white scroll, and all I could hear was my own voice, reading the following phrase aloud—'*My child is climbing the ladder. My child is coming to the realization that Christ is coming to take her Home.*' And then—BOOM—flash, I woke up. Just like that!"

Matt pauses two seconds. "Wow...um..."

"Matt, can you believe this? You know how I told you that God said He's 'coming' for me a few years back, and how that gave me so much hope this whole time?"

"Yeah?"

Should I tell him? Yes.

"Well, turns out He didn't mean He's coming to heal me. He meant He's coming to kill me!"

Act Two

"In the last days, God says, I will pour out My Spirit on all people. Your sons and daughters will prophesy, your young men will see visions, your old men will dream dreams."

— Acts 2:17

"Blessed are those who mourn, for they will be comforted."

— Matthew 5:4

"I provide water in the wilderness and streams in the wasteland, to give drink to My people..."

— Isaiah 43:20

"Place me like a seal over your heart, like a seal on your arm; for love is as strong as death, its jealousy unyielding as the grave."

— Song of Songs 8:6

15

The Cross-examination

The next day, New Year's Day, 2022

"Why? Honestly, why. Why does God allow so much unimaginable suffering if He loves us so much? Tired of it."

My voice is sharp, accusing, but my eyes are holding back tears.

I'm sprawled flat on our fancy blue living room couch in pajamas, eyes locked on the ceiling. Matt sits in an armchair beside me in dark navy jeans and a black jacket, his shoulders hunched like he's been listening too long.

Three hours and counting.

Because apparently, I'm having my "day in court" against God.

My cross-examination subject and God's star witness—Matt.

I've decided to steal a play from Job 31:35, where Job seeks a court trial against God to prove he doesn't deserve all his suffering. Job argues, "I sign now my defense—let the Almighty answer me; let my accuser put his indictment in writing."

I keep pressing my case. "There's pain, and then there's *pain*, right? And sometimes, there's just no point to what God allows. Isn't that correct?"

Matt hesitates, as if he's computing a diplomatic response. "Sometimes," he starts, "we only see after the fact how God redeemed our pain for good. Take my first cancer as a kid. Chemo meant a pile of pills that made me nauseous. If I threw 'em up too soon, I had to take 'em again. So Dad played Pokémon with me, keepin' me distracted from nausea as I swallowed each one, round after round, until they stayed down."

I stare at the ceiling, absorbing his words but refusing to meet his eyes.

"But one day, when Dad wasn't home, I wanted to try on my own. Maybe if I prayed, God—if He was real—would help me? I did, and for the first time, I kept all the pills down. Didn't need Pokémon after that. That planted a seed. I didn't become a Christian until college, but lookin' back, I see how God was always workin'." His voice presses through under the COVID mask he's wearing to protect my compromised immune system.

"So my suffering itself wasn't good, but God brought somethin' good from it. He flips evil on its head that way. He did that with Jesus' death to redeem us. He redeems our pain too, but in many cases, we'll only understand it lookin' back from eternity. But those times when God chooses to heal in this life—or redeem in ways we can actually see here—give us hope for the times when we can't see it."

He pulls out his phone. "Just made a devotional video on this. Listen."

Matt makes unique YouTube devotional videos for the youth group kids, blending Bible lessons with classic movies and superheroes. He presses play, and his voice fills the room:

> In the classic film *The Lord of the Rings*, Frodo looks at the impossible odds and overwhelming evil he's facing, and wishes the ring never came to him. But Gandalf encourages him, finding strength in the understanding that there's a more powerful sovereign force directing

all things, good and evil, for a greater good. We likewise can find strength in our greatest suffering, knowing that God is working out a powerful purpose. Thanks for tuning in, and as always, if you need me, I'm just one phone call away.

That's how he always ends his devotionals—"I'm just one phone call away."

I hate that he's right. Sickness bubbles inside me like a volcano ready to erupt, and tears finally escape down my cheeks.

"But I don't want either one of us to die, Matt!"

Yesterday morning, Matt sensed my desperation over the phone and offered to come over today to discuss that dream I had.

In person.

For the first time in four years.

When he arrived earlier, we discussed the dream ad nauseam. *What did God mean?* Is Jesus actually going to end my suffering by taking me home soon to Heaven instead of healing me here? Am I really going to have a severe chronic illness the rest of my life until I die?

Matt offered his best wisdom. "Some of my missionary friends believe God gives prophetic dreams today, but I've never had one. I can't say if your dream was from God or not, but even if it was, God didn't say *when* Christ is comin' for you in the dream, right? Jesus said not to worry about tomorrow, so take it one day at a time. We're all dyin' in a sense, and eternity should be our focus anyway. Look at me with this cancer. We'll walk through this grief together."

His words soothed me earlier. But now, desperation is rearing its ugly head again.

"Forget dying," I lament. "Let's say God's will is just not to heal me. Like, to let me suffer chronically with this illness my whole life. Because whatever this vertigo is, it isn't terminal, or I'd be gone by now. Wouldn't that mean He'd be wasting my talents?"

The Cross-examination

Matt replies stoically, almost like a computer output. "Maybe God doesn't need your skills."

I move my eyes off the ceiling toward his bald head shining under the lamp light. *Excuse me? Insulting? Out of character? But...it's kind of refreshing that he's standing up to my pride?*

He sees my furrowed brow and instantly digs up his Bible. "Psalm 141:5," he reads, "'Let a righteous man strike me—that is a kindness; let him rebuke me—that is oil on my head.'"

He's right. Again. Matt's a smart witness, but I won't be telling *him* that. God doesn't need *my* work. He can use whoever He wants. *But then why give me intellect and legal skills? To just rot in a bedroom? Why doesn't He want me to do fruitful work for Him?*

Matt adds, "Look, I'm not sayin' I'm all righteous. I'm tryin' to get you to see that God accomplishes the work and gets the glory, no matter whom He uses."

"Okay," I sigh. "But a lot of times, He withholds good things we desire too. Like marriage. Isn't that correct? And our loved ones He takes too soon." *Maybe cool the lawyer tone, Lara. The guy's going through cancer.*

"I get it," Matt answers, contemplating. "But as much as we want blessings in this life, the goal of the Christian life is a deeper relationship with Christ, not gettin' blessings. We have to focus on the eternal gifts He promises us in Heaven. This life is temporary—we won't get everythin' we want. God sees a million things we can't, and some answers may never come on this side of eternity."

Matt shifts awkwardly in his chair. Then, he adds, with some hesitation, "I know what you mean though. After bein' single for so long, I think marriage probably isn't God's plan for me. But...I do want it."

Woah...that was random. I thought he was too shy and/or holy to like girls? Is that vulnerability, or insecurity, all of a sudden? Theology is his comfort zone, but this topic seems to make him... shy again? Give him something, Lara. He's been helping you for three hours.

"Any girl would be insanely lucky to be your wife, Matt. I mean it. You have intelligence, character, kindness, courage."

He looks down, fiddling with his hands. "Thanks," he says stoically. *He seems kind of aloof; I can't read his straight face. Does he believe me? I can't see under that dumb mask.*

Even during our phone calls, when we strayed off theology, sometimes he spoke tersely with straight one-word answers—making it hard at times to tell what was going on in his brilliant mind. He's so tender and yet somewhat robotic and guarded at the same time.

"You can take off the mask," I offer, "as long as you don't have any COVID symptoms."

He peels it off, and I sneak a full glimpse of his full face for the first time in four years. His fair skin, Roman nose, and overall boyish looks peer back at me. His big warm brown eyes sit there, worn down but somehow still beaming with youthful optimism, telling the story of perseverance in great suffering. *He feels achingly familiar but like an entirely new thing. What's different? This is such a strange way to meet face to face again.*

"You're the first friend to visit my house in years, Matt. Can you believe it?"

He smiles gently then leans forward abruptly, wincing in pain and shifting his hand to his lower abdomen.

"You okay?" I ask.

He shrugs. "Yeah. Just pain. Comes and goes. I've lost a lot of weight too. From the cancer."

"I'm so sorry. You know, I'm sorry I called you yesterday morning at work. The whole dream thing was super strange, and I didn't know where else to turn."

"No problem. I told my students I had to step out because this is a girl I care about."

Matt darts a quick glance at me, then peers down at the floor. *Care about? That came out of nowhere. That's sweet of him.*

Then, all of a sudden, it's upon me. "Oh my gosh, oh my gosh."

The Cross-examination

Matt leans forward. "You okay?"

"Ow!" A sharp jolt zips through my skull, unleashing tidal waves of more vertigo and an electrical brain zap that crash into my brain all at once.

Out of instinct, I blurt, "Matt, do you mind holding my hand? It helps me feel steady." He shifts closer, scraping his chair against the floor. Without a word, his fingers lace through mine, firm but gentle.

"Sure thing."

"Thanks," I mutter, "Just give it a moment. I'm sorry if I scared you. This is what walking is doing to my brain now. Harder spinning, sharper brain zaps. Sometimes it's fewer zaps and more pronounced turbulence."

Another wave hits. I groan, squeezing his hand. My cheeks flush. "I'm so embarrassed."

"Don't be," he soothes, squeezing back lightly, as his symmetrical thin lips curve up into a warm smile. His hand feels safe, soft. *He's so darn nice.* He has this instinct to just sit with a sufferer. Even in his own pain.

I glance at his face again. *Wait... It's his circle beard. That's what's new! He didn't have that before in 2017. It kind of distinguishes and frames his face. I really like it on him...?*

"I'm sorry if I'm being too aggressive today," I say. "I want to cross-examine God on suffering, and He dropped an 'expert witness' on suffering right on my doorstep."

Matt chuckles. "Who, me? Nah. I'm used to debatin' atheists in PhD circles. This is fun, actually."

"You've been under questioning for hours now. Do you need a lawyer present, or are you just going to keep being annoyingly reasonable?" I flash him a cheeky smile. Then suddenly, I feel... self-conscious. *Are we still holding hands? Is that okay? Gosh, I hope he's not grossed out by my poofy, frizzy rags of a "hair do."*

Matt winces in pain again, his eyebrows furrowing.

"You don't deserve to go through cancer twice," I say.

"It's okay," he sighs. "For the Christian, there's always hope, Lara. My joy isn't based on whether I heal. I have eternity in Heaven. I read once that a pastor told a grievin' couple that their baby—who died two minutes after birth—wasn't born to live only for two minutes. It was born to live for eternity. Powerful stuff."

I study him, trying to grasp how he can walk around with cancer with such poise, as if facing death is just another item on his to-do list. He's like a wise old sage trapped in the body of a nerdy engineer, dropping wisdom like it's his side hustle. He reminds me of missionary Jim Elliot's words: "Walk as if the next step would carry you across the threshold of Heaven." Matt is cut from a different cloth; his entire countenance shines radiantly with Christ's peace. Even in this fire.

"Matt," I whisper. "You're the closest representation of Jesus I've ever met."

He smiles softly. "Suffering refines us, makin' us more Christ-like. I've had plenty of practice, I guess. But I'm no saint." He squeezes my hand as if to make a point. "I understand your grief—I could stop chemo anytime. But I want to fight. I've got my own dreams—returnin' to preach in Haiti, Vietnam. Growin' the youth group."

The kitchen door creaks open, and we instantly drop hands like guilty teenagers.

Mom peeks into the living room. "It's 10:30 P.M. Are you two okay in here?" Her voice is tinged with exhaustion, and it's clear she's ready to spot me back to bed then hit the sack. *Is Matt going to get the hint and leave? Do I even want him to leave?*

Matt turns to her, and smiles wide, unfazed. "We're fine Grace, thanks."

Mom lingers a beat then retreats, her eyes betraying her thoughts: *Hint not taken. Geeky engineers and social cues.*

I exhale. "Can we change the subject for a bit? Why can't we talk about puppies and butterflies sometime, instead of, you know, doom and gloom?"

Matt's eyes light up. "Sure. Hmm. Let's see. Butterflies are members of the order Lepidoptera," he declares, giggling, with somewhat surprising dramatic flare as if lecturing. "Their metamorphosis is biologically efficient."

"An expert are we?"

"I saved one when I was seven. Nursed it back to life."

"Oh, so you like saving things, do you?" I shoot him a teasing grin.

"Depends on who I'm savin'," he says, smiling wide. *Am I blushing?*

"Let's talk about bureaucrats and politicians actually," he adds. "Their stupidity should lighten the mood."

"I love chatting about policy and politics too! I'm a lawyer, remember?"

"*Ah*, but lawyers...can never trust 'em."

"Oh please, you love hanging out with me. You secretly want to be a lawyer, don't you? You love debating and writing. Your sermons are so well-written."

"I don't know about that, but I do know that a lot of people are dumb." *Ooh, is there actually pompousness in there somewhere?*

"I mean," Matt recalls, smirking, "I started analyzin' the data and putting up COVID updates on Facebook to help educate people way back when. But so many other supposed scientists were releasin' junky articles without supportive data." *What's the deal with his slight Southern affect? It feels like he slips in and out of it, and more so when he's relaxed or joking around. Kind of sweet.*

"I'm still trying to process the fact that you just said people are dumb."

"Am I wrong?" he says, giggling. "I mean...don't take me too seriously. I'm just bein' goofy."

"Matt, can you guess what role I played in *Cinderella* the musical as a kid?"

He pauses a moment then darts me a quizzical look. "The pumpkin?"

"Hard no," I pout, insulted. "The evil stepsister."

"Ooh, should I be scared?" He cocks one eyebrow teasingly. "Your personality doesn't align with traditional villain archetypes."

"You sure about that?" I reply. "The loony roles are always the most fun. I played an insane woman in an opera years ago."

"Fine by me. Sanity's overrated." *Hmm. I like this goofier side to him. Never seen it before.*

A quiet settles into an awkward silence, and I spot his signature navy Indiana Jones hat on the coffee table. *He's still wearing that number, eh?*

"Matt, can I just ask. Why do you like hats so much?"

He hesitates a moment. "In college, my hair started fallin' out—autoimmune thing, like my grandpa. I had weird patches of hair on my head while the rest of it was bald, so a friend told me to just shave it all. So I did. Now, hats keep my head warm." Something shifts in his expression—a flicker of vulnerability he quickly tucks away.

Then, he glances at his watch. "Well, gettin' late. I'll head out now. If you want, I'll come back tomorrow? New Year's week and all. Some visits will do both of us good for a change, yeah?"

"I would love that. Thanks so much for, you know, coming tonight."

He looks down, pauses a beat, then drags his gaze up to meet mine. "Sure thing. There's no place I'd rather be."

My cheeks instantly blush. *Woah, that came out of nowhere. Should I say thank you?*

He stands, shakes off his pants, and strategically angles on his beloved hat. *Wait, his phone isn't attached to his hip like years before? There are fashion miracles.*

He picks up his backpack and swings it over his right shoulder. At five-foot-ten, with a thin build but broad shoulders, he holds himself with quiet assurance, his posture straight but relaxed.

He tips his hat like a British gent, and he's off.

I lie in bed an hour later, replaying the night in my head. *There's no place I'd rather be... Why did my insides light up when he said that? Who sits with you for hours like that? Seeing him in person felt...surreal. He's somewhat robotic yet ironically so perceptive, almost like he sees right through me. And was that...humor?*

Then, like a lightning bolt, it hits me.

The dream.

Who cares, I've got bigger issues—I'm going to die!

My mental diary, rapid fire:

This is terrifying. Shocking. I had just come to spiritual acceptance of my illness for the time being. But to not heal at all—or worse, to die?! I didn't negotiate for this! Is *that* why nothing has worked? Talk about whiplash. All these years I thought God was telling me He was going to heal me. Why does He refuse to heal some of us? Jesus walked around healing people in the gospels?!

What is "Home?" The dream said, "*Christ is coming to take [me] Home.*" I've read descriptions of Heaven in the Book of Revelation, but reading and really believing it? Two very different things. And why now?!

God betrayed me. When the Holy Spirit originally said "I AM COMING" years back, I naturally assumed that meant to heal me on earth, not to take me to Heaven. Isn't He supposed to be the God who rescues, not the one who pulls a cosmic bait and switch?

God cannot take me so young. There's too much left undone. Marriage. Kids. The "perfect Armenian" life. I must have no worth if God's taking me out early.

God's timing isn't "perfect." Three years of agony on a bed and *now* He's handing me the finale like a closing scene in a tragic play. Why didn't He just spare me the suffering and take me out before? Why did He let me hope? He tells me now, when I'm trying to walk again and making my pain worse?

So much for being inspired by Job's faith. My vibe is less "[t]hough He slay me, yet will I hope in Him," and more "Please don't kill me, please!"

Why is God rewriting the script? And who gave Him my pen?

16

Not Funny

These past four weeks have been an intense crash course in serious grief.

Physical status: After Matt's visit, in a haze of sheer defiance, I decided I *have* to keep walking because I simply can't stay trapped in that bed forever. Every attempt to sit up hits me like a freight train—nerve pain, electrical currents ripping through my body, the world spinning harder, more severe turbulence. But I can't go back. And if I literally might be dying soon anyway, why not go out on my feet?

So I push.

Hard.

I wheel around in my wheelchair (with eyes forced open), or scrape my walker across the floor like I'm training for the world's slowest NASCAR race with Mom pacing behind me like pit crew. The route: Bathroom. Living room couch. Eat upright, use utensils like a real human, pretending the world isn't shaking. Lie back down on the couch for hours. Back to bed. Next day, repeat.

My muscles are non-existent, my legs trembling under the strain, but each day, I force myself to walk in greater increments until I feel extremely faint and simply cannot tolerate the shaking and pain anymore.

The result? Eighty percent of my day still flat on my back. It's been a rebirth of sorts—at least I'm on the living room couch and sitting up for short periods of time now. But it's not a real rebirth. I'm just *forcing* this.

Every time I lie back down after sitting up, it's the same drill. Nausea. Stabbing in my ears and brain. More severe earthquake sensations activated in my skull and the outside world. Harder spinning. But something in me has snapped. *Move or die.* So long as I don't have to go to the ER for blood pressure issues, I am going to keep sitting up then lying back down. Regardless of the rollercoasters.

Emotional status: The dream plays in my mind on repeat like a bad pop song. I thought I was grieving Matt. Now I'm grieving myself. "Lord," I beg in feverish prayers, "I believe You just told me it's Your will to take me Home instead of heal me on earth. So when are You 'coming'? Is it a heart attack? A seizure? I'm terrified! And am I really going to suffer with chronic illness the rest of my life until that inevitable moment? Please, don't come!"

Look, this whole "dream" thing is entirely foreign to me. We all know God spoke through dreams in Biblical times. It's all over the Bible. Job 33:14-16 even states, "For God does speak... In a dream, in a vision of the night, when deep sleep falls on people as they slumber in their beds, He may speak in their ears and terrify them with warnings." But growing up in "cessationist" church circles, I was taught that God stopped handing out visions and prophetic dreams after the Apostles. That sort of thing belonged to Bible characters in robes and sandals, not to modern-day women fighting chronic illnesses.

In more charismatic Christian circles, though, they believe God still speaks to people through dreams and visions *today*. There are hundreds of Christian denominations, and I judge no one. I can only speak to my experience.

When I first woke up to those definitive words—"*Christ is coming to take her home*"—I *wanted* to tell myself I was losing it. Initial thoughts: "You don't even have a terminal illness. Your brain might be playing tricks on you with a crazy dream that's not necessarily from God."

But, I couldn't fight it. I just *knew* the dream was from God, not a regular dream stemming from psychological angles. I've had countless nightmares about supposedly dying in car crashes, etc., and in those cases, I've always woken up and known it was just a dumb dream. This was *different*—an authentic experience with the Holy Spirit. *When you know, you know.*

But given that I've never experienced anything like this before, I sought counsel immediately, doing what any rational person would do. I hired a Christian counselor with a theology degree and even started making awkward phone calls to pastors I know, almost like dialing customer service for the afterlife: "Hi, I've got a question about this whole dying thing."

Their advice? Most were startled and said that even if the dream is from God, I should hold my interpretation loosely. But how loose can you hold something that sounds so terrifyingly direct? *"Christ is coming to take her home."*

No timeline. No conditions. Just a gut-punch proclamation. And let's just say I'm hoping Christ isn't coming anytime soon. *I have so much to live for. I'm too young. I just reemerged into the world again, Lord!*

Desperate for clarity, I turned to the Bible, the ultimate authority for Christian instruction. And sure enough, Acts 2:17 stood out like a beacon—"*In the last days*, God says, I will pour out my Spirit on all people. Your sons and daughters will prophesy, your young men will see visions, your old men will dream dreams." So while it may be rare for God to communicate in this way *today*, I found Biblical support for God doing so.

Then I sought wisdom from the Holy Spirit regarding the dream's interpretation, scouring every resource I could find by reputable theologians on the topic. All with my strained eyes on my phone lying in bed. I've been trying to get accustomed to electronics anyway—as much as I can tolerate—by keeping my eyes open for as long as I can and reading as much as I can. It causes me more pain to focus my eyes, but who cares at this point. Through all this, I found many modern theologians who believe God still uses dreams today to reveal His express will to believers.

I then found testimonies of countless modern-day believers who claimed they, too, had been given dreams from God, on a whole host of issues. Some credible, some not, using my judgment. But people all over the world today—from high-profile Christian thinkers like Lee Strobel to former atheists to former Muslims in the Middle East—claim to have experienced divine dreams from Jesus. Rare, but it does happen. *Okay, I'm not crazy.* People often testify that dreams from God have this unique, rare quality such that you know they are from Him. *Yeah, that was Him.* Dreams from God can warn us about future events or convey other messages like guidance.

But it still felt extremely strange that God would give me a dream about *upcoming death*. Matthew 6:34 and James 4:14 make clear that Christians should not "worry" about tomorrow and typically believers do not know what tomorrow brings. *So why this, Lord?* But I realized those verses are not mutually exclusive to God's choice to *give* a believer a specific prophetic revelation on any topic, as evident in the Bible.

I also found Biblical instances where God *did* inform someone of upcoming death. *Ah, so this has Biblical basis!* God told Ezekiel his wife was going to die. God told Moses he was going to die. Paul wrote in 2 Timothy 4:7 that he had a conviction (presumably from the Holy Spirit) that his time to depart this life was near, even though he knew full well that God could save him at any time. Peter wrote in 2 Peter 1:14 that he had a conviction his life was drawing to a close.

Long story short, while God typically does not reveal upcoming death to believers, He does sometimes. I debated all these ideas with a few pastor friends. *Who needs law; now I'm a seminary intern! At least I'm finally getting some real intellectual stimulation after three years of staring at a ceiling.*

I also read credible Christian articles on Godly dreams, which explained that such dreams are usually a part of an "ongoing conversation" with God, not just some isolated thing God says to you. In my case, I know God isn't giving me a theology lesson that He's coming to take me Home at some random point, young or old, just because we all die eventually. I already know that. *No.* This message was God speaking *specifically into my serious illness* in the context of God's prior communications to me the last few years.

I've come to discern that when God first told me "I AM COMING" a few years back, He did so to sustain me in the *context of my illness* and give me assurance that He *is* coming to end my neurological suffering. Otherwise, despair would have swallowed me whole. I clung to that hope. But apparently, it was never a promise of *earthly healing*, and I was wrong to impose that interpretation onto it. But isn't that what anyone would assume a loving God meant?

Now, God has clarified through the dream that He meant He's coming to take me Home—*i.e.*, that the end of my suffering will be in *Heaven*, whenever that will be. Whether I will die today, tomorrow, or next year, the dream did not say, but it meant I will not heal before I die. *Wow. Oh my gosh. But Lord, isn't it unfair to drop a divine death notice and then expect me to stay calm? If You're the Giver of life, why are You fixating me on death?*

Because I don't have a specific date, I've started grieving intensely, both my lack of healing as well as my upcoming death, whenever it is. The dream made it sound imminent though: *"Christ is coming to take her home."* God could have said, "Christ will not heal you and you should come to permanent acceptance of this chronic illness." But He didn't stop there. He focused on my *entering eternity.*

That's why I assume my death will be at least sometime relatively soon? Otherwise, God wouldn't have given me such a bold proclamation that He's actively *coming* to end my suffering. The dream even said that I'm "climbing the ladder"!

The Bible says in 1 John 4:1 that we must test all spirits by seeking God's discernment. As such, I've begged God to clarify that the dream was *not* from Him, or if I have gotten its meaning wrong. But alas, God has only confirmed my interpretation, dropping signs like breadcrumbs and whispering that He understands my grief. One might argue I'm experiencing confirmation bias, but if anything, I'm straining to convince myself *out* of such a depressing interpretation. Through tears in bed, I've been dictating everything He says into my phone. A few examples:

First—The morning of the dream, right after I called Matt, I opened my *Daily Streams* app to find the daily verse, Psalm 116:15—"Precious in the sight of the Lord is the death of his faithful servants." My heart pounded. I just *knew*. The devotional wrote, "Are you entering a new season of intense grief and sorrow? The Lord equips us to keep serving Him even as we walk through the darkest of valleys, especially that of death. His rod and staff will guide you."

Missionary Elisabeth Elliot's words sat there too—"I must not think it strange if God takes in youth, those whom I would have kept on earth till they were older. God is peopling eternity, and I must not restrict Him to old men and women." *Coincidence? Oh my gosh.*

Second—Four days after the dream, a card arrived in the mail. My friend had no idea about the dream, yet inside, Matthew 5:4 stared at me—"Blessed are those who mourn, for they will be comforted." Then she wrote, "God heals all wounds and grief in Heaven, and comforts us until that time." *This is from You, Lord. You are comforting me through this friend and she has no clue.* That night, Pops' Bible study rolled around. Matthew 5:4 popped up again. My stomach dropped.

Third—The first Sunday after the dream, two of my devotional apps featured the same verse of the day, John 14:3: "And if I go and prepare a place for you, I will *come back* and take you to be with me that you also may be where I am." *So God is showing me that the dream aligns with scriptural truth!* I never even knew this verse before. Turns out, when it's our time, Jesus actually "comes" to take us Home.

One of the devotional apps elaborated, "Even in the valley of the shadow of death, you can give your pain and sorrow to the One who will hold your tears and give you joy each day in Him." *Wow. Chills.*

Fourth—The next week, two friends separately emailed me the same Christian devotional out of nowhere, without knowing about my dream. It was titled, *When God Says No*. It explained that Jesus answers our prayers "yes" only if they align with "His will." 1 John 5:14. My gut twisted as I read the devotional—"We must accept God's sovereign plans when it comes to the timing of life and death, even for those who die young. Are God's plans and goodness limited to this side of the grave?" *But this is cruel, Lord. How can You say no to my healing? How can I accept my premature death? Please change Your will.*

Fifth—Two weeks in, while I was crying in bed in pain, a friend texted me her church's sermon, in which her pastor said, "Is God calling you to acceptance of a tough situation, like perhaps a chronic illness He will not heal until eternity? Would you still trust His good purposes?" My chest tightened. *What are those purposes? So...I guess this is it. God is confirming the dream yet again. I'm supposed to stop chasing healing. Lay down the therapies, and stop punishing my body into submission.*

Sixth—One morning, the raw cry of "My God, my God, why have You forsaken me?" pulsed through my heart. Hours later, a friend, without knowing, texted me a Christian article about "God's denials" which featured that famous verse where Jesus cried out to God (Mark 15:34). The article explained Jesus knows what it feels like to be forsaken, but that grief over upcoming death should not paralyze us. In that moment, it felt like God was whispering, *I see your grief. I know You feel forsaken because My will is hard. My Son knows this ache.* Later that night, during Pops' Bible reading, we came across Mark 15:34 again, and my tears flowed. *God is walking me through this.*

Finally—the most dramatic confirmation. One night at midnight I begged, tears streaming down my face, "Lord, am I crazy? Or was that dream really from You? Is all this just confirmation bias? Give me an extra-Biblical example of a time when You gave another believer a dream about upcoming death. I beg You."

I kid you not. The next morning, I woke up, opened my third Christian devotional app, and my heart almost stopped when I read the "story of the day." *The martyrdom of Saint Perpetua.* The devotion explained that God gave this woman in early church times a prophetic dream about her upcoming death, where she had a vision of herself *climbing a ladder* leading up to Heaven. She wrote in her journal in prison that she knew God was telling her she was going to be martyred instead of released.

My heart pounded as I considered the parallel to my own dream—"*My child is climbing the ladder. My child is coming to the realization that Christ is coming to take her home.*" While my situation is starkly different from Perpetua's religious persecution, God immediately answered my prayer that He *does* give dreams like this. All four years of this illness before the dream, God handed me themes of waiting, trusting. Now, since right after the dream, He's been bombarding me with signs in neon lights: "I'm walking you through this great grief."

Naturally, I told my closest friends over the phone, calling them for the *first time in years* and expecting them to think I was crazy. If God had told me I was destined to be a zookeeper, I wouldn't bother sharing. Who cares? But death? That's the kind of thing you don't keep to yourself. And if I'd had serious doubts whether the dream was from God, I would've buried it deep. Who wants to look crazy?

Not many friends believed me. Who can blame them? Especially nonbelievers who don't believe in supernatural experiences anyway. They chalked it up to cabin fever because I've been isolated forever. The Christian friends? Few believed God gives these kinds of dreams today. Their reactions came in six flavors, none particularly pleasant. I knew their words came from a place of genuine love and care, but despite their good intentions, I felt genuinely misunderstood.

"You've given up and have lost your faith." Talk about adding insult to injury and false "prosperity gospel theology." Like I'm not trying. I still have faith in God's miracles. I survived years on a bed thanks to a relentless belief that God would heal me. But He seems to be calling me to acceptance now, to know that that's not His will for me. It's easy to believe God can work miracles. What's hard is believing He is good when He doesn't.

"You must be depressed or even suicidal." This pierced like a knife. I *love* life. I've always been bigger than life. I've been fighting on a bed to save my life for years—why would I give up now, especially now that I'm willingly forcing myself to walk into more pain?

"Maybe you're just scared of death, so your brain made this up." If fear was running the show, I wouldn't be pushing myself to walk. My rational mind has no reason to fear upcoming death now that I'm moving my body.

"If you're angry, that's not the fruit of the Spirit, so the dream can't be from God." Sure. Because Job and Jeremiah were always sunshine and rainbows. Jesus himself was "a man of sorrows, and acquainted with grief[.]" Isaiah 53:3 (KJV). Anger is one of the stages of grief. Of course I'm angry!

"This is from Satan, not the Lord." Yes, 2 Corinthians 11:14 states that Satan "masquerades as an angel of light" to trick people. But I've prayed desperately for correction and discernment, and the sheep know the Shepherd's voice, especially while walking with Him through great suffering.

"God wouldn't inform you in advance." Really? How do you know? So long as a message aligns with Scriptural precedent (God informing people in advance that they will die), it seems fair game. God's not constrained by our boxes. The God of the Bible turned a woman into a pillar of salt, opened the mouth of a donkey to rebuke a guy, turned water into blood, told Ezekiel to cook his food over human dung, and sent a disembodied hand to write on a wall during a feast. God's ways are *not* our ways.

Despite all the skepticism, my conviction has not wavered, even though it seems completely irrational given that I'm not even terminally ill. Loneliness plagues me. *All my friends probably think I'm loony.* Did I have to be the one person God gives such a revelation to? A full-on divine mystery that makes me sound like I belong in a prophecy convention instead of a courtroom? And why are fellow Christians ironically so quick to dismiss supernatural experiences? We believe in Christ's literal resurrection from the dead.

I understand it's difficult to discern if someone's experience is real, hallucinated, or fabricated, especially if you haven't had one yourself. But often, people claiming to have had such experiences—like me—have nothing to gain and everything to lose by sharing.

Yet God has graciously met me even in my loneliness. One day I texted my dear friend Lisa that I felt sharply misunderstood, and my third devotional app later that day stated, "Are you feeling lonely because others don't understand God's private revelations? Remember how even Job's friends were unable to meet him where he was. Keep going, knowing God is intimately by Your side." *Wow, God is actually acknowledging my predicament straight on. This is so comforting.* And God has given me friends who are very compassionate, even though they don't fully understand. I don't blame anyone for not understanding; it's a truly rare spiritual experience I had.

Matt's been visiting on Sundays, too, to help me as I swing

between surrender to Jesus and rage like it's an Olympic sport. He sits there, like a sweet computer that processes all my problems as inputs, then spits out a theology of death and suffering. "We're all dying, Lara. Prophetic dream or terminal illness or not. Let's keep our eyes on eternity together. God doesn't want you to live in fear, even if this was a word from Him. Death is not the end."

He also speaks into my intense sense of betrayal by God, given that I believed God assured me on the bed that He was going to heal me *on earth*.

Matt has an answer for all my arguments:

Question: "God lied when He gave me that devotional years back which said 'Jesus won't let the boat sink.' Dying is the definition of sinking, Matt!"

Answer: "God probably meant He was sustainin' you such that your spiritual boat doesn't sink. You're still a believer after all you've gone through. If your illness ends with you in Heaven instead of earthly healing, that's the ultimate win. The Bible says death is the Christian's reward." *Is this guy unhinged? Can I get a refund on earthly healing then?*

Question: "Remember how you said, 'kings are made in caves, not palaces'? How can I do any work when I'm dead? What was all this supposed 'training' for?"

Answer: "Maybe He's been trainin' you for work in Heaven. For an eternal role. He's preparin' an eternal Kingdom, and we'll all have roles to play in it. God never promises a perfect life. He uses suffering to prepare us for the next. This life is a trial: the testing and establishment of the kind of relationship with Him we need for Heaven."

Question: "So much for all those devotionals He gave me years back about delays and waiting. Doesn't 'waiting' suggest a healing in the end?"

Answer: "Our treasure is in Heaven. That's what all Christians are ultimately waiting for. He gives us encouraging principles like 'wait and trust' along the way so we can persevere. But we shouldn't impute specific outcomes onto them." *Yeah, unless it's a direct statement in a dream, finally revealing His express will.*

Whether it's working or not, it's obvious God has parachuted Matt into my life (and house) at this exact juncture to give me Godly comfort, heal my emotional wounds, and focus me on eternity. I'm learning God doesn't always give up front answers that reveal the future *outcome* in your life situation (though He can), but just gives you *principles* to encourage you along the journey regardless of outcome, just like He did for me while I was on the bed.

Then, when He finally *does* answer with clarity, it can be through a direct, explicit word from God, like my dream, or an actual change in circumstance. However, during the *pre-outcome* phase when He's just giving you principles, it's very hard *not* to assume He's promising you a specific outcome.

Sigh.

My goals used to be simple.

Get healthy. Practice law again. Find a sexy spouse.

Now I'm going to have this illness permanently, and might even die soon.

Now what?

All I want now is for both Matt and I to live. I still want that "perfect" Armenian life. Don't I deserve that after so much suffering?

Old goals: Lawyer, world domination.

New goals: Stay upright and pray I don't meet Jesus yet.

And I'm staring down a new choice. If Jesus' answer really turns out to be "no"—no healing, no future, early death—do I still love Him? Or walk away?

I've been on this rodeo before—Aunt Jackie. God won that round. *Enough is enough. You've crossed the line this time, Lord.*

If I continue being angry, though, I will have no refuge or peace. Matt's attitude undergoing cancer intrigues me and makes me desperately want what he has. That thing Job ultimately had too—an unflinching belief that God is good and trustworthy *even* when He allows grave suffering.

Even death.

Will I ever get there?

One thing is for sure.

If life is a test, I'm failing the "stay chill" unit.

17

The Bag of Basic Blessings

I sit up straighter in the armchair, my voice trailing through the air as I sing *Misty*, a jazz classic about falling madly in love. *Does Matt think this is weird? Why did I pick all love songs? Who cares, I miss singing jazz. I can't believe I'm doing this.*

Sitting up, singing, for fifteen minutes.
Without a sharp drop in blood pressure.
Someone snap a picture before gravity remembers I exist.
At the end of his third Sunday visit, Matt proposed, "We can do this weekly? After I teach my Friday classes?"
So now here we are, our fifth official Friday hangout. Same routine each time.
Matt walks in, backpack slung over one shoulder. That Indiana Jones abomination perched on his head like it owns the place. Today, though, he's paler, slower. (Chemotherapy week.) He's lying here by my armchair flat on his back in his beige work trousers, on the same blue living room couch—Mr. Couch, as I call it now. It's our unofficial "sick kids" headquarters.
I've been using Matt's visits to practice increments of sitting up more and more until I get faint, letting our conversations or music

distract me from the extreme pain, brain zaps, and turbulence. Sitting up and forcing my eyes open still aggravates my brain in the same way, so I'm still bedridden the lion's share of the day. Sitting up or lying down, the outside world is still turning and shaking—nonstop—and harder when I sit up. Zero neurological relief.

I've had many moments of emotional weakness: *I just can't sit up anymore, this is too painful.* But then I slap myself back to reality: *Move or die.* I'm literally relying on God's sustaining grace moment to moment.

But here's the interesting part—no *immediate* fainting or steep blood pressure drops this last month, even after a maximum of twenty minutes sitting up while my brain is spinning—though I have had three close calls. And…we honestly have zero idea why. Maybe because my brain and body chemistry are more stable now because I haven't been on any drugs for a year now? Maybe because we stopped those migraine diets which stripped me of all nutrition? Again, no clue.

But amidst the chaos of forcing myself into these daily "sitting up exposures," my only way to express myself has been crooning tunes until I'm faint and flat on my back again, nauseous.

"I've been waiting to sing these jazz pieces to someone…I mean…Sorry, it's been so long." *Lara, you're probably making Matt uncomfortable.*

"No problem by me," Matt replies, smiling wide. "I could get used to this."

"I'd say you're my captive audience. Do you enjoy captivity?" I tease.

"Caught me."

I can't put my finger on it but there's a force bringing us together. We have this mysterious connection, an intimacy built on suffering. Apparently grief is a team sport.

"I need water," I announce, putting down my sheet music and pushing myself slowly off my chair. My muscles have gotten a bit stronger. I grab my walker and shuffle to the kitchen. *Look at me, strutting to the kitchen like a newborn giraffe on rollerskates. It feels so good to wear these jeans. I have a shape; I'm not a potato sack! So long, hippo pajamas!*

My weight is coming back slowly also—after losing twenty-eight pounds over three years—because we recently stopped the migraine diets. They didn't help anyway, so we gave up, figuring it's time to focus on my body, because my brain isn't healing regardless. My *body* desperately needs nutrition.

This slow weight gain is giving me the strength to keep walking—even with all the neurological agony. Eating *more* is quieting my extreme bouts of nausea too, even though I'm spinning even harder thanks to sitting upright. *This makes no scientific sense. This nausea aspect is a complete miracle.*

I even took a shower sitting up for the first time in three years, with Mom's supervision. (Chronic vertigo in the shower is basically "Survivor: Bathroom Edition." Think gripping onto walls to make sure my vertigo "boat" doesn't turn upside down, all the while feeling real water splash down over me. Think sinking ship in a storm, but with better hair.)

I come back and ask Matt, "Mind if I lie down now on Mr. Couch?"

Matt knows the drill. Tag team. He stands, offering his hand. "Here, let me help you," he says, gently holding my back as I recline.

"Thanks for when you hold my hand," I murmur, "I hope it's not a bother…I…like it actually. Comforts me."

"No problem," he says, sitting on the armchair next to me.

I orient myself to the horizontal position, bracing against the intense waves and brain zaps crashing into me from this recent "sitting up and walking" stint.

I exhale hard. *Distract yourself.* "Let's get back to the basics. Here's my take, Matt. If Jesus loves us, He owes every Christian what I like to call the 'bag of basic blessings.'"

The Bag of Basic Blessings

"The what?" A surprise laugh escapes him.

"The bag of basic blessings. You know—healthy childhood, good education, food, marriage, and kids. The starter pack. Sprinkle in a little suffering to keep us humble. But beyond that? Cruel."

His eyebrow lifts skeptically. "You know I do missions work in Haiti. The Haitians barely have rice and beans. But their joy? Intense. Here, people have everythin' but they've got no clue what real joy is."

"Sorry. Guess I majored in Entitled Brat studies. ...Ow!... Sorry. Brain zap."

He touches my wrist, as if to make a point, then slips his hand back. "Don't be too hard on yourself. You've suffered. A lot. It's natural to ask. To grieve. But again, we don't get all our desires in this life, right?" *I love when he says "right" to rally consensus with me.* Matt could probably pep talk a rock into believing in itself.

"Health and success are intoxicatin' until you realize they're idols that can be whisked away at any moment. Yes, God wants to bless us here, but He cares more about our holiness. Life's short, eternity is not. Live for the line, Lara, not the dot."

"Maybe the musical *Cabaret* has a kernel of wisdom for all of us," I reply. "It's got a famous song in it about how life is short from cradle to death." I start humming that famous tune.

"*Cabaret* isn't exactly what I had in mind." He giggles, smiling wide and arching his eyebrows. *I never realized before how catching his smile is. It almost has a magnetic warmth to it.*

"You're not gonna stop me from sing..." I resist smiling, then break into a laugh anyway. *How is he able to make me smile when I'm trying to complain?*

"Okay, forget *Cabaret*. Christians don't live for the dot, do they? We want happiness, not pain."

"The things that matter are the eternal things—faith, hope, love. This life is a rental, Lara. Don't invest in a rental."

"But Jesus wants us to be super grateful for His blessings, then tells us not to cling to them. He can't have it both ways. What's the point of caring about life if life's all about looking forward to eternity? Why don't all Christians just end their lives then? Makes no sense."

"Life is a precious gift—we don't waste it, but we don't idolize it either. Death, though evil, is just a doorway to eternity, not an ending. We look forward to enjoyin' eternal life free from death, disease, and sin. For Christians, thanks to Christ's sacrifice, life is a win/win—here and in Heaven. Christians need to have a good theology of death. A lot of people don't."

What a unicorn. Matt knows how to live meaningfully here but also long for Heaven. His longing for eternal treasures, rather than temporary ones, has such a credible force of persuasion because he's staring death in the face right now.

Suddenly, I feel unsettled. I need something. I move my right hand to the edge of the couch and look from Matt's eyes to my right hand several times.

He leans in and grabs my right hand almost instantaneously. *Ooh, quick study. Why do I need his hand?*

"Thanks," I whisper, feeling the warmth of his grip seep into me.

He squeezes my hand. "No problem."

"Do you ever question God's judgment for why you're suffering? I don't think real trust is possible, not unless He gives us the *why* for tragedies."

"I don't try to play God. I just trust He knows what He's doin'." His hand tightens around mine, a silent plea to believe him. *How can a PhD have such humility?* He's a walking oxymoron—a science and numbers guy driven by data, yet when it comes to Christianity, he has such humble faith.

"Jesus encourages us to ask why," Matt adds, "and sometimes He does answer. But achin' for answers will break us. He gives Himself in our suffering instead." *That's true at least. God has been right by me in all this strange grief over my future death, constantly comforting me in timely ways and grieving with me intimately.*

"But why has God chosen not to heal my neurological pain? Sitting up is making my brain worse."

"He could be doin' a million things—refinin' your faith, usin' your suffering to impact others spiritually, or fulfillin' eternal purposes we can't see. His economy is different. Tangible earthly blessing doesn't indicate God's favor. Just look at Job—faithful, yet God still allowed his great suffering. The idea that 'God is good so He doesn't want us to suffer' is not Biblical. Yes, He's good and He does heal some diseases on earth, but only if it's His will."

"But Matt, I'm angry. We might both die! What good are our degrees now?"

"I get it. I used to be controlled by anger. In my first cancer, I was so angry I asked Mom to bring me a hammer and a cardboard box once. Couldn't even pick up the hammer. Lost it completely. I used to trance out on the way to chemo to avoid the emotions."

I eye him. "Hard to picture. You look so strong now in this deadly situation."

He giggles. "Trust me, I'm not so strong all the time. Mom and the church ladies have been feedin' me nonstop lately. Sometimes we gotta ask for help, right?"

The conversation drifts and a few hours of rest later, Matt's eyes light up in a new direction. "Want to try sittin' up again? I have somethin' fun to show you."

He slides an arm behind me, solid against the small of my back, and helps me up. We sit side by side on the couch as he pulls out a theology comic book. *These exist?* He flips through pages fast, whispering jokes in my ear. Laughter bubbles up, unexpected and welcome.

Then suddenly, there's an awkward silence, and his brown eyes hold onto mine, intense.

I should look away.

I don't.

We snap our gazes to the front, both sitting frozen, side by side.

"I've only been on two dates before," Matt says, breaking the silence. "One tea, one ice cream." *Did he just bring up dating? Two dates? He's even more cautious and guarded (or innocent) than I thought? So if he's thirty-eight now, he's been single twenty years?*

"Girls are scary, you know," he adds. "Not so easy bein' 'round 'em." *Did he just wink at me? What is up with that random Southern affect he slips in and out of? Does he want to be in a western? I like that self-deprecating humor.*

"Maybe girls thought I was rigid or robotic or somethin'?" he considers somewhat stoically, shrugging his shoulders. *Maybe that's why he's never chased after love? Some inner fear that he was too different somehow? Or did the childhood cancer leave some emotional insecurities that left him scared to be vulnerable?*

I tease, "Maybe all those bimbos just didn't have enough intelligence, fire, and spark to date a chemistry professor like you. Get it? Fire. Sparks. Chemistry."

He grins wide. "Guess I need someone I have chemistry with... Get it?"

My cheeks instantly flush. We lock eyes again. *Did my stomach just turn a somersault?*

"Yeah, well, I wasn't allowed to even date in high school, so I have my own issues," I say, trying to look casual.

"And now?" He smirks, looking mildly concerned.

"What do you think?" I tease.

Suddenly, Matt winces in pain, throwing his hand to his abdomen.

"You okay, Matt?"

"Worried I'm gonna have an intestinal obstruction. That's a big fear whenever the pain ramps up. Haven't had one yet, which is surprising, but once things go south like that, it's...not a good sign."

"I'm so sorry. What was your hospital trip like last August?"

He sighs. "Rough. Couldn't eat. Drink. Vomiting. Intestines inflamed. They still don't know why."

"And now?"

"Right now, the cancer's stable, but three clinical trials have already rejected me—I didn't qualify. I'm hopin' my upcomin' surgery opens new options. The surgeons won't know until they go in. Best case, they remove parts of my intestine and lymph nodes, so we can test for a targeted immunotherapy."

My throat tightens. The reality of his diagnosis weighs on me, and suddenly, I'm fighting back tears. I instinctively grab his hand and slide closer to him.

"Why can't God just leave you with us? He's so selfish. He'll have you for eternity. Why can't we have you longer?"

Matt lifts his other arm and slowly puts it around me. "It's not wrong to ask. I've seen miracles. I took a risk moving to San Francisco in 2014 to lead the youth group, without having a job lined up. But something in my spirit knew God was going to provide. The day after I moved, Susan from church randomly called, asking if I'd be interested in this new faculty position opening up. There's always hope. Sometimes God brings it out of nowhere."

Is his arm around me?

"What are we going to do Matt? We're in a nightmare." A tear slips down my cheek.

"We're gonna keep trustin'. One of my favorite verses is Isaiah 43:2. God promises, 'When you walk through the fire, you will not be burned; the flames will not set you ablaze.' That's why we can have joy…even in the fire."

He pauses, lost in thought. "Think of it like…singing…but you know, in the fire."

"Singing?" I reply, wiping away a tear as a smile cracks through. "I guess I'm used to singing through fire already."

Matt inhales a breath and smiles softly. "Here, let's pray."

He changes his tone to one of reverence, thickening with emotion with every word. "Oh Lord, we've been suffering for so long.

We need your grace and your deliverance." His voice catches, then he starts again. "Take us through these challenging times and help us give one another the strength and courage to get through. In your Son's name we pray. Amen."

An isolated tear slides down his cheek. He lifts his arm off my shoulder and leans forward to snatch a tissue from the coffee table. He dabs at his face, turning away, his jaw tightening. *Is he embarrassed?*

"Sorry," he whispers. "See, I've got emotions too. But I've got to be strong...for the youth group kids...for my parents. I can't let anyone's faith fall through the cracks because of my cancer." *Is that why he's emotionally guarded sometimes? He internalizes his pain so as not to hurt others or be a supposed burden? Maybe another kind of trauma from the first cancer?*

"You know you don't have to be strong all the time, right Matt? Always putting others before yourself? Or like taking on so many responsibilities at church? You can complain. You can rest. You're human too."

He shrugs his shoulders. "Thanks. Yeah...easier said than done. I better get going," he rambles, standing somewhat abruptly. He slings his backpack over one shoulder like he always does, and puts his hat on.

He walks me to the door on his arm so I don't have to use my walker.

We embrace in a tight hug. *Ooh he's tall. I never really noticed that before.*

When he backs off, his chin grazes mine.

We freeze.

"Ooh, sorry," he murmurs.

"It's okay," I mutter.

We stand here.

Hanging in the moment.

Two awkward teenagers at a school dance.

Before I can say something, he asks, almost tentative, "How about... Let's do somethin' special on Monday, yeah?"

Monday? What's so special about...

18

My Funny Valentine

"Matt's coming over tonight? On Valentine's Day? Doesn't he always come on Fridays? I knew there was something more just from the way you would describe him, Lars!"

I read Sevan's text as I slip into a pink skirt, black tights, and a silky beige button-up blouse. My arm muscles are finally strong enough—I can dress *on my own* now, even as I push off circles in my vision. Looking at my reflection in the mirror, tears well up.

Am I a real woman again, wearing makeup? My fair skin, dark lashes coated with fresh mascara, and rosy, red lips bring a flicker of familiarity to the stranger in the mirror. *Finally, my reflection doesn't scream "medical drama" extra.*

Mom and Pops left ten minutes ago for Aunt Rosalie's—Golden Girl No. 4—for Armenian dolma night. They're comfortable leaving me alone now that I've almost "graduated" from the walker and can walk around in very slow increments on my own (leg muscles are slowly forming). I've recently discovered that if I clasp onto walls or waddle back and forth nonstop during any "sitting up" exposure, sometimes I can trick my brain into focusing on *that* bodily motion instead of the turbulence—and it helps me balance somehow even while the vertigo is rising.

Regardless, Matt's coming soon. *He can catch me if I fall.*

My phone buzzes again. My friend Miriam's text: "You deserve this. Just relax. Give the guy a chance. Wear the red dress—yes, *that* one—and let Cupid do his thing!" *The red dress? Oh my gosh, this really is a date, isn't it? Did Matthew John boldly ask me out? What does this mean? I mean, I really do like a guy with a big brain... It's so... Wait, what am I saying? Why is my heart racing?*

Goal: don't vomit.

I tie my hair in a loose bun, letting a few dark brown curls frame my face, then strategically display the giant red Valentine's pillow and fluffy pink blanket Auntie Arax gifted me last year in the living room. *If anyone deserves a magical night, it's Matt and me.*

Knock, knock.

My heart pounds as I waddle slowly to the door, clasping onto walls. I open it, and Matt stands there in beige work trousers, a blue button-down dress shirt, his regular black jacket, and his backpack slung over one shoulder. His signature wide smile falters at the edges, twitching nervously.

Nothing in his hands.

My heart drops.

"Hi Lara," he says, lips tight, glancing down at his feet.

"Hi Matt," I respond, gesturing him in.

He parks himself in an isolated chair, then anchors his gaze at his feet.

Mr. Couch sits empty—our usual spot. *He seems...nervous? I need a minute.*

"Be right back." I shuffle to the bathroom and close the door behind me. *He didn't bring anything. No flowers? No card? Does he even care?* I bite my lip. *Why are you so ridiculous? Calm down. You're just "hanging out." The guy has cancer. What did you expect, tickets to Paris? Maybe.*

I take a breath, square my shoulders, and head back to find Matt perched stiff in the chair, fidgeting with a Kleenex. He darts me a glance when I sit across from him in my own chair. I wrap the pink blanket tight around my legs. *Just friends.*

Silence.

We sit here frozen, glaring straight at each other, two deer caught in headlights.

I shuffle my feet. (My fuzzy pink unicorn slippers scream "cozy grandma," but at least my lip color screams "I'm trying.")

"Hi Matt," I try again, biting my lower lip.

"Hi," he says, flashing a tight smile, his hands locked together.

Silence again.

Seconds stretch into an awkward eternity.

I look down at the floor to avoid eye contact.

So does he.

So much for all the emotional intimacy from the last six hangouts. Hollywood lied—there's no romantic violin playing in the background.

And then, Matt abruptly moves. He rummages through his backpack, stands, and walks toward me.

"I got you somethin'." He smiles, bashfully, holding out an adorable white and black polka-dot stuffed animal puppy, and a beautiful red box of chocolates.

Relief floods my chest. *So sweet. Phew.*

"Oh, Matt. Thank you." I grin wide and clutch the puppy. "I'm naming him Fluffy."

His eyes light up. "Remember when you asked me why everythin' can't just be puppies and butterflies? Well, here's your puppy. God tells us He'll give us joy, even in suffering." He fumbles over his words, backing away from me and clasping his hands together again.

Silence.

Lara, change the energy. Say something.

"Did you notice, um, how I'm wearing makeup? First time in… Feels like I'm alive."

"Yeah." *Liar. Guys never notice these things.* "But you don't need it." *Ooh, that's kind.*

"For the record, I'm not high-maintenance," I tease. "You can take me out just for burritos sometime if I ever leave this dumb house." *Yeah, sure you're not high-maintenance. That's why you almost lost it at the thought that he showed up empty-handed.*

He cocks his eyebrows. "You do realize you're wrapped in a pink blanket with hearts on it. And pink slippers." I look down as far as I can go. *Touché.* I can't look down too far or my ear crystals will unlodge, causing a harder spin.

"Girly isn't the same as high maintenance, Matt. And I'll hurt you if you tease me again."

"Ooh, I'm scared. You can barely walk." He grins wide, taking his black jacket off. *Ooh. Edgy, dry humor? Ice is broken? Wait… The guy can flirt? He never showed me this side in 2017. Hmm.*

My eyes dart to his left ear, which is attracting my attention. *Why does it pop out slightly more than the right one? Is it a strategic antenna for theological debates? It's actually really… adorable?*

In no time, the awkwardness fades into deep conversation. Debating theology. Suffering. Our safe space. Common ground. We share some chocolates, and the smooth, velvety chocolate melts on my tongue, balanced by the satisfying crunch of roasted almonds. *I haven't had chocolate in four years. Delicious.*

Half an hour later, we've drifted to the dining room table, sitting next to each other at a close angle.

"Matt, I feel so abnormal. Do you ever feel that way?"

"Yeah. Like, why do I have to go through cancer twice? I've asked the Lord that a lot."

"It must be so incredibly hard."

He exhales. "Thanks. Small intestinal cancer is so rare that docs don't understand it. They don't even know how I got to Stage 4 so fast."

"I can't even imagine. Look at us Matt. This is so sad. We're both grieving."

"But we're also comfortin' each other. Blessed are those who mourn, for they will be comforted, right?"

His eyes brighten. "Here, let me show you somethin'." He pulls out his laptop, flipping to a CAT scan of his intestines.

"See these big yellow cancer blobs? Three weeks later—before I had even started chemo for this cancer—gone. Miraculously. God can do anything. My docs were baffled. Gave me a chance to witness to one of 'em actually. No idea if he took me seriously. Sometimes it's in our greatest suffering that God gives us the best opportunities."

Feeling stiff, I start rolling my shoulders and self-massaging my neck to ease my electrical nerve pain. When I grab the table to steady myself against a more acute vertigo wave, Matt's chair scrapes against the floor.

In seconds, he's behind my chair, his hands hovering near my neck. *What is he—*

His fingers suddenly press gently into my skin.

What on earth? Is Matt, the Godly, introverted PhD, actually massaging my neck and shoulders? In like a surprisingly suave kind of way? Plot twist I didn't see coming.

"This is what we do in Haiti after long days," Matt says. "A stress-relief line."

Yeah…I'm sure you do… This feels a bit…scandalous? Wonderful? Did he just cross the "no more than hand holding" barrier? Whatever, at least we're both more at ease now. Did he enroll in acting lessons lately?

He's so mysterious and aloof sometimes that I can't tell if he knows exactly what he's doing or is clueless. He's one of those intensely cerebral people who only say twenty percent of what they think, unless you explicitly ask or engage them.

Fifteen seconds tick by in silence, the gentle touch of his hands lingering. *Say something, Lara. Anything.*

I decide to sing a few bars of *My Funny Valentine*, chuckling when I get to the part about the lover's funny looks.

Matt chuckles as he massages. "Are you sayin' I'm funny lookin'?"

"No, it's a popular jazz standard. But I can tease you when I like." We both giggle and the tension cracks again.

"So, uh, Matt…favorite animal?"

"Eagles. I was an Eagle Scout. They remind me of strength and courage."

"Any others?"

"Hmm. Whales."

"Why?"

"During my first cancer, I watched *Free Willy* obsessively, then the Make-A-Wish Foundation sent us to Alaska to see the whales after I healed."

"Was it magical?"

"Yeah."

"Favorite ice cream flavor?"

"Mint chip."

"Me too! Favorite color?"

"Blue."

"Introvert or extrovert. What type?"

"I'm type Matt." *Touché.*

"Thing you hate?"

"Travel. The self-indulgent pictures, 'luxury' sights, airport lines." He stops massaging and slides back into his chair.

"I love travel! Think history. Culinary and cultural delights! Okay, fine." I roll my eyes. "Something weird about yourself?"

"My stubborn belief duct tape can solve anything." He giggles.

"Favorite sport?"

His eyes narrow playfully. "This interrogation is worse than the first time I visited you on New Year's."

"When I get nervous, I go into lawyer mode. Lots of vicious questions."

"I think you're tamer than you think." His eyes widen flirtatiously.

"But," he adds, "badminton. Couldn't run anymore after the first cancer because of back pain so I switched from soccer to the high school badminton team."

Okay, Lara, bring out the big guns. He seems open. Let's see what he's got.

"Can I confess that a few years back, I thought it was sexy when you used Inspector Gadget as a metaphor in one of your Bible devotional videos?"

Sexy? Really? You literally just told the youth pastor he's sexy? Does he even know that word? I think I meant attractive? Adorable? Either/or?

"That's a weird thing..."

He flashes an awkward smile and his left ear—the one that adorably pops out—goes bright red instantly. After processing what I just said, his lips curve into a huge grin. "But I'll take it." *Okay. Now I've warmed the guy up.*

He cocks one eyebrow. "But you know, you should be focusin' on the content of my devotionals." *He's got sharp flirtatious instincts. Who knew?*

"Don't get smart with me. I can break up with you," I reply.

Matt leans in, smirking. "We haven't even started yet." *Ooh, Matt: 10. Lara: 10. Why is this so exhilarating? I can't remember the last date who kept me on my toes. Wait, I can't remember my last date, period. Ugh.*

"Tell me something else I wouldn't expect about you Matt."

"Hmm, let's see. In college, I survived on eight dollars a day for food, just to see if I could for three months. Wanted efficiency in my cookin'. And I made a California proposition analysis series using stick figure jokes and flowcharts. Non-partisan." *Oh my gosh, that big brain is just so...*

"See? You were meant to be a lawyer or policy analyst," I tease. "Anything else I wouldn't expect?"

"I can sew."

"Don't tell me you're on a competitive knitting team too?"

"Nope. Just patches. Things fall apart, I fix 'em."

"No Versace frontlines in your future?"

"Don't know what that is. Been wearin' the same suits for years. They fit just fine. But every Christmas, Mom insists on buying me the 'trendy' stuff." *So that finally explains why some of his outfits are meh, while some are at studmuffin level!*

I turn to questions about his current job as a professor, shaping the minds of hundreds of students who go on to test blood in hospitals. He tells me about playing flute in the UCLA marching band and his experiences as a Christian camp counselor.

"So there I was," Matt recalls, giggling, "in front of a room full of kids, explainin' chemical reactions when—*BOOM!*—the beaker foamed over like a volcano. They went wild, cheerin' like I was a science magician. I gave a little bow, secretly prayin' the table wouldn't catch fire. The kids clapped and shouted, 'Do it again!'"

I smile, but the spinning and electrical pressure in my head overwhelm me. "Mind if we move to Mr. Couch now? Need to lie down soon. Feel really faint."

"Sure thing."

We get up and sit on the plush blue cushions side by side. A beautiful sunset paints a picture right outside the big windows. Hues of orange, red, and gold cut across the sky like an artist's bold brushstrokes. We watch in silence, soaking it in. *Good timing.* My right hand inches toward the empty space between us, and the ghost of his touch lingers in the gap. The air feels charged between us, like something has shifted. *Does he want to take my hand? I need... I want...*

"After being stuck inside for so long, and with my eyes closed, seeing all this feels unreal," I whisper. "The first time I saw myself in the mirror after everything... I bawled. My eyes are open now.

Open! I know I'm spinning harder as a result, but I don't have a choice. Whether I heal or not, I *have* to keep sitting up. But firecrackers are going off in my brain nonstop."

"I know, Lara." He slides an arm around me, as his other hand finds mine. *Finally.*

I feel so vulnerable. But so safe. Mr. Couch has become our sanctuary. A place of stolen moments. Giggles. Escapes. *And now, he's...holding me. In both arms.*

"The sunset's beautiful," Matt whispers, his eyes on me now.

I meet his gaze. *How come I never realized how handsome his almond shaped brown eyes are?* I falter, unsure whether to look away.

He doesn't look away.

Neither do I. *This is so intense.*

"You are too, Lara."

My heart flips...fast. *Did he just tell me I'm beautiful? Oh, when he says Lara in that deep voice...*

"Thank you, Matt. I..." My voice wavers. "I'm so sorry I'm an angry basket-case of grief these days. Where's old optimistic Lara? I'm still singing, but...pissy. I used to love the Lord so much."

"I don't see you as depressed. I see you as fightin'. For your health and life. And you're still talkin' to God." I arch an eyebrow.

"Okay," he adds, "maybe yellin'. But you haven't lost your faith. You could have walked away by now. Strength isn't measured by success; it's measured by courage and perseverance in faith, even despite great testing."

He sighs. "Look, maybe next time we can watch ten minutes of a terrible movie or eat yummy snacks. You know, normal people stuff. Whatever you can handle given the whole electrical wave sensitivity thing. Here, let's pray."

As Matt prays, the garage door rumbles open. *Mom and Pops are home.*

Matt's arm instantly slips off me, and he stands, awkwardly rubbing the back of his head. "I should get goin'. You need rest."

He helps me stand and I grip onto him for balance against the turbulent shaking of the room.

Our eyes lock, and there it is again—an electric pull buzzing between us.

He leans in.

Close.

Maybe nine inches from my lips.

Then—he steps back, exhaling.

"I have surgery comin' up. Let's skip next week, so I can rest up, yeah?"

"Of course."

He pulls me into a hug.

Neither of us let go.

I breathe in his scent—clean, fresh, familiar, comforting. A scent I've grown attached to. Almost an airy cologne but softer.

"What cologne do you wear, Matt?"

"Soap," he says with a smirk.

"Cologne isn't in your ideal bag of basic blessings?"

"You, my lady, should focus less on that bag thingy and more on the treasures you'll hold in Heaven." *My lady? He's giving off major British gentleman vibes which is so my gig as an Anglophile.*

As Matt drives off in his car, the thought hits me. *Am I going to die before this man visits me next?* Every goodbye lately feels like the end of a season finale. "Tune in next week to see if Lara's still alive!" *Ugh, I hate this feeling that the clock is ticking, but no one will tell me how much time I have left. Lord, why that dream?*

I shuffle to my room, catching Pops murmur a joke to Mom in the family room: "Those two are all well and good with their health issues, all they need now is a little romance and heartbreak."

Heartbreak?

19

Jekyll & Hyde

T he next few days, my heart and mind are a chaotic courtroom where I argue both sides of a legal case with the fervor of Jekyll and Hyde.
Woah… I have strong feelings for Matt.
Do I?
Oh my gosh…
Wait… I think I do?
I do like Matt.
Yes. I do.
I really like Matt.
Do I?
Yesss.
Woah.
Where did this come from?
I can't deny it. This guy is uniquely everything I've been… waiting for.
Loyal.
Courageous.
Witty.
Compassionate.

Humble.
Brilliant.
Godly.
Very Godly.
Talented.
Teaches children.
Preaches internationally.
Half Armenian...*check!*
Half Jewish... *Can't go wrong with the chosen people...*
Wise.
Unique.
Just plain different.
Wait...quirky.
Ah, yes. Quirky. That's it. Like me.

Wickedly attractive. Yes, he has a heart of gold, but has anyone noticed those dimples and that million dollar smile? How is this guy even single? He's literally the most handsome Armenian I've ever laid eyes on. Was his aura suffocating under that abomination of a hat all these years?

That thing deserves jail time.

Wait... How long have I felt this way? Have we subconsciously had crushes on each other all along? Is that why my heart would beat fast before every phone call on the bed?

Oh... I think I'm in...

I guess there's nothing mysterious about it. We both have bizarre illnesses no one understands. Being understood—really understood—is intoxicating. Emotional intimacy? We've had that for years now, starting with those phone calls.

And that deep voice...those intense deep brown eyes that see right through me...the way he says "sure thing"...and that adorably playful Southern affect...

Wait.

Lara, no.

What business do us two sicklings have "dating?" Are we nuts?

I have enough emotional baggage to start my own airline at this point; do I really want to check in a boyfriend with cancer into the mix? *Great idea. Fantastic.*

No, no.

This must be some sort of weird Florence Nightingale complex we've developed towards each other. But that jawline...

No. We are too different. We're better off as friends. Yes. Just friends.

The guy is a semi-stoic introverted engineering genius who probably thinks *Oklahoma!* is just a state and not a musical, while I'm as extroverted and emotional as they come. He hates law, I hate teaching.

Lara, you know none of that matters. And you would look really good with a tall and handsome PhD on your arm.

No. It's not wise to get invested in someone with cancer. Oh, the irony. Look who's talking—Miss "I'm gonna die, God told me."

The heart of the matter—should I really date this amazing man, knowing full well he could die on me? Or me on him? Can I even trust God at this point?

No.

I've done the whole "give and take away" experiment before, and I don't have it in me to do it again.

And isn't God's design for marriage aimed at achieving the "perfect Armenian life" anyway? A forty-year, stable commitment, popping out a litter of kids, and chowing down kebabs at picnics? Why would Jesus want us two sick kids to date and/or marry when either one of us might be checking into Heaven tomorrow? You're telling me God might want to slip in some last-minute nuptials before He takes me? Or him? God doesn't give marriage just for joy's sake. *Does He?*

Enough of this nonsense. I need to protect Matt. He doesn't know how complicated love is. He's too optimistic about life and too innocent. He trusts God *way* too much. I'll get over this. I have to. I don't even know him—not really. What if he's a secret spy? Or worse...a minimalist? Who's to say he isn't Matthew John from church, the secret serial killer lurking in plain sight?

Right?

Right.

Meanwhile, though my deep sorrow over my own future death persists, God has still been walking me through my grief, showing up in countless ways. For example, my friend Steven called recently on a Saturday: "While praying for you, I heard the Lord say, 'Jesus is interceding for Lara in her grief,' so I had to call you."

The next morning, my church's online sermon focused on Hebrews 7:25: how Jesus intercedes for us in prayer to the Father. *Wow. Not a coincidence. Good thing Jesus is my Advocate in this grief—because I keep showing up whiny, dramatic, and emotionally unprepared for trial these days.*

The day after that, on Monday morning, a Christian newsletter landed in my email inbox. It cited the same exact Hebrews verse, stating, "Are you grieving your death? Do you feel the Holy Spirit grieving with you? Jesus intercedes for us and comforts us with His peace." *No way. The theme of intercession again.* The devotion provided hope, setting forth Jonathan Edwards' famous argument that the joys of Heaven will be ever-increasing for all believers, giving us great hope when we experience earthly losses. It also cited Psalm 16:11: "[Y]ou will fill me with joy in Your presence, with eternal pleasures at Your right hand." *But what does this Heavenly joy look like, Lord? Are these eternal treasures actually better than the bag of basic blessings here?*

I also told Mom and Pops about my dream right after it happened last month. They haven't had experiences like this with the Holy Spirit either, so it obviously upset them. Pops' reaction—"Don't go loony on me, Lars. We've been through enough. Be grateful you're walking again." Who could blame him? And Mom's weekly interrogation—"Has Matt been able to help you with those strange thoughts, Hokees?" *They're probably thinking this is "Lara plays Mad Margaret," the real-life reprise. Ugh.*

I desperately wanted to give Mom the answer she wanted, but I couldn't. I knew the dream was from God. *Oh well, even Jesus' family thought he was "out of His mind" at one point.* Mark 3:21. I nonetheless agreed, at my parents' request, to book a few online sessions with a Dumford psychiatrist, the goal being to get me to somehow change my conviction (and make sure I'm not a loon).

The doctor listened, nodded, conducted standard testing, and concluded in our last session: "From what I see, you're rational. Clear thinking. No clinical depression or mental illness. You're bubblier than the pack of 'em despite your grave suffering. This dream issue appears to be a religious squabble, and it's been fun debating it with you as an atheist myself." Thankfully he didn't suggest any anti-depressants, because my brain certainly loves those!

Unbeknownst to me, though, God was already orchestrating something new behind the scenes.

Fast forward to this morning: a text message buzzes on my phone, and with it, the next divine breadcrumb.

My friend Lisa: "My Bible study group was praying about you and your conviction of death today. You won't believe this. A girl in the group suddenly said she was experiencing a vision and that she felt the prompting of the Holy Spirit to tell you something. Something big."

20

The Rainbow

I stare at Lisa's text, squinting hard:
"Lara, this girl in my Bible study has the prophetic gifting. I've seen her foretell events accurately before! Today, as we were praying about you, she said the Holy Spirit gave her a vision of a large scroll, then told her to tell you the following:

'HER STORY IS NOT OVER YET. GOD HAS A PROMISE TO GIVE HER FIRST.'

Then, the girl said she had a second vision right after, of a woman with brown curly hair standing in a field with a rainbow over her head. Lara, I never told the group your name or your hairstyle, or even the contents of your dream! Just that you had a conviction of a premature death."

I have no idea what to make of this. What does one do with this kind of prophetic poetry, packaged by a stranger and forwarded by a friend?

Lisa moves in more charismatic streams of Christianity. I've personally never had a vision or a direct "word from God" to give *someone else*—just that one dream. (To be clear, I'm not claiming to have the "prophetic gift" either. Just that the Holy Spirit gave me a direct revelation about *me* in a dream, just like He speaks personally to all believers in different ways.) But Christian "continuationists" like Lisa believe God gives some believers today the spiritual gift of prophecy, meaning they receive and then share "words" or "visions" from the Holy Spirit regarding *other* believers.

This idea has Biblical basis. In 1 Timothy 1:18, the Apostle Paul exhorts Timothy to hold onto "prophecies once made" about him. Paul also instructs the church to "eagerly desire gifts of the Spirit, especially prophecy" (1 Corinthians 14:1), and to "not treat prophecies with contempt" (1 Thessalonians 5:20).

Hmm. I don't even know this girl who had a vision of me, apparently. How does she know I have brown curly hair? And she saw a scroll like I did in my own dream… Was it the same scroll? Is it a comprehensive scroll containing all the events in my life or something? *Great, now I'm basically the heroine in a Christian detective novel.* But maybe she really does have a prophetic gifting? Why would she make any of this up?

But what does her message from God mean—

1. "Her story is not over yet."
2. "God has a promise to give her first."
3. Me standing under a rainbow…?

I have no clue.

Two hours later, my friend Toukhig texts me out of the blue: "Lara, I've been praying about your conviction of death. I really believe your story's not over yet. God's not done with you." *Wait. Your story is not over?*

The next morning, a card arrives in the mail from my friend Rachel. A delicate watercolor rainbow is arched across the front.

Inside: "I know your journey's been hard, but I believe there's more to come." *More to come?*

Then, around mid-afternoon, Pops calls me to the front of the house. "Lars, come look at this. Beautiful."

I wobble over and see it—a large rainbow blooming across the sky, perfectly framed for us to see from our front windows. Stunning.

I sit on Mr. Couch, feeling ambushed by hope. *Is this You, Jesus? Are You actually telling me I'm going to live a bit longer? That You have something more for me before You "come" to take me? What am I missing? I know my dream was from You. Was this girl in Lisa's group reading the same scroll You gave me? What on earth more could there be left in my story, if I'm going to die in the near future? How do I reconcile all this?*

I stare at the sky, then back at Rachel's card. Are all these rainbows divine breadcrumbs?

Maybe I'm just standing too close to a very enthusiastic sprinkler.

21

The Plot Thickens

My phone vibrates at 8 p.m. against the nightstand as I rest in bed.

Matt.

Breathe. Just Matt. It's not like you have feelings for him or anything. Wasn't he supposed to be resting up for surgery?

I swipe to answer. "Hey Matt?"

"Lara."

"Everything okay?" My heart stumbles. *Snap out of it Lara.*

"I don't know how to tell you this…" Matt exhales a shaky breath as I grip the phone tighter. "I landed in the ER yesterday. Couldn't eat or drink for over twenty-four hours."

"What happened? Your voice is kind of fuzzy."

"Sorry, there's a giant NG tube down my nose."

"I'm so sorry. Are you—"

"There's a really big obstruction in my small intestine. I…I've been scared this might happen. I can't pass anything through my system. Whatever I eat or drink just stays there. So I can't eat. NG tube is supposed to drain it all."

My stomach knots. "Wow. What does that mean for the surgery next week?"

"If I can't keep liquids down without vomiting, and if the obstruction doesn't resolve, they won't do it." *Oh no.*

"Once these cancers get to the point of causing obstructions like this, there aren't any great options. I've tried chemo for eight months now."

His voice is slower than usual, strained. "And if I can't eat at all because the obstruction doesn't resolve…this is…probably…the end for me. The docs are already throwing around the hospice word."

Hospice? My heart pounds. "Oh my gosh Matt. I can't believe this!"

A long pause stretches between us, filled only by the faint beeping of hospital monitors. I struggle to find words, anything that doesn't sound as hollow as I feel.

"I'm so incredibly sorry, Matt. I…How's the pain?"

"Bad. Even with morphine. Like a rock in my intestine. And this tube feels like it's drilling into my ribs and throat. Can barely move."

"Oh Matt, I can't imagine."

"But…" His voice softens around the edges. "If I do get out of this alive, Lara…I want to see you again. To take you on as many dates as I can… You know, in your house. As you are able." His voice, though weak, has a tint of joy in it. *Oh my gosh, he still wants to pursue this!*

"I'll sign a legal affidavit promising it," he adds, "And you know I hate lawyers." *Oh, that sense of humor.*

"I can't wait to see you either. But all I want is for you to get through this!" *I can't escape it. I want to see him. I need to see him. Wait… No you don't! Stop this!*

"Lara, we need a miracle. That's what it's down to. If this blockage doesn't resolve…"

"It *will*, Matt. God's got this. I'll be praying. Nonstop."

"Pastor Calvin and some youth group kids came by today.

Prayed with me." Calvin is our pastor who's been praying for our illnesses. Matt is his right-hand man as the youth leader.

"So many people are rooting for you. If I could get in a car, I'd be there."

"But Lara..." He hesitates. "What's going to happen to the youth group kids if somethin' happens to me? Can't let 'em down. I'm responsible for their...I can't bear the idea of anyone goin' down a wrong path because they're demoralized by this."

"Matt. Listen. You *can't* think about others right now. Don't save the world right now. Just focus on yourself."

"I know, I know. It's...hearing your voice helps me. A lot. I just... I just wanted to talk one last time. In case..."

"Matt! Don't. Jesus will save you. Stay strong, okay? We all admire your courage! And...thanks for calling. I love hearing from you."

"Sure thing."

Two days pass in a blur of intense prayers, until I get an email from Matt to the church listserv.

Subject line: *The Fruit of the Vine:*

> Lying in this hospital bed, unable to eat or drink for several days, I've been thinking a lot about the Last Supper—Jesus' final meal before His crucifixion, forever symbolizing His sacrifice for our sins. He told His disciples to remember this meal, and He said He wouldn't taste it again until the Kingdom of God comes.
>
> You can sense His deep longing for that day when He'll share this meal again with His friends. Given my condition, I have a glimpse of Jesus' intense longing. I would have savored my last meal more if I knew it was going to be my last for a while. But even my eagerness to eat again doesn't compare to Jesus' anticipation for the day when all His children will partake in that great wedding feast in Heaven.

I digest Matt's words (no pun intended), pressing a hand to my chest. His words are full of hope, even as his body gives up. *How does he even have energy to write?*

If Matt's faith is this strong dying on morphine, the rest of us really should up our game. His focus is *still* on Heaven rather than the dire situation at hand. *I want this courage. This peace. This desire for Heaven. This trust in suffering.*

I pull on my hair, my heart racing at the thought of him.

Great. I'm falling hard for a brilliant guy who's literally one bad bowel movement away from meeting Jesus.

Six days later, the buzz of a text from my phone shatters the quiet of my room at 6 A.M. I squint my eyes open and grab the phone.

Matt.

My fingers fumble to unlock the screen.

Text: "Still in the hospital. Things took a turn for the worse. Can't explain now. Haven't eaten a thing. Feeling weak, so I'm sending you a goodbye text just in case. Want you to know—whatever happens, you mean a lot to me. More than you know."

Goodbye?

22

On the Brink

My breath catches in my throat as Matt's "goodbye" text sears into me.

My vision blurs and tears spill down my face before I even realize I'm crying. Matt is my vision of clarity in a spinning world—literally and metaphorically.

No, no, no.

I try to text back something meaningful, poetic or prayerful, but every letter is a betrayal of what I actually want to say.

The day crawls by, like molasses dripping through grief.

Goal: don't have a mental breakdown.

I pace in and out of Pops' office, tugging my hair, waddling back and forth to brace against the hard turbulence in my vision. Eventually, I lie down in defeat. Even Pops' jokes can't draw a smile from me today. And Pops can find humor in a tax return.

Matt's dire situation has me staring straight into the face of death and eternity. This isn't theoretical anymore like my own dream of future death—it's real. Matt might *actually* be dying. Prayers sputter out of me in fractured fragments, half-whispers straining for coherence. If my life had a soundtrack right now, it'd be an endless loop of Darth Vader's *Imperial March*.

Will God be good if He takes Matt? No.

The next day, at 8 P.M., another blog post from Matt lands in my inbox. *He's still writing? Is this man for real? Did something turn around? Why hasn't he texted me?*

Subject line: *Only Death Awaits?*:

> Death is everyone's destiny—but not the end. Of course, we can't measure or study the afterlife. We need someone who's been there. Someone who's been dead, and comes back to tell us what it's like. *Ah, but can you really trust stories from people claiming they went to Heaven for twenty minutes? Perhaps just hallucinating, or dreaming?* No. We need someone truly dead for a few days. Someone who seemed reliable while alive, who demonstrated true power and knowledge. Someone who always spoke truth, even if it angered everybody.
>
> If someone like that came back to life, walking around and telling people what happens after we die, *that* would be someone worth listening to. Especially if His return completely erased His followers' fear of death. Every Easter, we commemorate the resurrection of the one person to ever walk the earth that could reliably fit that description. He knew what was coming, told His followers in advance he would be killed, and suffered not for Himself, but for us.
>
> Christians don't rely simply on blind faith. Our faith is grounded in historical evidence of a singular event in history—the resurrection of a man named Jesus. Jesus never promised us prosperity in this life. Only that we will come back to life, just like He did.
>
> It's exciting to imagine what Heaven will be like in all its glory—new sights, sounds, even senses beyond our understanding. Our new bodies all gathered around God's throne. Our scars long gone, yet seeing His there—an eternal reminder of the penalty He paid to give us a reward we could

never hope to earn. Today, in this hospital bed, I'm certain of where my hope lies: eternity. And thanks to God, I don't have to look to the future in fear, mistaking that only death awaits.

Thank God he's actually okay! Matt continues to face death so valiantly. He's the personification of Philippians 1:21—"[T]o live is Christ and to die is gain."

Maybe Matt's been right all along? Maybe this temporal life isn't about accumulating blessings but about preparing for eternity with Jesus—whether our time here is long or short? Maybe the only way to find the peace I so desperately crave—no matter which of us lives or dies—is to anchor my hope not in earthly happiness, but in the ecstasy of being with Jesus forever.

I sit with that thought for a moment. Let it swirl.

Then, grief crashes in like a monstrous wave, drowning me in its cold logic.

No. I'm not ready for that kind of surrender. Not strong enough, not mature enough. The moment I do, Jesus will hand me a terminal diagnosis, making good on the prophecy in that dream. He'll take my life—just like He's doing with Matt. Isn't that how God treats His most faithful servants? *Think martyrs.*

Nor is the cryptic "rainbow" message from Lisa's friend enough to convince me that God somehow has something more for me before I join the ranks above. Sure, God gave me rainbows as a promise of marriage years back, but I probably got that wrong too, just like I thought God wanted to heal my neurological agony.

Sigh. How can I trust any supposed promise of marriage now that God has affirmatively told me I'm going to die instead of heal? How am I supposed to juggle all these conflicting prophetic messages?

The only way to deal with all this grief at this point is to shove it down. Deep down. I've begged God night after night to change His will about my death from the dream. And now Matt? *I'm still a believer Lord, but I'm not sure I love You anymore. All this hurts too much, okay?* And if I have an early expiration date, I'm going to make sure I actually *live* first.

Forget surrender. I'm going full *bucket list*.

New goal: seek the bag of basic blessings for as long as Matt and I have left. Artisan chocolates? Strawberry cake? Delectable French pastries I can't pronounce? *Oui, oui!* Migraine-triggering foods of all kinds? I'm ordering. Via DoorDash (greatest invention of all time). If it's delicious and mildly reckless, I'm eating it—for the first time in years. This is my *comeback feast*. So long as my digestion tolerates the new foods, I'm all in, no matter how hard my brain spins on this turbulent airplane ride. *I'm spinning anyway. And I need to gain weight still.*

Three days later, around noontime, Matt's name lights up my phone. *I can't believe he's finally calling.*

"Matt! Please tell me something good."

His voice bursts through the phone, almost breathless, charged.

23

The Philippians 1 Dilemma

"Lara... The obstruction cleared!" Matt says, his deep voice uncharacteristically bright with disbelief.

"Are you serious?!" I reply, letting out a heavy sigh.

"Dead serious. Sorry, wrong choice of words." He giggles. *Oh, I've missed that giggle.*

"The docs were gearin' up for the worst—pain was gettin' worse by the hour, even with morphine. NG tube wasn't helpin'. Then boom, pretty miraculous. This mornin' the scans...the obstruction was gone. No explanation."

A sharp laugh escapes me. "Oh my gosh, Matt. Praise God!"

"Right? My Auntie Ann set up a prayer chain marathon. And now I can eat again. Soon, anyway. They finally took out that awful tube."

"Matt, I'm so happy for you!"

"Oh, and thanks for the whale stuffed animal you sent to the hospital. The Genesis 50:20 verse—I needed that reminder."

I smile, warmth spreading through me. "I remembered how the church was studying Joseph's story the same week you got diagnosed. So that verse felt fitting." I swallow hard. "Matt, I have to force myself to try to believe that verse. That God works all things for good. Even the bad stuff. But...I won't lie to you. Let's just say I've been spiraling spiritually the last few days, and I'm not proud of it. Bipolar emotions."

"Don't be so hard on yourself. Did you read my blog post about Heaven?"

"Yeah, I did. How on earth did you have energy to type it up?"

"Don't know, to be honest. God's just been sustainin' me through the ups and downs. By the way, the cat's out of the bag with my folks. Dad opened the whale package when it arrived and interrogated me on who sent it."

I slap a hand over my mouth, smiling. "Oh no. Am I in trouble?"

"Not yet," he chuckles. "The minute Dad saw the card, he said 'From a girl eh?' Then Mom said, 'This girl must like you, honey.' I told her the jury's still out on that one."

"Well, the jury can deliberate when you visit me next," I tease.

"I'll visit after surgery, first thing."

A few days later, Matt circulates yet another blog titled, *The Philippians 1 Dilemma*:

> During a dangerous time of imprisonment for the Apostle Paul, when it looked like his life could be over soon, he wrote a letter to a church, contemplating the possibilities of surviving or dying—'Christ will be exalted in my body, whether by life or by death. For to me, to live is Christ and to die is gain. If I am to go on living in the body, this will mean fruitful labor for me. Yet what shall I choose? I do not know! I am torn between the two: I desire to depart and be with Christ, which is better by far; but it is more necessary for you that I remain in the body. Convinced of this, I know that I will remain[.]' Philippians 1:20-25.
>
> This is an important passage for our deadly situations too. People are usually terrified of death. Some rich people spend thousands to cryofreeze themselves, hoping to be thawed out in the future after humanity discovers a cure for death. But these bodies aren't immortal.

And Paul here highlights a crucial dynamic for the Christian. On the one hand, we look forward to our reward in Heaven. On the other, we each have important work on earth to finish that God made us for, and no matter how deadly the peril, we want to remain until it's completed. Here, Paul knew that he still had work to do on this earth, so it wasn't his time to go quite yet.

In my case, this aggressive cancer generally doesn't respond to chemo, and people diagnosed at Stage 4 like me typically don't survive past six months. When we caught it nine months ago, it had already spread to three different places in my intestine. In fact, my first instinct when I saw the histology report, before I even met with my oncologist, was that I should probably make a goodbye video.

Then after a few days of that mindset, something changed. I can't explain it; it wasn't some new medical data I came across or new information from my oncologist. I was just filled with a strong conviction that I wouldn't need to be worrying about goodbyes anytime soon. I knew how impossible the odds were of surviving this cancer. It just didn't seem to matter anymore. It's the Philippians 1 principle: it was necessary for me to remain, so remain I shall. The more I found people praying for me all over the world, the stronger my conviction felt.

And then I saw the hand of God sustaining me. Chemo treatment was surprisingly easy. Far from knocking me down, I found myself largely unaffected by side effects. I had my normal amount of energy and minimal nausea. Scans were even showing that the cancer was shrinking in response to the chemo. But now, things have changed. The doctors take this obstruction as a sign that the cancer has grown. Maybe we've lost the progress we made initially. It's unclear, but I'm still here, nine months after diagnosis. Still remaining.

I could get discouraged, or I can say this is a battle worth fighting. As Paul fought to be reunited with those whose lives he had impacted, we also fight to continue our work on earth. There's pain in the fight, but joy in knowing God's work isn't in vain. So let's see what comes of my upcoming surgery, and where God takes us next.

My eyes shift off Matt's email.

This man might be the only person in the world who is more prolific in a hospital bed than out. So he has a conviction that he isn't dying anytime soon? That God might keep him longer on this earth?

Maybe God's miraculous save shows us this is true.

Lord, if this really *is* going to be a slow-burn romance where both of us keep dodging death, I'd love an advance script at this point.

And maybe a fancy costume budget.

24

On the Cheek

Smoke curls into the spring air, carrying the rich scent and sound of trout sizzling on the barbecue. The mountains in the distance stand tall beyond our humble backyard porch, their peaks kissed by the golden evening light.

Matt's hand is wrapped around mine near the grill, where Pops is at work grilling. The sweet breeze is laced with the faint fragrance of jasmine. *I love being in nature. I've missed this so much.*

A well-worn baseball cap shields Matt's eyes from the setting sun, but I can see the glint of something new in them. Three weeks in the hospital, walking the tightrope between life and death, and now, here he is.

Alive, despite the odds.

And the air between us?

Charged.

Very charged.

Different.

There's an undercurrent—like we almost missed *this*. Like everything could have ended before we even figured out what *this* is.

On the Cheek

He's thinner, his body worn, but there's a lightness, like a burden he's carried far too long has lifted. Even with a chemo pump strapped to his side today, his smile is genuine.

"So happy you're back, Matt. Now I can torture you with another 'bag of basic blessings' lecture."

His eyes twinkle as he steps closer to me in his beige khaki shorts and scuffed sneakers. "Careful—I'll bill you for emotional damages."

He wiggles his free fingers toward my waist, barely grazing my yellow lace dress with his feather-light touch. *Is this man actually full on flirting with me? Taking risks today? It feels like he's my... boyfriend? His confidence in God's miracles is oozing off him.*

"And I only accept torture if it's *pro bono*," he adds, smirking.

"Talkative today, eh? How does an engineer know what *pro bono* means?"

"Been watchin' a YouTube lawyer who analyzes famous cases. Fascinatin' stuff. I just might give you a lecture on tort law over trout."

He barely finishes his sentence when the ground beneath me feels like it's about to pull a cruel prank. *Oh no.* Intensely sharper earthquake sensations than the chronic normal (think turbulent airplane about to drop out of nowhere). Sharper spinning (think boat about to tip over in a storm). Here we go again—my body, the drama queen, stealing the moment.

The barbecue suddenly tilts at a hard angle in my vision. "Ow! Matt, hold me. Just had brain zaps. The vertigo level is rising."

Matt's reaction time? Olympic level. If they gave medals for catching dizzy girls, he'd be on the podium. He pulls me into his arms. "I've got you, don't worry."

After two minutes, the barbecue appears normal level again and I've dodged the immediate need to lie down. *When is this virtual reality life going to end? Wait...I don't want it to end, Lord! Just ignore the shaking. Distract.*

Fifteen minutes later, the perfect distraction sits in front of me.

I'm sinking my teeth into a juicy piece of trout in the kitchen, and a zesty burst of lemon and warm spices hits my mouth. "Outstanding, Pops! The lemony taste, the rich flaky texture, wow!"

While I'm writing a Yelp review out loud, Pops beams with pride but Matt sits there, silent, eating almost methodically with the efficiency of a machine.

Pops inquires, "You like it, Matt?"

A curt nod. "Yeah."

With me, Matt is easy, comfortable. With them? A little stiff. Pops joked privately last week, "That kid doesn't talk to me."

"Have you made trout before, Matt? How does this compare?" Pops asks.

Matt replies with stoic confidence. "Comparable to mine."

Good, bad? We don't know. Maybe he views eating as functional? While I'm a walking exclamation point, Matt's a human spreadsheet who communicates in bullet points sometimes.

Mom attempts to break his shell. "Matt, give me a *geelveh*," she says, which means *smile* in Armenian. Matt instantly complies, flashing a wide, almost too-perfect smile. *Introverts. He just doesn't know them yet.*

After dinner, Matt and I go sit down side by side on our usual couch in the living room, alone. His hand rests six inches away from mine.

"Surgery was a mixed bag," he explains. "Too much cancer to remove anythin' significant."

My heart clenches. "I'm so sorry."

"We did get a biopsy for further treatment options though. I'm lookin' into Mayo Clinic, MD Anderson, and Dana-Farber."

"What was the worst part? Other than the pain?"

"No food. Even after surgery, I had to be fed through TPN a few days to get strength back."

"I know what that's like. Remember my jaw debacle?"

"Yeah. I'm chuggin' Ensure Plus to bulk up now."

"We're basically an AARP couple. Between us, we could get a group discount at the geriatrics pharmacy."

We both laugh, then—his hand brushes against mine on accident.

"I like the sound of the word couple," he says, slowly slipping his hand into mine. A tingly sensation goes up my spine. *Are we officially a couple now?*

"At least I don't need my walker at all anymore. Separate from the neurological pain, my muscles have gotten stronger after all that atrophy. You can tell today, right?"

"Yup." His voice turns thoughtful. "God taught us a lot about prayer too. Each time when there was some new obstacle, a prayer group rallied and things changed. But the most miraculous was the obstruction."

"Matt, in your blog you said you have a conviction—maybe from God—that you're not going to die from this?"

He hesitates. "Yeah. I mean. Just have this feelin' I'm not goin' anywhere—anytime soon. Can't explain it." *Must be nice. I'm over here sending back my Heaven RSVP.*

"See? It's like my conviction from the dream, that Jesus is coming to end my suffering through death, not healing on earth. God gives us convictions!"

"But we have to hold our convictions loosely. We put our trust in the cross, not in outcomes."

"But I *love* life, Matt!" (Look, I know I sound whiny. Imagine if God actually gave *you* a divine dream prophesying your upcoming premature death. How would you feel?)

"We all die, Lara. God helps and 'saves us' in countless ways throughout our lives, but He can't save us from the last one—otherwise we'll never get to be in Heaven with Him. Heaven is Home." *Why do all our conversations sound like a sermon and a Rom-com had a baby?*

"Well, what about that verse, 'God has plans to prosper you' in the Book of Jeremiah? It feels like a lie when Christians die young."

"Faith isn't a transactional vending machine," he says, rubbing his thumb against my knuckles. "Christians suffer greatly. Hebrews says some of God's most faithful followers were sawed in two for their faith. And that Jeremiah verse was a specific promise to the nation of Israel. Yes, Jesus has plans for all of us, but that includes in Heaven. Eternal life starts the minute you are saved in Christ and continues right after death in Heaven."

I sigh. "Yeah. But it's still hard to comprehend His goodness sometimes."

"Why don't you just surrender? Let go of your picture of the perfect life and trust Him, whether God's really gonna take you soon or not."

I blink, my throat tight. "Not ready for that. I want to live. I want joy. I want filet mignon and trips to Florence and, a judgeship." *Have you learned nothing?*

"It's not bad to have dreams. But don't invest in a rental. Don't put your identity in it."

My eyes flick to his chemo pump sitting on his chest. "Thanks for all your help, Matt. I mean it. Fasting for me when my jaw was out, pouring out your time to help me grow, thinking about me."

"Lara...I...was thinkin' about you all the time."

His voice, deep and steady, wraps around my heart like a vine. *If this man gets any sweeter, I might have to check my blood sugar.* The stoic Matt, the one who usually guards his emotions behind a wall of stoicism, suddenly so open again, so raw.

I almost lost this man. His wisdom, his courage, his adorable popping out ear... The more I watch him wade through illness in Godly fashion, the more I'm...

"Matt, I...feel so strange around you too."

He gives me a quizzical look. "Uh, thanks?"

"Wait. No, no. I mean. Like I feel different around you. In a good way." *Lara do something. Twirl your curls. Anything.*

Before I know it, I'm diving in.

I plant a loud smack of a kiss on his cheek.

My eyes widen as I pull back, my hands flying to my face. *Oh brother. What's wrong with you? Are you a teenager with raging hormones? This is what happens when you don't really date for fifteen years.*

Matt is startled a second then smiles cheekily (yes, the pun is intended). He forgets to hide his emotions, letting them run wild on his face.

So much for what they taught us in youth group—"Don't chase boys."

Think Ruth and Boaz, ladies. We all know she laid at that dude's feet to get him to propose. Sometimes it's Biblical? Especially with clueless engineers who like you but don't know how to show it. Matt has "I want Lara" written all over that handsome face.

"Um, is it okay that I kissed your cheek?"

He stares at me for a beat, then smiles impossibly wide. "Go right ahead."

I exhale, laughing. "Kiss first, then ask questions. Turns out I'm passionate."

"I noticed," he chuckles, sliding an arm around my shoulder. *I love how his calm demeanor grounds me and absorbs my energetic disposition. And I think my excitable nature is loosening up his rigid, robotic side?*

"Don't think you're in the clear, Matthew. I can play hard to get."

"Looks to me like you're already gotten."

He gazes straight into my eyes, almost like he wants something. He leans in—

Then stops, his expression shifting as a flicker of pain crosses his features.

"Matt? What's wrong?"

He suddenly casually unbuttons the top of his plaid shirt, and I casually forget how to breathe. *Lord, have mercy! One innocent cheek kiss and now he's halfway to a sexy cologne commercial! Am I in a Christian devotional or The Bachelorette?*

"Let me show you somethin'." He points to a small, odd-looking circular port embedded in his bare upper chest. "Where they give me chemo," he whispers. "You can touch it."

I do. I feel the landscape of his skin, entering into his physical world in an intimate way. *He's letting me into his world.* His suffering isn't theoretical anymore; it's beneath my fingertips. There's literally poison coursing through his body. The chemo pump sits in a bag on his lap, connected to the port.

"It stings sometimes," he observes. "Wanted you to see it. There's no perfect life, Lara. I'm not in control of any of this. God is." He winces in pain again.

"Matt, you know you can complain to me, right? I want you to complain. Tell me how much that stings! Just shout it out! Don't worry about letting others down. You don't always have to be so strong."

"Oh, this sting is nothin' compared to that NG tube."

He buttons up his shirt and abruptly changes topics. "Listen, where would you want to go if I ever did take you out in a car?"

"Oh Matt, how would I survive the car ride?"

"I know. Just curious."

"Hmm, the grocery store. Used to love them. The food, the colorful produce. Nothing says 'dream date' like fluorescent lighting and a banana sale."

He taps my knee. "Okay. Well, now that your muscles are stronger, wanna try walkin' one block outside?"

"Sure. Would be nice to see if my muscles can tolerate the gentle incline. Haven't tried."

Matt guides me slowly down our front porch steps. I lace my fingers through his as I breathe in the crisp scent of fresh pine and earth. "Look, everyone's jealous of our romance," I whisper, gesturing to the empty street.

He chuckles. "Yeah, cause all we can do is walk up and down the driveway."

I stop on the last step, wrapping my arms around him as an anchor and savoring the view of the forest green oak trees standing tall before me. A bird calls in the faint distance.

Wow. A suburban block. A wave of emotion ripples through me, and my eyes well up with tears. "Do you know what it feels like to be outside of this house after years stuck inside? I thought walking around our back garden was emotional."

Matt tightens his embrace. "I'm here, Lara. I'm here."

The next month, God injects Matt with superhuman stamina because he finds energy to drive twenty minutes south every few days to visit me.

Does cancer come with secret energy boosts? The guy still holds down his full-time professor gig like he isn't juggling cancer treatments (and a girlfriend?). Even Pastor Calvin apparently raised an eyebrow: "Are you sure you're a cancer patient?"

Every visit, Matt's dry humor—like he doesn't even realize he's funny—lights me up. "All I hear is giggles," Mom mutters after he leaves.

And Pops' jealous reaction at first? "Oh, Matt's coming again?" (If Pops had his way, Matt would still be filling out an application form.)

"Pops listen," I said. "This guy's the *crème de la crème*, a handsome engineering PhD who moonlights as a missionary and likes politics, music, and theology just like me. Get with the program."

We haven't had the official "relationship" talk yet, but Matt's M.O.—*Let's keep walkin' together and trust God*. Cool, collected, trusting. Meanwhile, I'm in full-on "shove God's will down" mode.

I'm so tired of thinking about life or death at this point—for either of us. I don't want deep thoughts.

I want Matt's company.

I want life.

I want the bag of basic blessings.

Right before visits, I DoorDash a delectably fancy dinner or dessert for us, and morph into someone else. Sitting up or lying down, the world is still shaking and turning severely—nonstop. Regardless, I sit up, yell at my brain to calm down like it listens, use my "waddling" technique as a coping mechanism to balance myself against the waves, and sift through my closet like it's prom night (as if Matt of all people cares about outfits). Humming '90s pop love songs and summoning endorphins the whole way. *Finally. A good signal from my brain.*

At some point, Pops finally finds the sweet spot with Matt—Bible trivia. Matt is sharply introverted, but if you ask him anything about Christianity or science, he lights up like Times Square on New Year's and talks at a mile a minute. "Pop in a coin and he instantly fires up, like a rocket ship encyclopedia," Pops joked yesterday.

Matt's more comfortable now too. Last week, he sat in his unassuming posture—wearing his "Duct Tape Can't Solve Stupid But Can Muffle the Sound" sweatshirt—and cracked lawyer jokes to Pops.

"For someone who hates lawyers, you sure hang out with one a lot," I sneered.

"Can't lick 'em, join 'em," he replied.

Mom and Pops seem cautiously supportive of us "dating"—if you can call it that given that we haven't left the house—but they are giving off more "Lara needs joy" vibes rather than "this is a wise decision" vibes.

Matt and I haven't discussed physical boundaries since my "sneak cheek attack" either. We're Christians, so nothing remotely sexy is happening until "I do," folks. But let me tell you—I am aching for that first K-I-S-S. I refuse to initiate it, though. (Remember ladies, the Ruth technique only goes so far. "Hard to get" always wins in the end.) Who cares that Mom and Pops are literally in the next room? That's what doors are for. Isn't that how the Victorians flirted? With parents in tow?

Each "visit," when Matt holds my hand on Mr. Couch, I wait.

And wait.

And wait.

Matt sits there, arm around me, flashing that boyish grin, dropping the occasional kiss on my cheek.

Is this some form of righteous torture? Couldn't this man be just a *little* less Godly? Or shy? A tiny bit less patient? Why doesn't the Bible have a *When to Kiss Your Girlfriend* manual?

If Matthew John holds back much longer, I'm slapping a cheek tax on him.

25

The 19 Day Ban

"I don't think we should see each other anymore."

My words land like shards of glass.

I stare at Matt, who sits across from me, frozen—half quizzical, half deer caught in headlights. It's his classic "I'm confused" face. Half "computer processing," half "puppy left in the rain."

We've been dating for one month, and when he arrived five minutes ago, chemo pump strapped to his chest, I asked him to sit at the dining room table across from me. Not Mr. Couch this time.

"What do you mean?" His eyes narrow. "I'm confused."

My stomach twists. "I just...I..."

Silence.

"It's okay," he says, clenching his jaw. "You can be honest. I can handle it." His eyebrows furrow and his eyes plead—*I almost died last month. Don't take this joy away now.*

I inhale sharply. "This isn't about you, Matt. It's just... This is foolish. One of us is going to die, and the other will be left shattered. Why not stop now before our hearts break? It's irresponsible." My chest aches, hollow and raw. *I feel naked without his hand in mine.*

I have no idea what I'm doing. I've got the man of my dreams sitting across from me and I'm calling it off. But lately, I've started feeling the weight of the "dating."

Maybe it's because we're kissing on the cheek now.

Maybe it's some guilt for leading Matt on given my belief that I'm going to be checking in at Heaven's gate any moment, while he thinks he's getting a wife, given his conviction that he's not going anywhere. *I can't hurt him.*

Maybe it's that I don't trust God to let me keep something good permanently.

Maybe all of the above.

He exhales and his shoulders slump, relief flickering across his face. "So it's not about *us*."

"Right. It's not about *us*. It's…God's going to break my heart like the last four years. Why should I believe He'd let me keep you? It feels like He just wants me to suffer."

He hesitates. "Lara, I understand your concerns. I know we've been avoiding the hard questions. That's my fault. I should've brought this up earlier. I've got my own fears."

"You do?"

"I've always feared I'd end up like my grandpa, leaving my wife a young widow."

"Oh…I understand." *Perhaps his grandfather's untimely death is why he has that drive to never let others down?*

"Yes, we want to honor God as we get serious about a future together."

I furrow my brows. "Why would God want us to date, let alone marry? How are we supposed to build a life when we can barely take care of ourselves?"

"I don't claim to know the future or His purposes. But I do know God led us to each other in our pain."

Tears sting in my eyes. "We're not normal, Matt. We don't get to take these kinds of risks."

"But following Christ includes risks. Sometimes reckless risks that come from reckless trust."

I huff out a bitter laugh. "Well, why would you want to marry someone who claims she's going to die early when she's not terminally ill?" *I hate this insight. Lord, I wish You never gave me that dream.*

My emotional journey since the dream has been a severe storm—one moment, I'm clinging to faith consuming my Bible, allowing Matt's suffering and example of faith to soften me; the next, I'm spiraling through disillusionment at God's betrayal of what I thought was His original promise to heal me. Some days, I want to let my faith grow so strong that I can fully surrender—*even unto death*. Other days, anger overwhelms. Such is grief. A strong tide pulling me in two directions at once.

I blink back tears, refusing to let them fall, but my voice breaks. "And if Jesus does take me out of the game young, I'm worthless. A wasted life."

He cocks his eyebrows. "Oh, okay. I see your logic. So I'm worthless too then? Because I'm dying too?" *Why is he always right? I guess he doesn't use that Southern affect in serious conversations...*

"Forget the dream," I reply. "I still have no real diagnosis. I'm even attempting another drug again out of desperation, because sitting up and walking is agony. Hasn't helped. And I'm trying despite the fact that God told me to come to acceptance of healing in eternity." *Ouch. Brain zap.* I grip the table as the turbulence in my brain takes a sudden drop.

Matt nods compassionately as I press on. "So why would you love someone who's chronically ill? Wouldn't you have liked me better if I were still practicing law? I'm still bedridden seventy percent of the day, forcing myself to sit upright for longer periods of time every few hours, before I collapse again from the pain. Nothing's changing."

Matt narrows his eyes. "Are you really asking why I would

love someone with an illness when I'm actively hooked up to a chemo pump? Lara, love and marriage are about reflecting God's glory, not about health, certainty, or qualifications. It's about walking through whatever comes, together, with God at the center. What if you marry someone and they get a chronic or terminal illness four months later? Have you considered that?" *How can he be so mature for someone who's never even had a girlfriend?*

I pull on my hair. "Well…umm…oh, Matt."

"Life doesn't fit some stereotypical mold, right? This chemo pump reminds me every day."

His words hang in the air.

After a few moments, I exhale sharply. "Okay. Maybe we should just take a break. Pray about it. Just to make sure this is God's will."

"Of course. How long?"

"Nineteen days," I blurt.

He blinks twice. "Nineteen?" ("Matt classic confused face" activated again. ERROR 404: Understanding not found.)

I bite my lip. *Nineteen days? Where do you even come up with this stuff?* Move over, "ghosting," I just coined the dumbest term in dating history: the "nineteen-day ban."

Matt nods, standing abruptly. "Okay. Lara, listen. I respect your decision. And I'll be praying too. I have been." He slings his backpack over his shoulder and heads for the door. Sometimes this more rigid side of his personality takes over. When he's joking around with me, he's totally relaxed and free. But today, his computer-brain has been told we're on a break. *Translation:* he thinks he has no business staying longer.

He pauses at the door a moment, and turns back, hesitating. "Call me when you're ready… Or…"

Doubt creeps on his face as he stares at me across the room. I swallow hard. *Does he think I'm lying? That I'm ending things because of our lack of chemistry or something?* "But please.

Seek counsel from Christian friends. Don't just stay in your own thoughts, okay?"

"I will. Thanks for understanding Matt."

He steps out, closing the door behind him with a finality that makes me flinch.

The silence that follows is deafening, marking the start of a "nineteen-day ban."

My mind shakes as hard as the dining room table before me. Tears finally spill over now, hard.

Why did I cut it off? But how can I proceed if my heart doesn't feel settled? Lord, what is Your will in such a strange situation?

A few days later, I'm on the phone with Pastor Calvin. He doesn't do sugarcoating—he's an Armenian straight shooter in his sixties with brown eyes, a bald head, and stylish glasses. As I'm spilling my guts and worries, he asks in serious fashion, "Is this real, Biblical love or do you think you're just infatuated with Matt?"

I roll my eyes. "*Of course* I'm infatuated with him, Pastor Calvin! He's a five-foot-ten Godly, Armenian engineering genius with Biblical biceps and the kind of smile that belongs in a museum. Wouldn't you be?"

"I just want what's best for both of you," he replies, chuckling. "Who knows? Maybe this is God's will. Let's keep praying."

Oh, I'm praying all right. Still screaming at the ceiling like it's customer service and I'm on hold—"When and why am I dying? Why hasn't the dream come true yet? It's been three months—not that I want to die. Why is Matt dying? Is he even dying? Am I allowed to date this wonderful man? I wish I could believe You have a purpose for all our suffering like Matt says."

Days dissolve into one another, and soon, it's day nine of the "nineteen-day ban."

I'm on my "sitting up hour"—propped in an armchair like a wilted houseplant—listening to the rain pound against our roof, creating a steady drum roll echoing through the house.

Then—

Knock. Knock. Knock.

I shuffle to the front door, gripping walls at points to steady myself against the room's turbulence. *Is it Amazon?*

I peek through the peephole.

Oh my gosh.

26

Lion Number Two Needs A Haircut

I open the door—and there he is.

Matt.

He stands inches away from me on the front porch, a silhouette against the downpour, wearing dark navy jeans, that familiar black jacket, and his celebrated hat.

No warning. No umbrella. Just him—soaked but steady, backpack slung over one shoulder, eyes locked onto mine like he's seeing past everything I've ever tried to hide.

My heart immediately starts hammering. *I can't believe he's here.*

"Matt?"

He doesn't move.

Doesn't speak.

Just stands there like a stubborn statue.

"Do you—"

He cuts me off. "I know it hasn't been nineteen days."

Silence.

The rain cascades off his hat in sheets. Seconds later, he adds,

"But I want to raise somethin' else as we pray about this." His lips press into a firm line. "Can I come in?"

"Oh, Matt. Of course. Come in." *My heart is going to explode.*

He strolls in, dripping water onto the hardwood floor, bypassing the cozy familiarity of Mr. Couch and heading straight to the dining table. *Ouch. This is what you wanted, Lara.*

I follow, sinking into a chair across from him. It's only been nine days, but our separation feels like years. *It feels so right that he is here. Lord, is this right?*

He leans forward contemplatively, elbows on the table. "Lara, we've been walking through suffering together for so long. Remember the calls? Our connection. It's a natural outgrowth of where God's been leading us."

I want to speak, but all I can do is hold his gaze.

"You're a brilliant woman with imagination. And your strength in the face of everything you've gone through…is beautiful." *How does he respect my strength when I'm sinking emotionally?* I exhale, blinking rapidly.

"But Lara. You can't live your life on what-ifs and worries. I know I've got cancer, and you've got your own convictions. But God calls us to live for today. To not worry about tomorrow. I came across this verse the other day." He pulls out his battered Bible from his backpack, the pages frayed and worn with years of love.

A *battered* Bible. How can I argue with that kind of spiritual flex?

He flips to a passage and reads, "we must 'mak[e] the most of every opportunity, because the days are evil.'" His eyes lift. "Ephesians 5:16. One of my favorites."

For the first time ever, I don't have words. My pulse pounds in my ears.

"Look," he adds, "I don't want to put my heart in a box and leave it there. I don't think you do either. I'm willing to get hurt. I'm no stranger to risks."

The air between us is electric. *This man.* A C.S. Lewis meets... Indiana Jones? So much for his nonchalant "let's just trust God" nature. Today, he's teaching me that trust in Jesus is multifaceted, and involves not just surrender but also taking active risks, knowing God is sovereign and will guide our steps. Matt somehow balances both effortlessly.

"What I'm trying to say is... Don't make a decision based on your fears. God's perfect love casts out fear." I reach for his hand but stop short.

"Thanks so much, Matt."

"I'm not here to pressure you. I'll respect whatever decision you make. But I wanted to make my case."

I muster a smile. "I thought you hated lawyers?"

That familiar, warm smile creeps onto his face. "I do... Except this one."

A warmth spreads through me, melting the knot of anxiety in my chest. *He still has that adorable sense of humor. Even now.*

Then, as suddenly as he arrived, he stands, heading for the door.

"That's all I wanted to say. I just...needed you to hear it. In person...you know? Take all the time you need."

After Matt's visit, I feel weighed down and untethered at the same time. I seek wisdom, lying in my bedroom every day, watching Matt's entire YouTube sermon and devotional collection, taking in every eye movement, every gesture, every smile. All of his Godly wisdom. *I never said I couldn't watch him on the internet.*

Matt is exceptionally talented in Bible teaching. He has that rare ability to explain complex things in simple terms. His sermons are packed with wisdom, yet they bear a casual tone like you're having a cup of coffee with him, without a trace of moral superiority. *He would make a great expert witness in court. Lara, you want to date him, not direct examine him in court.*

Next up on my video cue—Matt cracking jokes about Daniel's experience in the lion's den in the Old Testament:

> I'm assumin' things were super awkward between Daniel and King Darius after the lion's den incident. Imagine Daniel goes back on the job after, Darius calls him in for a meeting, and they discuss lion cage maintenance. Daniel probably said, 'You know, when I was down there in the den, I saw quite a bit of rust on that lion cage door; probably should send someone in to repair it. And I think lion number two needs a haircut; his hair's gettin' kinda long.'

Oh, that situational humor slays me. Lord, this whole situation is so bizarre. Should I date this man even though I'm convinced I have a personal expiration date? On the one hand, Matt knows my conviction. Full disclosure. But what if he dies on me? What use is love with no future?

Are You setting me up for another heartbreak, just like my career and my chronic illness?

Are we just two ticking time bombs, foolishly in love?

27

Joy In Grief

On day thirteen of the "nineteen-day ban," I crack open my daily Christian devotional for my usual morning meditation, and it hits me with a message I wasn't quite expecting—"God gives us gifts and joy in our suffering and grief." *Hmm. Is Jesus trying to tell me something? This resonates for some reason.*

Hours later, a surprise package arrives from Sevan in the mail. The card inside reads, "Every good and perfect gift is from above. James 1:17. I hope these gifts bring you some joy in your pain, Lars." *Gifts and joy in pain? Either this is a coincidence, or the Holy Spirit microchipped Sevan and my devotional app. Thank you, Lord. You're still acknowledging my grief and pain in an intimate way.*

The next few days, I seek advice on the "Matt issue" from countless Christian friends via phone—trying to tolerate all the electrical phone waves in short bursts. To my surprise, almost every other mentor or friend drops the word "joy" or "gift" in connection with dating Matt. Unprompted.

"Take this gift of joy," they emphasize. "Move forward prayerfully, but it seems Matt is a gift from God in your pain." Auntie

Nanor—Golden Girl No. 2 and my personal "Godly Wisdom Central"—put it this way: "Perhaps God wants you to enjoy this gift, this joy in your valley? We had heard about those phone calls between you two!"

Okay, Lord. It feels like You're actually giving me the green light to move forward with this man. If this is right, please show me—unmistakably.

Sure enough, day seventeen arrives, and my phone buzzes. Text from Lisa: "Lara, I think I should share my Christian devotional with you today." I read it, and the lesson explains that God understands grief over death, which is why He gives His people gifts and joy in their grief to sustain them. *Gifts. Joy. Grief. Same words again.*

The lesson states, "Christians are called to have joy and grief together." *Joy and grief together? What an oxymoron. Hmm. Maybe it's kind of like singing in the fire, like Matt said a few months back.*

The devotional then recounts the real-life story of a Christian couple—both of whom had suffered greatly in life—who got married, only for the wife to be diagnosed with terminal cancer two months after. The message? God called them to embrace God's "gift of love" despite their grief. To find "joy in one another even in the sorrow, knowing there is purpose to their suffering."

I stare at the screen. I blink hard. I can't believe what I'm reading.

Gifts. Joy. Love. Cancer. Grief.

Oh my gosh. This is it. Lord, You just answered me!

So God actually *does* orchestrate romances like this! This kind of joy in grief? But why would God give that couple marriage even though He knew the woman would die shortly after? I guess God's telling me He *can* have a purpose for this kind of love story. Even though it's not the stereotypical "perfect life" ideal. Even a forty-year marriage is just a drop in the ocean of eternity, isn't it?

I feel this burden lift almost immediately. Can't explain it. Something just shifts.

My conscience *knows* the Holy Spirit just gave me the green light to date Matt. I don't know if this will lead to marriage or not, but I feel this strange combination of extreme joy and peace moving forward. *Thank you, Lord!*

But wait—does this message from God also mean that either Matt or I will die prematurely, like the woman in the devotional?

Otherwise, why would God answer in this specific way? He gives outcome-specific messages and parallels sometimes, like His Jericho promise to open my jaw on the bed... *Oh no...*

Am I willing to take the risk and trust God's ultimate plan?

I exhale hard and collect myself.

Okay. Let the record reflect I'm choosing to trust God.

But I'm reserving the right to appeal.

28

From Test to Testimony

A group of ten people sing in a circle, belting at the top of their lungs in our family room, singing *Because He Lives*. It's an old gospel favorite, one that declares the bedrock of our faith: that because Jesus rose from the grave, there's no reason to fear what comes next. Not tomorrow. Not suffering. Not even death. It's the kind of song that wraps around you like a warm blanket in the cold—simple words carrying eternal weight.

Harmonies rise and fall like a choir. At the rate this is going, Pops might accidentally host the first ever "evangelical" Broadway revival in his house.

So, I've never met missionaries before.

But these singing missionaries are next level.

The moment this pack of smiling thirty to forty-year-olds stepped into our house, they brought their own weather system—a warmth, a light. Maybe "sunny with a chance of unsolicited prayers." They have this tangible energy I can't quite describe in words—this deep, inner joy. *Peace.*

It's been a week since our "nineteen-day" ban officially lifted. I looked Matt in the eyes and said, "Time to reopen this case. New evidence suggests God wants us swooning." I also told him

I couldn't wait to flirt again—respectfully, of course. Think Song of Songs meets Sunday brunch.

My rationale: the Holy Spirit gave me the green light, and the reward is greater than the risk here. If this life really is a blip in light of eternity, and if I'm going to make a serious attempt to live for eternity instead of the "bag of basic blessings" on this earth, I have to trust God and risk being vulnerable to emotional pain.

Today, Matt is introducing me to his friends visiting from out of town. They're the folks Matt travels to Haiti with for missions work—the VIPs of his world. (Don't worry, I'm on my best behavior. Let's just say it's a performance so holy, even nuns are taking notes.)

As we sing, I waddle back and forth to keep up with the ocean waves and earthquakes, trying to keep it "subtle." *Lord, help me. So embarrassing.* My striving against the ocean waves has gotten somewhat better from a *balance* standpoint, but the neurological sensations themselves have not changed at all since getting off that master bed. A bout of severe nausea instantly hits me. *Just pretend you're on an airplane.*

We all sing the last line again, proclaiming that our Savior lives.

As everyone settles into their chairs, Winston Bui—the Vietnamese group leader in his fifties—leans forward. "We sing this in Haiti on every trip, in Creole." His brown eyes burn with a passion that commands attention as he tells me about his team's Haiti ministry helping destitute Haitians, and how Matt preaches as a lay pastor there. *Maybe these missionaries take risks going to dangerous places like Haiti because they truly find their security in Christ, not in the blessings of this world.*

Winston turns to me. "The Haitians always line up asking for copies of Matt's sermons. No one ever asks me! Good thing I'm humble." Laughter ripples across the room. Winston's charisma could probably sell me a used car I don't need and convince me it's part of God's plan.

"And we always host 'Ask Matt' sessions where people can

ask their deepest theological questions." I smile inside. I can tell Winston is acting like a wing man, thinking, *Matthew finally has a girlfriend. Big stakes.*

Matt chuckles, a little embarrassed, sitting in his khaki shorts and sneakers, sporting yet another **Camp Arev** shirt—his fifth in rotation recently. I'm convinced he's secretly their paid mascot.

"Been to Haiti eleven times," Matt says. "Not even my forte. My body hates the heat, the travel. But God uses me there, in my weakness."

Elisha, a girl in the corner wearing vibrant purple artisan earrings, speaks up.

"Lara, a cute Matt story. We were playing cards once. I was so close to winning, just missing one card. Round after round, Matt kept stacking up cards. When I finally won, we all looked at his hand—he could've won ages ago. But he let me have it."

I glance at Matt, who's glowing now, so alive in their presence. It seems God is using these friends as a gift to lift Matt up in his suffering. It's working.

They listen compassionately as I share my story, my struggles, my convictions as well. Elisha nods. "You know, Matt kept urging us to pray for years for a girl named Lara. When I heard you two were dating last week, I thought, *Ohhh...*" She winks at me.

Team member Brian shifts topics. "Matt, what are the worst of your symptoms?"

"Abdominal pain, burnin' around my ostomy site." His ostomy bag now holds his bowel output since the surgery, when they pulled his intestine slightly out of his body so that it can serve this function. His skin is somewhat discolored today—a typical chemo thing.

"The first chemo made me so sensitive to cold, I couldn't even touch the fridge. There's some neuropathy in my feet, like I'm walkin' on coals sometimes. But honestly, pretty negligible side effects compared to my first cancer. I've still been enjoyin' gardenin' in my backyard, and even drove myself six hours to **Camp Arev** right after chemo one round. Probably not the smartest move, but I've done stupider things." He giggles. "Had an awesome time with the kids."

"You're a light, Matt," team member Tim remarks.

Matt grins. "I finally got my gastric tube out, so now I have one less tube stickin' out of me. They just yanked it out and slapped gauze on the hole to stop my stomach from leakin' out all over the place. Now I'm waitin' for my stomach to close up on its own." Matt's tone is "scientific casual," almost like reading off a grocery list. *Does Matt ever really complain?*

Winston says, "Any hope with treatments, buddy?" *He keeps calling Matt "buddy." Kind of cute.*

Matt shrugs. "The genetic testing wasn't great. Nothing promisin' for immunotherapy. There's a KRAS mutation, but it mostly tells us what won't work. My oncologist just sent my records to the Institute of Cancer Research in Maryland. All the other trials have said no already—all focused on large intestinal cancer, so I'm disqualified. I'm also worried about getting another obstruction again."

Winston sighs. "Listen buddy, we believe in miracles and we know God is sovereign. But you've got to turn your test into a testimony, no matter what." *Test to testimony. Hmm.*

Matt's been saying all along that God uses our suffering as a testimony of His sustaining grace and love amidst our trials. One of the hardest parts of my illness has been this inescapable conclusion that I have no *purpose* anymore. Maybe *suffering itself* is a work with great purpose that God calls us to?

Matt smiles. "You love that line—test to testimony. God must have some purpose for this cancer. I'm willin' to trust."

"Glory!" Winston exclaims, and the group erupts into cheers and laughter.

Team members Mitch and David smile at me. Mitch says,

"That's what Winston says *every time* he wants to proclaim God's goodness: Glory!"

The Haiti team's joy lingers long after they leave. The following week, still stirred by their faith, I feel an inner prompting to study 1 Peter.

There, the Apostle Peter encouraged early church believers, who were experiencing great persecution for their faith, to remain steadfast. In 1 Peter 1:6-7, he writes, "In all this you greatly rejoice, though now for a little while you may have had to suffer grief in all kinds of trials. These have come so that the proven genuineness of your faith—of greater worth than gold, which perishes even though refined by fire—may result in praise, glory, and honor when Jesus Christ is revealed." *Genuine faith is of greater worth than gold. Hmm.*

Then, my friend Steven randomly texts me his Christian devotional, which says: "Costly sacrifices and suffering for the sake of the gospel are required today, even in countries without religious persecution. Jesus allows other kinds of severe persecution in His people's lives, sometimes in the form of sickness and bereavement, to test their faith, refine their character to His, and give them the unique privilege of taking a clear gospel-proclaiming Christian stand in life despite their losses."

Steven also himself writes, "Try reading 1 Peter, Lara. It might comfort you as one reason you're suffering. The early church believed it was an honor to share in Christ's suffering. By proving their faith was genuine even amidst suffering, they had the privilege of testifying to the world that God's love is great and real, which authenticated the gospel." *Woah. Steven has no clue I'm already studying 1 Peter right now. You must be emphasizing this to me, Lord. Didn't Winston say "test to testimony"?*

Maybe one good purpose God has for my suffering (even if it's not religious persecution *per se*) is that I'm testifying, to myself and my community, the genuineness of my faith, God's sustaining grace and power, and Jesus' all-surpassing worth—all because I'm remaining a Christian in this fire. Matt always says, "We follow a suffering Savior. We're called to suffer alongside Him sometimes as a witness to the world of His own crucifixion and love."

Wow. It sounds like suffering really is a work with *purpose* that Christ calls us to? *Oh Lord, help me take this to heart!* Is this why 2 Corinthians 6:10 states Christians must be "sorrowful, yet always rejoicing"? Because our pain has purpose?

The Apostle Paul wrote his chains "served to advance the gospel." Philippians 1:12. And in Acts 5:41, the Apostles "rejoic[ed]" in being flogged "because they had been counted worthy of suffering disgrace" for Christ. They were not masochists, rejoicing in the pain itself. They rejoiced because their suffering was directly linked to the proclamation of Jesus.

Hmm. I've never seriously considered suffering in this light before. Finally! God just gave me one tangible reason for suffering that is actually clicking at a heart level rather than intellectual mumbo jumbo. Thank you, Lord!

But would it be possible for me to actually get to a humble place where I can "rejoice" in the midst of all this grief?

What I really want is kisses in grief...

29

Victorian Fantasies

"Kitten?" I ask.

A dainty box of freshly baked red velvet cupcakes sits on the kitchen counter, with the word "*Kitten*" piped across each one in delicate pink frosted swirls. The sweet aroma of cocoa, vanilla, and creamy buttercream wafts through the air.

Matt leans against the fridge, arms crossed, smiling like he just pulled off the heist of the century.

"You bought me Kitten cupcakes?!"

"I'm gonna call you Kitten from now on. Does my girl like it?"

"Kitten," I repeat, tasting the word. "I love it! I have fluffy hair, like a kitten's."

He smiles wide, running a hand over his bald head. "Got more than I do. Kittens are harbingers of death and destruction you know, and I'm allergic to 'em."

"Oh!" I gasp, poking him in the ribs. "So, I'm ferocious and you're allergic to me. That's what you're saying?!"

"Not exactly...but close." He giggles, grabs a cupcake, and takes a giant bite, smearing frosting on the corners of his mouth.

"I even have a little scar on my lip from when a cat scratched me when I was two."

I arch an eyebrow. "Well, I've been researching nicknames for you too. My favorites so far are Gumdrop, Creampuff, and Trouble. For maximum embarrassment."

"I know...I'm always in trouble."

"Hmm...Trouble," I reply, sizing the name on him. "Trouble it is!"

We walk to the living room and plop onto Mr. Couch, where Matt tenderly presses a soft kiss to my forehead. "Trouble it is," he says.

This sunny May afternoon (at the end of our fifth month dating), Kitten and Trouble have the house all to themselves.

Mom: vacationing in Hawaii with Sevan.

Pops: tackling his famous three-mile walk at the park.

Trouble: still hasn't kissed Kitten on the lips.

If he waits any longer, I might have to stage a power outage to see if my man gets braver in the dark. I even spritzed on a non-chemical perfume from Mom's stash earlier. Will it work? If this doesn't work today—paired with my orange floral-print lace dress—I just might have to purchase "Kiss Me Now, You Fool" by Dior.

Matt turns to me, lacing his fingers through mine. "You smell different."

"Like 'good' different or 'wash it off now' different?"

"Good."

Matt's visiting me today after a youth group graduation event, where he handed the kids individual gifts to show his support. Mark Twain once observed, "The most interesting information comes from children, for they tell all they know and then stop." Matt loves kids—and identifies with them—precisely for that reason. He has zero patience for the pretensions of adult society. Unlike yours truly, who loves a good societal function to dress up for and parade in.

"Babe, feel like being adventurous today?" I ask, testing the waters.

He gives me a look like he knows whatever it is, it will be a bad idea.

"Sing with me."

He hesitates a second, then replies, "I don't mind singing. Really liked middle school choir."

"Full of surprises, are we?"

Long story short, we casually duet three Disney karaoke songs on YouTube. If casual means several key changes that sound more like key witnesses refusing to cooperate in court. Turns out Trouble has pipes though! *I'll have him singing real show tunes stat.*

After our impromptu "concert," Matt shares how he conducts his finances, telling me he donates monthly to missionaries around the world. (I'm currently investing in DoorDash deliveries—we all have our callings.)

After a while, I crave a shift—something lighter, something mine. "Matt, you make me feel like spring."

"Yeah, it's spring outside." He tilts his head, giving his signature quizzical look when someone around him just said something illogical.

I roll my eyes and poke his chest. "No. *You* make me feel like spring." My fingers find his biceps. "And I love your muscles."

He laughs. "I've lost seventy percent of my muscle mass thanks to chemo. Kitten, why do we have to date amidst cancer? I wish this was all over."

I poke his chest again. "That's why your name is Trouble." I peer directly at his lips. *Let's cut to the good stuff.* He tickles my waist with a feather light touch, and I squirm, laughing, "All this oxytocin is going to heal your cancer but kill me."

"Not so sure that's how biochemistry works, sweetheart," he deadpans.

"Don't ruin my fun with your facts, Trouble."

Recently I've discovered a fun way to flirt with him—just say something illogical and it gets his juices going.

But after a brief moment, Matt grabs my hand, eyes serious all of a sudden. "Lord, please let us live long enough to enjoy this."

And just like that, when I see the intensity in his eyes, my heart explodes and words start escaping my mouth.

"Matt, I…"

"Yeah?"

My heart starts pounding.

"I'm…"

His gaze sharpens. "Yeah?"

"I'm in…"

"What is it, Lara?"

"I'm in love with you."

He raises his eyebrows and sits there a few seconds, stunned. Then he exhales a slow laugh, shaking his head. "Do you know how long I've waited to hear that? I'm madly in love with you too."

Madly? This man keeps checking off my Jane Austen fantasies. I don't know if he was waiting for me to say it first out of respect or what, but either way, I can tell a sudden wave of confidence just rolled over him.

He leans in to hold me closer. "We never dated, did we Lara? We just fell in love."

I gasp, letting out a breathy laugh. "How does an engineer have such a way with words?"

He winks at me. "I'm Trouble."

Matt, in his own right, has found this unexpected knack for handling me with a romantic touch that always catches me off guard. Zingers you would never expect from an engineering genius. I'm learning to blossom that instinct, but it comes out more naturally than I expect every time. *He makes me swoon.*

He cups my face now, his thumb tracing my jaw.

"Matt, what does this mean for us?" I ask, my heart fluttering all sorts of sensations.

"We start talkin' marriage, Kitten. You never know where God will lead us. I knew this was where we were headin'."

My heart thunders. "Oh Matt!" I stand up and disappear into my bedroom. *Good. Pops isn't home yet.* When I return, I hand him a rolled-up, light brown parchment with frayed, soft edges, its surface adorned with faint floral embossing, reminiscent of paper from the Victorian era. A deep burgundy ribbon secures it, lending an elegant touch.

"I wrote this last week. Open it."

Matt unties the ribbon, amused. "You wrote this in cursive with a quill, didn't you?"

"You know your girl's an Anglophile. It's a Victorian style love letter. Will you read it aloud?"

"You know you're doin' somethin' right if your girl writes you a love letter."

He reads, slowly:

> *Matthew, you must see the strict possession you now hold over my heart which leaves no space unoccupied. Thy name is sweet music to my soul. You are an excellent creature, whose mature and powerful presence absorbs my flighty and desirous heart. With one quick word you satisfy me.*

His voice softens, growing more tender with each word.

This is my dream.

My "perfect Armenian life."

I've found my unicorn, a quirky and musical Christian Armenian nerd, just like me. My own Darcy, reading my deepest emotions. This feeling is a thousand times better than sitting in front of a warm heater on a rainy day eating chocolates.

He continues:

'[Your] eyes are like doves by the water streams, washed in milk, mounted like jewels.' Song of Songs 5:12. Your compassion knows no end, and your heart of boundless love casts shades of rest over my weary desert land. '[You are] radiant and ruddy, outstanding among ten thousand.' Song of Songs 5:10.

Halfway through, he stops reading and peers at the ceiling. A tear slips down his cheek. *Oh my gosh, I didn't expect that much of a reaction. Yes!*

"Oh, Lara. This is...beautiful."

"I've always wanted to include quotes from Song of Songs in a love letter, and I genuinely meant every word!"

What a day for escape.

For imagination.

For love.

No talk of cancer.

No talk of spinning.

No chemo pump on his chest this week.

No death.

Just...joy.

When he's done reading, I can't resist and drop an exaggerated pose. "Trouble, Trouble, why art thou a Troublemaker? Why can't you be some other name?"

Matt stares at me like I've lost it. I gush on. "Denounce thy father and refuse thy name, or if thou wilt not, be but sworn my love—"

He smirks, pulling me into his arms. "You're ridiculous."

"And you love it, Romeo."

He leans in—a fraction. Three inches from my lips.

My breath catches.

And then it sounds.

Pops' key jingles in the front door lock—two feet away from

us. *Perfect timing. Lord, I prayed for a kiss, not "deliver us from temptation via Pops."*

Pops waves then slips into the kitchen, closing the door behind him.

Matt jests, "Isn't this the part where you take some Shakespearean potion thingy? Well, if our love story's gonna involve feudin', it might as well involve some shootin' too." I furrow my eyebrows, confused.

"I grew up watchin' *Andy Griffith*," Matt explains, "and one time, he said somethin' like that in this *Romeo and Juliet* bit he did." *Oh, so that's where he gets that Southern affect thing! My boyfriend has been moonlighting as an old-time Southern sheriff.*

"Are you advocating violence, Romeo?"

"You're the one always hittin' me on the arm."

"It's called flirting. Okay, that's it. Your insane levels of cuteness appear to be toxic to my overall health. I'm about to prosecute."

"Will the verdict involve wedding invitations or are you breakin' up with me?"

"No, but if *you* dump me, I'll hurt you."

"You're a lawyer; you know murder is a crime, right?" He arches an eyebrow.

"Shakespeare did say the 'course of true love never did run smooth.' Maybe I'll kidnap you into Kitten Territory and deal with your crimes there."

"Crimes?" He scratches his head. "By the way, I did watch an *Andy Griffith* show once where the male lead told his girlfriend he saw her in eggs or somethin'."

"Are you saying you see me in eggs?! I give you a Victorian masterpiece and you tell me you see me in eggs?"

He giggles, and I stare deep into his eyes.

I wait.

My eyes dart to his lips.

Nothing.

Not even a twitch.

Come on, Matt. Love letter from girl in gorgeous orange dress *equals* kiss the girl with dramatic bravado. Even in your analytical, data-driven brain, surely you know this?

Nope.

He's literally clueless.

Apparently, he's got other plans. "So, uh, Kitten, there's this Facebook setting…people click it to announce they're a couple." He shifts his feet and bashfully smiles. *Why so shy? I literally just proclaimed my love for crying out loud. How is he so bold and shy on and off? He's such a paradox.*

"If you're asking if you can add me as your girlfriend, the motion is granted."

Matt and I are polar opposites in many respects. I'm an actress chasing the grandiose, while Matt's grounded, pragmatic, data driven. But his non-earthly eternal worldview makes it feel like he's almost living on his own planet, even for a Christian. That's the part of him that gets me and makes this click perfectly—it allows him to step into my fantasy worlds. (And, he also loves his own fantastical *Dungeons & Dragons* expeditions on his weekly online game nights with his nerd crew.)

Turns out, God moonlights as a stand-up comedian—only He would think to pair an energetic, emotional, over the top artist with a reserved, stoic genius.

Recently, though, our differences have led to some miscommunication problems (hilarious now, not so hilarious then). Sometimes his logical, no-nonsense way to view the world paired with his minimalist—and at times terse—speaking style rubs me the wrong way when I misinterpret his intentions. Like last week. Holding hands in the garden.

"Matt, look at the lemon tree," I gushed, my voice full of wonder. "It's like something out of a dream—the green buds, the citrusy smell, the smooth texture of the leaves. It's just gorgeous!"

He glanced at me, his expression flat. "It's a lemon tree."

Was I being ignored or mocked? My inner lawyer went into full "objection" mode. What followed was a marathon three-hour discussion about communication—clearly I'd misinterpreted his tone. I told him that some of his anti-lawyer jokes bothered me too. *E.g.*, "Most lawyers are experts at talking without saying much." I couldn't tell if he was cracking a joke or throwing shade at my entire career (though he might have had a point). Luckily, we worked it through calmly and thoroughly, clarifying our intentions and apologizing.

"Lara, you know PhD stands for 'pig headed dummy' right?" He giggled. "I say a lot of stupid stuff. Don't take me seriously."

I, in turn, apologized for overreacting. "I come from a long line of overreactors. Remember that scene from *Father of the Bride*?"

Turns out love is less like a perfectly choreographed Victorian waltz (*sigh*) and more like an impromptu tango—sometimes graceful, sometimes a tangle of missteps, but always growing.

"Trouble, will you slow dance to *I'll Be Seeing You* with me? One of my favorite jazz numbers from the '40s. Sad but beautiful."

"Anything for my girl." Every time he calls me "my girl" (it's his thing lately), I feel like I've stepped into a '50s sitcom and we're two teens chewing bubblegum and going steady. *I love it.*

Soon, the music plays softly on my phone and Matt circles his arms around my waist. I reach up and drape mine behind his neck, crossing my wrists and balancing myself against the turbulence shaking the room. Matt's strong and steadying arms hold me up and we sway slowly in a circle at a snail pace.

Before the dream from God (and my illness), I was never present in the moment, rushing from one shiny event or achievement to another. Now, I'm *hyper* present every day. Tasting food, smelling flowers, listening to harmonies, or ripping open beautiful cards. *Who knows, I might die tomorrow.* Today, I'm dancing.

"You good?" he whispers in my ear now, his breath warm against my skin. Heat flushes through me at the nearness of him. *I'm in a romantic '40s film. This is just... Wait...*

"Don't turn too fast or lean me back or forward. I have to stay upright. I don't want an ear crystal to fall out."

He tightens his hold, grounding me. "I've got you, love."

Love. The word lands like a pebble dropped in still water, sending ripples through me. *Where did that come from?* Kitten, my girl, and now *love.*

When the song's over, I slip out of his hold and bring over a big box from the dining room table. "Last surprise, I promise." I lift its lid to reveal twelve chocolate covered strawberries and a bottle of non-alcoholic champagne. Matt can't have alcohol due to the liver damage (first cancer) and I can't have it due to migraines.

"You know I prefer grape juice, but I'll try it," he says, winking.

"Sometimes, Trouble, it's good to indulge. You spend all your energy giving to others. It's okay to relax and enjoy the finer sides of life for *yourself* sometimes. Luxury chocolate strawberries are a timeless classic in the bag of basic blessings."

His gaze lingers on me, something unreadable but joyful sitting in his eyes. "You're teaching me how to live, Kitten," he says softly.

I swallow hard, unsure if I should say it.

I do.

"And you're teaching me that it's okay to die."

Suddenly, the room feels heavier.

The next day, Matt's Facebook relationship announcement goes live. Nearly 400 people react—likes, comments, emojis galore.

> *What a delightful surprise in your journey! Keep fighting!*
>
> *So happy for you! Sweetest couple ever!*
>
> *God's blessings! Enjoy each other and spoil her Matthew.*
>
> *It's about time you two—still praying for healing.*
>
> *Look at this gift God brought through your suffering! Miracles!*

Consensus seems to be: How did an introverted engineer like Matt—who never even seemed interested in dating before—find his first girlfriend in the middle of cancer? And what are the chances that Lara—who's been bedridden for years—suddenly has a boyfriend right after starting to walk again? Is this luck or divine intervention? Only God could orchestrate such an unlikely romance in these circumstances.

As reactions flow in, I text Matt immediately.

Me: "The post on your wall has more likes than mine. People clearly like you more. Betrayal at its finest. Stop being so adorable."

Matt: "I thought we're in the same relationship?"

Me: "Facebook creates two separate posts. So be a gentleman and let me win."

Matt: "Love isn't a competition."

Me: "Yes it is. Actually, competing with you is kind of sexy."

The following week, I mail Matt five bright pink, glitter-doused, strawberry scented "Victorian" style love letters addressed to "*Matthew Trouble, PhD, Property of Kitten, JD,*" guaranteed to embarrass him in front of his roommates. With microscopic Kitten shaped stickers inside. *This will drive him mad.*

On the outside of one envelope, I write in bold black sharpie: "Infatuation: the act of being unbearably physically attracted to Matthew John, without any due regard to his inner character or heart."

He texts me upon getting that one.

Matt: "You're impossible, you know that?"

Me: "You love it."

Matt: "Gonna punish you by charting our compatibility with a scatter plot. Maybe it's time for some evidence-based romance."

While we're busy flirting, we have zero clue that there's trouble in paradise.

Indeed, Mom returns from Hawaii a week later looking less "aloha" and more "I need a lawyer."

30

Finally!

"Vayel, get in here," Mom barks.

She's back from Hawaii, digging her hands into her hips, her eyes locked on Matt like he owes her rent.

"Matt, I didn't appreciate something," she starts, her tone a cocktail of seriousness and sweet. "I woke up in my Hyatt hotel room a week ago to a flood of texts from church ladies from LA, Fresno, San Diego—'Congratulations! So happy for them!'" Mom sighs all theatrical, throwing her hands up like she's presenting Exhibit A.

Apparently, there's a courtroom trial today in our family room.

Prosecutor: Mom.

Defendant: Matt, sitting on the couch at my side wearing **Camp Arev** t-shirt No. 3,023 and a face of the falsely accused.

Presiding Judge: Pops, sipping his Armenian coffee like it's a gavel in disguise.

Mom continues her opening statement with vigor. "I nearly had a heart attack thinking you two got married without telling us! I called Lara, who told me about the Facebook relationship thing, but I was rattled."

Mom's distress level ranks somewhere between "the house is on fire" and "someone ate the last piece of baklava." *Not this again.*

"Mom," I groan, already tired of this retrial. "I already cleared this up with you. Case closed. Double jeopardy rules apply."

Matt's expression screams *objection sustained*, but he bites his lip to avoid laughing.

"Mom, you really think Matt would elope?" I add. "I mean, *I* would—so romantic." I shoot Pops a wink. "But I don't think Matt's the type."

Pops chokes on his coffee, trying to suppress laughter, the kind that could be considered contempt of court if Mom had her way.

"Listen, Matt," Pops interjects, his diplomat face on now, trying to set a new tone before Mom really turns into Armenian Judge Judy. "We know you wouldn't elope. But we realize we should've had a formal discussion with you about your intentions."

Mom narrows her eyes, torn between applauding Pops' diplomacy and shooting daggers at him for hijacking her cross-examination. Classic co-counsel conflict. *But wasn't Pops the judge?*

"We have some concerns," Pops explains. "It's all well and good you two have been lifting each other up. But you have cancer. Lara's still very sick." He pauses, carefully choosing his next words. "We're worried about whether this relationship makes sense...and the risks if something—"

"Happens to you," Mom cuts in sharply, reclaiming the floor like a seasoned litigator.

"Completely understand your concerns," Matt nods solemnly, all composed. "And I apologize—I should have taken the initiative to clarify with you earlier. I'm datin' your daughter with the intention of marrying her."

Marriage. Oh my gosh. Matt, I hope we're moving in the right direction. I'm still worried one of us is going to croak any minute. Would God really give us the gift of marriage too?

I have no clue where we're headed, but I know what I *want*. I want us both to live, to have Armenian Jewish babies, to feel the exuberant joy of feeling blessed by God, that feeling I had in my childhood. I want peace with the Lord, and I really *do* want to love eternity more than these "temporary" blessings. But I desperately want life too.

Pops eyes Matt like he just offered to buy me with camels and gold. "I see."

"In my first cancer," Matt adds, "I saw miracles. My spine was infected, and the doctors debated if I'd die from the infection or cancer first. I won that debate I guess! Apparently I'm tough to kill." Matt giggles, casually dropping a "doctors thought I'd die" bomb like it's just another Tuesday. He's had this thing—a verbal and physical swagger of sorts—since I told him I'm in love with him. His confidence is just blooming in a new direction.

Pops exhales. "Must have been terrifying."

"Jesus has rescued me from impossible situations. And while I don't know what He will do here, I know that if He wants to make a way for us to be together, He will."

Matt is a "Why not?" kind of guy, as one pastor once described him. When his church team in Los Angeles considered feeding the homeless in a dangerous area, others worried about safety. But Matt just said, "Why not? God's got this." He takes bold risks when it comes to God, from Haiti trips to six-hour drives to camp with his chemo pump actively feeding him poison.

Cancer, ironically, seems to be pushing him further into that mindset. Now, he's taking a risk to be my husband even as he's terminally ill. Funny, considering how rigid he is in other areas of life—avoiding dating for twenty years, his never-changing fashion, and his unrelenting dedication to grape juice. *I wish he had a "why not" attitude when it comes to kissing.*

A longer discussion ensues as Matt, ever the calm apologist, lays out theological reasoning like he's defending a doctoral dissertation. Except, the thesis isn't about eschatology or atonement theory. It's titled, *Why Dating Your Daughter is God's Plan: A Biblical Defense of Love in the Midst of Terminal Illness.*

Mom listens, arms crossed, eyes narrowed—not in hostility, but in high-powered maternal analysis. Twenty minutes later, she softens somewhat but tries again. She spent four years keeping me alive. She's dotting all her I's.

"Well, what about Lara being in musicals? My father was strict. I just want to be sure…" *Ah, yes, forget finances or health. The real test of character—will Matt endure me belting out show tunes at all odd hours?*

Matt's face lights up with cautious amusement, then a wide smile. "You know I saw her *whodunit* murder mystery play in 2016, right?"

Mom bursts into a guilty giggle. And just like that, Matt strikes the winning blow in this very odd courtroom—he's charmed the prosecutor. *It's that darn smile. He should have it trademarked.*

Trial adjourned: not guilty?

"Let's take it one step at a time," Matt assures, "but now you know my intentions."

Pops, who's been quietly sipping his coffee like a UN mediator, snorts. "Grace, don't you want to lose our PSI status?"

Matt gives me a side glance. "PSI?"

"Parents Seeking In-laws," Pops announces proudly, as if he's pitching a real Christian dating app.

Minutes later, Matt and I retreat to the living room, closing the door behind us.

"How's my girl?" Matt says, as we sit side by side on Mr. Couch. "I think that went okay, except the musical theater interrogation. Now I see where you get it."

As I slap his arm to punish him, he pulls out his laptop and shows me the sermon he's preaching on Sunday at church. "Is this part too much? Tryin' to draw attention to how sometimes we care more about worldly things than actual worship—like how Jesus scolded the Jews for turnin' the temple into a house of robbers."

I read his sermon aloud: "Let's ask ourselves. Is our church so busy preparing to sell food at our Armenian food festival that we don't have time to pray for each other? Can you hear Jesus saying to us, 'Is this gonna be a house of prayer or a house of sou boreg?'"

I burst into laughter. (*Sou boreg* is a scrumptious Armenian dish made of cheese and filo dough that the church ladies meticulously cook for our annual festival.)

"Babe, I love your sense of humor."

"I'll take that as you like it? Good."

He shuts the laptop abruptly.

He pushes it aside.

He hesitates a second.

He leans in.

He cups his hands on my face.

Then, without warning, he darts forward and—

BOOM!

His lips crash into mine.

My heart immediately races. *Is this really happening?* I instantly pull him in closer, and his hands thread gently into my hair. *This man is hitting me with a Rom-com kiss like we didn't just talk theology?!*

After a few blissful seconds, our lips part. He backs off, and just sits there smiling at me, his cheeks somewhat flushed.

"Finally! You Troublemaker!" I gasp, my hands flying up in the air. "Where did that come from? You made me wait five months for that!"

"Now that we had the big talk with your parents, I felt it was time. Everythin' at its proper time, Kitten. Patience."

"How about everything in its wrong time?! I was about to file a missing affection report."

"Have to set an example for the kids at church. If they ever ask me how I courted you, I want to honor God."

"Yeah, yeah, yeah. I can't believe our lips are on a first name basis now!"

"Just promise me no more nineteen-day bans. Got that?"

"Trouble, listen," I ramble, still in shock, wanting more. "We *need* to have an intense fight right now so that we can smack lips passionately afterward in the rain. Okay? Does that make sense? Is it raining?"

He eyes me, communicating *you are ridiculous.*

"*Please*. Just one simulation. I want to play the romantic lead."

"We're kissin' now. That's good enough. I'm not required to play any roles." He leans in for another kiss.

"Nuh uh uh!" I push him away. "If you don't cooperate, I'll retaliate. I'm good for your sanctification, because now you have to exercise self-control."

"Well, if you don't cooperate, I'm gonna explain the rapture to you in stick figures."

He pulls me in and finally plants another tender kiss on my lips. *I could get used to this. I feel like Liesl in the Sound of Music kissing Rolf. Finally.*

My heart is still fluttering, but my memory flashes back to something powerful. *I want to know.*

"Matt, do you remember that one phone call when I was on the bed, when I asked you why you generously keep helping me? You got really flustered and said, 'Lara, I love...' And then you stopped cold. Do you remember that? In the moment it sounded like you were about to say 'I love you' and then stopped yourself, but I wasn't sure. I did tell Mom though."

He pauses a moment. "Lara, I won't deny it. I even told Winston about my strong feelings for you after that camp trip we took together in 2017. There was something captivating about you—something rare and beautiful—that I'd never encountered before. But you got sick a few months later. I didn't know what to do."

"Oh, Matt, I think I fell for you right there on the bed, during those quiet phone calls when my heart would beat way too fast before you got on the line..."

"I waited five years for you, Lara."

Suddenly, the floor flips upside down without notice. "Ow...

Oh gosh, I need to lie down. My brain is shaking like mad. Been an hour sitting up."

He sighs. "I finally kiss sleepin' beauty and she faints instead of wakin' up."

We lie down side by side on Mr. Couch, fingers intertwined, too exhausted and in pain to speak another word. An hour long nap later, I cue up NSYNC's *This I Promise You* on my phone, a pop relic from my middle school heart, long before chronic illness and grief rewired my playlists.

Matt stirs from his sleep, turning onto his side to face me. *I want to kiss him.* But there's a problem—I can't turn my head, or my body, left or right while lying down or it will dislodge an ear crystal. So I stay frozen, heart racing again, wondering how we can close the space between us. *I've waited for this.*

Somehow, he understands. He slowly props himself up on one elbow, his torso twisted away somehow as he lowers his head only. And then, his lips gently meet mine.

And stay.

Two.

Full.

Minutes.

Our lips don't move.

Neither do we.

Not even a millimeter.

His body angled like a broken triangle, my body locked in place.

We're not kissing—just lips, pressed and locked—still, sacred, suspended in something deeper.

This isn't about passion.

It's about presence.

About promise.

I don't know if we're even kissing or praying.

Probably both.

The music swells, as the lyrics fittingly promise love to one's lover until the day one dies.

Goosebumps break out across my skin and gratitude flows through my veins. *Thank you, Lord Jesus. This has been five years in the making.*

When the song ends, we head to the door, where I stare into his large brown eyes. "Trouble, have I told you your eyes are like beautiful chocolate almonds?"

"I didn't know my eyes were edible?"

"Thanks for loving me, Matt."

"Always." *Ooh, I like this new upgrade from "sure thing."*

When he's gone, I head to the bathroom, torn between screaming into a pillow and composing a sonnet.

He kissed me.

He kissed me.

He kissed me!

Then, I overhear Mom talking to Pops. "They're in love and this is what love is. It poses risks. Anyone could get sick once you marry them, and you have to stand by them." *Really?* Are my Armenian parents actually open to this, given how risk-averse we are? Feels like God's hand is at work. Mom went from Judge Judy to "love conquers all" real quick. *Maybe Matt's testimony strengthened her faith for a moment.*

Either way, Matt's first kiss started a countdown I didn't know I was on. Six weeks later in July, I'm peeling ribbons off a large box.

First green ribbon... Off.

Second blue ribbon... Off.

Third pink ribbon... Off.

Am I auditioning for the ribbon Olympics?

31

The Box in a Box

I sit upright on our family room couch, slowly unspooling a ribbon from a big green box. I'm donning sparkly white diamond earrings and a red cocktail dress cut to my knees. It's my big 3-5.

My *first* birthday off of a bed in four years.

Matt and his family sit across from me, perfectly still. My parents sit on the opposite side, mirroring the tension. *Why is everyone so quiet?*

It's the big meet—Mom and Pops finally meet Anna and Joel, Matt's parents. "No better time than your birthday," Matt insisted three weeks ago.

Matt sits forward on the other couch in his Sunday best, his knee bouncing like he's trying to shake off nerves.

Fourth purple ribbon... Off.

Fifth yellow ribbon... Off. *Is everyone breathing? Or have we decided oxygen is optional?*

Finally, I lift the lid, revealing a glossy little red square box nestled inside.

Before I can even process it, Matt springs up, snatches the box from me, and looks around the room: "I think there's a proper way to do these things, right?"

He grins.

Wider than the Nile.

Wait.

Small.

Square.

Box.

Oh. My. Gosh.

!!!

He kneels down on the ground on one knee, right in front of me.

My heart stops.

He opens the box.

A ring.

A princess-cut diamond radiating a million stars right into my eyes.

One million emotions tumble through me.

Love. Joy. Fear.

This is my dream. Am I allowed to say yes, Lord? Is he really proposing the first time our parents meet? Does God want this? What if I die on him? What if he dies on me? I desperately want to marry this man!

As the shock flashes across my face, Matt says, "I know," a nervous giggle slipping out. "We've been through a lot together." *Oh, that giggle. My Trouble is proposing!*

Matt clears his throat. "Lara, I don't know what will happen today, I don't know what will happen tomorrow, but no matter what happens, I know I want to face it with you. So, my sweet Lara...will you marry me?"

I glance at Mom and Pops.

Beaming.

Anna and Joel.

Beaming.

My sister. Matt's sister.

Beaming.

Lara, STOP overthinking this.

Suddenly, it bursts out of me: "Ayo!!"

Cheers erupt. Cameras flash. *Oh, I probably should have said yes in English, for the sake of the non-Armenian speakers in the room.*

Matt slips the ring onto my trembling finger, and it twinkles brilliantly. We're still staring at each other, frozen in this wild moment when Anna's voice cuts through—"Shouldn't you two seal that with a kiss?"

Matt, still kneeling, moves in for a kiss.

I melt into him.

Fireworks.

Butterflies.

The whole circus.

Heck, even peacocks.

Everyone knew but me. "The ring is stunning, Matt! I cannot believe this! Thank you!"

"Always," he replies, and it kills me every time. "I got it from your Aunt Arax who made it in Alaska." *Mental note: call Golden Girl No. 1 to thank her later. Is this really happening? I'm too shocked to even cry!*

No time for pleasantries. Mom, Anna, and Joel are already dialing the Armenian and Jewish diaspora.

392 cousins and 513 aunts later, Mom is too elated to remember her traditional left-eye kiss. Kebab preparations hit overdrive. Pops takes full command of the grill like he's manning a military base. The kebabs don't stand a chance.

"Matt, will you sing Nat King Cole's *L.O.V.E.* with me?" I burst out, vibrating with excitement and disbelief. I flash the karaoke microphone my friend Jamie gifted me today. *Nice timing, Lord.*

Thirty seconds in, Matt's plowing through. *Nicely done,*

Trouble. Our duets are getting better. Way to sing with the punches. Such a quick study. How did I find a guy willing to sing jazz with me?

The air soon thickens with the intoxicating aroma of sizzling meat and rich Middle Eastern spices that waft through the backyard and infiltrate the house.

Joel, apparently self-appointed videographer, struts around in high-tech video-recording gear, ribbons flapping from his chest like war medals. He's a charming, tall Jewish engineer with a full head of wavy, silver hair, big brown eyes, a gray mustache.

When our impromptu "performance" is over, Matt announces our engagement on Facebook—"The verse that comes to mind on this special occasion is Ephesians 3:20-21: 'Now to Him who is able to do immeasurably more than all we ask or imagine, according to His power that is at work within us, to Him be the glory[.]'"

Nice try, Satan. God turned our suffering into a love story. We're really singing in the fire now! Engaged—cancer and all. Better luck at the millennial, you dimwitted fiend.

Anna swoops in with baby photos of Matt, and I all but bask in them. Big brown eyes, rosy lips, a full head of shiny brown locks. "All the moms thought he should model," she declares proudly.

"Missed his calling," I tease. Anna flips the page to one picture from 1998, where lo and behold Matt and I are surprisingly slammed right next to each other, ages ten and fourteen, in a standing group photo in front of a gigantic graduation cake at our church, CACC.

"Babe, what are the chances? I didn't even know you until we met as adults decades later. Wait. Wait... Look at my face here. I'm glaring at *you*. I *know* that look. I was *so* crushing on you. Look at the way I'm angling to be by you!"

Matt smirks. "Lara, you were a fifth grader. You were eyeing the cake."

"And you apparently were a seductive eighth grader," I reply.

Matt rolls his eyes. "I hated those sorts of graduation luncheons.

Gimmicks like banquets, encouragin' people to attend church only once a year to show off their kids."

Later, during dinner, Joel bites into a juicy beef kebab and hands Pops the Merlot bottle. "You know," he recalls, "Matt came to me last month and said, 'Think Mom's grief might lift if she were to say, plan a wedding?' I told him, 'Yeah, that just might do the trick.'" He smiles wide, in an infectious smile all too reminiscent of Matt's.

One *My Girl* slow dance, an hour nap to rest my brain, and fifty kebabs later, I grab the mic once more. Joel doesn't miss a beat, sitting in front of me, camera at the ready. *I could get used to this guy.*

"I have a special song for Matt, on behalf of my family," I announce. Clearing my throat, I start belting out *Consider Yourself* in a cockney British accent—a classic song about making someone feel right at home, as if they are part of the family.

"It's from the musical *Oliver!*," Anna exclaims.

"Yes!" I reply.

But the show doesn't end there.

Two weeks later, during our family engagement party at our home, I hand Matt, my newfound co-star, his surprise engagement gift—a tongue-in-cheek script I wrote for us to perform about the surprising path that led us here. *He knows he has no choice.*

Pops all but glows as Matt and I perform on our makeshift kitchen "stage." Mom giggles, wiping her hands on her apron while assembling chicken kebabs for her entire Sadakian family. Mom's four Golden Girls and my cousins roar at each ridiculous joke, and Joel records the whole skit, with the same video-recorder and camera ribbons strapped to his chest. A giant red velvet cake sits next to our Armenian coffee bar, with an inscription in white frosting:

PhD + JD + Ayo = Love.

After fifteen minutes, I deliver the closing punchline—"*Weddings Today* interviewed Lara and issued a heart-wrenching story: 'From bedridden to bride. Don't give up girls, there's a man for everyone!'"

When the crowd erupts into cheers, I'm drunk on pure joy. *This is our first family party in five years. Thank you, Lord.*

Joel snickers, nudging Uncle Albert. "Just as Lara got out of bed, my son plotted to get her back in."

"Joel!" I exclaim, rolling my eyes.

"My son didn't have a romantic bone in his body until he met Lara," Joel adds.

After dinner, the entire Sadakian clan links hands and dances in a circle around Matt and me, swirling in time to a lively Armenian folk tune pulsing through the speakers. *At last, a glimpse into the "perfect Armenian life," in all its noisy, joyful glory.*

"Do you two realize your love story is miraculously backwards?" Aunt Rosalie teases as she dances past us. "Engaged without ever leaving this house!"

Suddenly, the familiar grip of a 9.0 earthquake episode creeps in. I clutch Matt's arm. *Not right now, not right now. Don't shout.* My vision shakes harder, lightning flashes before my eyes, and I press my fingers to my temples, trying to brace against it.

"Oww..." *An ear crystal must have popped out.* Luckily, no one hears me over the shuffle, but Matt decodes my face instantly with that knowing look, the one that sees past the smiles to the struggle beneath. He grabs onto my waist.

"You okay?"

"The circles, the loud music... Time to lie down."

As he brushes my hair from my eyes and cups the back of my neck to stabilize it, a wave of grief pinches my heart. *I just want to be a "normal" bride. One whose brain doesn't drown her in waves nobody else can see.*

The truth is, God has not healed me even though I've been off the master bed for seven months. I'm still bedridden seventy percent of the day. No changes; sitting up still feels like my body hired an electrical contractor without my consent. I'm just forcing myself to get up every day, and stay up as long as I can, even though the world's spinning out of control, whether lying down or standing up. But God is helping me push through; no sharp blood pressure drops after just twenty minutes of sitting up and I can force myself to sit up/walk amidst the hard turbulence for an hour and a half *maximum* before needing to lie down again.

"I thought you healed?" my extended cousin asks, noticing my stiff demeanor all of a sudden. *Do I lie, or be honest?*

For the last seven months, I've been living a double life. Outwardly, I smile, I laugh, I play the part of "fine." And because I'm trying to grab that joy, people assume I'm "healed." They don't believe me when I say nothing has changed. If I'm honest, I *want* everyone to pretend I'm healed sometimes—just to escape it. I wear my smiles like armor, a shield against questions I don't have answers to. But pretending comes at a cost. It's lonely to feel unseen. Thank God I have Matt. *Will I ever come to terms with this chronic suffering?*

I respond honestly. "Yeah, the floor is constantly moving up and down, left and right, and it just flipped a full 360. I know you can't tell. It's okay."

I take one look into Matt's eyes and forcefully remind myself. *You have to stay positive. God told you to have joy in grief, remember? Focus on how you are literally engaged.*

The next four weeks past "Ayo" contain more surprise gifts from God.

First, Nerses—my former pastor who used to play piano to my vocals in our Armenian jazz band years ago—surprises us by playing piano on FaceTime while I serenade Matt with some jazz vocals. Talk about the perfect engagement hype crew. *Praise Jesus and pass the sheet music!*

Then, Joel sends me a YouTube video he created titled "It's A Love Story"—a full-blown cinematic montage of our two parties with dramatic credits and a swoon-worthy musical score so emotional it could make a stone cry. What better in-laws could an actress ask for? It feels divinely arranged—like Jesus himself yelled "Action!" and handed us all SAG cards.

Matt and I start premarital counseling with Pastor Calvin at my house too. During our first session, Matt shows me his packet where, under "Name of Spouse," he'd written: Kitten. I, in turn, tell Calvin, "FYI, I prefer using the *Kitten International Version* for these sessions. I believe it says 'husbands submit to your wives.'" Calvin half-laughs, half-grimaces, and turns to Matt, "We've got our work cut out for us."

Matt replies, "You don't know the half of it. She had Dad sneak into my house and put up a giant human-sized MEOW sign up. Thought I was getting robbed when I got home from work. And she keeps saying she wants to be the appellate court in our relationship. Apparently, my decisions are subject to review." *That was a joke, Trouble.*

Then, when Calvin reads the standard blurb in the premarital packet about how marriage is a bond for "sickness and in health," Matt deadpans, "I think we've got the sickness part down."

We also start getting to know Matt's parents more and more. Because chemo treatment is draining Matt's energy more than usual, every two weeks Joel now drives him to the chemo infusion center where they pump him full of poison for three hours. Afterward, they visit us on their way back home. It's become our sacred "coffee and story time" ritual.

As soon as they arrive, Pops bolts for the kitchen, pulls out his "impress-the-guests" coffee machines, and brews fancy drip concoctions like he's about to host the world's most high-stakes barista competition. He's reached his promised land, shedding his

"Parents Seeking In-laws" status, and he's not taking it for granted. Joel, for his part, is a walking TED Talk of stories. He could talk about the history of paperclips and still make it fascinating.

This typical scene plays on repeat biweekly:

Joel sits at our kitchen counter, snatching a cup of dark coffee from Pops' hand, grinning like a kid who just found extra candy and jesting, "Vayel, did you know that on the eighth day God made coffee?"

Pops nearly chokes on his specialty Armenian crumpet, letting out his hearty belly laugh that could make an entire church choir clap along.

Pops and Joel then proceed to debate a random topic like smart fridges.

Meanwhile, Matt—sitting next to me on the family room couch with his chemo pump attached—sneaks quick kisses without shame, giggling between.

I feel *zero* embarrassment and secretly rejoice that my plot to flourish Matt's romantic instincts is working (*e.g.*, "Babe, think feelings, not flowcharts").

Joel rolls his eyes, spouting, "Oh, don't mind us. We're not here or anything."

Matt gloats, grinning like the Cheshire Cat without saying a word.

End scene.

Each biweekly two-hour visit feels like God's gift of joy wrapped in a bow for both families—sitting down over coffee, trying to catch a breath in the chaos. Anna visits often, too, for wedding planning. Only God's timing and provision could bring these two sets of parents together—*both who know the pain of watching a child's suffering, and right as they are walking through it.* God truly can pull water from a rock in the middle of a desert. Just ask Moses.

Apparently God can pull lace out of nowhere too. After calling eleven bridal shops—all of whom politely said "take a hike" when

The Box in a Box

I asked for a special fitting at home to avoid car rides—I'm ready to elope in pajamas.

Then, the miracle call comes. Her name is Rin, a soft-spoken Thai seamstress with a heart as warm as her kitchen. She hears my story and says, "I'll come to you—with my newest lace collection. And I'll bring fresh pad thai too." Mom nearly cries. *Is Jesus dispatching angels in measuring tape and noodles now?*

Another divine delivery. Another mercy.

Within hours, our living room transforms into a battlefield of beauty—twenty contestants (gowns) draped across couches and armchairs, a jungle of tulle, satin, and sequins. Auntie Astrid—Golden Girl No. 3 and ball of charisma who's been like a backup sister to Mom—instantly takes command like the general of glam. "Try this next one, Lara. It shouts princess!" she trills, holding up a monstrously fluffy gown like she's emceeing a couture game show. One by one, I transform from "Big Bird Chic" to "Disco Disaster," all in the name of finding *the one*.

Until—Rin lifts up a gown. Pure white silk, soft beading, delicate lace patterns, and a train that floats like it's auditioning for a Victorian period drama.

When I slip into it, the room stills. Time tilts. My reflection catches in the mirror—radiant.

Whole.

Beautiful.

Stunning.

Astrid gasps like she's witnessing a birth.

Anna clutches her chest.

Mom wipes a tear from her eye and murmurs in Armenian: "As megeh." *Translation*: "This is it."

Without missing a beat, Astrid pivots to Rin and starts negotiating prices like she's part "sweet Auntie," part "mob boss at a flea market."

But amidst all these joys, there's nonetheless a lingering, unspoken heaviness.

At our third premarital counseling session with Pastor Calvin, we discuss how even the slightest car motion will skyrocket my neurological pain. We consider some serious logistical dilemmas—like, can I survive a car ride to a wedding venue, or are we saying our vows between the tomato plants in the backyard? (I haven't stepped into a car since Dumford years back.)

And post-nuptials, how will I get all the way to Matt's house in Daly City? Either he moves in with us, or we start researching the market price of an extremely patient horse.

More importantly, while Matt's cancer is miraculously not growing thanks to chemotherapy, he still hasn't found a clinical trial. The Maryland one, yet again, rejected him. Now he's doing follow-up on a new, very promising trial out of UCSD. But will they accept him, and before we wed?

Calvin tries to set our expectations amidst all the uncertainties, focusing our trust on God and reading us a quote from C.S. Lewis' "The Four Loves":

> *Love anything, and your heart will be wrung and possibly broken. If you want to make sure of keeping it intact, you must give it to no one, not even an animal. Wrap it carefully round with hobbies and little luxuries; avoid all entanglements. ... It will not be broken; it will become unbreakable, impenetrable, irredeemable. To love is to be vulnerable.*

Vulnerable.
The word settles in my chest like a weight.

32

God's Wild Ride

"My lady, your chariot awaits. Got a surprise for you." Matt stands at the foot of the front porch, hand outstretched like a true gentleman, his voice all honey and mischief.

My stomach turns. *How will I do it?*

After being engaged two months, Matt's feeling bold today, trying to get me into his car for the first time. We've been discussing this possibility for months. *I have to try. But how am I going to handle a car's electrical energy and motion?*

"Babe, I want to try. I do. Just need a moment. My brain's on fire."

"If the pain gets too high, we'll turn right back."

Matt helps me down the porch and into the passenger seat—slowly, carefully. Being in this enclosed space again, the weight and gravitas of the car's metal structure instantly strikes me. The smell of leather and even his car air freshener evokes intense nostalgia. *This is insane. If Mom and Pops knew we're here, they'd have instant stress diarrhea.*

Two seconds later, we're buckled up. "Taking risks together, right Kitten?" he asks, putting his keys in the ignition. *Risks. Sounds riskier than I can afford.*

"Let's just try," he adds. "Very slowly. Think of it like bein' in a wheelchair."

The engine roars and before I know it, we've pulled out of the driveway.

Distraction, Lara. Humor. "Okay, Trouble, fun fact—I was once a certified criminal behind the wheel. Got three traffic tickets."

"Yeah I know, my fiancée's a felon."

Foot by foot, we roll down the block at seven miles an hour with Matt's hazard lights on, like it's normal. A snail passes us and gives us the side-eye.

Soon we reach new streets, rolling past the humdrum of suburban life. The world drifts by. Trees swaying like they've known me my whole life. Houses standing like old friends. There's no way to describe this feeling—maybe nostalgia with a side of blasting off into a new adventure in a rocket ship. *I'm three blocks away from home. For the first time in four years.*

Three minutes in, reality strikes. My brain spins harder, more violent. Larger earthquakes activate, shaking the car doors in my vision. I clutch onto my seat. *Don't faint, don't faint. Please, Lord, help me. Sustain me.*

A few blocks later, Matt announces, "Almost there."

"Go slow around the turns. Please."

He turns left and enters a familiar parking lot. He parks, and the sound of the engine dies in the quiet air.

"We're here," Matt says matter-of-factly, with a tinge of excitement.

Then, my voice cracks when I see it. "Safe—"

Matt gets out, sprints to my side, and opens my door to help me out.

Before I know it, I'm stepping into the outside world.

And it hits me.

The outside world.

Four years in hiding, shut away, and now here I am.

In a parking lot.

Standing!

And it's my favorite season: fall.

"Safeway!" I blurt out.

"Wait...the ground is shaking. Hard. Matt..."

He instantly clasps onto me. "Let's start walkin' so you distract from the sensation."

A short walk past the clunky automatic doors, I lose myself.

Rows of crisp red apples, bright oranges, and luscious blackberries stare at me like inviting hosts. *Oh, the colors! The colors!*

I yank my COVID mask off without thinking and breathe in the supermarket air. "Matt, do you see this apple?" I exclaim, dragging Matt over and leaning onto him like an anchor. "An apple!" I press my fingers against the cool, smooth surface of a juicy, red Honeycrisp apple.

I turn my whole body slowly to my left. "A shopping cart!"

Then slowly to my right. "A cereal box! No...the deli!"

Then, I reach the promised land.

"Pumpkins!"

My fingers land on the raw, curved ridges of three bright orange pumpkins, their bumpy, sturdy shells affirming their glorious presence. *This is it. Peak grocery store joy.*

"Matt, we have to get a pumpkin. And pumpkin spice tea! And cornflakes, and—oh my gosh—look at this place!" If fall had a mascot, it would be me right now.

Within seconds, Matt's lips meet mine, and I forget everything. I'm breathless. *He remembered I love grocery stores.*

"I love you so much, Trouble."

"Love you too, Kitten."

I keep moving so as to avoid the earthquakes pounding in my brain and vision. "Babe, follow me!" I urge, dragging Matt. "Produce aisles are super romantic."

We walk through the aisles one by one like it's our first date.

Our first real date. It feels like going back in time—like we're a brand-new boyfriend and girlfriend pair exploring together. *I can't believe normal people take this for granted.*

At the checkout fifteen minutes later, Matt buys me my favorite mint chip ice cream, pumpkin spice tea, and a pumpkin. But as he's handing over cash, something harder hits.

Oh no. Too good to be true. My spinning sensation enhances to a level nineteen, like a Tilt-a-Whirl at a theme park.

"Woah, Matt. I need to lie down. Like right now. I'm gonna—" My face goes white-ash, my palms go clammy, and my ears start ringing like a bad cell phone connection. Matt's face instantly goes from "Isn't this the best day of our lives?" to "Did we accidentally drink expired milk?"

"Here? In front of everyone?"

"Just anywhere," I ramble, clinging to him as the cashier stand takes a dramatic, nausea-inducing upside-down spin. "Just… outside."

So, like any modern-day knight, Matt marches me out the automatic doors.

"On the ground?"

"Yeah, I can't get to the car." *Lord, please help me.*

He gently lays me down in my faded jeans on the unforgiving gray asphalt by the cart return area—a perfectly reasonable place to have a crisis. The ground is rough and unyielding. Tiny pebbles press uncomfortably against my back, and I smell a mix of rubber tires and faint gasoline. And then—because Matt's a "why not?" kind of guy—he actually lies down right next to me, with his chemo bag on his chest. *We look like two drunk yoga instructors.*

After an awkward thirty seconds, Matt speaks up. "Enjoy the blue sky, Kitten. God's got us, don't worry." *Thank God my fiancé doesn't care what people think. If anyone asks, we're testing gravity.*

We're a mess.

We're probably a hazard to society.

But in this moment, he's here.

I'm here.

And for once, we're on a *real* date outside my house. Nothing says romance like holding hands flat on asphalt next to a cart return.

Ten minutes later, Matt stands up like he's about to fight a bear, scanning the parking lot for anything that could be a danger—a speeding car, an angry shopper, or a security guard who's rationally scared of us.

"Take all the time you need."

When we finally arrive back home, I'm not surprised to see Mom and Pops on the front porch, flailing their hands like we just returned from war. *Guess they figured it out. But wow. I feel... human again. Forget climbing mountains; I went to Safeway and lived to tell the tale. Just no ER, please Lord. They can't help me.*

Matt drags me up the porch and Mom rushes over and kisses Matt's left eye like he's a war hero.

Matt did it. He helped me travel somewhere outside this house, excruciating or not. I don't know why I agreed—probably because he understands I'm not doing this to heal—but because I'm desperate to *live*, every chance I get, until...

Pops claps Matt on the back with pride, but his eyes evidence a tinge of jealousy. "She never wanted to get in a car with me."

"I'm spinning so hard," I groan. "I need to lie down."

"I need to change my ostomy bag anyway," Matt replies. "Give me twenty."

He heads to the bathroom, and I collapse onto my bed with Mom's help. *I can't believe I got into a car. Wait...is my blood pressure dropping?*

"Mom," I say, nausea rising like bile. "Can you bring the blood pressure machine? My left leg's gone numb and I just had four brain zaps."

Thirty minutes, seven saltine crackers, and two seven-ups later, and my blood pressure is somehow stable again. We have no clue why. That's the problem with this disease. We still don't know what's exactly wrong with my brain. But the neurological pain is still climbing, like a ladder with no end.

"Mom, the bed is shaking so hard under me. Earthquake... Ow!"

"Distract yourself, Hokees. Maybe sing something," she replies.

Suddenly Matt's cloudy voice rises from the nearby bathroom. "Why is this leaking?" His voice cracks as if he's struggling not to snap. I know him too well. He rarely complains, and when he does, I know he's at a breaking point.

My heart sinks. *Is it really responsible for two weak people like us to get married? My brain is punishing me for even attempting normal life.*

Even Safeway isn't safe for me.

Matt comes in and collapses right beside me on the bed, his chemo bag resting on his chest. It's part of him now. A badge of strength and vulnerability. A perfect irony. Side by side, we stare at the ceiling.

"It's burnin' again," he mutters, pointing to his skin area around his ostomy bag, where his intestine is literally sticking out of his body. "I can't even go to the bathroom like a normal person. And my nose is bleedin' from the chemo." He blows into a Kleenex.

"I know, love. I'm so sorry. You're so strong. I admire you. And I love when you complain to me. Give me your emotions. It helps me understand your struggles better."

As we lie here, hurting together, minutes stretch into a painful silence. I don't want to bring up serious topics, but I need to. There's something weighing heavy on my heart.

The day after the engagement, God gave me the concept of *surrender* in two of my daily devotional apps—*and* in Lisa's random text message to me to "surrender this engagement to the Lord." It was unmistakably a thematic message from God.

But the devotionals were not cheery ones—they were about surrendering because "even if the outcome is not what we desire—God knows what's best." Was God suggesting we won't make it to the altar? It felt cruel for Jesus to drop "surrender" on me because Matt had literally just proposed. Am I giving Matt up or marrying him?!

So, on and off since that message—even despite all the excitement and wedding prep—I've been convinced that one of us will expire before we reach the altar, and that Matt was probably just a "good gift" God gave to me on the way to my own demise. Or his.

This is so confusing. God gave me a promise of marriage in 2017, so why is He asking me to surrender marriage now? Why not tell me, "Jesus delivers on His promises. Enjoy the promised land!" Or not say anything at all and just let me trust? Lord, You gave me assurances months ago that it was okay to date this man. So why *surrender*?

How can I trust God's timing and goodness now? God's ways are *not* our ways. In the past, I'd read about (1) Dietrich Bonhoeffer, who was executed in a concentration camp while he was engaged to be married; (2) a Christian couple who died in a car crash on the way back from their wedding reception; and (3) a woman who lost her Christian fiancé to a heart attack three months before their wedding. *I never used to be filled with doubts like this. It's because of that dream, Lord.*

There's still no sign of a clinical trial for Matt yet either. Is Jesus going to come through on his rainbow promise to me or is He going to take one of us Home? Which is it and can it really be both? When is my dream actually going to come true? Could I have been wrong that it will be soon? It's been ten months now, but I'm still…breathing.

And if I'm honest, my bucket list attitude the last eight months—*i.e.*, "I'm gonna seek happiness and blessings by DoorDashing churros"—hasn't given me any internal peace either. I'm *still* afraid of missing out. Because, let's face it, this isn't the "perfect" Armenian life. My fiancé has cancer. I've got a conviction I'm going to die. This isn't a feel-good family sitcom, folks.

I clear my throat and nudge Matt gently. "Babe, last week I asked God to comfort me that we'd make it to the altar. And then, this morning, two different friends randomly texted me the same verse: 'Not my will, but Thine, be done.' And then my daily devotional verse today—'Not my will, but Thine, be done.' That's not a coincidence. The devotional was about how God doesn't always give us the outcomes we want—like when Christ begged God to take His cup of suffering away. I don't feel called to break off the engagement, to be clear. But it feels like God's preparing me for something I don't want to hear. Like that we won't make it to the altar. Sounds like He's asking me to surrender to His will in obedience, even though it will be a tough outcome, just like Christ did."

Matt contemplates. "So, I agree God speaks through coincidences—sometimes. My senior year at UCLA, I realized electronics had too much control over me, so I asked God one night to help me stick to a new commitment to take a forty-day break from video games. The next day, I'm not even jokin', my laptop died. I did my schoolwork on the library computers and decided to devote my free time to God the rest of that quarter. Was liberatin' actually."

"See!"

"So I'm not sayin' God's not speakin' to you. What I am sayin' is God doesn't always give us clear glimpses into *outcomes*. He gives us principles to trust Him by, like surrendering your will to His, no matter what the outcome. The Bible isn't a magic eight ball."

"I disagree, babe. God gave me the Jericho story on the bed, and it was an explicit *promise* of a specific outcome—opening my jaw up. He delivered on that promise exactly as He said He would. Sometimes He *does* give us parallels that explicitly promise future outcomes. Good or bad."

"Maybe—but not always."

"So how are we to know what He's telling us in any given instance? If it's a prophecy or just a principle? In the past, *surrender* has always translated into an ultimate 'no' for me. God never gives me my heart's desires—He told me to surrender the career, to surrender healing. And here I am. Without my career and without my health."

"Stop gripping so tight. Let go of your control, your plans. Focus on God's wild ride. Like today. I drove slow and steady but was in control, right? You never know what blessings God has for you—here or in Heaven. The Christian life is about taking risks as you surrender to *His* will. You have to let Him drive."

"I'm tired of risks. My boat is always about to flip over. I live in a science fiction reality. And God's timing stinks sometimes. I'm like Pavlov's dogs, conditioned to believe He'll take good things away at the worst possible moment. Had to quit the job, remember?"

"I get it. I was diagnosed with my first cancer on Thanksgiving day. That didn't feel like good timing from our human perspectives either."

He pauses. "Look. Let's keep trustin'. Remember, Heaven is not a consolation prize, even if one of us really does die. The ecstasy you'll experience in Heaven far surpasses anything you can imagine here. That bag of blessings thingy you're obsessed with? Just a taste of what's to come. God promises, 'No eye has seen, nor ear heard, nor the heart of man imagined, what God has prepared for those who love him.' It's 1 Corinthians 2:9. Sleep on that, Kitten. I want you to really think about it."

"Thanks for always patiently talking me through these things. What would I do without you, Trouble?"

"Always."

33

Sick High Glamor

"**D**ad?"

Joel pops out from behind a giant oak tree some feet ahead of us, angling his camera.

FLASH.

Matt stops walking, yanking me to a halt beside him. He presses the tip of his blue cane into the gravel, the sharp end scraping against the soft, pebbled path. Lately, he's been needing a cane; his body is worn down from a relentless year and a half of chemo. I cling to his arm for dear life, trying to steady myself as the towering oak trees around us tilt and sway in my vision, threatening to collapse. *This will calm down. Just keep waddling.*

Twenty feet in front, Joel stands like a National Geographic photographer who's been camping out all morning waiting to snap our elusive "Sick Couples in the Wild" photo shoot.

FLASH.

A magical dark green forest encircles the three of us—a living cathedral of ancient oaks and fragrant eucalyptus, steeped in the earthy perfume of damp soil and sun-warmed leaves.

Matt's expression shifts to his signature quizzical look. "Dad, how'd you get here? You knew we were comin'?"

"Just ask your girl," Joel replies.

Today, I'm taking a big risk. I'll pay for it, but I don't care.
I want to keep *living*.
Risks.
Even amid excruciating chronic pain.
Live for eternity, not security and comfort here.
Let God sustain you with His daily grace.
The days are evil, so make the most of them.
Why not? (As Matt would say.)

A month after our epic Safeway adventure, I forced myself to try another close car ride to a big lake two miles away. It was agonizing, but worth every second being outdoors. I had to lie flat on my back for three days after, with all sorts of enhanced brain zaps in my body and brain.

Now, it's November, and after another month waiting for my brain to calm back down, I've gotten aspirational. I texted Joel last night, asking if he would snap us some surprise engagement photos at a breathtaking and small historical park called the Pulgas Water Temple. Four miles away from home.

Earlier this morning, I asked Matt if he would drive us here just for a "visit." After driving fifteen miles per hour with blinkers on, we just arrived.

"Thank you, Joel, for making this happen!" I shout. My feet wobble beneath me as the ground shakes hard. *Focus on the moment, not the earthquakes. Maybe four miles was not the brightest idea.*

The park, sparkling in its serene silence, is almost a sanctuary. Not one other visitor here at 11 A.M. *Luck? God winking?*

I visited this park alone once, years back, ironically one month before falling ill. *Stunning,* I'd thought. I'd walked these same paths, felt the breeze on my face, the earth beneath my feet. But now, I'm here again—*alive.*

I yank Matt along, his blue cane doubling as my anchor while I flit around in a frenzy of excitement, half distraction from my brain, half genuine awe and wonder. The leaves rustle underneath my feet. *Ah, the air smells like fresh earth.*

"Oh, babe look! Birds! Do you see them?"

"Yes." *Oh, those one-word answers with that cheeky smile.*

"The forest!" I exclaim, laughing now. "The water! The marble temple!"

In no time, Joel clicks into photographer mode with speed and precision.

"Matt, put your cane down a second," Joel directs. "Stand to her left. Hand on her hip. Yes, like that." (FYI: We're both dressed in casual, autumn wear that wouldn't exactly make the final cut in a VOGUE shoot. But hey, at least we're serving "Sick High Glamor" with confidence.)

FLASH.

For the first few snaps, Matt stands stiff as a board, acting like it's a corporate headshot. Meanwhile, I pose like I'm starring in a Jane Austen adaptation.

Joel and I speak telepathically—*does Matt like the surprise or does he think photo shoots are pointless "worldly affairs"?*

"Come on, Trouble. Give me some fashion poses. Anna didn't say you were a baby model for nothing."

He's such a trooper for indulging me today. The last few weeks were rough. Matt had just uploaded a Christian devotional video on strength and courage—*Star Wars* themed, of course—when the familiar pattern struck again. Matt ended up in the ER, with astronomical kidney pain this time.

Every few months since cancer first reared its ugly head, like clockwork, Matt finds himself in a sterile, fluorescent-lit ER waiting room. And yet, the timing of Matt's devotional was uncanny, like God was encouraging him to do precisely what Matt just shared with the world: *Have courage.*

Matt later downplayed the debacle on Facebook: "Hi everyone, I was hospitalized last night. The cancer started blocking the urine flow from my right kidney to my bladder, creating a urinary obstruction. Fortunately, a quick little operation adding kidney stents this morning fixed the problem, and I'm back to feeling 100 percent. Thanks for all your prayers."

Matt's ER update was so breezy, you'd think he was announcing a new *Star Wars* premiere, not a medical crisis. He's the living picture of Psalm 112:7: "They will have no fear of bad news; their hearts are steadfast, trusting in the Lord." It's not over, though. He'll need these kidney stents replaced via surgery biannually. *Another body part. Another loss.*

I jostle Matt to try to loosen him up. "This is our forest fairy tale babe!"

"I doubt hobbling with a cane is part of the fairy tale aesthetic," he deadpans.

But ever the good sport, Matt starts smiling genuinely.

FLASH.

We move to the next few spots, each one more picturesque than the last.

A rustic vintage bench with red and orange leaves scattered on top.

A giant reflecting pool that screams Victorian England, holding crystal clear murmuring waters that dance with the faint rustle of the trees.

A lovely big oak tree nostalgically embracing a blue checkered cobble stone path.

"Lara, chin way up please. Look at Matt," Joel demands, and I freeze. The tilt of my chin, too much of an angle, will send my ear crystals spiraling into a harder rollercoaster.

"Sorry Joel, I can't."

"That's fine," he replies, unfazed. "Matt, put your cane down again and lean down to kiss her."

Matt cups my face in his hands. His lips come close, hovering for a beat, just long enough to send a thrill through my veins. He kisses me tenderly.

"That's right," Joel yells from ten feet away.

FLASH.

FLASH.

At this point, Matt's working the camera, rolling with the snaps like we hit the right buttons on a computer. Input: act romantic and suave. Output: acting romantic and suave. *Such a coachable actor. Impressive work, Trouble.*

Joel shouts, "Engineer by day, model by surprise."

FLASH.

As the sky shifts from cerulean blue to a beautiful golden haze, gratitude fills my heart.

This.

The wonder of the outdoors.

Another real date with my sweetheart outside my house.

My father-in-law snapping photos in a private engagement shoot in a Victorian style park.

The cool, crisp autumn air pressing against my skin.

I am alive! With a fiancé!

There's no denying it. God's fingerprints are all over today. *Oh Lord, why can't I always have this faith and joy? Please forgive me.*

Twenty minutes later, Matt winces. "Kidney hurts."

I glance at Joel. "We're done."

"Wait, one more spot," Joel says, eyes glinting. He points toward the grandiose white temple, standing tall against the sky like something from another era. Its elegant marble Roman-era columns cast long shadows that ripple across the reflecting pool.

We walk over, and my fingers brush against the smooth white stone, feeling the weight of time and history. Matt reads the inscription carved into the stone, which I hadn't noticed years ago:

> I PROVIDE WATER IN THE WILDERNESS
> AND STREAMS IN THE WASTELAND,
> TO GIVE DRINK TO MY PEOPLE
> ISAIAH 43:20

My heart skips a beat. *This sounds familiar. Wait.* "I came across this verse this morning when reading Isaiah! I thought it was so beautiful."

I pause, calculating. "Babe, what do you think about making this...our wedding theme? How God gives us...streams of water in the wilderness—how He sustains us in the desert?!"

Matt sizes up the idea. "Hmm...I love it, Kitten. Joy in suffering. God's gifts of joy amidst grief." *Joy in grief. What God's been teaching me. If only I could surrender to the grief part.*

"Matt, I wasn't sure if we should push our limits like this today, but maybe God had a specific reason for bringing us here."

Matt kisses my forehead softly.

"See, love, I'm trying," I add. "Joy with grief. Like Paul wrote, 'sorrowful, yet always rejoicing.'"

Christianity presents some hard dichotomies. One second, you're mourning; the next, you're called to rejoice because you cling to how God really must have a good purpose for all of it. *Easier said than done, but I must try harder.*

"Proud of you Kitten. Stay strong like this. One day at a time, right?"

"I can't believe the wedding's set for March!" Anna found a hotel three miles away from my house for the wedding, four months away.

"Stay right there, you two," Joel suddenly yells, breaking the spell.

He's crouched down on the ground in front of us, camera aimed up.

FLASH.

"Okay," Joel says, standing up and smiling wide. "Got all the shots. Now who needs an ambulance?"

34

Streams In the Desert

"At Christmas, Matt's Auntie Ann gave me a blanket that his grandma knitted long ago for Matt to give to his future wife! And Judge Santin sent us matching *Matt & Lara* ceramics. She's my former boss who tried desperately to find me an Armenian guy for ten years."

I pause for a breath and glance around at my ten closest girlfriends. Each one is dressed in a shade of rose gold and seated around our dining room table, which, at the moment, looks more like a work of art than a place to eat. Goodies, drinks, pictures, games, all ornately decorated in rose gold and sage green, my wedding colors. The enticing scent of vanilla and chocolate wafts from the cupcakes and cookies stacked in the center of the table.

Bachelorette party time.

Sixty days out from the wedding.

Goal: embarrass a certain someone.

Yulee holds up the plate of cookies, sparkling with frosting. "Lara, these are adorable. What is Isaiah 43:20?"

"I had our wedding verse stamped on them. Matt's been my fountain of water in my desert of suffering." The girls look at me with an unspoken understanding, the kind only the closest of friends can share.

Evelina winks at me sarcastically, biting into one. "Nothing says holy matrimony like sugar and Scripture. This cookie is so good, it might just convert me."

To my left, in front of Mr. Couch, sits the absolute grandeur of a towering display of two hundred rose gold balloons, all molded into a giant, glittery six-foot-tall heart structure. The sight is pure magic. Almost like Pinterest threw up in here.

My internal logic when ordering: *Why not? Joy in grief. God invented balloons, didn't He?* Pops' take during installation: "Are we hosting the hot air balloon festival?"

Tonight, I'm focusing solely on joy. And earlier this week, we got some big news that's really helping.

Miriam leans over, grabbing my attention over the chatter. "How's Matt feeling lately?"

I sigh a breath of relief. "I'm not sure if I told all of you, but UCSD just told us Matt's biopsy matched their clinical trial requirements. Finally, an open door!"

Since the news, a weight has been lifted off me. *Matt will live.* And last week, my second daily devotional app featured Psalm 37:4: "Take delight in the Lord, and He will give you the desires of your heart." Two hours later, my friend Sona emailed me a beautiful encouragement, citing that same verse. I started to wonder if maybe God was saying, *Take heart, My child, you will in fact get married.*

The party hums on, and after forty minutes of post-dinner bed rest in my room, I hear it.

Knock. Knock. Knock.

The excitement in the girls' voices rises from the living room.

"Get ready ladies!" Mandy shouts.

"Shhhhh," Jeaneatte instructs.

I anxiously get out of bed and shuffle into the kitchen, where

Joel and Anna have been chowing down on kebabs with Mom and Pops.

"I'll catch everything, don't worry," Joel reassures. He's wearing his usual casual jeans and gray button up, camera in hand. They all slip into the living room, but I stay behind, leaning against the closed kitchen door, listening to the madness unfold while I hide.

As soon as Lori opens the front door as planned, I hear that unmistakable nervous giggle. *How will you deal with all these women surrounding you now, Trouble? Good. You deserve some punishment.*

In seconds, Matt is seated on Mr. Couch behind my monstrous balloon display, being serenaded by ten women, each soloing their designated verse of "Matt's Girl." It's my "exceedingly creative" version of *My Girl* by The Temptations, butchered for maximum drama. Eighty percent of the women here? Musical theater lovers.

Mom yells out, "Aw, Matt's singing too!" *You've got to be kidding me. Oh, my heart.*

When the last verse begins, I bust open the kitchen door and walk out onto the "stage" singing my solo verse, donning a pink "Matt's girl" sash and white cocktail dress.

FLASH. *Joel doesn't miss a beat.*

When the song ends, Pops' roaring laughter vibrates the room. "With Lara, every day is a surprise!" he blurts as he claps.

Olivia teases, "How surprised are you, Matt?"

"I didn't expect this much!" Matt replies, his voice both amused and overwhelmed. *I know you're mortified by the five million balloons, Trouble. Live a little. You'll pay for that later.*

Anna giggles, insisting, "You have to expect the unexpected, Matthew."

"Ladies, let's go!" I shout. *We didn't practice this for nothing.* As self-appointed director, I instruct the women to line up for our ridiculous '90s Britney Spears dance number. (More "let's wave our hands" than "dance," but hey, participation trophies exist for a reason, people.)

As the girls line up and the music starts, Matt's face registers the five stages of grief.

Denial: "They won't actually dance."

Anger: "Why is this happening to me?"

Bargaining: "Maybe if I pretend to enjoy it, they'll stop."

Matt's face twists as we execute the worst "dance" moves this side of a talent show. I can't help but enjoy torturing him. This is the guy who once lectured me on the logical fallacies in a Backstreet Boys song. I do my very best to enjoy the movement without looking down or up, or bending forward or backward. *Don't let an ear crystal loose, Lord, please. Not tonight.*

By the third verse, Matt's lips finally relax into a casual smile, and we're belting out the final line of the song.

FLASH.

FLASH.

It's over.

"Time for my solo," I say, grabbing the karaoke mic and stepping forward.

All I Ask of You echoes through my microphone now, shifting the collective mood to something slow, something tender. It's one of Matt's *Phantom of the Opera* favorites. I gaze at Matt, and his eyes soften as I sing to him those famous lyrics, where love promises safety and light in place of fear.

These words aren't just lyrics—they capture the steady, faithful love Matt has shown me all these years. When the song ends, I ask Matt to join me in a slow dance to Céline Dion's *Because You Loved Me.*

Time stands still as we turn slowly with the music, holding each other up. The warmth of his body presses against mine as my friends blow delicate bubbles all over the two of us, each bubble shimmering under the light, drifting about us like enchanted dust.

It feels as though we've wandered into a dream—where love

leads, music permeates like perfume, and every moment sparkles with quiet delight. *I don't want this to end.* I take in the familiar scent of soap on his skin and use his body as an anchor against the turbulence.

FLASH.

FLASH.

At the third chorus, I declare, "Ladies, sing!"

Voices instantly harmonize, as this moment suspends in time and downright magical lyrics about giving your lover strength and hope in their weakness.

I pull back, eyes searching Matt's face. *Oh!*

"Why are you crying?" I whisper, brushing a tear sliding down his cheek.

"I'm dancin' with the love of my life amidst cancer. God gives joy in suffering, Kitten."

A chorus of "awws" erupts around me as the ladies literally swoon. Joel shouts, "Turn around, you two!"

FLASH.

FLASH.

One decadent chocolate mousse cake, ten Kitten-shaped cake candles, and one hundred **FLASHES** later, the party's over.

I lie here flat on my bed now, the sheets cool under my skin. Exhausted. Warding off pain. Nonetheless—wistful, grateful.

"Had a little too much fun tonight, eh Kitten?" Matt says, strolling into my room with a big box.

"My deliciously royal balloon arch terrified you, didn't it?"

"Got glitter in my lungs. Here, I brought you somethin'."

He hands me a silver metal keychain with a sage green tassel with an inscription—*Streams in the Desert, Matt + Lara 2023.* My fingers brush over the delicate engraving.

"Our wedding favors! Oh, beautiful!" I ponder how Elisha from the Haiti team worked tirelessly with her Haitian artisans to make these. He sighs, placing the box on the dresser and sitting on the bed beside me. His sigh is content, but I hear the exhaustion beneath it.

"You did so good without your cane today, love," I say.

"Thanks. Energy levels are up and down. Sometimes I don't need it."

"I still can't believe you matched the UCSD trial. Unbelievable. You've waited a year and a half for this news."

"I know. So grateful. We'll see what comes of it."

His fingers trace the outline of my hand, making me feel like I've been dipped in warm honey.

"You're so handsome, Trouble."

"Don't use your charms on me," he says, winking. "Lara," he expresses, his words thick with sincerity now. "I know it sounds cheesy, but…you're my dream girl. You brought out the Romeo in me. I needed the right girl."

"Well, if you're agreeing to play Romeo, I'm going to need a bigger balcony for our next 'Romeo and Juliet' reenactment. One that holds all five million balloons."

Minutes later, Matt sits at my desk and writes a Facebook post on his laptop—

"Friends, here's an update. The tumor testing came back, and it looks like I'm a match for the promising UCSD immunotherapy clinical trial I was most interested in. UCSD is going to do one more test to confirm. Pain's been down a bit, and I've been more active. My CAT scan last week showed the cancer is stable; no new spots of growth. Thanks for every prayer. Everything is falling into place before the wedding."

Meanwhile, I open my cards from my friends. Miriam's card strikes me, as its cover states on purple floral print paper—*You are a true love story*. Then, I grab the poem the ladies wrote in secret together for me to read later. The last line strikes me again:

Close your eyes and feel the wonder of the beautiful love story God is writing and you are living

Oh my gosh. A love story! A coincidental theme. God is encouraging me. I immediately flashback to when Lisa's friend gave me a "word" from the Holy Spirit exactly a year ago that my "story isn't over," which my friend Toukhig texted me also a few hours later. Now, God is making good on His promise. He has written a love story for me, with Matt and me in the starring roles. *This clinical trial will heal Matt soon. We will marry. Thank you, Lord!*

But alas, one month later, sweet anticipation quickly gives way to something more solemn.

It's 8:30 P.M. on a Tuesday and I'm pacing the family room like something caged, the sound of my footsteps hammering on the ground.

My eyes dart to the clock, a constant reminder of every passing hour.

I shoot Mom a frantic glance. She folds her arms tighter, like she's holding herself together so I don't have to.

One month before the wedding.

And the groom is missing.

"Where is he?"

35

The Meltdown

"Where is he? Should I call Joel again?" My voice cracks as I tug at my poofy curls and brace onto a wall to steady myself. "He's not answering my calls. What if he's at the ER?"

Thirty days out from the wedding and my groom's either got freezing feet or is playing a very committed game of hide-and-seek. I've been calling and texting him for five hours straight. No response but voicemail. He was supposed to come over tonight.

I've exhausted every option—friends, co-workers, his two siblings.

Nothing.

Even his parents don't know where he is.

Is he working late at his work lab without telling anyone? Where else could he be? His roommates already moved out to prepare for my move in, so maybe he's alone at his house?

"Maybe nothing's wrong," Pops reassures, switching off the television. "Maybe he fell asleep. Maybe he's having a movie marathon."

"He's a minimalist. He doesn't even own a TV," I insist. "And five hours? He's always reachable. He answers my texts within thirty minutes. Something's wrong."

"Okay. Call Joel again."

"I just did. He might drive to Daly City to check, but he's not sure. Wait...it's Joel."

My pulse races as I swipe my phone to answer. "Joel?"

"His sister's driving to his house to check if he's there," Joel replies. "I'll let you know."

An hour passes.

Nothing. *What if it's another intestinal obstruction like a year ago? I don't even know how we've warded them off so far. But wouldn't Matt have called me?*

Another hour crawls by.

Nothing.

Finally, 10:30 P.M.

I'm flat as a pancake in bed when *thank God*, a group text pings from Matt's sister—"Hi guys, I knocked, no answer. I let myself in with the code and found him in his bedroom, lying in the dark, wide awake. He's okay physically. Talked to him a bit and just left. Lara, he's going to call you."

I blink at it, confused, numb. *Thank God! Why didn't he call me? Or come over?* And then, my phone rings.

Matt.

My heart stutters as I swipe to take it. "Babe, don't you ever do that to me again! Why weren't you answering your phone? Are you okay—"

"Lara."

I stop mid-sentence. Something in his voice is distant. His tone cuts through me like ice.

"What is it? What happened?"

His voice cracks, thin with defeat. "The UCSD clinical trial team. They said no. The second confirmatory test. It didn't match. I'm not a match. They emailed me this afternoon while I was at work. I thought the chances of this happening were really slim."

A weight drops in my gut. I don't realize I've stopped breathing until the air fills my lungs again.

"What? I—wait, I thought it had worked out?"

He exhales hard, his voice thick. "One test matched, but the second one...it just came back negative. There's nothing left. I've been rejected by so many trials. This was the most promising option."

A nauseous heat floods my body. I can barely hold on to the phone with my clammy hands. "Oh my gosh, Matt. I—I'm so sorry. I thought...you were so hopeful about this one." *Lord, why? Why now? One month before the wedding?*

"Yeah. I really thought this was the one, especially because the first test matched," he replies. "I even posted on Facebook that *everything was falling into place.*"

"I know, Matt. I know. Oh...we will find a treatment, love."

"What's the point?" he asks, his tone turning uncharacteristically sharp. "What am I supposed to do? All this research. All these denials. I don't know how to keep doing this."

He sounds so small, so lost. It's a side of him I've never seen. Matt rarely shows doubts about God's sovereign control and plans.

"I'm not a rock, Lara," he chokes out, almost bitter. "Everyone thinks I'm invincible. A superhero. I'm not. I can't be strong all the time."

"Oh love, you don't have to be strong! No one's expecting you to be strong for everyone. You're putting that burden on yourself. You can be weak. You can relax. You can complain. Wear your emotions. Let your hair down. Well, maybe not your hair." *Was that a slight giggle? I'll do anything to hear that Southern affect again.*

I press on. "Matt, we all admire your courage. But it's not your responsibility to take care of or save everyone. God's sovereignty, right? You're always putting others first. Like when you drove the youth group kids to camp three times in two weeks that one summer because their parents couldn't, despite your agonizing back pain. You're so nice that you forget yourself. I want my Prince Charming to bear his deepest emotions to me. To go weak and let *me* take care of *him* sometimes."

"Oh, Lara, I know you're right," he says, exhaling hard. "I need you, Lara."

"I need you too, Matt. I love you so much."

"You know, there's something else weighing on my heart too," he adds.

"Now we're talking, Trouble. Spill! What good is a cat unless she shares the burden?"

"When I was a camp counselor years ago, I did my best to help this one kid who was having issues with his parents. Divorce, adultery, neglect. A mess. He was crying in the corner during a game session, and I sat with him and encouraged him as best I could. We stayed in touch, and he told me when he started college that I had helped grow his faith. Last week, I found out from a camp friend that he's left the church."

"Oh, I'm so sorry to hear that."

"I just wish I had done something more for him. Did I leave him behind in some way? Let him down? Maybe if I had been a better counselor…"

"Oh, love, you can't place this burden on yourself. What did I just say? God is sovereign and you did your best. I'm sure that kid will find his way back to the Lord. We will pray together for him."

"I know. This has just all been so hard. I should've called you earlier. I'm sorry. I just…I lost it. Got home, threw my phone across the room. Haven't lost control like that since my first cancer."

"You don't need to apologize! I'm so sorry I overreacted too. You know Kittens are emotional and ferocious."

"I love you, Kitten. Guess all I needed was to hear your voice."

"Matt, your voice got me through three years on a bed. Don't you forget that."

I lie flat on my back, tears stinging in my eyes.

"But you can't die now. Everything is about to change next month."

We both had the night to sleep on it. Reality has sunk in.

Let's just say I'm not so hopeful at the moment. Neither is he.

Matt came over an hour ago, but all I want to do is shout Job 10:3—"Does it please You to oppress me, to spurn the work of Your hands, while You smile on the plans of the wicked?" *Matt is going to die. We're out of options. Are You going to do a flat out miracle on my fiancé, Lord? I just started trusting You again! Like really trusting You.*

Matt sits across from me in the corner, his spine rigid against the chair.

After a long silence, he answers me. "I don't know why I'm not a match. But it's too late now. I can't fight with a dead end."

His shoulders sag beneath the weight of his grief. We sit with it for a while, letting the heaviness settle.

Eventually, our conversation drifts—grief, theology, pain, the usual. Matt speaks in slow, measured tones at first, his words weighed down by his ache.

But as we talk, something shifts—not a sharp turn, but a quiet easing, like the first break of light through storm clouds.

"Listen," he murmurs, a subtle hint of hope emerging in his voice. "We just might make it. You never know." *I don't know how he does it. How can we have joy in this grief now? What if he has another obstruction again?*

Minutes later, he abruptly gets up and walks to the bedroom door, gripping the handle.

"Lara," he says, his voice quiet but firm. "I may not know what's going to happen tomorrow...or even next month... But I do know one thing—God always writes the best stories."

I muster as genuine a smile as I can.

He hesitates, eyes cloudy. "But," he adds, his voice lower, tentative, "would you still marry me Lara, if you knew…I'd definitely die from this cancer?"

The air between us becomes electric, instantly charged with fear, longing. My throat tightens, and the tears I've been holding back spill over.

"There's only one answer to that, Matt. You know what it is."

He rushes to my bedside and puts his hand to my cheek. "Oh, Lara."

I close my eyes and rest my hand on his, letting myself believe—for just one moment—that our love will outrun even death.

36

If Just One More Life Is Saved

"Oh look, Matt, God placed you at a table with two lawyers. Appropriate punishment."

Matt and I are standing in the middle of a swanky restaurant humming with conversation, the clinking of silverware, and the buttery scent of garlic bread.

Matt's arm is steady under my grip, his strength amidst chemo still surprising. No cane today. Meanwhile, I'm clinging to him like a human life vest, praying I don't face-plant into a bread basket. I focus on the red heart-shaped balloons bobbing near the ceiling instead of the shaking ground. If I look down, the whole world might flip over, and I can't afford that tonight.

Three days ago, after the UCSD trial denial, Matt turned to me, his eyes soft but insistent. "Would be so good to spend time with our church family at the church Valentine's dinner." He rarely makes requests of me. How could I have said no?

The problem?
The drive.
Burlingame.
Eight miles from home.
The longest I've attempted.

But something in me said I *have* to do this.
One real romantic night out.
Away from Mom and Pops.
The pain would be worth it.
So...
Side streets.
Blinkers.
Crawling through fifteen-mile an hour zones.
Stopping halfway to collapse at Sevan's place for two hours.
Somehow, we made it.
And now, three minutes after arrival, we're spotting our designated table.

"Should we pinch ourselves?" I say, sitting down and clutching the white table linens, stabilizing myself against the giant waves in my vision. *Focus on the joy. Play "socialite extrovert" to distract yourself. Smiles and cheer. Old Lara.*

"I think we're actually here," Matt whispers back.

Our mutual Armenian friend Aren, a *former pastor*-turned-*lawyer*, sits at our table. A sarcastic straight shooter you can trust with the tough questions, he's been like an older brother to me since childhood and coincidentally attended Stanford Law with me. The *pastor* part of him gets Matt, and the *lawyer* part of him gets me.

Aren and I slip into old rhythms, reminiscing about our law school days between sips of ice water. *It feels so right to be part of my church community again. I'm back for the first time in five years. Wow.*

Twenty minutes in, a waiter slides a plate of bruschetta onto the table. "This is heavenly," I murmur, turning to Matt. "Okay, be honest with me and Aren here. Do you regret dating a lawyer, Matt?"

Matt leans in, giggling. "I plead the fifth." *You'll pay for that later, Trouble.*

"I still can't believe you two made it," Aren remarks, shaking his head.

"Thanks, Aren," I reply, sticking my fork into some Caesar

salad as a coping mechanism. *I wish I could stab this vertigo instead. Ugh. The room is shaking so hard. Distract, distract.* I take a swig of water.

"By the way," Aren teases, giving off *I can't wait to roast Matt* vibes. "I saw Joel's YouTube video of Lara's bachelorette party. Imagine that—Matt listening to Britney Spears while girls sing at him. Wish we had *Matt-thought* bubbles for commentary. You hate pop, don't you?"

Matt rolls his eyes then smiles wide. "Mostly illogical stuff. Let's just say it was educational."

I glance around the room, letting nostalgia wash all over me. I used to eat at restaurants all the time while working at the law firm. It feels like I've stepped into that old life, almost like a dream. *If only.*

Aren leans in again, arching his eyebrows. "You know, Lara, when Matt first told me he was visiting you every Friday a year ago, I thought, 'Classic Matt. Always the goody two-shoes deacon visiting sick church members constantly, making the rest of us look bad.' Then I found out you two were dating and I went, 'Ohhh.' Pretty sly there, Matt!"

Aren laughs as Matt's cheeks blush at a level that would make a tomato jealous. "It's amazing what God's doing in your lives," Aren adds, eyes sincere now. "Just think of the testimony your wedding will be—how God brought two people together in suffering. It's like He's saying: 'I'm the God of the universe. I can give my gifts anywhere. In any setting, life or death, pain or suffering.'"

"Thanks Aren," I say, squeezing Matt's hand.

Later, as dinner winds down, it's clear why Jesus brought us here. We needed this. This reminder of joy. This reminder that God hasn't forgotten us, even after the UCSD rejection. *Joy in grief. Okay Lord. I see the pattern. You really do want this joy thing happening amidst this grief thing.*

Matt turns to me, tentative. I know those puppy eyes. He wants something again. "Lara, I know this is a big jump. But what do you say I drive you to my place and you can stay for a few weeks? Just until your brain calms down? It's the same distance back to your parents' place anyway."

Am I hearing correctly?
Alone time.
With my fiancé.
In his house.
My pulse stumbles.

My brain screams, but my heart… Oh, my heart. Can I even plausibly resist this? Every single car ride (I've done four so far) has severely enhanced my brain zaps, spinning, and pain. *But that darn smile. Lara, you have nothing to lose.*

If I go home, I spin. If I go to his house, I spin. *This isn't about healing. Just trusting God to sustain you in your suffering until it ends. Dead or alive.*

Do I take the risk?

I can't stop reading Matt's scribbles in a notebook:

> My childhood suffering turned me to God, and that brought me great joy. As a result, I told myself—If just one more life is saved because of my suffering, I am happy to go through it again. So never be discouraged by suffering or persecution. One day we will all be together in Heaven, and we will see all the people who came to Jesus because of our hardships. We will see how God was using all of our pain and losses to accomplish far more than we could ask or imagine.
>
> - Sermon in Haiti, Matthew Silverman 2016

Matt's signature sits there on the page, handwritten five years before his second cancer diagnosis. *"If just one more life is saved because of my suffering, I am happy to go through it again."*

Hmm. Maybe Matt's current cancer really will impact others' lives through Matt's testimony in his suffering? Remember what Winston, the Haiti team leader, said months back—"test to testimony."

I take my eyes off the notebook, and it hits me.

I made it. I said yes to those big Matt puppy eyes and here I am.

Sitting in my fiancé's kitchen.

In *his* house.

Reading his sermons.

Some sixteen miles away from home.

Wow.

My first week here, my brain felt like it was spinning in a blender set to high, forcing me flat on my back for fifteen hours each day like the "good ol' days." The drive left my nerves screaming like sirens. I even considered going to the ER for some form of sedation, but what would be the point? Somehow, God sustained me as I pushed through. *No more long car rides, Lara. But wasn't it worth it?*

Now, I'm midway through my second week and the storm inside my head has settled into a slightly *less violent* tsunami after a week of pure bed rest. Right now, I'm trying to sit up again for an hour.

Goal: ransack my fiancé's house like a detective obsessed with the case—devouring every memento of my man like a nosy historian.

The house is a cozy three-bedroom, two bath exuding "little British cottage" vibes, thanks to the Daly City fog rolling in like a soft gray blanket, the crisp ocean air curling through the windows, and the bright blue ocean view in the distance. *What a whimsical oceanside paradise. I can work with this!*

Inside, the place is pure Matt. Video games, board games, comic books, science textbooks, puzzle collections, and brain teasers scattered across shelves. Countless **Camp Arev** t-shirts draped over chairs in the master bedroom. Coupons, lab work, and pill bottles stacked on the counter beside the refrigerator, which houses a healthy stash of applesauce, two large bottles of grape juice, and medicinal syringes. The bare walls evidence simplicity and functionality. *That's my man.*

I flip through another notebook now, finding more of Matt's handwritten sermons, and scribbled lists of people's names and their prayer needs. My heart swells. Because of his own suffering, Matt holds endless compassion for others. *I want to be this selfless.* Anna once told me Matt mentored other kids with cancer even during his first cancer. Last week, he visited a few other sick church members to encourage them. My man doesn't just survive; he gives.

"Just got off my online review session with my students," Matt declares, rousing me from my thoughts as he walks into the kitchen from the hallway. "Thanks for waitin', Kitten." He moves around the kitchen with ease, tossing red and green bell peppers and tomatoes into a pan with the confidence of a TV chef. The sizzling sound and intoxicating aroma soon fill the air. "Whippin' up a quick spaghetti."

I watch him, entranced. *My man can cook. Thank God he's not on chemo this week and has strength.* As he cooks, I reach into my pants pocket, brushing my fingers against a small bottle. *Not yet. I want the moment to be right.*

After a quick dinner, Matt proposes, "It's sunset. I want to take you out for a quick surprise. You think you can walk three blocks?"

"Oh! If it's really only three blocks. If it's uphill, I can't. I'll need to lie down right after." *I want this.*

"It's flat. You should be okay."

I cautiously grab my coat and trust him. We step outside, hands laced together. The neighborhood is pure charm—each house painted a different bright pastel color. On the third block,

Matt slowly guides us left, and I can hardly believe what unfolds before me. The wide ocean sits there in front of us, vast and wild, like a vintage painting. My breath catches as I watch the waves crashing against the jagged rocks.

"Oh my gosh, this is absolutely breathtaking. You live this close to an access point?"

"Wanted to catch the sunset for you."

He stands behind me, arms wrapped around my waist, head resting against mine. The breeze from the ocean washes over our faces as we watch the waves roll over and a beautiful sunset painting the sky. Deep oranges and rich reds gradually melt into shades of pastel pink and purple, creating a mesmerizing gradient that seems almost otherworldly.

"Does this compete with the sunsets at your parents' place?" Matt whispers into my ear, his breath warm.

"This is paradise, love. I have no words. Haven't seen the ocean in five years. I couldn't ask for a better Valentine's week. Thank you."

"Always."

"Babe, wait, hold my hands out like we're on the Titanic helm! Remember that scene?"

"Wanted to forget it."

"Come on, Trouble."

"You really want to be on a sinkin' boat?" he replies, reluctantly holding my arms up.

"Come on, let's live out our fantasies babe! Imagine we're the greatest lovers of all time. Darcy and Elizabeth, Queen Victoria and Prince Albert, Aragorn and Arwen!"

"Prefer Matt and Lara," he deadpans.

We stand here a few minutes, breathing into this escape from reality. Our world narrows down to the crashing waves and the rhythmic rise and fall of our chests against one another.

Until, something shifts. I feel it before he even speaks. *I know him.* I turn around and his cloudy eyes peer back at me.

"Matt, what's wrong? Other than the obvious."

He sighs, long and deep. "I don't know what other trials to look into. Been searchin' for so long." Exhaustion settles over his face. He is pushing his limits, working full time even in his pain, living in a body that's been poisoned by chemo for almost two years now. But I sense far more vulnerability in his emotions since the UCSD denial. The truth is, my grief over our future has intensely resurfaced again too. But today, it's my turn to be strong for him.

"Babe, let's focus on how your scans show no new cancer growth. Almost two years. That's a miracle. God's protecting you."

"I know."

"You were supposed to die six months after diagnosis. There must be a reason you're still here. Remember you had a conviction last year that you aren't going anywhere?"

He exhales, rubbing his temples. "But what if I don't make it, Lara?" *Oh, my heart. He almost never suggests that possibility.*

"Then Matthew, listen to me. We'll go down in style together—preferably with a musical number."

He shrugs his shoulders. *He needs more.*

"Look, let's go back and rest; it's getting cold and I'm losing steam. Starting to feel really faint."

Fifteen minutes later, Matt is sprawled out on his couch while I'm waddling to my backpack. "Keep your eyes closed; I'm coming," I say. Thirty seconds later, I'm seated on the couch pressing a sticker onto his right arm and holding it down with a cold, damp paper towel. "Done. Open your eyes."

Matt glances down. "A...fake tattoo?"

"Yes! A kitten with a heart!"

He shakes his head. "You evil cat." A thin smile creeps onto his face. "You always cheer me up, Kitten...except when you're babblin' about the bag of basic blessings."

"Watch it, I'll tickle you. I also want to give you this."

I pull out a small bottle from my pants pocket. "Here. Your new prescription."

He pops it open, spilling out the first tiny capsule and reading it: "Kitten RX?"

"Each blue capsule has a note inside with something I adore about you. Open one every morning, okay?"

He chuckles. "I love it."

He peers up at the ceiling, rubbing his chin like he's considering a major life decision. "Listen, Lara. Been thinkin'. I want you to join me on my youth group Bible devotionals from now on."

I blink. *Bible devotionals?* "Really?"

In seconds, my brain kicks into overdrive. "Wait...what a perfect way to combine music and theology together. Think musicals!" *I've been craving intellectual projects of any kind my brain can handle, and this just might be a starting point.*

"When did Broadway come into it?" Matt asks, scratching his head, giving off "I regret my last life choice" vibes.

"Babe. I have ideas! Think *Annie. Oliver! Cabaret...* Okay, maybe not *Cabaret*. Your devotionals are so creative—*Lord of the Rings, Batman*, superheroes. But it's time for some show tunes. The people need this. Trust me. But, I really need to lie down now. Help me push off the couch?"

Two hours later, I'm sprawled across a bed, hollering to Matt in the next room.

"Babe, I've got it all planned out! First, we'll do a spin on joy in suffering with '*You're Never Fully Dressed Without a Smile*' from *Annie*. Then, a twist on *The Sound of Music*. We'll call it 'The Sound of Worship.' You like it?"

Matt chuckles from across the hall.

"And," I add, "oh my gosh—'*Les Miserables*'! Nothing speaks suffering like a little French tragedy."

Matt strolls into my room. "Good work, love. Looks like we're the ambassadors for joy in suffering now, huh?"

"Yeah," I say, rolling my eyes. "Because every girl dreams of being the poster child for doom and gloom. Next up: '*The Dying and Disabled: A Musical.*' Catchy, huh?"

"No more snark, Kitten. But look, none of that Britney person in these, okay?"

We dive into drafting our first devotional, with me tossing out ideas lying down and Matt typing beside me like he's on a mission. The next thirty minutes involve nine rounds of:

Me: "Can we add this other song in this paragraph too? It's a solid metaphor."

Matt: "No, Kitten. We're writing a devotional, not a Broadway show."

Me: "So no costumes? What if we—"

Matt: "No." (With a wide grin)

Me: "Come on, just imagine a dramatic key change on that hope-inspiring song from *Annie* about the sun coming out tomorrow—right when the Apostle Paul gets shipwrecked."

Matt: "You need a nap."

Me: "You need vision."

Matt: "And you need limits."

By the ninth round, we're up and recording the video together, ending with a marvelously dorky vocal duet of *It's a Hard Knock Life*. At midnight, after some video editing, Matt posts the devotional on YouTube/Facebook, with the caption:

> I just finished my first joint devotional with a special someone. It's called *Joy In Suffering*. Tough one to put together given the UCSD denial, but being able to have joy in the midst of these hardships is part of what it means to follow Jesus. Let's see what lessons we can learn from the classic musical: *Annie*. And as always, if you need us, *we* are just one phone call away.

Oooh. It's "we" now!

But next time, he better let me sneak in a bridge and key change, or I'm rewriting Exodus as a tap number.

37

How Great Thou Art

I walk down the aisle.
   One step forward.
   Another.

My friend Toukhig sits in her pew staring back at me, her face streaked with shock. I swallow hard and keep moving.

Third step.

Fourth.

I keep walking.

Auntie Nanor turns in her pew. Her jaw drops and her eyes widen, filling with relief, disbelief, maybe both.

My pulse pounds in my ears and I can barely breathe.

The congregation stands, their voices rising in unison, pouring out the familiar hymn—*How Great Thou Art*.

No, I'm not walking down *that* aisle.

This isn't a wedding march. This is something else entirely.

After five years of isolation, I'm stepping back into my first church service at CACC. The sanctuary swells around me, vast and unchanged, yet older, heavier. The air hums with memories pressing down on me. The beautiful rainbow-colored glass windows peer back at me in all their glory.

I cannot believe I am back in this sanctuary.
Where I was baptized.
Where I grew up.
Where I sang Christian jazz duets with Pastor Nerses a decade ago.
Where I silently prayed for a husband.
Grief and joy intermingle as emotion overwhelms me.

My chest tightens. *Something's missing.* I imagined this moment so many times, lying in that dumb bed for years. I thought coming back would mean healing. I thought I'd feel…whole. Triumphant. Not grieving. For Matt's life. For mine.

A tremor rolls through me. An episode coming on. *I can't do more of these car rides. My brain is going to explode. I better not collapse and create the world's most dramatic church scene since Lazarus. Or Safeway.*

This morning was my last day at Matt's house. He looked at me, reaching for my hand. "Kitten, how about we take another risk? Stop at church on the way back to your parents' place? It's three miles, and we'll have to stop anyway for your brain to rest before the rest of the ride. You can lie down in the prayer room if you need to."

Every bone in my body wanted to say yes. So I did.

I grip Matt's arm now, digging my hands into his sleeve. "Hold me," I whisper. The sanctuary floor shakes violently beneath me, tilting, shifting. My stomach clenches as Matt's arm tightens around me. *Am I going to vomit?*

The congregation keeps singing *How Great Thou Art*—voices rising in unison, praising God's greatness with every word.

How fitting. Lord, did You time this song for us? Even when we stumble in late, even when we fall apart, You're still walking with us, doing miracles bringing us here? Yes, Lord, it appears You are great.

Finally, we make it to an empty pew. I sink into it, gripping the wood as if it might anchor me. I lean into Matt, his presence solid, his love undeniable. The same love that made this possible, and which initiated my emotional healing after the dream God gave me a year ago.

But the physical sensations overwhelm. Twenty minutes into the service, I can't focus. The room is turning in 200 mph circles, and the floor is shaking harder and harder beneath me. I clutch the pew like it's a flotation device. *The boat is going to flip over, I can feel it. I'm one rogue wave away from going under. Just stay calm. You are finally at church. A miracle.*

Then—BOOM.

Lightning flashes inside my skull, sharper pain sears my brain, and the sanctuary spins a full 360-degrees. *Who knew church could moonlight as a Six Flags ride?*

"Ow..." I grunt. "Matt, I feel really faint."

He leans in, whispering, "Hold on to me. We can leave whenever you need."

Maybe if I really do lie down in the prayer room, I'll earn double prayer points—like lawyer billable hours, but holier.

I cling onto Matt, distracting myself with the sheer fact that God actually brought me back here. Although the storm inside my head stays the same, I somehow dodge a fainting episode for the next twenty minutes. *Thank you, Lord. I will lie down immediately at home. Push through.*

When the service is over and everyone else shuffles into the community auditorium, the sanctuary falls completely silent, thick with the afterglow of reverent worship. Only Matt and I remain, seated side by side in this smooth, timeworn pew, both a little unsure what to say.

"Matt, I...want to walk to the front. To the foot of the Cross symbol. Help me."

He helps me to my feet, his hands steady as he leads me forward. The red velvet steps loom ahead, rich and familiar.

"Matt, help me kneel. I can't bend down alone. I have to stay upright on my knees but I can't do it alone, so you have to balance me."

He lowers me gently, his grip firm under my shoulders. I sink onto the first step, fighting for stability despite the turning floor beneath me.

"Keep my head and chest upright, babe. We can't trigger the ear crystals."

He kneels beside me, bracing me with an arm around my waist.

"Matt, please pray." He looks at me, eyes dark, filled with something deeper than love—something closer to faith.

"Heavenly Father," he starts, "Your mercy brought us here today. We praise You for these miracles, for bringing us together. You know our hearts, our fears, our grief. We pray You would grant our desire to marry and give us strength as we move forward. Give us courage and hope. The kind only You can give. Amen."

I clear my throat. "Lord, I praise You for bringing me back here and giving me Matt's love. I beg You to grant us marriage. I also ask one more thing. Would You show me You love me? Prove it to me, Lord. It's so hard for me to believe that when You allow all this uncertainty and loss."

On our return drive, as Matt drives snail-pace to my parents' place, my white-knuckled hands clutch my seat as I brace against brain zaps and aftershocks. Then, I glance right—and freeze. A sign. A gigantic, bright yellow banner hanging prominently on a church building:

GOD IS LOVE.
HE LOVES YOU WITH EVERLASTING LOVE.

Hmm. You're already answering me, Lord? Nah, just a coincidence. Churches feature this sort of stuff all the time.

The next morning, I wake up in bed at my parents' home to see a group email on my phone from my musician friend. It's a short Christian inspiration snippet which says, "God loves you with an everlasting love." *No way.*

Then, Matt shows up wearing a **Camp Arev** shirt. The logo? 1

John 4:16—"And so we know and rely on the love God has for us. God is love. Whoever lives in love lives in God, and God in them."

I ask him, "Did you intentionally wear that shirt today?"

"What shirt?" He glances down, baffled. "No?"

Ten minutes later, I get a personal text from Auntie Nanor randomly—"Praying for you today, Lara. I hope you know and feel God's incredible love for you."

Wow. Thank you, Lord. You just bombarded me with four different love notes. I guess it's true. You don't love us more or less based on whether You heal us or take us Home. If only I could get that through my thick head.

As Charles Spurgeon—a famous theologian who struggled with multiple serious ailments—once preached, "The Christian may not always be healthy, but he is always loved."

Even so, as I stare at Auntie Nanor's words—*God's incredible love*—my mind still spins into sharp anxiety of a most irrational kind. *Is one of us going to literally die in the next few weeks before the wedding date?* Months ago, God had asked me to surrender—and in my experience with God, surrender and acceptance have always come cloaked in an ultimate "no."

I can't help but doubt and ask.

Will God's incredible love carry us all the way to the altar?

38

Miracle of Miracles!

Lying here alone in my hotel room bed at 6 A.M., one quiet word rises in the stillness of my heart—unspoken, yet unmistakable:

"REJOICE."

It's You, Lord. I know that voice.

Minutes later, a text from my friend Nancy lights up my phone—"Lara! Psalm 118:24 is on my mind for you today: 'This is the day that the Lord has made; we will rejoice and be glad in it'" (KJV).

I blink. *You've got to be kidding me.*

Still processing, I instinctively open my third daily devotional app to find the same exact verse: Psalm 118:24.

Same word: *Rejoice.*

At this point, I half expect to open the room minibar and find a miniature bottle of champagne labeled "Rejoice."

Because it's finally here.

The morning of my wedding.

March 4, 2023.

MIRACLE OF MIRACLES!

And apparently, God is not subtle.

A wild rush of peace and excitement surges through me. I bolt upright like someone just flipped the power switch on my soul. I start spinning harder, but who on earth cares—*I am actually getting married today! And God just told me He's rejoicing with us! Is this literally happening?*

I hurl the covers off, slam on the lamp, and scramble for a pen. Matt *must* know, given how irrationally anxious I've been the last few days.

I scribble "REJOICE!" across a hotel notepad in frantic block letters. It looks like a cross between a ransom note and an over-enthusiastic church banner.

Then, I call Anna, breathless. "Favor, Anna. Can you sneak a note to Matt, so we don't see each other?"

Seven hours later, I sit on a chair in a holding room, beaming pure joy in my elegant lace wedding gown, heart ricocheting between my ribs, refusing to be tamed. An explosion of cheers and applause rumbles through the wall. "What was that?" I ask the wedding coordinator.

She peers through the cracked door, and a sly smile forms on her face. "Matt just walked into the ceremony room."

I exhale a laugh, trembling on the edge of tears. *Ah, yes. My rock star groom, basking in the love of 290 people in the audience—our church and friends, his youth group, his Haiti missions team.*

And in minutes, I get to marry him. *The man of my dreams.*

The air shifts, time leaps.

I'm not in the holding room anymore.

I'm on stage up front, my hands locked with Matt's facing him, as the lace train of my wedding dress flows majestically off the stage like it's auditioning for a fairy tale. Our voices belt out one of Matt's favorite worship songs with everyone we love—*Happy Day*.

The hotel ballroom around us dissolves. It's no longer four

walls, chairs, and carpet—it's something sacred, transformed by a sanctuary of voices worshiping, clapping. The veil between Heaven and earth feels tissue-thin.

I mouth to Matt: *Is this really happening?* He nods emphatically, eyes full of fire: *Yes!*

I spot Pops reading our green wedding pamphlet in the front row, which states, "Our wedding theme is Isaiah 43:20, which encapsulates how God graciously gave us the gift of love in a season of intense suffering for both of us. God gives His children 'streams in the desert,' meaning the hope, joy, and love we need to persevere through our greatest trials."

When the song fades, Pastor Calvin steps forward to preach as Matt and I sit down on a plush velvet couch on stage. *We've come a long way from Mr. Couch.*

"Wow," Calvin begins, voice steady, reverent. "You can say it's a miracle we're here today to enjoy this special wedding. Sometimes we wonder about God's mysterious ways when we consider Matt and Lara's health. But we are reminded how precious the gift of marriage is, given that life is so fragile."

Matt squeezes my hands. My heart explodes. This moment—this wild, improbable moment—is what happens when you think your story is over.

But God flips the page.

Calvin continues. "In Isaiah 43, God says, 'See, I am doing a new thing!... I am making a way in the wilderness and streams in the wasteland.' Indeed, you two have been in a form of exile, but through it all, God brought you together—even when you had given up hope for marriage. And now, God is saying do not fear the upcoming uncertainties, for He will continue to provide for you." The room murmurs in agreement.

Twenty minutes pass in a blur, and the vows are upon us.

As we stand facing each other, Matt reaches into his pocket and pulls out a folded piece of paper, flashing the back to me first. I gasp. It's my own note in my handwriting: "REJOICE!" My frantic, all-caps scribble now immortalized in the most romantic moment of my life.

Matt giggles, flips it over, and begins. "My sweet Lara," he says, voice thick with emotion, "we've been through the impossible together. And yet, during the hardest times of our lives, God brought us together. So today, I promise—"

His voice cracks, a tear slipping free. "I promise to walk through life with you. To lead us with all the wisdom God has given me. To always encourage you and lift you up. Always protecting, always trusting. Always hoping, always persevering. And as we walk with Christ together, no matter what trials we face, wealth or poverty, sickness or health..."

He stops cold, giggling at "sickness." Then, he adds, "Through the biggest storms and the greatest victories, for as many years as God gives us on this earth, I will always be by your side as your faithful husband."

My heart tumbles and my breath shakes. *I am undone.*

Then, my turn. I unfold my vows and turn to the audience with a cheeky grin. "Matt *Trouble* Silverman. I can't believe we are standing up here right now. This is truly a miracle of miracles. Praise the Lord! Our gracious God dropped you on my doorstep in my time of greatest suffering. You are the most unique man I've ever met. Is it your brilliant wit, your infectious smile, your intellectual prowess, your sacrificial heart, your courage and strength in facing adversity? *Hmm.* Nah, I think it's mostly just your insanely handsome good looks." Laughter ripples through the room.

"So, I vow this day to make illogical arguments that drive you nuts. To crack jokes at 3 A.M. when you're trying to sleep. To force you to sing an entire musical score with me every two weeks." Matt sighs dramatically. The audience snickers again.

"But most of all," I say, voice softening, "I admire your relentless pursuit of Christ-likeness. I vow to serve God with you, and to do my best to remember that—no matter what—the sun will come out tomorrow, because with God, eternity awaits."

After exchanging rings, Matt lifts his foot, poised above a thick napkin pouch on the ground holding shards of glass. With a swift stomp—

CRACK!

The glass cracks, shattering sounds burst through the air, and the crowd erupts into cheers and applause. We're doing this Jewish tradition because one of its meanings is accepting the fragility of life. As our wedding pamphlet declares, "Life is fragile and short, but we can still rejoice when things break, because as Christians we have hope in a glorious eternal future without suffering."

Seconds later, before I can even process Pastor Calvin's words—

BOOM! Matt's lips press firmly into mine. He's kissing his bride, sealing our vows with fire. *Finally. The good stuff.*

Calvin's voice booms over the cheers, the joy, the music, and the wild, heart-pounding wonder of it all—"I present to you for the very first time, Doctor and Mrs. Matt and Lara Silverman!"

𝄞

Matt grips the microphone like a man about to deliver the greatest speech of all time, his grin stretching wide enough to split his face.

"Now, you all know Lara loves musicals. And half of my family is Jewish. And you just can't have a proper Jewish wedding without a little *Fiddler on the Roof*, right?"

The guests murmur in anticipation. After four hours of sheer collapse—our "rest break"—Matt and I are back on our feet in the reception hall now, standing beneath the breathtaking chandeliers, lit like Broadway hopefuls about to make our grand debut.

Our duet song? *Miracle of Miracles*—one of Matt's *Fiddler* favorites.

Could there be any other choice?

Matt sings first, describing how, like Daniel in the lion's den, Matt felt God's presence in his hardest moments and came out the other side by nothing short of a miracle. A few stanzas later, he passes the microphone to me, and I sing about how God came through on His rainbow promise of marriage to me. Then our voices blend together in harmony for the final verse—a heartfelt declaration that the greatest miracle is this love between us: the gift we never saw coming.

A thunderous applause erupts as we press our microphones together in victory. There can be no doubt—God is supernaturally preventing 10.0 earthquake episodes in my brain right now so that I *can* rejoice, even amidst my chronic turbulence. *Miracles.*

As the excitement settles, Pastor Greg offers the blessing before dinner, and ironically quotes Zephaniah 3:17: "[God] will rejoice over you with singing." *Rejoice. There's that word again. Thank you, Lord. I hear you, loud and clear.*

Then, it's time for the speeches.

First, Pops grabs the mic with a flourish. "A year ago, I asked myself, 'Who is this young lad stealing my daughter's attention in my own home?' But now? I'm certain you two are a match from God. But Matt, you've got no clue what journey you've undertaken. Being a lawyer, Lara can carry an argument much further than the typical engineer would desire. Here's a critical tip for the road—my daughter is always right, even when she's wrong."

The room roars with laughter. "Lara believes the sky is the limit, and you'll have to tame her expectations from time to time—but let her fly the rest of the time."

Matt's brother Jeff roasts Matt next, then Sevan strides up with a wink. "I always told my sister she'd marry a teacher. Revenge is sweet." *Touché.*

Anna steps up, declaring, "I always wanted a second daughter, and now I've found her."

Then Joel activates his timeless "Joel-esk" wit. "You two beat the odds. You fell in love without dating, without ever leaving the house, and sometimes without even getting off a bed!" Cheers ripple through the audience.

Next, Winston, the Haiti team leader, takes the mic like a preacher who's about to change lives. "Matt Silverman, you're the man, the myth, the legend. You are a *significant* and *powerful* life. You are a *gift* to the nations, to Vietnam, to Haiti. The Lord is doing powerful things through you. Buddy, you're turning your test into a testimony. Glory!"

Finally, Judge Santin, my former boss, strides up, exuding the energy of a woman who has receipts. "You all should know Lara was laser-focused on marrying an Armenian Protestant man," she begins, her tone precise and measured, like she's building a case. "He had to be devoted to God. Family. Kind. Brilliant. Accomplished. Social. Had to be gorgeous. So let me tell you what lengths I went to in order to make that happen. Even though I'm not even Armenian." The guests lean in, curious.

"First, I ate at the famous *Carousel* restaurant in Glendale, *scanning* the room for potentials. Then I loitered outside an Armenian church in Burbank like a *detective*. I eventually enlisted my own husband, who, while giving a keynote at an International Armenian Lawyers Association event, forced Lara to stand up in front of three hundred lawyers as he announced—loudly and proudly—that she was *very* single and *very* eligible."

The audience loses it, bursting into cheers.

This isn't a wedding speech. It's an *exposé*. And honestly? I'm loving it.

But Judge Santin isn't finished. "Don't worry, I've got the mother lode. Then I dragged Lara to Justice Mike Crinkle's retirement party in Fresno. *One thousand* Armenians in one room. That's right." The crowd is in stitches, clapping wildly and clinking silverware.

"We approached every age-appropriate man and asked, *Are you single? And are you eligible?* Because we've got a fine woman here. But let me tell you—Lara was extremely picky. Her usual complaints—*Not smart enough. Kinda dull. Neck is too thick. Too much of a jock. I like nerdy.* She earned her nickname which was Goldilocks."

Judge Santin turns to Matt and concludes tenderly, "At the end of the day, I failed. Because I didn't know Matt. But I'm so glad Lara found him herself, because he's perfect for her on every dimension."

As cheers and applause crash through the chandeliers, the night barrels forward—a blur of food, laughter, jazz solos from yours truly. A delightfully nerdy magic trick where Trouble yanks a garter out of a *hat*—did you expect anything else? (Because let's be honest, no self-respecting bride does a real garter toss.)

Countless friends rush up to us, eyes shining, repeating the same theme—*we could feel the Holy Spirit's intense presence today.*

Indeed, miracles abound on full display today. God's practically rolling out the red carpet and blasting trumpets:

Matt and I are still standing.

There was a time when neither of us could eat a single bite (think jaw debacle, NG tube). Now? We sit here devouring filet mignon.

Despite exhaustion, cancer, and spinning, we dance on and off until 11 P.M., God carrying us through every step, every breath, every break.

And as the music fades, as the guests slip into the night, and as the last echoes of laughter dissolve into silence—

A quiet truth settles in.

We made it.

This isn't just a wedding.

It's a miracle of miracles.

And to top it off?

We're alive.

Act Three

"Rejoice in the Lord always. I will say it again: Rejoice!"

— Philippians 4:4

"About midnight Paul and Silas were praying and singing hymns to God, and the other prisoners were listening to them."

— Acts 16:25

"Therefore we do not lose heart. Though outwardly we are wasting away, yet inwardly we are being renewed day by day. For our light and momentary troubles are achieving for us an eternal glory that far outweighs them all. So we fix our eyes not on what is seen, but on what is unseen, since what is seen is temporary, but what is unseen is eternal."

— 2 Corinthians 4:16-18

39

Rejoice!

My paint brush drags a deep blue across the canvas of my half-finished painting of the English countryside. Rolling hills, an old stone cottage, and a looming, ominous fog—a perfect manifestation of my obsession with all things British.

Goal: finish this painting before Trouble gets home.

Date: late April, second month of marriage.

My gaze flicks to the left of my chair, where a black Victorian iron candle sconce on the wall casts a warm glow with colonial charm, while two towering gothic lanterns loom like watchful sentinels. To my right, the hand-stitched blue and green quilt made by Auntie Astrid cascades over an armchair like a domestic relic, whispering, *You live here now.*

A laugh bubbles up as I add another stroke of blue paint. *Who even am I?*

Four years ago, I couldn't care less about interior design, and now I've draped Matt's former bachelor pad in peak British cottage core. Me, a woman who once scoffed at throw pillows, now curating an aesthetic. Ironic doesn't quite capture it.

Our family room, a haven of cottage core floral fabrics, features a dark blue fireplace mantel, its surface lined with rustic black candlesticks, an antique Victorian clock that ticks in measured patience, and three baskets of dried flowers and herbs that give off subtle scents of rosemary, thyme, and lavender. *I can't believe we live in our own little home now.* (Though I do fancy calling it a "cottage." Why not?)

You can see that after pinning Matt down at those nuptials, I wasted no time.

First, I devoured my fictional *How to Be a Good Wife* manual, edition 6.79. Then, I set to work transforming our house into a Victorian fever dream.

Baroque framed wedding photos? Up. Glossy pictures of my sexy spouse preaching in Vietnam and Haiti? Up. A completely unnecessary but deeply satisfying number of antique Victorian teacups? Check!

And then, on a whim, I ordered an acrylic paint set.

Me. Painting. I used to hate this medium of art.

Yet here I am, brush in hand, transforming this blank white canvas into something vaguely resembling art. Either Matt Silverman is my muse, or marriage triggers latent talents. I'm still investigating.

Married life, generally, has been…rich. Every morning, I pinch myself. *Did God really grant my desire this time?*

We didn't get a honeymoon because (a) I can't travel, and (b) two days after the wedding, Matt had his biannual kidney stent replacement surgery. Some couples sip champagne in Paris. The Silvermans battle surgical procedures. But we didn't care. We were married. *Married!*

Married life is surprisingly…ordinary also. Gasp! Us? Normal? Most days, we're busy fighting customer service reps to activate our wedding gift cards or debating whether to host a housewarming party. (Matt's take: "Let's just turn the heater on and call it a day.")

There are *some* perks to being a sick couple in matrimony, though. Think permanent slumber party vibes, constantly lying down together, resting, on our queen bed. At night, I indoctrinate him into musicals; he retaliates by forcing me to watch *DuckTales*. (Compromise in marriage is a tricky art—endless negotiations, zero leverage. Matt thinks he's winning this battle, but wait until he wakes up singing *Edelweiss*.) I've learned Matt's desire for wisdom has no endpoint. Matt lights up during every *DuckTales* episode, pointing out implicit moral lessons (*e.g.*, implications of stealing Scrooge McDuck's fortune). Meanwhile, I focus on more pressing concerns: consuming popcorn.

Matt, in his own right, is learning the perils of living with a wife who sheds sharp hair clips like a molting porcupine. Last week, he accidentally sat on one in bed.

"Ow—these things have fangs?"

"That's a hair clip, darling."

"Designed by an engineer or villain?"

His education in *living with a woman* continues daily. Like when he questioned when I tried straightening my curly hair on my own last week. (I'm trying to expose myself to more and more electronics to see what my brain can tolerate.)

"You know it's the same strand on the head, right? Just flatter?" Matt asked.

Then he got even more confused when I curled that freshly *straightened* strand into big *curls* with a *curling* iron.

"So girls spend time," he asked, eyebrows furrowed, "to press their hair flat only to make it curly again? Logical stuff."

"Curls on straightened hair are far superior to regular curls, Matt!"

Men are a mystery. Matt drools over my "natural beauty," giving five hundred compliments like I'm some kind of mythological goddess whenever I look like a sleep-deprived potato sack in one of his **Camp Arev** shirts, with an unhinged Armenian poof and no makeup. But the second I put on ten layers of mascara and that sexy red dress? Crickets. (Other than saying I look "extra eyelashy," with a giggle.) Someone should run a double blind study on engineers' preferences.

Matt's also learning to cope with my *lawyer-infused* methods. When picking a couch color, I made him debate all angles with me, Supreme Court style.

"You can submit all opposing arguments to me by Sunday babe, but I choose Puma Ash."

"It looks gray?"

"It's elevated gray."

"You mean gray with a superiority complex?"

As for our wedding gifts? Also a trial.

"Order in the court," I declared, holding up a supposedly *state-of-the-art* giraffe shaped dish rack. "We're here today to adjudicate the defendant's charge of being a useless wedding gift. All in favor of a return, say aye."

"Objection. It's functional, so it's a keeper," Matt replied.

But beneath the laughter and joy, there's still a lingering whisper of something darker. We're not out of the woods. Matt still battles kidney and abdominal pain. No new clinical trials in sight. His cancer still isn't spreading, miraculously, but the chemo devours him every two weeks, relentless. At least it's working to control the cancer. How long will that go on?

We also conveniently avoid all talk about our dreams for the long-term future. Too painful.

Yet Matt remains unfazed. Luckily, he's got a spiritual speed dial of six pastors he talks to, including Winston, Aren, and Calvin. Matt's even joined his other friend Aren's *Grooms with Grit* Bible study for husbands navigating marriage. (I told Matt I'm starting my own group—*Wives with Wit*. But membership remains exclusive to me.)

As I swipe a bright red brushstroke onto the canvas now, completing some flowers, my phone buzzes.

From: "*Sexy Husband.*"

Yes, after the wedding, Matt changed my official contact name in his phone to "*Lara Beautiful Wife*," so I returned the favor, Lara style. Surprised?

His text: "Home in twenty, Kitten. Can't wait to see you. Why are you so beautiful?" (Marriage has turned Trouble into a full-blown romantic. If I was reaping dividends while we were engaged, now I'm cashing in a fortune.)

I set my paintbrush down and waddle to the bathroom to wash off the paint, catching a glimpse of my new sign on the door: *The Loo*. If I'm going to pretend to be a Jane Austen heroine in this "cottage," I'm committing.

When I rush outside to get the mail, the ocean stretches before me in the distance in endless hues of blue and green. The wind carries a salty, crisp bite, filling my lungs with fresh air as I admire our new *Silverman Cottage* sign on the front door. *How did I end up here?* In this perfect little oceanside house with Daly City fog reminiscent of the British countryside? With *this* view, *this* man? *I'm living my Victorian fantasy. Thank you, Lord!*

Back inside, I shuffle past our Kitten-remodeled bookshelf, stacked high with my well-loved copies of Austen, Brontë, and Dickens. Nestled among them—as if they, too, survived the Victorian era—are Matt's board games and comic books. Nothing says *Regency drama* quite like *Batman* brooding next to *Pride and Prejudice*. (FYI: Mom has earned widespread acclaim recently as my interior decorating "assistant." Because apparently, I *too* am here only for decoration. I still can't bend down, forward or backward, or look too high up or down without spinning harder.)

The master bedroom awaits me, a sanctuary of wooden flooring, vintage oak drawers, soft linens, and two more black Victorian candle sconces. I collapse into bed. *It won't be long before Trouble walks in, demanding a snuggle.*

The fading sunlight weaves through our delicate lace curtains and ivy-framed windows. While lying down, I spot Auntie Nanor's wedding card perched on my bedside table, setting forth this verse—"This is the day that the Lord has made; we will rejoice and be glad in it" (KJV).

Rejoice.

The same word and verse God pressed onto my heart the morning of my wedding.

And now?

It lingers, insistent.

A command.

A challenge.

I stare at the ceiling, weighing the evidence, pondering the very fact I'm a married woman. Against all odds, against every grim prognosis, against every whispered doubt that we'd never make it. *This is indeed a time to rejoice.*

Lord, have I learned anything else on this journey? I exhale, pressing my palms against the blankets. *Hmm.*

Lesson one: *Nothing will stop God's will.*

Not sickness.

Not suffering.

Not even death knocking.

All things *are* possible with God because He is sovereign and "does whatever pleases him, in the heavens and on the earth." Psalm 135:6. He knows how to give good gifts and whether His people are living or dying, He'll provide—if it's His will.

Matt should have died six months after diagnosis. That's not melodrama, it's medical fact. (Statistics for small intestinal cancer.) Yet here he is, two years later. The "he almost died" obstruction crisis when we first started dating should've taken him. The kidney failure, the chemo, the exhaustion—none of it broke or stopped him from dating me. God literally kept Matt alive to marry me.

And me? I should never have survived three years completely bedridden. Three years. Without a single blood clot or bed sore. Despite the fact that I have a genetic marker for blood clots. Given that I wasn't moving my head or body *at all*, my survival was an absolute miracle (through Mom's tender, loving care). Doctors opined I wouldn't live past six months if I didn't move. But I outlived their predictions. And that's not even mentioning the jaw miracle where I was able to eat again. God literally kept me alive to marry Matt.

Lesson two: God keeps His promises.

Looking back, the pieces fit together with mystifying precision:

2017: God promised me, with a sign of rainbows—*You will marry.*

2020: Mom told me she saw a rainbow right after one of Matt's hopeful text messages while I was bedridden. *I didn't think much of it at the time.*

2022: The Holy Spirit gave Lisa's friend a vision of me standing in a field under a rainbow, right around the time Matt started visiting me in person. The Holy Spirit told her to tell me: *Her story is not over yet. God has a promise to give her first.* Then, two other rainbows followed.

2023: The poem my friends wrote at my bachelorette: *Feel the wonder of the beautiful love story God is writing and you are living.*

And let me tell you, God delivered on His promise abundantly:

I prayed for a smart man—I got a brilliant PhD/professor.

I prayed for a Godly man—I got a youth pastor and preacher who could out-quote Spurgeon.

I prayed for a talented man—I got a man who shares my love for comedy and music as a flautist.

A memory from my 2016 Bible study years ago seeps in, where an acquaintance observed: *People always say you have to put yourself out there to find a Christian spouse, but they forget God's grace is enough. He'll provide if it's His will.* That night, I remember getting into my car after the study, and the first song on the radio was *Your Grace is Enough* by Chris Tomlin. I wept tears of joy and wrote that encouragement from God in my journal at the time. *He provides all right. I found my man while on a sick bed!*

Lesson three: God orchestrates resurrections in dungeons.

At my absolute lowest—when I was newly grieving God's message to me of death instead of healing—God sent me a gift package in Matt. Out of nowhere. *Right after* that dream. A kind, wise, compassionate man who knew the ache of deep grief and was uniquely shaped to share my pain and remind me I wasn't alone in grieving death. Only God's creativity could have come up with this union at that specific timing. God gave Matt a surprising resurrection too—the chance to marry despite being terminally ill. God plants miracles in the cracks of tragedy.

Lesson four: *Suffering really does have purpose.*

God chose not to give us one another while we were healthy. Now, I see one reason why. Our wedding wasn't just about us. It was a megaphone declaration of God's glory: a testimony that God doesn't abandon His children. That even in suffering, He provides streams in the desert.

I remember praying years before ever falling ill—*Lord, let my future wedding be a testimony of Your glory.* He answered all right. Be careful what you pray for! People watched our story unfold and saw the impossible circumstances through which God brought us together.

And they marveled.

Not at us.

At God.

At God's glory and power.

It's finally dawning on me. God really *can* bring beauty and purpose out of and even in suffering. It's not just a *cliché*. When God's people experience blessings even amidst grave pain, it points to the presence of a good and loving God who sees their pain and walks them through it. Armenian culture would say, *Don't marry amidst terminal illness, are you crazy?* But 1 Corinthians 1:20 states, "Has not God made foolish the wisdom of the world?"

So what does this all mean, Lara? Turns out Matt was right that the Christian life is not for the control freak—it doesn't fit into perfect little boxes with clear, predictable outcomes. It's a wild ride, with Jesus at the wheel. How could I have been so arrogant, so blind?

And if Jesus gave me this loving *yes* to marriage, could that actually mean that His *refusals* have loving, good purposes too? But we just might not understand how, in our human accounting. That's what Matt's been saying all along...

Oh no, I'm still not spiritually mature enough for *that* question, Lord. Not when it comes to You saying *no* to *life* at least. *Lord, change me! You've shown me now how you retroactively use suffering for powerful purposes.*

Maybe I don't have to have all the answers anymore. Maybe I can just loosen my grip—a little—on what happens next. Matt might not die. His conviction last year that he will "remain" might be right? And maybe that dream I had of my own death won't come true anytime soon because God just granted me a promise. What kind of promise would it be if He snatches it back immediately?

Either way, I can't keep living in *maybe* anymore. God never gave me a specific time in that dream. As a result, I spent all of last year foolishly predicting my own death date, convinced I wouldn't make it to the wedding. All it did was steal my peace. The timing is in God's hands; I don't want to live in fear of imminent death anymore. I have to try to let go.

For a moment, I do.

I close my eyes and exhale.

But—*Lord, I still just don't understand Your ways.*

Why *that* dream? Why not something gentle, reassuring? Why not a dream that said, "Accept your illness and rejoice that you will heal in eternity?" That would have given me peace and acceptance in the "now" rather than instigating fear about my future.

Instead, You said I'm *climbing a ladder* and then—*Christ is coming to take me home.* How could I not spiral into wondering *when* I will die and believe I would never get married? *I'm sorry, Lord. Am I the only Christian who finds Your communication confusing sometimes?*

You also gave me a word of *surrender*, and I thought You were saying *no* to marriage. *Surrender. Not my will, but Yours, be done.*

And yet—at the same time—You sent me all those other positive signs, indicating "Yes!" *The rainbow vision from Lisa's friend. The "love story" coincidences. The "desires of my heart" verse.*

One moment, green light. One moment red. It's difficult to discern Your will, Lord, because sometimes You give us outcome-predictive encouragements—like your rainbow promise to me in 2017 of future marriage—but other times, you just give us principles to walk in faith by. I guess Your word of *surrender* turned out to be the latter, instructing me to trust Your outcome, whatever it is.

I *still* don't know when to tell the difference. Trying to discern God's will is one of the hardest parts of the Christian walk. "God is not the author of confusion, but of peace" (1 Corinthians 14:33) so what am I missing?

Maybe it's not about figuring out God's will, or about getting a clear message. Maybe it's about trusting regardless of whether we understand His communication perfectly.

The garage door creaks open, jolting me out of my thoughts. *He's home.* Matt's footsteps echo down the hallway until he strides in.

"There's my girl."

It's his signature greeting, every single time.

His gaze shifts left to a new plaque hanging on the wall:

BEWARE KITTEN TERRITORY

"Kitten territory?" he asks.

"Gotta keep my boy in line."

"Are we at installment four of your Victorian shopping spree yet?"

"Installment three. Think of it like a historical restoration project. Notice anything else?"

He scans the room, then his eyes land on the vintage brown sign over our bed. He reads it aloud:

> *I have found the one whom my soul loves.*
> *Song of Songs 3:4*

"You like it?"

"Love it. It's a beautiful verse, Kitten."

"So what's it gonna be tonight, Trouble? *DuckTales* or *My Fair Lady*?"

He pauses then gives me that subtle tilt of his head, a plea hidden behind amusement. I know that look.

"*DuckTales?*"

40

The Love Story Goes Marital

I'm in the kitchen at 10 A.M., smearing peanut butter onto sliced bread, making lunch for Trouble to take to work as he rushes out. Fog curls outside the window, wrapping this May morning in a wet, gray hug. Second month of marriage.

Peanut butter.
Jelly.
A banana.
Grape juice.

Always the same. Partly because of my man's dietary restrictions from cancer, and partly because my man's a creature of simplicity and habit.

Church. Family. Students. That's his holy trinity.

Plus peanut butter.

"Don't forget your hat," I say, handing him his brown bag lunch and crawling back into bed. He slings his backpack over one shoulder and leans over me on the bed.

"Got chemo today," he says casually. "Dad will drive me straight from work if I need it, okay?"

He presses a kiss to my nose. Lips. Forehead. Lips again. It's his ritual. Never forgets. A kiss in all the right places, like he's memorizing me before walking out the door. I love it. *Finally Lord, your casting is on point. Being a wife—a role I'm absolutely loving.*

"Don't work too hard, Trouble," I mutter.

Trouble. My nickname for the man who insists on being everybody's hero, while cancer is actively trying to kill him. *By nightfall, if I get my way, our hero will be stepping into the spotlight… Will he rise to the occasion?*

The front door clicks shut, and he's gone.

An hour later, I'm back in the kitchen frying Jewish latkes (potato pancakes).

Goal: don't activate the fire alarm like last time.

As the potatoes and onions sizzle in hot oil, a savory caramelized scent mingles with the starchy, buttery depth of potatoes.

The weird part? I'm enjoying this. Another plot twist no one saw coming.

Reason one? *Challenge.* Watching Matt whip up sourdough from scratch last month lit a competitive fire in me. He made it look easy. Too easy. I wanted in. So I learned. Slowly. Now, I cook as much as my strength and brain allow and he's reaping dividends. *That rascal knew exactly what he was doing.*

I usually stand for half an hour to an hour to prepare part of any meal, then lie down, spinning harder after that focus and exertion, then get up hours later to finish the rest. Matt fills in for anything I can't do, *e.g.*, bend to pull a tray in or out of the oven.

Reason two? *Purpose.* Feeding a special someone feels like a tangible purpose I haven't had in five years. Something small packed with meaning. Years ago, I laughed at the idea of being domestic. *"Lara Palanjian, cooking? Please. I have better things to do, like DoorDash and a legal brief."*

Now? Lara *Silverman* gets it. I'm here feeding my man like he's a spoiled Roman emperor, at my own choosing. Every dish feels like one tiny piece of the puzzle keeping him alive. He's been gaining weight lately, so Operation "Lara is the perfect housewife" just might be working? Maybe.

(FYI: I concluded last month that if I can't find my worth in law, it's wise to find it in wifedom, and that includes making the most delicious meals this side of a *Food Network* lawsuit. Because if I'm not famous for winning cases, I'm going to be famous for winning taste buds.)

Reason three? *Creativity.* Cooking is my new "stage." I can't act in a real production for obvious reasons (still largely bedridden, no car rides). But I can cook. At my own pace. And if I can't beat illness, gosh darn it I'm going to beat eggs. Cooking is now art. Beauty. Sanity. Control. God's creation. It's navigating the grief of losing my career by reminding me I'm more than just a one-dimensional career woman. International recipes and paintings are my means to travel the world—without moving. Today it's Israel. Yesterday it was Greek gyros. Last week I nearly blacked out making a beef bourguignon for my "French-themed" night to surprise Trouble.

I carefully place another latke down on a napkin to soak the oil. *Hmm. I hope these turn out okay.*

Hours later at five, a text buzzes on my phone.

From: *Sexy Husband*: "TBA 15 minutes."

I drag myself off the bed and into the kitchen again, still nauseous and spinning harder from earlier. I had to lie down and cope with the intense pain in my brain for four hours, thanks to the exhaustion of making latkes just for an hour.

As I'm washing dishes, Joel walks through the front door, smiling wide like he's about to deliver the crown jewels, followed by Matt, who looks like he just wrestled death and came out with a participation trophy.

"Told you I always bring him back," Joel chirps, sipping from his ever-present blue coffee mug. Joel is the human version of that unshakable mug—always full, always stable, never spills. It's like he decided long ago that nothing, not even his son's second cancer, would break him. He glides through the house, taking out heavy trash bags, fixing things I didn't even know were broken. *Thank God for Joel.*

Matt crashes onto the couch, kicking off his shoes and beloved hat. "The nurse laughed at the kitten tattoo on my chest when she changed my chemo port," he groans.

I snort, brandishing a spatula from the sink. "Excellent. You deserve it."

"This is gettin' out of hand," he whines. "I'll get my revenge on you, you evil cat!"

Joel arches an eyebrow, watching our dynamic unfold like he's observing a rare species of lunatics in their natural habitat.

Minutes later, we're downing latkes. Joel, bless him, eats like it's his last meal. Whether he actually loves my culinary concoctions or just pretends to, I'll take the win. After dinner, I drop a towel on the floor. "Babe, can you get that?" I ask. Matt, knowing I can't bend in any direction without the vertigo sharply worsening, scoops it up without hesitation. Joel, meanwhile, is now emptying the bottom dishwasher rack because I can't bend to reach that floor.

"Oh, by the way," I say casually, trying not to press my luck. "We have to film one scene tonight, Trouble."

Matt instantly groans like I just sentenced him to hard labor. "Kitten, I told you. I'm not an actor."

Last month, dictating on my phone in bed, I wrote a tongue-in-cheek "movie" script about being newlyweds, with tons of fake arguments we're supposedly having. I don't know what that says about me, about Matt, or about both of us. *Art. I need art. If I can't be in a play or in court, I'm bringing a play to this fake cottage. We're in the business of rejoicing, people.*

"I wanted a wife, not a co-star," Matt laments, eyes twinkling with *Can I get away with saying this?*

"You should've read the fine print. That's it," I exclaim, tickling him hard until he's laughing so hard he's gasping for air.

In no time, the three of us settle into our roles in front of our kitchen counter. Matt, the reluctant star; me, the overzealous playwright; Joel, the long-suffering third wheel and cameraman who keeps us both sane. Matt eyes Joel, giving off "I signed up for this chaos, and only half regret it" vibes. *Thank God Joel loves videography. It's almost like he auditioned to be my father-in-law and was the perfect man for the role.*

Joel shouts, "Lights, camera, ACTION!"

Me: "Matt, I just spent the last 4.6 hours setting our meal itinerary for Pastor Calvin's visit. Beef and chicken kebab, salmon, trout, hummus, rice, yogurt soup, kofte, choreg, red and white wine, sparkling apéritif, Armenian coffee and baklava."

Matt: "I thought we were just makin' self-serve sandwiches."

Me: "Self-serve sandwiches? Do you really want to tarnish our reputation? This menu is part of my *perfect housewife* initiative, so don't ruin it!"

Matt: "Last time I checked, Calvin's fine eatin' sandwiches."

Me: "Didn't you read the *Newlywed Guide* Section 3.8 Subsection (B)(1)(r)? *Never* serve a casual meal to a pastor—especially in the Armenian community."

Matt: "Casual is fine."

Me: "Casual is not Biblical! Proverbs 21:20 says the 'wise have wealth and luxury.' Check the New Living Translation."

Matt: "You're takin' that way out of context."

Me: "Lawyers don't do context."

Matt: "That's it. I'm done, I refuse to sing one more musical."

Me: "What? Oh no, we're having our first fight! Someone get me my 'marriage works if you try hard manual'! I think there was something about forgiveness in the Bible but I forgot the point babe!"

Matt: "Forgiveness can't help if our marriage lacks efficiency. I plotted the cost of your spending versus the length of our fights, which are consistently longer than the national average."

Joel shouts: "Cut!"

If Matt and I were giddy teenagers when dating, we've now evolved into our new roles with surprising ease. I'm finally getting "domesticated" as Mom victoriously joked last week, while Matt is expanding his horizons, leaning into newfound acting skills. But after twenty minutes of today's "horizon-expanding" escapade, Matt, face pale, is about to pass out.

"Good work, Trouble. Okay, okay. Let's go lie down," I say. *Have mercy; he's on chemo.* We collapse onto bed, holding hands, as Joel heads out.

When the silence settles, I ask, "How was work today, love?"

Matt sighs. "Went to lunch with the department."

"All five of you?" His "department" consists of a quintet of middle-aged women who've essentially adopted him as their honorary son.

"They started girl talk, so I zoned out and started calculatin' divisions of prime numbers." He giggles like a guilty kid caught with his hand in the cookie jar.

Five minutes later, he's out cold. His head rests against my shoulder, his chemo bag wedged awkwardly between us. I watch him sleep, tracing the soft curve of his fingers, feeling both sadness and overwhelming gratitude.

This is love. Not candlelit dinners at five-star restaurants. Not glamorous parties where I parade him around like some trophy PhD husband. This is the real thing—his cheek pressed to my shoulder, the sound of his soft breaths filling the room. Love is a man with chemo fatigue still agreeing to act in his wife's play because he knows it gives her joy.

Perhaps God's purpose for marriage is entirely different than what I thought. It seems He does have a purpose for a marriage like ours that isn't conventionally "normal." Here we are—both deeply broken by illness, yet profoundly bound in love within a God-ordained union.

Sure, we have blunders here and there. Take our ongoing cold war over the thermostat. I have hot body flashes from migraines and his body always shivers due to chemo. Thus, the weekly passive aggressive scene:

I stomp into the bedroom, wiping sweat off my forehead.

"Can we turn the heat down?"

He looks up from his laptop, his face stoic with a hint of irritation. "We just turned it down."

"I'm hot."

"I'm cold."

"Where's your sacrificial attitude as a husband? Have you never read Ephesians?"

"Pretty sure the Bible doesn't cover thermostat settings."

"If you're not willing to freeze for me now, what won't you be willing to do for me in ten years?"

Cue my dramatic exit with the flair of a woman wronged, while Matt giggles in victory.

But the real tension comes from outside. My parents, bless them, haven't quite mastered "leaving and cleaving." Last week, I casually mentioned we had ants. The next day, they showed up armed to the teeth with ant traps and enough bug spray to fumigate the entire block.

Mom: "Where's the queen, Vayel?"

Pops: "We must go for the source!"

Matt: muttering stoically, "Doesn't work."

Then there was the time Mom and one of her Golden Girls conspired to "optimize" our kitchen organization. Matt opened a cabinet later that night, pulling out a measuring cup like it was some ancient artifact. "Can't find any plates."

For any *real* squabbles based on miscommunications, Matt and I communicate and resolve them immediately—because as an emotionally ferocious wildcat I apparently can't sleep otherwise.

But even our most "heated" discussions are not real fights, and I'm not intentionally romanticizing our marriage. It's honestly a byproduct of marrying Matt Silverman. His whole "earthly things are inconsequential" *chill* vibe is infuriatingly effective at keeping the peace. All couples should try it. I've come to the conclusion that if everyone lived like Matt, ninety-nine percent of marital fights would vanish. *Don't invest in a rental.*

And when you're staring down mortality, petty squabbles over who last cleaned the Brita filter seem exactly that—petty. Instead, we cling to each other. Every moment feels urgent, precious. If everyone lived like they were dying next month, the world would be a kinder place.

These are our days. Matt goes to work and church, and humors me by starring in my "film." Playing Hamlet. Sherlock Holmes. He even walked a makeshift fashion runway in our living room, making him the first engineering PhD to moonlight as a VOGUE model. Sacrificial love at its finest.

Luckily, all my friends have made a point to visit me at our little "cottage" too. *What a gift to fellowship with them these days.*

And then there are the funerals. Matt's been to three in the last two months. Just acquaintances from other churches. Cancer doesn't stop Matt from showing up for others. His choice to attend reminds me of Ecclesiastes 7:2—"It is better to go to a house of mourning than to go to a house of feasting, for death is the destiny of everyone; the living should take this to heart." *Lord, help me do so.*

𝄞

I hit "send" and watch my email swoosh into the ether.

"Babe, just sent the film to our listserv!" I shout with pride, lying in bed.

I reread my email—"Presenting our new feature-length movie, *The Love Story Goes Marital!* The family fun comedy you didn't know you needed. Viewer sarcasm required."

The last few weeks, Matt taught me videography and I turned our play into a full-length film. It still hurts my eyes to stare at any electronic screen for longer than twenty minutes, the static glow of the monitor clawing at my brain. But I've found a system: thirty minutes of intense computer editing lying in bed, then rest for three hours, rinse, repeat. Despite electrical sensations from the computer work, more vertigo and nausea, it feels *so* good to be doing *some kind* of work.

Four hours later, Aren's name lights up Matt's phone. The pastor-turned lawyer from church. Matt swipes to answer. *This is going to be good.*

"You two are hilarious," Aren laughs over the speaker. "Never in a million years did I think I'd see Matt Silverman doing a fashion show on YouTube. God's miracles."

Matt goes beet red. He points at the phone and then at me, mouthing, *You owe me.*

"Aren," I joke, "We've got problems. Whenever I win arguments against Matt, there's no judge to announce the winner. I wish marriage were more like a court of law."

"Yeah, seriously," he laughs. *From one lawyer to another.*

When we hang up twenty minutes later, Matt turns to me. "You owe me ten seasons of *DuckTales*."

"Oh, please. You looked fantastic in that sequined blazer."

"I looked like a disco ball."

"A stylish disco ball."

The truth is, I feel ridiculous too. These skits are silly and so far from anything I thought I'd be doing with my life. I miss law. The order, the logic, the writing, the sense of justice and solving problems. But then there's this other part of me—the part that's grateful I can even sit upright long enough to do something creative these days.

Years ago, while strictly bedridden, God gave me a word through a timely sermon: "[You] will see the goodness of the Lord in the land of the living." Psalm 27:13. And here I am. Still spinning, in severe pain and mostly bedridden, yes. Still wrestling with a brain that feels like it's been rewired by a drunk electrician. But, I'm married. Standing. Walking even. Phone calls and washing my head still trigger electric sensations in my brain, but God sustains me somehow each time. It's not the life I planned, but it's the one God is shaping, purposeful in ways I may never fully grasp.

Every morning, I wake up, swing my legs over the edge of the bed, and pray, "Lord, help me tolerate staying upright for an hour." And somehow, I do, before needing to collapse again. I'm seeing real truth in Lamentations 3:22-23—"[H]is compassions never fail. They are new every morning." *Keep your focus on eternity, Lara. Try. These symptoms are of this temporary world. Don't invest in a rental.*

I just might be getting closer to coming to terms with this illness?

Matt nudges me out of my thoughts. "You know they're gonna roast us in the YouTube movie comments."

"Oh, absolutely." I grin. "But we're giving the people what they need: joy."

41

Honeymoon's Over

"Ow!"

Matt's grunts pierce through our bedroom—gut-wrenching cries every fifteen minutes I've never heard him utter before. He's wincing in pain, sprawled in his navy-blue joggers on the bed beside me, clutching his abdomen.

It's August 20th—five months into marriage.

Goal: minimize my husband's agony *asap*.

Back in June, we traveled to Sevan's wedding in sunny Palo Alto and even went a few more miles down south to Matt's parents' home for the first time. It felt like a miracle and worth sustaining the agonizing pain of getting into a car again—a chance for a kind of honeymoon. Since pulling off our wedding, we've both learned to embrace *risk* even more so.

We played tourist, donning matching Hawaiian outfits and staying in hotels as rest breaks on the way to and from, allowing my brain to rest from the car's motion every ten miles. Every time my brain started shaking harder during a drive, I silently repeated my new favorite verse—God is an "ever-present help in trouble." Psalm 46:1. Matt had not landed in the ER for months, a record since his diagnosis two years ago. "Havin' a wife is my good luck charm," he'd joked.

But now, that fragile bubble has burst. The summer honeymoon is over, literally and figuratively. His latest CAT scan results came back yesterday.

Cancer growth.

The chemo has stopped working.

For the first time since his diagnosis.

His oncologist, Doctor Kranter at Crescent Bay Medical, laid it out in his clinical tone this morning. "There's cancer growth I haven't seen before. Your severe pain this week is likely from progression. The body builds resistance to the chemo's effectiveness. Luckily, I don't see obstructions, which is surprising. But I'm switching you to a new chemo—oral pills, mostly, so no more pump. This second chemo might buy you 120 to 150 days."

I glance at Matt's pale face now, hours after that call. *How much longer can Matt keep this up?*

Bitterness rises inside me. *This cannot be happening.* The man I love is both mine and not mine, because our time together is now bound by a ticking clock: 120 to 150 days.

Was Jesus bribing me? Did He give me one yes—a wedding—to be followed by a thousand nos? I had risked falling in love. Can I really risk my husband dying?

"Ow," Matt grunts again, the intensity of his pain rising. "Can you bring me my pain meds? I think it's time again."

I rush to his side with the pills and his water bottle. The pain meds were controlling his pain before. Not anymore. So Kranter hiked up his doses.

A few hours later, Matt is a tiny bit more relaxed, sitting up. "I think this higher dose is finally kickin' in." He exhales hard. "Well, I don't know where we go from here. It's unlikely this second chemo will work. The first regimen was way stronger." His voice is hollow, almost like he's talking to himself.

"We'll just keep searching for clinical trials, love," I reply, stroking his bald head with feverish vigor. "I know you've been trying nonstop."

"I just wish we could be normal," he mutters. "My intestines are stickin' out of me." He never complains to the point where hearing him complain feels unnatural. His shirt rides up just enough for me to see the angry red skin surrounding his ostomy, a sharp, raw reminder of everything that's wrong in our lives.

"I'm so sorry," I reply, grabbing his hand. "You don't deserve this. Any of it."

He exhales sharply again. "Wanted to take you to Haiti, Vietnam. All those places we could do missions together."

I bite my lip. "I know."

Silence.

We're on a first name basis with uncertainty now, kind of like living in a never-ending cliffhanger. At least before, we were relying on the first chemo to keep cancer growth at bay. The band-aid has been ripped off.

"Lara," he asks, hesitating somewhat. "If something…really does happen to me, how do I let the youth group kids watch me die without losin' their faith? I know I always bring this up but—"

I remind myself of everything Matt has taught me. "Babe, God's in control of their faith, remember? You told me your favorite doctrine is perseverance of the saints. Once God has you, He never lets you go. None of this is your fault or in your control." *He still thinks he's somehow letting others down. How can I change that?*

Matt nods, his expression tight. "I can't leave you behind either. Just like my grandpa left my grandma too early. I have to take care of you. We were goin' to—"

"And now we have a new plan, Trouble," I cut him off, forcing the words through the ache in my chest. "This new chemo agent just might be God's surprise deliverance. You never know. We'll fight back with joy, like you taught me. Singing through fire, remember?"

Three days later, we find ourselves lying side by side in bed, seeking solace in each other once more. But this time, he's the strong one.

"I used to be a genuinely happy person," I pout. "Now I'm so jealous of healthy families who can work and get in cars without penalty. I don't want to watch church on Zoom anymore. I want to be there with you every time."

"Try not to let bitterness consume you, Lara."

"But I'm even failing at faith babe. You're the perfect Christian, never getting mad at God. If you get any holier, I'm gonna start sprinkling holy water on myself to keep up."

"Lara, stop. I'm not perfect. Don't idolize me. I'm a sinner like anyone else."

"See, even when I compliment you, you stay rooted in the gospel."

"Don't be so hard on yourself or compare yourself to anyone else. God's completin' His good work in you, even now."

"But Matt, I'm so worried. I know you've had a conviction of healing, but... remember last year God showed me that couple in that one devotional? The wife died of cancer in the end. What if—" My voice breaks. "What if that's us? What if He's been preparing us all along? Either you die...or I randomly die? I still believe that dream was from the Lord."

Matt sighs. "God doesn't always give us direct answers. He just comforts us. God was probably just showin' you that other couples have walked similar paths through grief. He gives principles, not always outcomes."

"But God sometimes *does* speak into situations with predictive outcomes. One time God told me to be brave while I was bedridden, and then stabbing leg pains hit right after out of nowhere. How are we supposed to tell when He is informing or warning us in advance of specific outcomes, versus just giving us guiding principles?"

"There are no clear-cut answers. At the end of the day, we hear from Him but then we hold our convictions loosely, with humility. Remember, Paul wrote that in Heaven we'll understand more clearly. Read 1 Corinthians 13:12—'For now we see only a reflection as in a mirror; then we shall see face to face.'"

"If that's the case, I can't wait to be done with *this* part of faith training." I exhale hard. "I'm so sorry for my bitterness, love. I can't even sing worship songs. Whenever I hear 'God is good' lately, I cringe inside. I don't know how to change."

"It's okay. I get it. We're goin' through a lot, Lara."

Even married now, I'm riding on the coattails of Matt's faith. He gives me constant grace, remaining patient in my emotional outbursts without judging me.

But tonight, I still feel like a rubber band stretched too thin. I get up and rush to the kitchen, desperate for some semblance of control. *Brownies. I'll make brownies.*

Something I can do right. Something I can control.

I heat a pot of Victorian tea and get to work. Soon, the rich aroma of chocolate rises. But when I peer into the oven door, my heart plummets. I can spot from an angle that some of the edges are burned to a crisp. Before I realize it, I'm sobbing, my hands trembling as I frantically start mixing a new batch, desperate to make it right.

Matt walks in, his steps cautious, like he's approaching a wounded animal.

"Why are you cryin' babe?" he says, bending to pull the tray out of the oven for me.

I plunk the mixing bowl down onto the counter. "Brownies are bad; starting over." Matt looks at the edge of the brownie tray, looking confused. "They're fine."

"Oh Matt," I say, another sob bursting out, "this joy stuff is impossible sometimes. Don't take this the wrong way, but I don't want to be a cook, a painter, or a filmmaker. I wanted to be a lawyer. Does God really have to humble me like this? He couldn't just let me lose a job and give me another one? Why give me talents and then make me too sick to use them?"

Matt wraps his arms around me.

"I haven't accomplished anything in six years. I can't even make brownies."

"Lara," Matt says, looking me straight in the eyes an inch away from my face. "Do you love me for my PhD, or my heart?"

"Both," I pout sheepishly, avoiding eye contact.

"I asked which one."

I roll my eyes, a small, unwilling smile tugging at my lips. "Your heart."

"Good. Then stop puttin' your worth in things that don't matter—law, cooking. Even bein' a good wife. It's all pride. God's proud of you because of your perseverance in Him and suffering His will, not because of what you accomplish in this temporary world."

He pulls me in tighter. "Look, God's using your suffering to prepare you for an eternal role in His Kingdom. Paul wrote that our 'light and momentary troubles are *achieving* for us an eternal glory that far outweighs them all.' Focus on that this week: eternal glory. Okay?"

Hours later, I pray, raw and desperate. *Okay, Lord. Make me love eternity more than work, health, or life. I'm open. It's taken me a year and a half since that dream to even get to this place where I can ask genuinely.*

Before we sleep, an email pings on my phone from my friend Tim, who is sharing his latest Christian song release with his email list. Title: *Valuable*. I click play, and the theme in the lyrics washes over me like rain after a drought—*You're more than your achievements. You're a child of God. That's where your worth lies. In Christ alone. In His eternal purpose for you.*

Tears spill down my cheeks. The timing is uncanny. *I know this is meant for me, Lord.*

Then, I open my second daily devotional app, and I can't believe what I'm reading:

> Are you grappling with serious illness? Jesus remains enough when we or our loved ones lack good health. He wants you to release your bitterness and to know you have value regardless of circumstances. It is often when our longings are not fulfilled that we bear more fruit for God's Kingdom and are being prepared for roles in God's Kingdom. Keep your eyes focused on the eternal glory to come.

I close my eyes, clutching my phone to my chest. *Wow, Lord. What are the chances? Matt just said all this. I know You see me and are trying to change me.*

The next week, I listen to countless sermons that dive deep into 2 Corinthians 4:17-18, the verse Matt highlighted: "For our light and momentary troubles are *achieving* for us an eternal glory that far outweighs them all. So we fix our eyes not on what is seen, but on what is unseen, since what is seen is temporary, but what is unseen is eternal."

I learn that God, here, is not diminishing the severity of our earthly pain. It's real. It's agonizing. But He *is* maximizing our perspective so we see that the coming glory will far outshine this temporary suffering. Interestingly, God wants us to *share* His glory in Heaven. John 17:22. And He actually uses all our suffering here on earth to somehow *create* that glory and *prepare us* for that glory.

So all our suffering here has precious purpose because it mysteriously "achieves" our glory in Heaven? Okay, this is yet another reason God allows suffering that's finally clicking at a heart level.

Three reasons and counting at this point: Testing and proving the genuineness of our faith as a testimony to the world (*test to testimony*), showcasing God's glory and power, and somehow creating our eternal glory.

But the math here is downright mysterious. How can suffering create glory? Maybe that precise calculation is one of those "secret things" that "belong to the Lord[.]" Deuteronomy 29:29.

Or maybe part of the answer is that suffering forms in us the Christlike characteristics we need to thrive in our eternal roles in Heaven. I recently listened to Pastor Joe Sweet (of Shekinah Worship Center) preach that "this life is just training for reigning, the dress rehearsal for your eternal assignment." *This is what Matt's been saying—God's preparing me for an eternal role. Maybe this makes some sense now...*

Scripture affirms this idea. Revelation 22:3 and Isaiah 65:17-23 make clear we will "serve" under Jesus in Heaven, stewarding His "new earth." Similarly, 2 Timothy 2:12 promises that "if we endure, we will also reign with Him." If we're to be entrusted with any kind of authority, wouldn't we need the kind of humble, Christlike character that can handle it? The Bible is direct about how that character is formed: "[S]uffering produces perseverance; perseverance, character; and character, hope." Romans 5:3-4. In other words, we're "training for reigning." We're building up hope and joy in Christ and His eternal purposes *alone*.

Jesus even underscored this point in His explanation of the parable of the talents. It seems our faithfulness to God's will for our lives on earth isn't pointless—it's formative. Just as the master in the parable told his servant, "'You have been faithful with a few things; I will put you in charge of many things'" (Matthew 25:23), our present obedience somehow shapes our eternal assignments.

Hmm. This is a pretty revolutionary way to view suffering, and something I've never really meditated on before. Wow, Lord. Maybe I wasn't slapped on a bed for three years for nothing. Only God knows how I'm really changing...am I?

At the end of the day, however suffering ultimately transforms into glory, I've learned a big lesson this week. Christians are spiritual stock investors, trading present pain for eternal gain. Buy low, rejoice high. Every tear, every ache, every heartbreak is a deposit in a glory we cannot yet grasp.

A heavenly stock market where crying in the shower actually increases one's net worth? I'm in.

Eternal glory. Something to focus on.

Turns out God's portfolio has a miraculous return on investment—it's 100 percent long on the redemption of suffering.

Maybe Jesus really *is* the Redeemer?

42

The Caged Bird Sings Indeed

Day 13 on new chemo

Our doorbell rings, cutting through the silence.

"Who's here on a Sunday afternoon?" I mumble, pulling the comforters up to my chin.

Matt groans, swinging his legs over the edge of the bed and heading to the front door. "If it's Girl Scout cookies, we're buyin' 'em out."

It's Labor Day weekend, 2 P.M., but while the world blasts music in backyard barbecues, we're in pajamas, silent and emotionally drained, even after watching church on Zoom in bed. There's a heaviness in the air. Matt is fighting severe kidney pain from his third biannual kidney stent surgery last week. And the chemo clock countdown relentlessly ticks in my head: *120 days max.*

I hear the creak of the front door open, and Matt's voice, brighter now, summons me. "Lara, come. Looks like we've got a big surprise."

Curiosity yanks me out of bed. I change into some jeans, and waddle into the family room, bracing against the turbulent sensation of the room shaking.

And then, I see them.

The Boldi kids.

Four of Matt's prized youth group kids, with their parents in tow.

"The Boldis!" My voice oscillates between surprise and disbelief. *And is that a cello by our couch? I've seen surprise visits, but a surprise cello? That's next level.*

Rubina, their mom, strides towards the kitchen counter with two giant Trader Joe's bags dangling from her arms. She unloads crackers, smoked salmon, cheeses, sourdough bread, chocolates, and those fancy bottles of sparkling juice that make you feel rich.

"Thought you could use some cheering up on the holiday," her husband Armen comments. "Hope we're not imposing."

"No, not at all," Matt replies, his face lighting up.

"You didn't have to do this Rubina, thank you!" I exclaim, gluttonously examining the food. *Is that the scent of smooth dark chocolate with sea salt?*

"Nonsense," Rubina replies, placing a homemade lasagna dish into the fridge to boot. "Church ended, and we wanted to drop by with some goodies."

All the church ladies have been bringing food on and off to help us out, but not usually by such wonderful surprise. Armenian women express love through cooking. Still, I often find myself wondering, *God, why not just heal us? Asking for charity is so embarrassing.* But Matt calls out my pride, saying, "They want to be Jesus' hands and feet comfortin' us. God's grace at work. Let 'em help. You're makin' your symptoms worse cookin' all the time."

Rubina's eighteen-year-old son Andrew plops a massive fruit basket on our dining room table. "This was outside your door."

Matt tears open the card on top. "It's from Toukhig and her daughter," he reads softly. "Thanking me for teacher appreciation week."

I smile inside. God is clearly using Matt's youth group to encourage us today.

After Armen leads a short Bible meditation, Andrew's eyes

glint with mischief. "So, Matt, how about some music? Got your flute? Lara, how about some vocals?"

"Oh, nah...it's okay," I reply quickly, feeling uncharacteristically shy, but secretly wanting to belt out a Broadway chorus.

"I'm in," Matt counters, reaching for his flute on the fireplace mantel.

Andrew grins wide. "Do you mind if I open your keyboard?"

Within minutes, the Boldi kids are pulling out instruments like they're headlining at the Hollywood Bowl. Ethan and Christine on cello and clarinet. Nicholas wielding a glossy gold trumpet.

"Do you kids just carry these around?" I ask, bewildered.

Nicholas smiles. "You never know when a jazz session might break out."

"Jazz?" I blink. "I didn't know you guys like jazz."

Before I know it, Andrew's fingers are gliding effortlessly over the keyboard through a smooth jazz lick I almost recognize, blending seamlessly with his siblings' instruments. Forget von Trapps. This is the Armenian Jackson 5.

But four.

And classier.

"Is that *Just a Closer Walk With Thee?*" I inquire.

"Yeah." Ethan nods warmly, looking up from the bow on his cello.

Rubina commands, "Join in Matt and Lara!"

Without thinking, I pull up the lyrics on my phone. In minutes, my solo vocals soar above the chaos as Matt's flute flirts with the melody, light and playful.

For the first time in weeks, a rush of endorphins—nostalgia, joy, that familiar excitement of performing—flushes through my body. I'm literally singing lead vocals in a full-blown jazz gospel band, right here in my own family room.

Forget streams—this is a waterfall in the desert. What are the odds that Matt's youth group kids would be jazz prodigies? *I finally feel part of my church community again. If I can't go to church, church is coming to me!* (And did anyone tell these kids they should audition for *America's Most Talented Youth Group?*)

All the while, Rubina and Armen film us on their phones, smiling wide with pride. At the third verse, I catch Matt's face. The battle for his life has been intense—loss of muscles and strength, crushing pain, chemo. But now his eyes shine with happiness and his demeanor is relaxed, almost as if he's forgotten his kidney pain. He's reliving his marching band days while I'm reliving my jazz choir days.

When the song ends, Rubina proposes, "Maybe you all can perform this at church sometime?"

"Yes!" I blurt, without thinking, then my heart sinks. *When? I can't get in a car anytime soon because I pushed it way too hard this summer.*

Matt nods. "Why not? We'll find a way."

I immediately stroke Matt's bald head out of sheer joy. (Somewhere post-"I do," I started rubbing Matt's shiny dome, and well, never stopped. He enters—I stroke. He leaves and comes back—I stroke. A reflex. Touch is my love language, and let me tell you, that lack of hair is a *gift*. No barriers, just pure skin-to-skin connection with his big brain. VIP access to the smoothest stress ball ever.)

Matt's face flashes one emotion—embarrassed. *Deal with it, Trouble.*

After the Boldis leave, the house feels quieter but fuller. I immediately slap a piece of smoked salmon on sourdough and pop it into Matt's mouth. "Babe, savor the rich woodsy smokiness!"

Matt, mouth still open, collapses onto the couch. "Talk about God's timin', eh, Kitten? Still sustainin' us." *Thank you, Lord, for parachuting the von Trapps...I mean...Boldis...into our home today.* Who knew smoked salmon and a jazz band could double as a grief support group?

Matt adds, "Guess we needed a reminder to climb back aboard the joy train. God pulls joy out of grief better than a magician at a sold-out show." *Joy in grief. Our old friend.*

I've seen God's other unexpected gifts of joy and provision recently too. Take our new Christian housekeeper, Darcy. A lovely woman Anna found for us who helps in ways I can't—like bending down to clean the bathrooms or the laundry. What makes Darcy even more special is that she prays with us during every visit, bringing comfort and grace into our little home. If all these miracles keep up, I might start recommending suffering as a fast-track to divine housekeeping.

The following day, Matt suggests we finish that one Bible devotional we've been putting off because we've been too caught up in our gloom. It's called "The Sound of Worship." We finally film it, talking into Matt's camera:

> A worship-centered life helps us persevere through suffering, shifting our focus from temporal, earthly things to the permanent eternal gifts and love God has in store for us. In Acts 16, we find Paul and Silas, falsely accused and in prison. But verse 25 says: 'About midnight, Paul and Silas were praying and singing hymns to God, and the other prisoners were listening to them.' Beaten and chained, they worshiped through the fire, and even their jailer wanted to be baptized after witnessing their faith. In times of distress and grief, worship helps us persevere and encourages others in surprising ways. Never forget how God can turn your test into a testimony.

In the last line of the video clip, Matt stares playfully into the camera. "So, how do we worship through the fire, Lara?"

I immediately start singing that classic number from *The Sound of Music* about starting with the basics—ABCs for reading, and solfège for "praising."

"Do-Re-Mi-Fa-Sol-La-Ti—"

"Do!" Matt finishes with a proud smile.

Day 31

The garage door grinds open, and my heart leaps into my throat, my grip tightening on what I'm holding. *Matt's home. What will he think?*

I'm perched on the edge of our guest room bed, half-hidden in the shadows, my pulse thrumming like a hummingbird caught in a jar.

The front door creaks open, then closes with a clap. Even with his hiked-up pain medications, Matt continues to drive in to work for short "in person" stays to give lectures when he can.

His keys clatter onto the kitchen counter. "Kitten? Grabbed In-N-Out. Had some strength for the drive." The scent of grilled beef, freshly baked buns, and grilled onions instantly hits my imagination.

Matt's footsteps start down the hall toward me. My heart pounds harder, each step sounding like a countdown to this room until—

He arrives, stopping in the doorway. "There's my gir—"

He freezes.

His gaze drops to the object in my hands, and his brow furrows.

Slowly, his mouth opens, then closes, like he's trying to form words but the sight of me has temporarily fried his circuits.

"Is that...a violin?" His voice goes up a pitch higher than usual.

I can't help it—I laugh. "Yes!"

He blinks, taking me in like I've just dyed my hair neon green. "You...bought...a *violin*?"

"Yes!" I run my fingers along the violin's smooth wooden surface. "We're on the joy train again, Silverman. And that includes taking risks, right?"

Every time I choose joy in grief proactively now, I'm learning to trust God's Word over what my feelings are shouting at me about whether God is good. *And if we're counting down from 120 days, we're going down with music. Why not?*

Matt's expression finally shifts from shocked to amused. "Others impulse buy candy. My girl goes straight for the midlife symphony and a full-blown life goal."

His face softens with curiosity, as he reaches out to touch it. "So…did you wake up this mornin' and think, 'My life's missin' a violin'?"

"Last week, I saw this YouTube violinist play a haunting Chopin piece. It was so beautiful it gave me chills. And then, it hit me—I want to learn to play. It felt like, I don't know. A God thing. Or maybe not. Wanted to surprise you."

"Have you ever played before? You haven't told me anything?"

"Technically, yes. For four months when I was nine. Then I quit lessons so I could pursue acting and singing. Haven't touched one in twenty-seven years. Didn't even own one. But something last week just clicked. So I bought one off Amazon. I've already started teaching myself! Tons of free beginner videos on YouTube."

Matt's eyes shift to concern. "Don't push too hard, okay? Worried about your neck. And the spinning."

"I've got it under control," I reassure, though not entirely sure. "Turns out I don't have to bend my neck too far down. It's one of few instruments where I don't have to look down while playing, so it works! No 10.0 earthquakes yet. Just 6.0…"

"Good. Because I don't want to find you passed out in here after attemptin' some epic concerto."

"Noted. No concertos…yet. I mean, I promise not to be perfectionistic about this."

"I'm sure. And if you have a fainting episode playin' Hot Cross Buns, I'm gonna have to call 9-1-1. How do we even explain that?"

Ordering a violin was impulsive, sure.

But will Matt take kindly to my next overture?

43

Marie & Louis

Day 45

"This must be the wrong house."

Hudson smirks, taking a cautious step back on our front porch.

His wide eyes dart from me to Matt. His two little kids cling to his legs, their faces frozen in a mix of awe and confusion. Mel, his wife, tilts her head, quizzical.

Hudson and I have been good friends since we worked together as lawyers in Judge Santin's court chambers a decade ago.

"No, Hudson, it's me, *Lara!*" I spread my arms as if that will somehow explain everything. *I can't believe we're doing this.*

I touch my dress, the sheer *volume* of it, and burst into laughter.

I'm drowning in a monstrous sea of opulence—an ocean of pink satin and lace ruffles rising like waves, cascading crinoline, pearl accents, puffy sleeves, and a neckline so extravagant it could double as a serving tray. The three feet wide hoop skirt underneath could host its own cocktail party. A powdered blonde wig teeters atop my head, a tower of perfectly sculpted curls that belongs in a royal portrait.

Matt, standing stoically next to me, looks even more absurd.

His embroidered royal blue coat with white buttons and ruffles, breeches, and knee-high stockings scream 18th century opulence straight out of an aristocratic nightmare, while his powdered white wig tilts ever so slightly, like even it knows this is not Matt's scene.

"Okay, okay, come inside before the neighbors think we're starting a revolution," I say, shooing Hudson's family inside. They're not dressed up in costumes for our little Halloween get together.

Matt wishes he weren't either.

My hoop skirt catches the edge of the door-frame, nearly knocking my pumpkin display. Matt winces as one teeters dangerously, painted with the name *Silverman* in swirling black script.

Inside, our "cottage" overflows with Kitten-styled autumn charm. Orange, yellow, red, and green leaves cascading across our fireplace mantel, fake floating candles dangling from the ceiling, and colorful glowing pumpkins on the kitchen counter, modeling right next to the caramel apples Matt surprised me with earlier. *My favorite*. The dining table rocks an ornate orange and black leaf-and-pumpkin runner.

Hudson crosses his arms. "So what are you two supposed to be? Historical Barbie and Ken?"

"Wrong monarchy," I say, wagging a finger. "Guess again."

One of Hudson's kids sneaks behind Matt and tugs on his coat-tails, curious. "Are you a pirate?"

"Close enough," Matt mumbles.

Mel's eyes light up. "Marie Antoinette and Louis XVI!"

"Bingo!" I exclaim, my hoop skirt swishing dangerously close to our coffee table. Matt groans, probably calculating the cost of replacing half the furniture.

Hudson chuckles, eyeing Matt's stiff shoulders. "What'd she have to promise to get you into that?"

Matt exhales sharply. "Sacrificial love. If I fake a gout attack, you think she'll let me change? I'm just tryin' to survive until the French Revolution reaches me."

We all know this isn't exactly Matt's vibe. He hasn't worn a

Halloween costume since fifth grade. Despite his literal brilliance, he's a simple man, giving no importance to pomp and circumstance—or costumes. In fact, parading around as 18th century French royalty is the antithesis of his values. Yet here's my man, playing along, because he's the kind of guy who'll set aside his pride to let me joyously drape him in absurd gold embroidery.

Since the Boldis' visit, we've challenged ourselves to find joy again—not in spite of the sadness, but alongside it. *Joy in grief.*

It's not easy. I see it in Matt's eyes every day—the weight of the unknown pressing down because the second chemo has no guarantees. And yet, Matt carries this quiet strength, a deep instinct I'm starting to recognize even in myself. Despite the uncertainties, despite facing death, despite the pain, we will *not* be defined by illness.

And I've come to another important realization lately. God calls us to have joy in grief not just for joy's sake. It's about embracing the abundant *life* God wants for us. Because Jesus died and rose and is alive today, we too will *never* die. Jesus promised, "I am the resurrection and the life. The one who believes in me will live, even though they die." John 11:25.

Luke 20:38 also states, "He is not the God of the dead, but of the living, for to Him *all are alive*." In fact, there's a saying that dying Christians are ironically moving from the land of the dying to the land of the living.

So, why not live with joy like we're fully alive today, as we'll always be?

Why not? Why not laugh, dance, enjoy—even while the clock ticks? Even while Matt's technically "dying"? So, as the cancer worsens, we're pushing harder to live. And if we're not dressed like French monarchs, are we even trying?

These costumes are my megaphone—we're living big, bold, and unapologetically. (Sure, I'll admit there was a pinch of "let's squeeze in all the blessings we can before one of us hits the pearly gates" in my calculation to buy them. But hey, I'm still learning to live with the hope of eternity at the forefront. Character development takes time, people. Think baby steps, big costumes.)

The doorbell rings again and Judge Santin sweeps in like a storm of charisma, dressed head-to-toe as Mario with a red hat, a fake mustache, and the kind of swagger only a federal judge can pull off. Her husband trails behind as Luigi, looking just as enthusiastic and game for the adventure.

"Lara!" Judge Santin's eyes sparkle, taking in the scene. "Is this what you've been up to since you left chambers? Living out your Marie Antoinette fantasy?"

"Guilty as charged," I cackle, attempting another curtsy, though the skirt decides to rebel again and nearly knock over a lantern. Matt rolls his eyes. "This dress has its own zip code," I confess bashfully.

Judge Santin glides to the kitchen counter and sets down an enticing chocolate cake. "Time for an epic cake party reunion," she says. The nostalgia hits me. Back in chambers, cake parties were our tradition. Whenever we needed a sugar-fueled break, Judge Santin would produce some ridiculous confection, and we'd eat like the world was ending.

I glance at Matt, who's now quietly unbuttoning the top of his embroidered coat like he wants to be released from a medieval torture device.

"Matt, how do you feel surrounded by five lawyers? Need therapy yet?" I ask.

Matt smirks. "I'll have my people call your people."

"Are those gyros?" Judge Santin inquires, her attention shifting. The smell of warm pita bread, spiced meat, and garlicky tzatziki sauce fills the kitchen, mingling with the earthy aroma of fava bean soup simmering on my stove—a Middle Eastern favorite of beans, garlic, and lemon.

Minutes later, the dinner table is a lively buzz of chatter. Matt, however, is quiet, his shoulders still tense beneath that elaborate abomination of a coat. He sips his soup, glancing around like he's waiting to escape. Not an introvert's comfort zone—new crowds, costumes. *He'd rather be giving a sermon.*

Then Judge Santin's husband, a man blessed with the uncanny ability to put anyone at ease, asks Matt about Haiti. Suddenly, the stiffness melts, his face lights up, and Matt launches into an animated story about building schools and medical clinics. My heart swells with pride. I remember the endless debates we had in chambers a decade ago about who my future husband would be.

But as I'm settling into the moment, halfway through my second gyro, a 9.0 earthquake hits my brain, enhancing the turbulence in my vision. The room tilts hard, and I grip the edge of the table.

"Matt, I need to lie down." Matt's by my side in seconds, his hand steady as he guides me to our bedroom. I sink onto the bed immediately.

"Here," he says, grabbing my water bottle. "Drink. And please, change out of this monstrosity. It's probably making you dizzier."

I gulp the water obediently, trying not to laugh. "Thanks for putting up with all this, Trouble."

"You're welcome, your majesty. I'd fight for your honor in any century, but next time, can we please just hand out candy like normal people?"

I giggle, resting my hand over his as he sits right by me, his legs hanging off the bed. "Normal? Nah. That's too normal."

His expression softens, intensity rising in his eyes. "We're not done fighting, Kitten."

For a moment, everything—the ruffles, the costumes, the noise from the party—fades away. It's just us, in this fragile, uncertain space, encouraging each other.

"Good. Neither am I."

Half an hour later, we're back in the kitchen and Judge Santin is gleefully slicing into her masterpiece of a cake while Hudson's kids salivate. As she cuts, the heavenly smell permeates the room—rich cocoa, the tang of fresh strawberries, and sprinkles. "Patience, my apprentices," she says, wielding the knife like she's conducting surgery. "The best cakes require precision."

𝄞

The Santin chambers Halloween party was only the start of our Silverman "fall parties" extravaganza. We've packed my favorite season, committing to six more gatherings in the coming weeks—despite the fact that Matt's strength has been steadily declining and that the second chemo doesn't seem to be working.

He's started vomiting more—something new—leaving us uncertain if it's a side effect of the new treatment or a sign of further cancer progression. He's napping more due to his fatigue levels, and to make matters worse, yet another experimental clinical trial rejected Matt's provisional application. Our prospects are looking increasingly grim.

Nonetheless, every party, every dinner, every time I stroke Matt's bald head in public is a deliberate act of rebellion. A deliberate *yes* to *joy*.

On my self-designated Sadakian "cousins night," Matt and I make sangria and tacos. Each sip, each bite, each head stroke is a toast to the moment—to *now*.

On Armenian "pizza night" with our families, I go entirely overboard in the best way, baking chocolate mousse, banana cake, and pumpkin spice muffins for dessert. As I rush around the kitchen fighting off spinning attacks, Matt eyes me—*I told you to rest.* Then—"We could've just done Safeway cookies and grape juice."

On the morning of Matt's 40th birthday, the house hums with quiet anticipation of another win coming—the kind that happens only when love and mischief intertwine. I've orchestrated a superhero-themed surprise party with Anna, enlisting the youth group kids to wear superman capes.

At 5 p.m., while Matt is napping, some forty people tiptoe

through our front door in the dark and hide in our small living room. Matt, blissfully unaware, finally stumbles into the room with groggy eyes, and the room erupts into cheers. I toss him his Spider-Man shirt, and his face lights up with that boyish grin. Then, Joel slaps in a video I made on his large monitor, and the faces of the youth group kids light up the screen:

"Happy Birthday, Matt! Thank you for believing in me when no one else did."

"You've changed my life with all your lessons, Matt. I'll never forget it."

"I don't know where I'd be without you. We're holding you in prayer."

Their love shines—funny stories, quiet gratitude, deep admiration. When it's over, Matt blinks hard, his voice catching. "This... means everything." *I hope he sees now he can let others be strong for him sometimes.*

These are God's victories amidst grief. Matt's life motto is probably, "No soul left behind," and here he is, still growing these disciples even in his pain. Just as God "showed [Joseph] kindness and granted him favor" even in his prison, God is doing the same for Matt in his prison of cancer. Genesis 39:21.

Sure, it feels absurd hosting more parties than a healthy crowd. Matt and I are like two dying iPhones, perpetually hovering at two percent battery. But somehow, God's grace is this miraculous, never-failing portable charger that keeps us going. Turns out God gives us way more than we can handle (contrary to that popular saying that He supposedly doesn't).

But when He does, we need not fear because "He gives strength to the weary and increases the power of the weak." Isaiah 40:29. This Biblical promise keeps proving itself true to me.

And I'm finding that surprising clarity comes with knowing your time is limited, a sharp-edged awareness that life is just *preparation* for eternity. When you stop clinging to the illusion that you'll live on this earth forever and you're not afraid to die, that's ironically when you really start living. You start choosing life—not just for the here and now, but for eternity.

Nor does it matter when your last day will be on this earth because even if you die tomorrow, that wouldn't be the end. *Talk about a strong antidote to fear.* Jesus died to give us that abundant life in both the here and now, *and* in eternity. He explicitly said, "I have come that they may have life, and have it to the full." John 10:10. We're leaning ruthlessly into that promise. Every party reminds us: *Live. And live in view of the life to come.* (We're focusing on that *eternal glory* I learned about recently.)

And our family Halloween party? That's the crown jewel.

Our parents lounge on the couch, sipping my British wassail concoction with spiced cinnamon, cloves, and apples. Pops' booming laugh bounces off walls while our nieces (Matt's sisters' kids) tear into candy bags. Matt and I, of course, present as French royalty again.

"My darling Louis," I say, striking a pose. "Shall we dance? Imagine glittering chandeliers, Versailles courtiers—"

"Lost me at chandeliers," Matt says, his lips twitching into that almost-smile he displays when he's about to cave. "Okay Kitten," he huffs, standing.

"Follow my lead, Louis," I say, yanking him into a clumsy waltz as Joel (of course) records on his camera. "Step. Glide. Now *you* twirl because I can't!"

"I feel like the court jester," Matt deadpans.

I catch sight of Pops' bright red shirt and giggle. Given that Matt and I are royalty, there was only one fitting costume choice for the parents—and Golden Girl Auntie Arax who's in tow tonight.

That's right. I turned them into a humble pack of M&Ms, tossing them their matching colorful shirts the moment they walked in the door.

As Marie said, let them eat M&Ms.

44

The Wardrobe

Day 60

"Does it have to be now, Kitten?"

Matt groans dramatically, lying in bed at 3 P.M.

"Yes," I reply, grabbing a black scarf off the dresser.

Matt slowly sits up, arching a skeptical eyebrow. "Why do I feel like this is gonna involve glitter or feathers?"

I laugh and wrap the scarf around his eyes. "Shush. Trust me."

I drag a blindfolded, half-protesting Matt into our guest room. "Ready?"

"Not remotely."

I whip his blindfold off with a flourish. Matt blinks, his eyes adjusting to the scene before him—the bed buried in piles of brand-new men's clothing.

Sleek business suit jackets.

Tailored dress trousers.

Slim-fit blazers.

Coats that scream "I drink single-origin coffee and make more than you do."

"What's all…" He steps closer, eyes flicking from pile to pile like he's trying to process an optical illusion.

"Happy birthday, Silverman," I beam. "There comes a time in every marriage when the woman tries to change her man. I'm starting with outfits."

(Let's be honest: Matt's academic, utilitarian style is quirky with a side of adorable, but his suits and shirts are in tatters, and he's turned "absent-minded professor" into a full-blown fashion crisis. Time for a Kitten-inspired makeover.)

His brow furrows, but there's a flicker of other things—hope, confusion, awe—all shining in his eyes.

"Just wanted to spoil you. Remember I told you your birthday gift from me was gonna be private?"

Matt stares blankly at the clothes, his hands hanging limp at his sides. Silence stretches, and my stomach knots into a pretzel. *Does he hate it? Think it's too much? This is either going to end well or in a theological debate on why budgeting is Godly.*

Finally, he presses his lips together, his eyes shiny.

"Matt? What's wrong? Do you hate it?" *Is he tearing up?*

He shakes his head and swallows hard. "No. No. It's... Been thinkin' for a while now that maybe I needed...you know...an upgrade. But I couldn't bring myself to spend the money. Felt selfish." A tear slides down his cheek out of nowhere. *Stop the presses! He's actually conceding he needs a wardrobe upgrade?*

"Oh, Matt." I reach up and wipe the tear from his cheek.

"But," he says, "I'm so happy I have a wife who's takin' care of me now. This is...amazing. Thank you." Matt literally only seeks treasures in eternity, as Luke 12:33 instructs: "Sell your possessions and give to the poor. Provide purses for yourselves that will not wear out, a treasure in Heaven that will never fail[.]" *Is this same man happy-crying over new dress pants now? I don't even know who we are anymore. Somebody hand me an Oscar in the "wives changing wardrobes" category.*

I sigh, relieved. "Trouble, you're officially being kidnapped by my fashion choices henceforth."

He chuckles, running a hand over the first clothing pile. "I mean, some of my shirts probably were carbon-dating themselves."

"Oh, love—it's *okay* to embrace blessings in your life! God delights in giving you good gifts *here* on earth too. Don't refuse them. You can allow yourself to receive, too. You're not letting anyone down if you put yourself first sometimes."

The contrast is beautiful. I'm encouraging him to savor God's blessings in the here and now, while he's inspiring me to get excited about eternal blessings. He teaches me to find beauty in simplicity, and I show him the value of dreaming big.

And just like that, the Trouble fashion show begins. I hold up shirts and jackets, darting around like a stylist while he changes.

While putting on the first blazer, Matt whines, "I'm not really a blazer guy."

"You're not really a fashion guy. This is a makeover monarchy, not democracy. And I'm the queen."

"Not that Marie woman again."

Next, he tries on blue skinny jeans.

"Is this a pair of pants or a blood pressure cuff?" he exclaims, simultaneously getting a red sweater stuck over his head.

"This is it. This is how I go. Death by fashion!" he giggles, trying to tear the sweater off.

Next up—a light pink suit jacket he refuses to entertain for more than five seconds. "Please?" I beg. "You look so hot in pink. Do I need to blindfold you again to make our decisions easier?"

"It's a hard no. It's better than that Louis nightmare, but I draw the line at pink."

"So you'll wear twenty-year-old cargo shorts, but *this* is where you draw the line?" I roll my eyes. *What's up with men and pink? God made sunsets pink!*

Next up—a blue checkered wool sweater that gives off catalog model vibes.

"Am I givin' cozy lumberjack or depressed poet?" he pouts.

"A little of both, and I'm into it."

"I feel weird."

"It's called style. Welcome to the other side, Silver."

Finally, Matt steps in front of the mirror wearing a dark green flannel shirt and tailored dark navy jeans, and I gasp. The shirt fits his broad shoulders perfectly, and the jeans hug his frame just right. *Goodbye, baggy 2003 denim. Hello husband goals.*

"Turn around," I order, twirling my finger.

He spins with mock drama. "Well?"

"Handsome as ever. We're keeping both. Non-negotiable."

After thirty minutes, the room looks like a hurricane of fabric and price tags, but Matt stands in front of the mirror, adjusting the collar of a slick, dark blue suit jacket, his eyes expressing a stark confidence.

"Violation of Cuteness Code Section 5678," I shout, tickling him. "Prepare to be prosecuted."

"Do I have to be? I'm exhausted," he whines, as I plant a quick kiss on his lips.

"Is it normal for the prosecution to kiss the defendant during arrest?" he asks, tilting his head. "That usually results in a mistrial."

"In this court? Absolutely."

Three hours later, resting in bed, Matt's face tightens and turns pale, and without warning, he lurches forward. I quickly grab a bag, holding it out just in time as he starts to vomit.

And just like that, PRADA meets Pepto.

Some people bond over exotic vacations. We bond over who can find the vomit bag fastest. Honestly, the intensity is kind of romantic.

Such is the reality of marriage amidst suffering. One moment, modeling. The next, vomit bags. But lately, I've realized that the unglamorous parts of our marriage surprisingly give me so much purpose.

While I was completely bedridden, I prayed for God to redeem my suffering, and one of the ways He answered was Matt. In Matt, I've found a partner *and* a ministry—a shared calling to extend love, compassion, and tangible help to a fellow sufferer, just like he does for me. It's a unique and profound purpose—channeling our understanding of pain into service for one another.

This appears to be the fourth reason I've discovered in practice for why God allows suffering: equipping us to effectively comfort others in ministry (2 Corinthians 1:3-5).

For me, that means supporting Matt however I can even with my own limitations. Whether it's helping him through nausea, massaging his feet during neuropathy bouts, or simply being there emotionally, just as he is for me. He, in turn, picks up every single item I can't bend over to reach, and when one of us is too weak to rise off the bed during the day, the other ensures basic needs—water, food, comfort—are met. These small acts, born out of necessity, are sacred expressions of our love.

Serving one another in the trenches has also forged a deep, sacred intimacy between us. Every human heart longs to be truly seen and loved not only in strength or beauty, not only when it's easy or deserved, but in weakness, in brokenness. I'm learning Jesus calls us into marriage not to fulfill our desired checklist of earthly milestones but simply to serve one another in this fallen world, just as Jesus sacrificed for His church through His death on the cross. Turns out marriage, at its core, really *is* just a forum for servanthood and sacrificial love, because *those* pursuits refine us into Christ's selfless image.

Who needs champagne and Italy when you've got Pedialyte and a husband who sacrificially laughs at your bad jokes while he's taking your blood pressure? Our days look vastly different from any normal ideal, yet, in this imperfect life, loving each other sacrificially is a source of true joy. I guess generic comfort and happiness are *not* the same as deep blessing and joy. Perhaps the joy I've sought my whole life isn't in the "perfect Armenian life" but in the hard, holy work of loving others sacrificially...just like Christ did. *Hmm.*

In the same vein, perhaps the "perfect life" I've idealized—a life filled with elaborate dates, travels, and neatly checked boxes—is not at all what God desires for us. Maybe the "perfect life" in God's eyes is one paradoxically marked by suffering, because that's how our character is most deeply transformed, shaping us for eternity. (Remember folks, you want to cash in on that *eternal glory*. That's the *real* investment.)

According to Romans 8:29, one of God's explicit goals is to conform our character to that of Christ. Why, then, are we surprised when God calls couples to love each other in the hard day in, day out of suffering? When we're frustrated with one another, we learn Christlike patience. When we're weak, we learn to rely on God's strength and sovereignty like Christ did. God uses suffering, then, in a redemptive way by changing our character.

Indeed, Matt and I have been discussing lately how, just as fire purifies gold by burning away its impurities, God allows our trials in order to shape, test, and refine both our character and faith. Job himself said, "[W]hen He has tested me, I will come forth as gold." Job 23:10. The Bible explicitly promises such testing. 1 Peter 4:12 states, "[D]o not be surprised at the fiery ordeal that has come on you to test you, as though something strange were happening to you." We recoil from this idea because we hate suffering, but Scripture emphasizes this idea repeatedly. *E.g.*, Psalm 66:10, Zechariah 13:9, Proverbs 17:3.

Faith and character grow the same way muscles do—by pushing against resistance. The more they are tested, the stronger and more resilient they become. Would you trust a gym coach who never challenges your muscles to grow? We only really find out whether we have *real* faith that God is good when our circumstances scream the opposite, right?

This is turning out to be the fifth reason for suffering that's finally clicking at a heart level. *Okay, Lord, You're refining my character and faith, making me more like Jesus through all this testing. Help me desire this above all. I'm still struggling with bitterness, even despite knowing these redemptive reasons for suffering.*

Will I ever actually surrender to Your will fully? Let me come forth as gold, Lord! Preferably 24-karat.

Worse comes to worse, at least I'll make it out as gold spray paint from the Costco clearance aisle. Not quite Job-level refinement, but hey—still shiny under the right lighting.

45

The Silverman Show

Day 81

I grip the vintage-style microphone, its silver finish glowing under the glare of my new "spotlight," *a.k.a.*, my desk lamp.

The sequins on my hot pink 1920s flapper dress itch against my skin, and my earrings—a pair of absurdly long gold tassels—sway against my neck. I take a breath and launch into the first smoky notes of *Georgia on My Mind*, a Ray Charles jazz classic. My voice bounces off the walls of my "music room"—formerly known as our guest room.

Now? It's my new stage. A rack of old musical theater costumes lines one wall, their sequins catching the light and giving off the faint and disgusting smell of mothballs.

My audience? A tripod-mounted iPhone camera peering back at me.

Three months ago, I caught the jazz bug from the Boldis, who unknowingly reminded me of my first love. Painting? Cooking? *Nah. Boring. Let's get back to the good stuff. Performing. Where my soul wakes up.*

So, I did what any sensible chronically ill person does. I threw myself headfirst into creating a 1920s jazz YouTube series.

Ordered a cheap Art Deco-style mic. Asked Mom to haul over my ancient musical theater wardrobe. Converted a whole room into a makeshift jazz club. Well, jazz club-ish. It's less "Great Gatsby" and more "budget Gatsby meets Craigslist."

Bottom line—I started posting videos of myself singing jazz numbers on Matt's Christian devotional YouTube channel. As the old adage goes, if you can't practice law, sing. Paul even wrote *while imprisoned*: "Rejoice in the Lord always. I will say it again: Rejoice!" So by golly, if I'm in this prison of an illness stuck at home on a bed, I'm going to entertain the masses.

Isn't that precisely what Romans 8:37 means by "we are more than conquerors" in Christ? Serenading the airwaves with jazz so smooth it makes Satan choke on his pitchfork? Paul wrote a million epistles on house arrest. This is my house arrest contribution.

So here I am today, crooning the 34th number in the series, taking "singing in the fire" to a whole new level.

"Take two," I mumble, shaking out my hands. The green screen on the wall behind me is courtesy of Joel—my 24/7 sarcasm and tech support hotline. He set it up as a means for me to add backdrops to my videos. *Gotta love engineers.*

Matt's Christian devotional YouTube subscribers must've been confused at first. One minute, they're watching Matt preach in his Indiana Jones hat—"God is good, even in suffering." The next, they're knee-deep in me crooning *Fever* in a sequined dress so bright it could blind Moses. We went from "praise Jesus" to "pass the martini" real fast.

Just imagine someone tuning in for Matt's "Five Biblical Tips for Staying Humble," only to be greeted by me in full flapper gear, belting out *It Don't Mean a Thing If It Ain't Got That Swing*. They probably thought they accidentally subscribed to "The Holy Spirit and All That Jazz" channel.

But the kicker—God even got on board. Blasphemy? Hear me out.

A week after I started this little jazz venture, a box of vintage flapper hats randomly showed up at my front door. Feathered headbands, sequined cloche hats, the works. My sister's mother-in-law, who knew nothing about my project, had sent them, claiming they'd belonged to a sweet old lady in her church who'd wanted her costume collection to go to someone "young and creative" after she passed. The timing? Uncanny.

God winking at me? They literally completed the aesthetic I wanted. I knew God was saying, *Look, I know what you and Matt are facing. Take this gift of joy.* That box was so on-the-nose that I half expected to find a note inside saying, "From God: Keep jazzin' for Jesus."

Who would've thought God would conspire with me to do 1920s jazz club covers? This takes "God works in mysterious ways" to brand new heights. You can't box Him in—after all, "all things have been created through Him and for Him," including music. Colossians 1:16-17. Worship isn't just about gazing at God in isolation; it's about using the gifts He placed in us for His purpose.

From that hat box on, let's just say I ran with God's encouragement.

Maybe a little too far.

One day, while rearranging my props, I noticed an old sign I'd bought when Matt and I first got married. It was hanging above the fireplace, almost waiting for this moment: *The Silverman Theater*. That's when I decided to rename Matt's channel. He didn't even blink. Just that easygoing smile: "Whatever makes you happy, Kitten."

And that's how *The Silverman Show* YouTube channel was born. I immediately started working on five other musical showcases—opera, oldies, musical theater, reggae, pop.

Cycle: record one song a day for one hour standing up, collapse back into bed. Edit the video later for one hour in bed. Then rest. (I've been trying to "expose" my brain to even more time on electronics. It's still painful, so I do small amounts at a time with breaks.) *Keep going, Lara. Maybe you'll win a Tony Award for Best Bedridden Actress—nominated for her riveting performance in "Bedridden, but Make It Inspirational."*

Then, another surprise landed. "Have you...noticed the subscriber count goin' up a bit?" Matt asked one day, showing me the YouTube analytics.

"People are actually subscribing?" I gasped. "Oh my gosh. This...might be...a ministry opportunity!" The idea hit me—use music videos to hook people, then sneak in Christian content. Plant more seeds. Forget *test to testimony*, we're doing *jazz to testimony*. This is the best whiplash ministry strategy west of Matt's well-written sermons. *Why not?*

We started with a video of me interviewing Matt as he discussed how he came to faith as a scientist. He explained:

> I used to think science and faith were like oil and water, never meant to mix. But the deeper I studied science, I realized it actually supports faith. Take the universe. The constants of physics like gravity and the speed of light are perfectly calibrated. If they were off even by a hair, life wouldn't exist. It's like someone tuned every dial just right. That kind of precision doesn't scream 'cosmic accident.' It sounds more like intentional craftsmanship. Like someone wanted life to happen.
>
> I also considered how DNA is like a biological code—an actual language made up of billions of instructions. That's when it hit me: code doesn't write itself. If there's information, there's an informer. If there's a message, there's a sender. It felt less and less reasonable to believe that the most complex code in the known universe came from nothing and no one. It pointed me to design. A mind behind it all—eternal, uncreated, and powerful. And what society doesn't tell you nowadays is that

most scientists before the 21st century believed in a higher power. Science is a process to determine truth; it isn't the truth itself.

In our second video, Matt explained he came to know Christ after studying the Bible for an entire year and taking stock in the overwhelming rational and historical evidence that this man named Jesus—who claimed to be God—actually did rise from the dead. First, he explained there's no record anywhere of anyone surviving Roman crucifixion, and that several extra-Biblical ancient sources confirmed Jesus was dead. Second, there were early reports of eyewitnesses to Jesus' resurrection within months of His death; this wasn't just a legend created centuries after Jesus' life. Third, Jesus' disciples were courageously willing to be martyred for their faith *after* touching and eating with the *resurrected* Jesus, even though they all deserted Jesus out of sheer fear when Jesus was arrested to be crucified. Something must have changed to impact their attitude: Jesus' literal resurrection.

"No one would die for somethin' they know is a lie, right?" Matt asked the audience. Finally, Matt said he found it deeply compelling that the God of Christianity doesn't just allow suffering in this world. He entered into it when He suffered on the cross. "That's not a distant God who ignores suffering. That's a God who bled for us."

Lucky for Trouble, I then roped him into some musical Christian parodies I scripted. We made fun of illness using Disney and pop songs to teach that we can be patient in suffering because we have hope in eternity without suffering.

Backstreet Boys, *Cinderella*, you name it, Matt sang it with me (or just stood in the background as a somewhat confused but adorable prop behind my vocals). His self-proclaimed favorite so far has been my rendition of *Today I Met the Matt I Want to Marry*.

Despite the occasional furrowed brow, the poor lad never says no, even in his extreme pain, except when he attempted to refuse my *Billy Joel-inspired* parody making fun of Satan.

"You want me to sing *what*?" he exclaimed, a cheeky half-willing grin peeking through. (He has sharp performing instincts—I've seen that spark in his eyes when he's preaching.) Matt did say once though, "I wanna make sure you're not doin' all this to prove somethin' because you're not working, love. Don't overwork yourself."

"No, I have genuine joy," I replied. "I may not be practicing law right now, but I feel like God's got a hidden purpose in this creativity."

Long story short, we're taking this "caged bird sings" thing to the bank (without the funds). Like Paul and Silas singing in prison, we're blending comedy, theology, and music into something uniquely ours. *Joy in grief.* Jesus is making us "fruitful in the land of [our] suffering," just like He did for Joseph. Genesis 41:52.

This all goes to show that God works through our secular platforms in surprising ways, and that our worldly positions and talents are just tools God uses to spread His gospel. For me, jazz led to sharing Christian inspiration.

For Matt, it started when he shared scientific COVID-19 updates on Facebook and attracted hundreds of new random followers years back. As Matt preached at church recently, "I started askin' God what I should do next given that I had the attention of all these people interested in my opinions. Then sure enough, I was diagnosed with cancer and all of a sudden, all these people I didn't even know—Christian and non-Christian—were following and commenting on my testimony as a Christian navigatin' cancer." *Test to testimony.* Imagine that. God using evil for good. Genesis 50:20. You never know when God will bring forth a harvest.

"Take three," I say now, hitting the record button again. My voice fills the room, low and smoky. For a minute, I feel alive, transported to a jazz club with clinking glasses. And with that, I'm done recording *Georgia On My Mind.*

This is how our nights unfold in our cozy cottage in England (though Matt prefers to pretend we live in Daly City). The music room is my domain, where I either sing or wrestle with my new passion (and arch-nemesis)—the violin—while Matt sits in his office grading exams, writing sermons, or plotting his next *Dungeons & Dragons* campaign with his nerd crew. Or, we just nap together when the pain requires.

Just last night, I was screeching my way through something that might be considered Mozart. From the next room, Matt yelled through the wall, "Sounding good, that's my girl!"

"Liar!"

This saint of a man—talk about sacrificing your eardrums. Some nights, Matt even pulls out his flute and joins me. Our duets are another tangible gift from Jesus in our mutual sorrow.

Indeed, the violin's tone, with its haunting beauty, has become my voice for emotions too deep for jazz to carry—an intimate vessel for my sorrows. I hadn't even touched a violin the last twenty-seven years. Isn't it funny how God orchestrates things, leading us back to the right path at the perfect time? How He plants seeds today for tomorrow's unexpected surprises?

Like that car ride back in 2017—Matt and I crammed into the same car going to camp, getting to know each other. Without that foundation, I doubt we would have connected so intimately during those phone calls while I was strictly bedridden.

Jesus sure has a way of bringing joy and resurrection out of nowhere. In fact, aren't all these recent creative ideas—cooking, painting, script writing, filmmaking, jazz, violin, *The Silverman Show*—proof of that? They just popped into my head as gifts from God, the same way He brought Matt into my life unexpectedly. Maybe Jesus wants to bless us in surprising ways, reminding us that we don't have to chase after some idea of a *perfect life* with the "right" earthly blessings.

I'm starting to believe that the best gifts come when we're not even looking.

46

Jazz & Joy

Day 109

The blasting sound of a big swing 1940s jazz band swirls through the CACC church sanctuary, filling every corner with life.

The band?

The talented stylings of the four Boldi kids, with the Silvermans in tow.

Nicholas' trumpet soars, bold and brassy, while Christine's clarinet snakes underneath. Ethan's cello hums beautifully, grounding the chaos. I belt out my vocal solo, swaying my hips and snapping my fingers like I'm not in church. *This is what Heaven must sound like—a lot of music and a lot of joy.*

The sanctuary is packed. Mom, Sevan, her husband Rob, Pops, and the Golden Girls sit in the front row clapping along like a jazzercise class. A few brave souls sway in the 25th pew while others look ready to file a complaint with the church deacons. *Don't worry, parishioners—jazz ain't airborne.*

This church hasn't seen jazz since 2014, when Pastor Nerses and I shook things up with some jazzy worship songs. Now here we are again, a decade later, breaking the unspoken rule that reverence can't groove.

We made it to church months back to perform a Boldi/Silverman rendition of *Just a Closer Walk With Thee*. Today is our encore, during Advent.

We are performing a very sassy, borderline rebellious rendition of *God Rest Ye Merry Gentlemen*—think '40s jazz club. It's like we're saying, *Yes, we love Jesus, but we also think He'd appreciate a solid trumpet solo.*

I'm donning a floor-length ruby dress with an Old Hollywood drape, and a "subtle" black derby style feather hair clip—an ensemble screaming "Ella Fitzgerald fan club president." Matt, playing his flute at my side in his pinstriped new blue-and-gray suit, half looks like he just stepped out of a speakeasy. His gray Sinatra style hat sits in the front pew. No cane today. Just raw energy somehow gifted from God for this moment.

"Hit it, Andrew!" I shout, waving my arm like a bandleader. Andrew launches into a fiery piano solo that's so alive I'm pretty sure his fingers are applying for their own Social Security number.

My heart swells. I took a risk with another straight three-mile car ride, and I'm *back*. To be soloing up here like my healthy days—it's a resurrection. With a bittersweet edge, sure. Because even in this moment, the church is spinning all around me. I wanted a real comeback—one without illness, or frankly, intense grief. But this is nonetheless still a miracle. God's miracle of *sustaining grace*.

Indeed, how on earth am I forcing myself to sit up and walk for two years now—even though doing so is still making me spin harder and enhancing all my electrical nerve pain? And now, I'm on a stage again? It really *is* true that "this all-surpassing power is from God and not from us. We are hard pressed on every side, but not crushed; perplexed, but not in despair; persecuted, but not abandoned; struck down, but not destroyed." 2 Corinthians 4:7-9.

Given that I'm literally rowing against endless severe ocean waves, Psalm 77:19 also hits comically close to home—"Your path led through the sea, your way through the mighty waters." It's not just metaphorical—God is sustaining me through the vertigo waters moment by moment.

"Hit it, Nicholas!" I bark now. His trumpet cuts in, soaring through the air like a hot knife through butter. Joel, as usual, films from the front row next to Anna, his ever-present video-recorder angled just right.

When the song ends, Matt and I make our way to the pulpit. He grabs the Advent candle holder and lights the candle, a symbol of light in the middle of our own darkness. My heart squeezes, full and broken all at once.

"Today," Matt announces, "we light the Advent candle of joy."

A week ago, Pastor Calvin called us. "You two want to do the Advent reading this week? The theme is joy."

Joy. Of all themes. Ironically, we were in a really dark place when he called. Vomiting. Crying. Grieving. But his ask reminded us of our wedding theme: God gives us streams of joy in the desert. We knew we had to say yes. *Test to testimony.*

Matt now reads Isaiah 35:1-2—"The desert and the parched land will be glad; the wilderness will rejoice and blossom. Like the crocus, it will burst into bloom; it will rejoice greatly and shout for joy."

When it's my turn, I grip the pulpit, steadying myself against the rising waves of vertigo. "God doesn't just give us joy when things are perfect, He gives joy when we desperately need it. Joy is us today, playing jazz and taking risks even if it aggravates our pain, because we've got God's miraculous stamina. Joy is Christ empowering me to learn violin while my brain is on fire. Joy is being stripped of my career and health, but learning deep lessons about eternity I never knew. We're here today, testifying about joy from our prison of pain. Think Paul and Silas, folks. Sorrowful yet always rejoicing. They go together. Like jazz hands and church."

As the crowd chuckles, Matt finishes. "Mary and Joseph's marriage didn't look like they'd planned that first Christmas. Their child was born in scandal and a stable. Yet, through their obedience, God brought the world salvation. He brings joy in the most unlikely places. This reminds us that even when our situations don't go as planned, God can bring great joy and purpose out of them. This is why even in suffering, Christ's birth is still the season of joy."

After the service, the church's community auditorium buzzes with warmth. Auntie Nanor rushes up, clutching my hand. "You're exuding God's joy!"

Auntie Arax chimes in, "I loved your YouTube musical Christmas card." Auntie Rosalie adds, "That video with you two singing *Baby, It's Cold Outside*—adorable!" *Thank you, Golden Girls. They always lift us up.* My heart is so full.

But half an hour later, a random acquaintance sidles up and my smile fades. Her sarcastic laugh and words land like a slap: "Well, of course you're happy this year. You're married this Christmas."

I freeze. *Yeah, marriage cured global hunger too.* I'm fighting tooth and nail not to focus on the fact that Matt might die, and that God's joy is independent of earthly blessings. But here it is. The assumption that my joy is tied to circumstance, that marriage or any other earthly joy is some magical fix-it-all—the end-all, be-all of Christian joy.

Sometimes we Christians just don't get it. All our earthly roles—wife, mother, educator, and so on—are temporary assignments, not eternal identities. Paul would be flatly unimpressed with how the church idolizes marriage. God wrote, through Paul, that singleness is equally "good" (1 Corinthians 7:8, 32-34).

A tear threatens to betray me, but I shove it back. *No. I know where my joy comes from now.* Then—another acquaintance walks up. "You look great, Lara! You're all healed now!"

"Thanks so much. But, um, actually, I'm still spinning and bedridden most of the day."

She waves me off with a laugh. "Oh, it's all in your head. Why aren't you working yet?" *Ah, there it is*—the phrase that has haunted every person with a chronic illness since the dawn of time—"It's in your head." *Perfect. I'll just pop it out and give it a good rinse in the sink. Problem solved.*

An hour later at home, Matt and I look like two rag dolls tossed onto a shelf, lying flat on our bed. The walls spin acutely harder, and my brain throbs with electrical currents, brain zaps, and more earthquakes. I hold back the sob clawing up my throat, but it breaks loose anyway.

"What's wrong, sweetheart?" Matt asks.

I sigh heavily. "I had so much joy today, babe. I really did. I pushed through, got into the car again. Only you understand what it costs me. The courage it takes to choose pain for the sake of living. I love our church community, so don't get me wrong. Everyone has the best intentions. But some people don't want to believe in chronic illnesses. They're shocked when I say I'm still hurting."

"I know, Lara."

I wiggle my legs, wincing as that subtle movement sends another wave of vertigo crashing into me. "I know my illness is invisible, so it's hard for people to understand. They see me standing, singing. Who can blame them for thinking I'm fine? It probably makes them sad to think I'm in pain, so it's easier to dismiss it."

I pause, biting my lip. "But what bothers me is when they suggest I'm lazy for not working, like I'm sitting on a beach sipping margaritas. How am I going to write a legal brief in seven days while my vision is shaking up and down? Video editing for half an hour is one thing. You know I have to lie down for three hours after any two hours sitting up. If they believed me, I wouldn't have to fight to explain myself."

"I get it," Matt nods, like he's taking notes for a dissertation titled *How to Survive Marriage with a Chronically Ill Jazz Enthusiast*.

"Remember when Carol told me she saw me as sick last time? That was the first time I felt truly seen, understood."

"She gets it because of her daughter's illness. She's lived it. And it's okay to have grief alongside joy, right? Don't feel like you have to put on a front, smilin' all the time. Be genuine. If you're suffering, tell people."

These are the unvarnished struggles of living with chronic illness, a life suspended between hope and heartbreak. Yet God continues to provide for me through the compassion of a husband who intimately understands physical suffering. Last year—my first year off the bed—my focus was singular. Walk again no matter what and strengthen my body. This year, I've tried a few random therapies again. None of it bore fruit.

Yes, God is miraculously sustaining me as I've been walking for two years now—but I've seen no habituation (healing) of my brain, eyes, or ears. "Walking" vestibular therapy is supposed to train your brain and calm vertigo down eventually. But it just *enhances* it for me. I have to slam back down on the bed each time, and I still don't know why my brain isn't habituating. I'm still bedridden most of the day except when I'm up forcing the vertigo, and my head still shakes on and off involuntarily while lying down.

The truth is, I'm not surprised. Not because I don't want healing—believe me, I do—but because in that dream two years ago, God called me to acceptance. And that call has been the hardest truth I've ever had to reckon with. What does a person do when they believe God has called them to stay permanently in the storm, not to chase the shore?

The sorrow of His "no" still weighs heavy on my heart daily. If it weren't for that word from God, I'd still be clawing my way through every possible option. I spent five years doing just that—researching, fighting, trying therapies, begging. And I'd do it again in a heartbeat if God had left it ambiguous, or if I believed He was asking me to try again.

A friend (out of love) recently said, "No one can help you if you don't want to heal." Those words landed like a hundred knives sharp with misunderstanding. As if I don't want healing? I don't even know how to give up—I've spent too many years warring against my body to know how. But what am I supposed to do—keep fighting with the Almighty Himself? Somehow change His sovereign plan?

I realize how counter-intuitive this is in modern society where health and success are prized above all and you're supposed to "chase after healing and not give up," etc. Even Christians can and should desire healing because Jesus healed the sick.

Unless God expressly reveals His will to the contrary. Here's the impossible space I live in: wanting desperately to heal, but feeling called to lay down that fight. For as many Christians there are in the world who will tell you they *don't know* God's end plan for their chronic pain, there are countless others who testify to an unmistakable call to acceptance. I've read their testimonies, and they've been a balm to my weary soul. A reminder that I'm not alone.

I've also started taking serious inspiration from the Apostle Paul, who had his own chronic affliction and begged God three times to heal it. God explicitly refused, in order to teach Paul to rely on God's all sufficient grace and strength alone, and so that *God* got the glory for everything Paul accomplished. Paul finally accepted that it was part of God's plan, and even began to "boast" about relying solely on God's power. In 2 Corinthians 12:9-10, Paul writes, "I will boast all the more gladly about my weaknesses, so that Christ's power may rest on me... For when I am weak, then I am strong."

Our society sees weakness as a flaw. But Paul saw it as an integral part of the Christian life. We were never meant to be the source of our own strength. We were created to worship the One who is. The weaker we are, the clearer that truth shines. Thus, one way God redeems our pain is showcasing His glory. One might ask, as I have, "Why does God selfishly want more praise at my expense? Isn't that egotistical?"

But He is teaching me that desiring more of His glory actually "transform[s] [us] into His image with ever-increasing glory" (2 Corinthians 3:18)—even through tears. His glory—which He is rightfully due as the almighty Creator of the universe—is tied to *my* good because it gives me more of what my soul was made to crave. He created us explicitly to desire and praise Him. Isaiah 43:21. Think of each person like a sunflower that must bend toward the sun (a phenomenon called heliotropism). The sun isn't being selfish by demanding the flower turn toward it—it's simply the sunflower's source of life, warmth, and growth. Just as the flower flourishes in the sun's light, we were designed to thrive in His glory.

Ultimately, if God wants to surprise me with miraculous healing, or nudge me to research random therapies again, He can. God knows how to speak to His sheep. But until that day, I think I'm getting closer to real surrender. So here I am, still walking, praying, waiting. Not waiting for healing, but waiting to see how He'll turn my pain into something beautiful, even if that beauty looks nothing like the healing I once dreamed of.

On a different note, the deep connection Matt and I share through our mutual suffering has illuminated a parallel truth about my relationship with Christ—one that is entirely reshaping how I view my illness. Just as Matt and I "get each other," I don't think we can truly grasp Jesus' crucifixion without bearing our own crosses and submitting to God's will just like Jesus did.

Suffering, then, is a means to experience deeper intimacy with Christ, *because we are walking the same path He did.* In Philippians 3:10, Paul writes, "I want to know Christ—yes, to know the power of His resurrection and participation in His sufferings, becoming like Him in his death."

This in no way means we seek out suffering. Rather, when we do suffer in this fallen world, it's a means to experience deeper fellowship with Christ. I feel that intimacy every time the Holy

Spirit draws near with timely comfort in my pain. This is the *sixth* tangible reason God has given me now regarding why God allows suffering. *Six and counting.*

An hour after talking with Matt, I open my devotional app and it features Philippians 3:4-10, where Paul counts all the reasons he had to "put confidence in [his] flesh" but nonetheless concludes, "I consider everything a loss because of the surpassing worth of knowing Christ Jesus[.]" *Thank you, Lord, for reminding me at a timely moment yet again.*

My worth, identity, and joy must come solely from Christ, not health or work. I can't let others' opinions, at church or otherwise, sway my outlook. We're all growing and works in progress. *Does this mean I don't need to fear missing out anymore, no matter what the future holds? Because even if one of us actually does die, Christ really does remain the truest joy?*

On that score, even months into marriage, I remain deeply convicted that the dream I had about *my* future death was from God—despite having misunderstood what God was communicating about whether Matt and I would marry. I've pleaded with God to clarify whether I might have misinterpreted the *meaning* of the dream as well, given that I'm still alive. But the conviction remains—and God never gave a timeline.

Tellingly, though, God continues to comfort me in deeply personal ways, not just in my grief over Matt's potential death, but in the sorrow I carry over my own.

Just the other night, Matt and I couldn't help but wonder—wouldn't we expect God to give me a dream like that only if my death were imminent? The next morning, my third devotional app curiously stated, "The valley of the shadow before death can be a short season, or a long one. But even in the heartbreak, God wants us to live fully alive in Christ every day, living moment to moment for Him." *Hmm. It feels like you are giving me a message about the timing of my dream, Lord.*

A few hours later, a complete stranger named Sara called me.

She told me she was a Christian, and oddly enough, a friend of one of my *non*-Christian friends who had apparently told her my spiritual struggles months ago.

Sara told me she knew believers in her church in the Philippines who had similarly received insight from the Holy Spirit about their future deaths. Rare, she said, but real. The timing of this unexpected phone call was uncanny and comforted me yet again that I'm not alone.

Sara even sent me a video testimony from a man named Eric Stogner, who shared that God had once given him a dream foretelling his wife's death. He had never had visions or supernatural dreams before, just like me, but this one was unmistakable. The revelation filled him with immediate sorrow and grief, and five months later, his wife passed away. And yet, he said the advance notice, as painful as it was, became a strange kind of mercy. It prepared his heart.

In all events, I'm noticing a shift into a less angry heart space concerning Jesus' plan to "take me home," whenever that is. Maybe—just maybe—that's okay…because we're *all* dying?! I'm not saying "who cares, this life stinks and I want out." Rather, this life is *not* the be all, end all. Our citizenship is in Heaven. Philippians 3:20. My emotions still jostle somewhat violently between great grief and acceptance, for both me and Matt. But *something* in my heart is shifting. And while friends sometimes urge me to live in the here and now instead of getting excited about Heaven, they're missing the point. When you're grieving a loss of any kind in this life, eternity isn't some distant dream; I'm learning it's the only hope sturdy enough to hold you through the fire.

Day 124

"Matt, are you okay?"

Mom's worried voice slices through the warmth of the living room.

Matt has been shifting on the couch for half an hour, his hand gripping mine, his face tight with discomfort. His jaw is set, his eyes unfocused. We're watching *Matilda* at my parents' place, but he hasn't laughed once at Danny DeVito. His attention is somewhere far from the screen.

It's December 23, around 8 p.m, and four days ago, we made the courageous trek by car to my parents' house, hearts full, trunk stuffed with gifts. Our first Christmas as husband and wife. A memory in the making.

"What's wrong babe?" I whisper now, afraid of the answer, stroking his head.

Matt winces, pressing a palm to his abdomen, clenching his teeth. "Hurts. Something's off."

Fifteen minutes pass.

The pain doesn't.

He's hunched over now, head in his hands, knuckles pale. I rub his back in slow circles, as if I can will the pain away.

Mom's eyes dart to me, then back to him, twice. Her voice cuts through the silence: "Matt, it's time we take you to the ER."

Oh no.

Is it beginning to look a lot like Christmas...or death?

47

The Night Before Christmas

The next morning at 7 a.m., December 24

My phone rings.

It's the call I've been dreading—from Joel, who stayed overnight with Matt at the hospital. *Bad news? No news?* My stomach knots as I answer on FaceTime, breath already held.

On Joel's FaceTime screen, Matt is curled into a fetal position on his hospital bed, his head pressed back into the pillow like he's trying to disappear into it. My heart sinks.

"Babe, how are you feeling, my sweet love?" I whisper.

Silence.

Then, barely audible, "Hurts."

I ask Joel, "The meds aren't working?"

Joel shakes his head and explains. It's Matt's first bowel obstruction in nearly two years—since his intestines launched a full-scale protest shortly after we started dating. This obstruction proves the second chemo wasn't our miracle. Scans now show further cancer progression.

Doctor Kranter had told us this chemo regimen would statistically buy us 120 to 150 days. It's been 124.

The symmetry is eerie.

Cruel.

The next morning—Christmas Day—another phone ring.

This time, it's Matt himself, calling from his hospital bed, his voice inexplicably stronger. Joyous, even. "Soon, we'll be together again," he says, resolute. "God's not done with us. Merry Christmas, my sweet girl."

He sounds like a man with renewed hope, and I desperately want to believe him. *Is the Holy Spirit assuring him he has more time? Will this obstruction clear?*

Still, as I sit alone today on Christmas morning, the ache in my chest burns. What kind of hope is this, on our first Christmas, Lord? Separated, uncertain, hurting. I know there are reasons for suffering, but must they really demand my husband's pain like this? Or worse, his death?

Hours later at night, my friend Rachel texts me her church's Christmas sermon on the Book of Habakkuk to comfort me. Habakkuk was a prophet watching his nation crumble under rampant injustice, crying out to God with raw questions about why He allows evil to thrive. But by the end of the book, Habakkuk's heart shifts—not because his world changes, but because he anchors his hope in God's goodness rather than his circumstances.

Before I listen, I open my *Daily Streams* app, and Habakkuk 3:17-18 stares back at me: "Though the fig tree does not bud and there are no grapes on the vines, though the olive crop fails and the fields produce no food, though there are no sheep in the pen and no cattle in the stalls, yet I will rejoice in the Lord, I will be joyful in God my Savior."

Thank you, Lord, for calling my heart to Habakkuk today. Whenever I read parts of Scripture that dive headfirst into suffering, it's like chugging spiritual Gatorade. Electrolytes for my soul. Frankly, I don't want to read about Jesus turning water into wine on a joyous occasion. I need help dealing with my suffering. Especially on Christmas.

I play the sermon, and the pastor's voice fills my heart with truth:

> Habakkuk's journey reminds us that even when circumstances are tragic and bewildering, our faith can flourish if we trust that God's ways surpass our understanding. Habakkuk moves from confusion to worship, praising God even without answers. We, too, must let go of the need to know why and trust God's goodness based on His Word and character, not our circumstances.

What are the chances this pastor would preach this on Christmas Day of all days? It almost feels divinely arranged for me today.

Lately I've been begging Jesus for answers again—*Why might You take Matt? Or me? Or both?* Clarity hasn't come. But when the Holy Spirit speaks to me in these coincidental ways—working through Rachel and my app—I recall Elisabeth Elliot's words: "God, through my own troubles and sufferings, has not given me explanations. But He has met me as a person[.]"

This has been true in my walk as well. I keep trying to act as judge but God keeps banging the gavel: "You're not even licensed in eternity. Trust Me." *Okay Lord, so You're telling me to stop obsessing over the "why."*

I once believed freedom came from unraveling answers. But I'm starting to believe that true peace is to be so convinced of the goodness and glory of God—as His Word assures—such that even in the dark, I can believe His motives are loving. This is the paradox of faith. To praise when we do not feel a molecule of gratitude. To accept His will when it hurts. To trust He's doing something good, though we can't see any good in it.

Lord, I want to get there. I'm still begging You to shape me into someone who doesn't just endure suffering, but who finds real joy within it. Someone who doesn't swing wildly between grief and joy, but can hold both at once. I feel like I'm flopping between the two like putting on those good old theater masks—tragedy and comedy, each taking turns under the spotlight.

I do feel some growth. Some of the reasons You allow suffering—they aren't just concepts anymore. They're becoming real to me, reshaping the way I see You. And yet, still, one question lingers, pressing at the edges of my faith.

You won't actually cross the death line, will You?

48

Stayin' Alive

"Joel, shake your hands left!"

I'm shimmying in my in-laws' living room inches away from Joel, my hips swaying dramatically to *Stayin' Alive* (by the Bee Gees) blasting from my phone speaker.

Some daughters-in-law drag you to brunch.

Others take you shopping.

I force Joel into impromptu disco routines. Since Trouble is out of commission, I've recruited Joel as my new but temporary co-star. I'm not sure if Joel agreed out of genuine disco fever or sheer inability to say no to me. Hopefully both.

Joel flails his arms around, his face a mix of genuine amusement, forced enthusiasm, and mild regret.

"Now shake your hands right!" I exclaim.

Anna, my enthusiastic videographer, giggles behind her phone camera. "Move those hips, Joel! Feel the groove!" she hollers.

It's been a few days since I made the trek down here to spend the rest of the holidays with Matt's family, just after Matt was discharged from the hospital. Thankfully, the obstruction cleared, but Matt is on a strict liquid diet now, in order to prevent any further obstructions. I've been lying flat as a pancake for four days to compensate for the long car ride, but now the ocean waves are settling somewhat back down to their chronic level.

Yesterday, we unwrapped gifts under my in-laws' Christmas tree to make up for Christmas Day. Matt—drained, hungry, but still smiling—opened a package of letters from his current and former students brimming with encouragements. A reminder of all the lives he's touched, even as his own hangs by a thread. Now, he's upstairs in the loft sleeping.

Though Matt is out of the hospital, we now know the second chemo was a bust. So even in the warmth of being together for the holidays, there's an unspoken tension in the family, like we're all holding our breath, afraid of what's coming.

Bottom line—Lara must lift the family mood.
Solution—the Bee Gees.
So here we are.
Shimmying.
Laughing.
Stayin' alive.
Literally.
Metaphorically.
Why not?
Live.
Auntie Ann glides by. "Looking good, you two!"

Having her, Uncle Ted, and Cousin Joey here this week has been such a comfort. Auntie Ann is an aerospace engineer and university professor—a literal rocket scientist—who once shuttled Matt to our sister Armenian church while he studied at UCLA. That's where he became a Christian. Now, she's constantly setting up Zoom prayer meetings for him.

"Cooper, get out of the shot!" Anna commands. The Silvermans' overenthusiastic Australian Shepherd, a Blue Merle blur of fur and boundless energy, has decided he, too, must boogie. He jumps into the frame, his tail wagging like he's leading a canine revival of Saturday Night Fever.

"He's got more rhythm than you two," Anna teases, as we shake our hands above our heads.

"Cooper's not bound by the chains of dignity," Joel laments.

Joel acts like he's just enduring this, but I catch that tiny, familiar smirk—like Matt's. The one that screams, *I'm too cool for this, but secretly love it.*

When the song ends, Joel takes a long sip from his reliable coffee mug like a man who's seen too much.

"Thanks, Joel," I say, needing to collapse, the turbulence of the room rising sharply from the two-minute stimulation. "This will be featured in my YouTube oldies collection."

"Great. When do I get my royalty check?"

I laugh, trudging towards the upstairs loft and passing by Joel's extensive vodka collection—three cupboards of elite bottles from every corner of the globe. "So, *this* is where you keep your life choices, Joel?"

"And where I question them." (He loves vodka. But in a "sweet Jewish uncle" way, not a "call the intervention team" way.)

Upstairs, I find Matt sprawled in bed on a video chat with Pastor Calvin, telling him that Ephesians 6:12 was on his mind during his hospital stay. That verse says Christians are fighting battles "against the spiritual forces of evil in the heavenly realms," likely in countless ways they can't even see.

Ephesians 3:10 also states God is making His wisdom "known to the rulers and authorities in the heavenly realms" *through* the lives of His believers, which are on display to angels and demons. 1 Corinthians 4:9 echoes this idea. Matt explains that this means that keeping our faith amidst suffering boldly declares God's power and sustaining grace to those spiritual beings. *So God uses our pain to showcase His glory even on a cosmic level? Wow. That's wild theology, but it's right there in the Bible.*

As Matt talks, I'm reminded of something strange God told me years ago while strictly bedridden. One night I cried out, desperate to understand why I was so severely ill. Four days later, Lisa texted Mom to tell me she had woken up with the word *bondage* impressed on her heart, for *me*. She didn't know what to make of it.

But later that week, two other Christian friends—separately—texted Mom to give me Luke 13:16, where Jesus said of a crippled woman, "Satan has kept her *bound* for eighteen long years." *Bondage*, again. It felt like God was opening my eyes to a deeper reality that sometimes, suffering has a spiritual dimension we can't see—just like God allowed Satan to torture Job, without Job even knowing. Job 2:6.

I didn't understand it at the time, but it's dawning on me as Matt explains: Satan wants to destroy our faith by taking us captive to illness or other kinds of suffering, but God remains sovereign, using evil attacks on His children to showcase His glory *even* to the cosmos.

We barely hang up with Calvin when Winston FaceTimes us. *Is it pastor office hours?* Luckily, God keeps giving us intimate time with friends who let us vent, grieve, discuss the hard questions. Calvin. Winston. Aren. The pastoral dream team—like therapy, but more Scripture and less copay.

Tonight, Winston asks if there's any way we can do a Haiti fundraiser at our church. Matt's eyes flicker. "Wait. Our one-year anniversary is coming up in March. What if we combine 'em somehow?"

Winston's eyebrows shoot up. "Anniversary fundraiser? I like it, buddy."

The conversation spins into planning mode, ideas flying back and forth. And this time, I'm not asking, *Will we make it? Is this God's will? Will we be too sick?* Instead, I find myself calm, reflective, even hopeful. Even if it never comes to pass.

"Why not?" I say aloud, surprising even myself. *More joy is on the way?*

A few days later on New Year's morning, Matt posts a Facebook update, downplaying his pain as usual:

Well, it's a new year, with new opportunities and adventures. It's particularly special starting off the year as a married man, and Lara and I are enjoying amazing family time. I landed in the hospital with an obstruction, but thankfully, it cleared up faster than expected. Treatment has been taking a larger toll on me, but we're still looking into clinical trials and I'm ready to start teaching next semester. Lara continues making wonderful music videos, and we have some fun projects coming up. We have some challenges, but I'm looking forward to what God has in store for us this year.

Meanwhile, I email out my *Stayin' Alive* video and vocal cover, giving people questionable fashion choices as I croon in outrageous disco outfits looking like I just escaped a '70s time capsule.

And the irony is not lost on me. We're stayin' alive, all right.

I laugh as I post it to YouTube, but inside, I'm proclaiming to the world—Still here. Still fighting. Still finding joy and *living* despite dying. *Joy in grief.*

Hours later before bed, Auntie Ann steps into our loft with enthusiasm and urgency.

"Matthew, I just got back from a conference. Ran into an old acquaintance with connections to a pharmaceutical company—Axelrodis. She's willing to pull some strings to try to get you compassionate use access to their latest experimental immunotherapy for colorectal cancer." My breath catches as I turn to Matt.

Auntie Ann has spent years researching treatments for Matt's disease. Maybe this one will finally stick? Her networking skills are so good that she could walk into a coffee shop for a latte and walk out with free tickets to a Michael Bublé concert.

Matt sits up, eyes focused now. "Would I qualify if it's for large intestinal cancer though?"

Auntie Ann replies, "Right, it's not designed for small intestinal cancer, so we need compassionate use access. That means approval from Axelrodis, which I'm hoping we can get through my friend, and approval from both Crescent Bay Medical's Institutional Review Board and your doctor. That's Doctor Kranter, right sweetie?"

Matt's eyes burn with new intensity—hope, skepticism, and desire all in one. "I'll email him now." *New year, new hope? Please, Lord, let this be real.*

Auntie Ann's chance encounter feels like divine timing? But we've been wrong before.

Still, if we've made it this far—through ER visits, late-night prayers, and questionable disco moves—then maybe, just maybe, we might keep stayin' alive a little longer.

49

Can't Get a Break

"You watching monkeys again, Trouble?"

I step out of the bathroom, rubbing my hands with a towel. It's after 8 P.M. on February 1, and our master bedroom is dim except for the blue glow of Matt's phone screen. He's reclining against his pillows in his blue button-up plaid pajamas, eyes locked on whatever primate antics he's found this time.

"Yeah," he whispers, contemplative. "Calms me. Makes me happy."

"I got you something," I say, pulling out a silver chain and fastening it around his neck. An eagle pendant gleams in the light. His fingers trace the metal, his expression unreadable, his eyes foggy.

"Symbolizes strength. Courage," I murmur. "You're my Eagle Scout."

His lips twitch into a soft smile.

"I was thinking of that verse," I add. "They will soar on wings like eagles, they will run and not grow weary—"

"They will walk and not be faint," he finishes.

We're together again, in Daly City, after a month apart. January was a cruel thief, robbing us of time together. I got a nasty flu so I stayed with my parents to shield Matt, and he had back-to-back hospitalizations. First, the cancer started pressing into his *left* kidney as well, so he needed an emergency surgical stent operation for *both* kidneys this time. Then, a nonstop obstruction cycle began:

> *Matt's intestines revolt*
> *He starts liquid diet to clear said revolt*
> *Revolt clears*
> *He tries to eat solid food again*
> *Matt's intestines stage another coup*
> *Repeat*

Put simply, he can't eat solid foods anymore. Due to severe abdominal pain, vomiting, and his recent obstructions, he has to stick only to soft foods to prevent further obstructions. *Soft eggs. Pudding. Pureed chicken. Watery soups. Apple sauce.* Not exactly a menu out of *Le Cordon Bleu*. But Matt? He never complains.

His weight is starting to plummet, and the chemo is starting to eat at his liver too. Lab results are off, for the first time in a year.

Thankfully, Auntie Ann's friend miraculously got Axelrodis on board, so that's one really big victory. But we're still stuck in limbo, waiting day in, day out for the green light from Crescent Bay Medical's Institutional Review Board and Doctor Kranter on whether *they* approve the use of the immunotherapy on Matt as well.

But right now, none of that matters.

We're here.

Together again.

Finally.

Matt rubs his thumb over the eagle pendant. "Do you love me?"

I softly gasp. He's never asked me that before. His blank face betrays a need, perhaps reassurance of something good in this world.

"Yes, I love you so much, Silverman. More than the British love tea." I lie down beside him and clasp his hand.

"Sometimes I just need to hear it again. An anchor in the storm, you know?"

"Totally. I'm here babe, I'm here. You're my anchor too."

This is still our marriage. Lying in bed half of the day to rest our bodies and brains, holding hands, willing the pain to pass. Our normal. A normal we need.

Two minutes pass in silence.

Then Matt's voice wavers, soft, almost breaking. "I can't believe Harout died."

My stomach knots. Harout, a fellow Armenian youth pastor at Matt's old church in Los Angeles. Thirty-eight years old. Brain cancer. Died in six months. Over the holidays. Leaving a wife and two children behind.

I'm at a loss for words.

Matt exhales hard. "All the churches were prayin' for him."

"I know, love. God's ways are so mysterious. He seemed like an amazing man."

Another quiet settles, heavier than the last.

"Babe," I finally whisper, "should we even do the Haiti anniversary event in March? Given everything you went through last month? It's okay if you want to cancel. It's okay to let people down sometimes."

His jaw tenses, considering. Then, after a long pause, he says, "We should press forward. God'll give us strength."

I search his face. "Oh Trouble, I don't know how you even taught all of last month. Literally from those hospital beds on Zoom."

"Good distraction from everythin'," he replies.

He waits a few seconds, then adds, "Lara. This Axelrodis thing is very risky. My body's already wrecked. The treatment shuts down your immune system. No guarantees it'll work, especially with all my obstructions."

"We should try it though, right babe?"

"Yeah, it's all we've got. There's nothin' wrong with beggin' the Lord. Here, let's pray."

We hold hands, eyes shut, and Matt prays. Harout's death apparently didn't shake Matt's faith. Just his resolve to smile.

We drift into sleep, until an hour later at 9:30 P.M., when Matt stirs.

He shifts, throwing a hand to his chest. "Chest pain. Feels like I can't breathe."

My eyes fly open and I sit up immediately, bracing against the turbulence of the room. "What do you mean?"

His head tilts back against the pillow, his eyes locking onto mine, fear flickering there. My pulse jumps. "What do you mean you can't breathe?"

"Don't feel right."

"Is it the meds? The chemo?"

"Don't know."

Three minutes pass. Nothing changes.

"Babe," I say, my voice tight, slapping a blood pressure cuff on his arm. "Should I call an ambulance?"

He doesn't answer. It's answer enough.

As I'm calling, Matt looks up to me, his eyes gleaming frustration.

"This isn't fair," he blurts, his voice cracking, sharp. "We just got back together." He's never voiced a complaint like this during emergencies. The January hospitalizations have finally shaken his patience. How could they not?

Within minutes, the house is swarming with paramedics.

Flashing red lights.

Voices barking instructions.

Matt heaving on the bed, gripping his chest.

I call Anna and Joel, my heart racing. "Matt's going to the hospital."

"We'll meet him there asap," Joel says.

As they wheel Matt toward the ambulance in a wheelchair, something shifts in his expression—there's fear, but also a flicker of courage. "I'll be back, love."

"Think eagle, Trouble! God will give you courage!" *Good timing on that eagle, Lord. Please keep him safe.*

And just like that, we're separated again.

The silence that follows swallows me whole.

This isn't just a rollercoaster. It's a radio stuck on the same loop of a tasteless song. I sink into a dull, familiar jadedness. *It almost feels normal to have my husband whisked away.*

𝄞

Matt shivers under a blanket at our kitchen table, trembling in the relentless Daly City cold.

After the episode last night, he came right back at 6 A.M. this morning. The doctors couldn't diagnose what caused the breathing issue, only that increasing his pain meds made it stop. A mystery with no answer. Another crisis averted but never resolved.

And for his grand return? A "welcome home" gift wrapped in crisis, tied neatly with a bow of cold—the electricity shut off this morning without warning.

No heating.

No fridge.

Our food is spoiling, rotting by the hour.

Luckily, Matt's sister and her husband are coming over soon to help clear out what we can salvage. I stand at the stove, flickering a lighter beneath a pan so I can cook soft scrambled eggs for him. This electricity debacle is adding fuel to the fire, except there's no fuel and no fire. Just our diminishing emotional reserves.

I set Matt's eggs down on the table and rub my arms, scavenging around for a second sweater. Then I open the fridge and take one whiff. "The yogurt is probably a biohazard now. I told you DoorDash is one of life's necessary blessings. We just might need it now."

Matt half smiles then shrugs. *He looks so muted, so exhausted.*

Twenty minutes after breakfast, Matt's sharp, guttural yell

from our master bathroom floats down the hall. My stomach drops.

Matt doesn't yell. Not when they botched his IV. Not when he lost seven pounds in two weeks. Not even when they said the cancer was growing again.

I rush in to find him standing shirtless, hunched over the sink, his ostomy bag clutched in his trembling hands. *He's trying to change it.* His skin is damp, nearly translucent, his teeth chattering. The chemo makes him cold already, and he doesn't have his regular body weight to keep him warm anymore.

"Bag broke. Twice," he laments, looking down, his voice sharp. "I'm freezing. There's no heat."

I swallow hard. "It's okay, love. I'm here. How can I help? Please. Tell me."

His eyes flick to mine, wet with frustration. He didn't sleep a wink last night in the hospital.

Suddenly, he chokes it out—"God's abandoned me."

I freeze.

Matt has never cracked. Never questioned. Never allowed himself to doubt. Turns out he's human after all.

"What am I supposed to do?" he blurts. "I need Doctor Kranter's approval, and they keep telling me he's still traveling. The Institutional Review Board process could take months. Bureaucratic jumbles. They might never get back to me."

He looks down again, his voice turning softer, weaker now. "I texted Winston earlier. If God doesn't break a bruised reed, why are we breaking?" His tone is not one of accusation. It's a genuine question to His Lord. The God he loves.

Hours later, Joel comes over, our emergency help-line hauling in blankets thick enough for snow. He tosses them over us, joking about how he's prepping us for the next ice age. I giggle with Joel. Matt doesn't. He stares past us, his fingers clenched in the fabric. I've never seen him like this—so taut, so hollow.

After four grueling, frostbitten days, the electricity finally flickers back on. We react like wrongfully convicted prisoners granted parole—disoriented, suspicious, but overwhelmingly grateful.

Relief.

Sweet relief.

But later that same night, another disaster.

I burn my hand on a hot pan while cooking Tuscan chicken, the pain a white-hot sear. I yelp, sprinting to the sink, shoving my palm under cold water.

"Matt, it's probably second-degree," I grit out, crying, while he calls the advice nurse for me. *What's next?* If our life is a comedy of errors, the errors are the script, the set design, and the director.

The next night, we finally have some much needed quiet time together lying down in bed. Matt decides to reflect on Psalm 91, which states:

> Surely [God] will save you from the fowler's snare and from the deadly pestilence. ... You will not fear the terror of night, nor the arrow that flies by day ... 'Because he loves me,' says the Lord, 'I will rescue him; I will protect him, for he acknowledges my name. He will call on me, and I will answer him; I will be with him in trouble, I will deliver him and honor him. With long life I will satisfy him and show him my salvation.'

A few minutes into our reflection, Nancy, one of the youth group moms, texts him the same exact verse as a comfort—Psalm 91.

"Matt," I exclaim, heart jumping. "This isn't a coincidence. God's speaking to you! Look, Nancy's timing—God's promising you'll be healed! What else can it mean—the verse explicitly says, 'I will rescue him' and 'deliver him' and save him 'from the deadly pestilence.' I know this Psalm doesn't apply to you just because it's in the Bible. But it *does* apply when God gives it to you specifically as a promise."

Matt's eyes fill. No answer, but I see it—he wants it to be true. Every fiber of his being is clinging to the possibility.

"Babe, you've had a conviction of healing all along. God's encouraging you given what you're going through now."

Matt exhales, long and slow. "He's speaking to me, yes. But I don't feel like this is a promise of healing specifically. That conviction I had that I would 'remain'? It's fading. I somehow knew two years ago that I'd be around longer. But now, it feels different."

"But babe—look at the words—"

His jaw tightens, his face flustered now. "Lara, this could just be an encouragement from God that He will comfort me in the pain, not a guarantee of earthly deliverance."

A beat of silence. Then his voice hardens—rare, but unmistakable. "Stop pushing your theology on me, okay? You're acting like my pain and sorrow don't matter because you think I'm *definitely* going to heal."

He looks away.

His words slap me across the face.

My pulse spikes.

"That's not what I mean, Matt! I'm trying to encourage you about healing, not dismiss your grief."

What's a wife supposed to say? "You just might die"? Aren't we supposed to believe in Christ's miracles? How are Christians supposed to encourage their sick loved ones? My parents always encouraged me I would heal—and I believed it with every fiber until the Lord expressly told me otherwise.

Absent an express indication that God's will is to the contrary, it seems right to encourage Matt that he will heal. Especially given his original conviction of healing, and the fact that God has kept him alive despite terminal illness for so long.

Are we really supposed to just throw up our hands and say— "We don't know the outcome, but God will do what's best"? *That doesn't feel right. But am I trying to control this because I love him so much?*

My cheeks heat. Before I can stop myself, the words spill out. "Well, have you noticed you never *ask* about my symptoms? We only talk about your cancer and pain. Unless I bring mine up explicitly." My voice shakes. "I know you say you don't want sympathy, but I ask you every day how you're feeling, and you like and need it."

"That's because you never *want* to talk about your symptoms. You escape them. So what's the point in asking you?"

"I talked about them for four years. Then God told me *no*. What am I supposed to do? Tell me what you would do if God called you to acceptance."

"Maybe He is."

Matt falls silent.

So do I.

We're worn down.

At breaking point.

Is Matt's conviction of healing really fading? Could this be like my situation where God originally told me He was "coming" to encourage me generally, but I incorrectly assumed God was promising healing specifically?

We've never had a fight like this in one year of marriage. But even the strongest bonds fray under enough weight. Given our sinful nature, Christian spouses are bound to take pain out on one another and misunderstand each other's needs at times.

Seconds of silence stretch into minutes and exhaustion wins. Matt drifts into a kind of depressive sleep, hunched upright on his pillow, while tears slip down my face in the quiet of our dim bedroom.

Forty minutes later, Pastor Calvin texts both of us, and the buzz of Matt's phone shifts him awake from his nap. Calvin encourages us to persevere, citing Paul's declaration in Philippians 3:13-14—"Forgetting what is behind and straining toward what is ahead, I press on toward the goal to win the prize for which God has called me Heavenward in Christ Jesus."

Matt reads the text and turns to me, his voice raw with tenderness. "I'm sorry, Lara. We're breakin' down. And this reminds us to stay focused on eternity. To keep perspective that these trials are temporary."

I break down instantly because I realize—I am hurting my husband.

"I'm so sorry, Matt. I love you so much. I can't believe what I said. And you're right. Our hope isn't supposed to be in earthly healing, but in Heaven. Eternal glory, right? My mentality is hurting you…a lot."

"Lara, it's…I just…I need you to grieve with me sometimes, that's all. Instead of rejoicing about an outcome we don't know will come."

"I hear you, love. I'm so sorry. Look. I won't tell you going forward if I still think this Psalm 91 coincidence from Nancy's text means God is explicitly promising to heal you. I don't want to hurt you again."

He squeezes my hand. "You can still tell me your beliefs. Your hopeful nature is a gift. It's just, sometimes I need to sit in the grief. Make sense?"

"Of course."

A beat later, I say the only thing I can think of: *"DuckTales?"*

50

A Musical Love Story

I stand before the tripod in my music room.

My silky, yellow A-line dress pools at my feet as my satin, elbow-length white jazz gloves wrap my fingers in elegance.

The melody of the timeless jazz classic *They Can't Take That Away From Me* flows from my lips as the camera records, filling the space with quiet intimacy.

And then, mid-phrase, I turn—

Matt.

Standing in the doorway.

Watching me.

That look—those eyes of adoration that make my breath hitch.

My breath snags from emotion and I can't get out the next note.

"Oh, Lara," he offers. "You're my *Maria* from *The Sound of Music*. I was suffering, and then you came into my life, bringin' music and joy."

I close my eyes for a second, swallowing the weight of his words. "Matt... I... your words of affirmation mean so much to me. And *you* taught me how I can actually have that joy in the middle of grief."

After everything—the hospitals, the waiting, the disasters—we need tonight. A stolen pocket of time where sickness doesn't own us.

Valentine's Day.

I pause the recording, and Matt grabs my hand, leading me toward the kitchen in his indigo jeans and green polo, a mischievous twinkle glistening in his eye. "Time to feed my girl. I whipped up somethin' special."

"I thought we were going to cook together?"

"Don't worry, I had some strength."

The moment we step into the kitchen, the scent of chicken parmesan hits me—crispy breaded chicken, rich marinara, and melted cheese, all blending into hints of garlic, basil, and oregano.

"Oh, love, it smells wonderful! Thank you so much."

On the dining room table, a dozen red roses sit in a crystal-clear glass vase. The faintest hint of their intoxicating fragrance drifts through the air. *This is so Old Hollywood romance!* Then, he slides a familiar pink box toward me.

Red velvet cupcakes. *My favorite Daly City bakery.*

"Babe, you didn't have to, this is so—"

"Shhh," he murmurs, pulling out my chair, nudging me down with gentle insistence. "Let me spoil you tonight."

"Thank you!"

"Always."

We eat—at least, I do. Matt in contrast, picks at tiny, puréed bits of chicken from the freezer. Still, he watches me with pure contentment, as if my joy can be swallowed in place of his own. For dessert, Matt grabs a cupcake. "Just one bite," he says, carving off a thumbnail-sized taste. It's all his system can handle.

After dinner, I slip away into our bedroom and return to grab his hand. "Follow me, Trouble. My turn."

He chuckles down the hall until I dramatically push open our bedroom door. And as I do, the world slows.

Soft, flickering candlelight from ten vanilla scented candles bathes our otherwise dark bedroom, casting gentle golden shadows across the walls. Crimson, heart shaped velvet petals lie scattered across the bed. (I still like pomp and circumstance; I'm an actress, not a minimalist. What did you expect—subtlety? If there's no dramatic lighting, is it even love?)

On the dresser, a six inch by six inch wooden box—with words engraved on it—cradles a single glowing red candle, its flame a heartbeat against the dark.

Matt takes it all in, eyes growing wide. His gaze lifts to the words shimmering across the wall from the candle box, like a sacred vow:

I LOVE YOU MATTHEW
ISAIAH 43:20

"See, babe?" I whisper. "You're still my stream in the desert. You're still here. Still alive."

He pulls me close until our heartbeats align. I tap my phone, and the soft, emotional notes of *Can You Feel the Love Tonight* spill into the air. One of our favorites from our wedding playlist. We sway together, not circling but just holding each other, lost in the quiet rhythm of love.

"I love you, Lara," he says, pulling back and reaching to his bedside drawer, revealing something of his own. He hands me a beautifully crafted photo album wrapped in fancy, textured blue leather, with high-quality gilded pages inside. Across the cover, these gold-embossed words shimmer:

A Musical Love Story

I gasp. "Matt—"

"God's still writin' it, Kitten."

I flip page after page, photo after photo of our stolen moments, our journey, frozen in time. I clutch the album to my chest, holding this night, this love, this gift of *joy*. "This is the most beautiful gift I've ever received, Matt. The title is so thoughtful."

My heart is going to explode tonight. God wrote us a love story at death's door. He scripts "glory" right when we'd cue "despair."

After a few moments, Matt exhales hard, breaking the magic somewhat abruptly. "Need to lie down, I'm exhausted."

He heads to our bathroom and smirks, looking at the MEOW sign Joel sneaked in a year ago. "Isn't it time to take that thing down?"

"You don't want to be thrown into the Kitten dungeon, do you?"

He giggles, disappearing into the bathroom.

"Matt," I call after a minute, lying down in bed now. "We're almost out of toilet paper. But I just refilled some." (You know you're married when Valentine's Day segues from candlelight to toilet paper real fast.)

His voice drifts through the door, laced with sarcasm. "Turns out there are stores. You know, where you can go and pay and they give you the stuff."

"Yeah, yeah, yeah. Be careful, or I'll make you lie down on a Safeway pavement again."

"Anything but another nineteen-day ban."

While waiting for him, I flip to one of his YouTube devotionals on my phone. (I'll admit: so I can watch that handsome face.) *Why can't I get enough of this man?* Even when I kiss Matt, it always feels like it's ending too soon. Like there's always an itch for more. Do other couples feel this way?

Interestingly, C.S. Lewis wrote, "If we find ourselves with a desire that nothing in this world can satisfy, the most probable explanation is that we were made for another world." He also wrote, "All joy emphasizes our pilgrim status; always reminds, beckons, awakens desire. Our best havings are wantings."

Maybe my longing for this feeling of permanent love and joy *in Matt* will only find its final satisfaction in eternity? In Heaven, finally experiencing *God's* glory? Ecclesiastes 3:11 says God has "set eternity in the human heart[.]"

Matt steps back into the room, arching an eyebrow. "You're watchin' those for *spiritual content* these days, right Kitten?"

"Shut up, Silver. I've got to squeeze in all your cuteness now because word on the street is that no one's going to kiss me in Heaven."

He sits beside me on my side of the bed. "What am I, chopped liver?" He giggles. "But, technically, you're right. In Heaven, Christ will be the church's bridegroom, and the church will be His bride. You and I won't be married there, but we'll be reunited. There'll be a wedding feast of the Lamb—Jesus—instead. Our temporary marriages on earth are a precursor to our unity in Heaven with Jesus."

"Sadly, I'm aware," I whine dramatically. "I found it today—Mark 12:25. We're all doomed." *Lord, I'm gonna kiss Matt up there whether You like it or not. I'm willing to negotiate some of my eternal rewards—if I have any.*

Ladies, stop lying to yourselves. Every Christian wife is wondering why Jesus takes away this beautiful gift in Heaven. Theologian John Piper posits that the eternal joys awaiting believers will be so intensely pleasurable that they will far surpass any pleasure we experience now, meaning earthly marriage cannot contain the fullness of God's eternal joys. 1 Corinthians 2:9 certainly supports this idea.

This is an absolutely breathtaking Scriptural promise but so difficult to believe when you love your spouse so much.

Matt chastises me, touching my nose with his finger. "We'll all be baskin' in God's love and glory. So…you probably won't care about me anymore."

"Ha! See!" I throw a pillow at him. "No kisses in Heaven! So let me get this straight. Streets of gold, angelic choirs, and eternal peace, but God draws the line at kisses? I need a courtroom debate with Apostle Paul immediately. Didn't he end his epistles instructing people to greet with a 'holy kiss' or something? Maybe there's hope."

"Kitten!" He tickles me. "So, now you've finally learned there's no perfect life on earth, so you've moved your target to your perfect version of Heaven?"

"Look me in the eyes, Silverman. Do you or do you not want to cuddle me in Heaven? That's a yes or a no question."

"Look, we can't really understand it. But we know that Jesus' love and our mutual agape love for each other will be so intense that it will be beyond marriage. Marriage is about intimacy and deep connection. And marriage here is just a foretaste, an anticipation of that deep love we'll have in eternity."

I roll my eyes. "Well, will I still get to sit next to you at the Heavenly potlucks? Or, if I accidentally trip and fall into your arms, will that count as unlawful post-earthly affection? These are the *real* theological questions. Maybe I need to consult Aren. I need a lawyer's take."

"We'll have all of eternity to be together."

"Fine. Now kiss me. You're negligent. Been twenty minutes."

"Right then. Envision the grand stage, dearest! Let your bow weave a tempest of passion spun from the echoes of a thousand forgotten symphonies!"

Mary, my exuberant violin teacher, bellows through my Zoom camera in a thick, Scottish accent, waving her hands enthusiastically.

"And, if you miss a note or go weak at the knees from nerves, make it so dramatic they think it was intentional!"

Three months ago, I started taking real lessons. I found Mary's YouTube channel while teaching myself, and something in me said: "Hired." She's a petite, vivacious Scottish lady living in a cottage in Ireland, with long shimmering silver hair and bright blue eyes—like a character in a *Lord of the Rings* movie. A retired concert violinist, her fantastical encouragements are exactly my vibe. God couldn't have paired me with a more fitting teacher—someone who speaks the same theatrical language as my soul. Another *gift* from God in my pain.

Today—while Matt's writing a political proposition analysis, his mind deep in logical analysis to solve real-world problems—Mary and I are preparing to dazzle 'em. I'm prepping a full thirty-minute, fifteen-song violin set I'm *determined* to play as guests arrive at our one-year anniversary Haiti fundraiser.

Why not take the risk of playing a new instrument in public, even though I've only been at it for months? Singing and acting is my "safe" space. Violin? Let's just say I'm not well-seasoned yet—more like a bland, undercooked chicken breast that still needs salt, pepper, and oregano. But I'm definitely improving, so…Why not?

Is this a new *"my worth is not in perfection so let's take risks"* Lara or the *"tick it off the bucket list before I waltz into Heaven"* Lara? I *think* I've almost outgrown the latter…?

Either way, I can't believe I'm about to play a full concert *while spinning*. (And if I fail miserably, at least the church has a solid prayer team.)

I stand up taller and tighten my grip on my violin. "Don't worry Mary. Mozart's got nothing on me. Well, except for the whole child prodigy thing."

51

The Days Are Evil

Matt's voice rings steady through the CACC community auditorium.

"A lot of people look at what we've been facin'—cancer, neurological challenges—and ask, *How much can you really do?* But Ephesians says we must make the most of every opportunity because the days are evil. Time on earth might be runnin' out, but here we are, makin' the most of every opportunity. We're still here. Still fightin'."

Matt grips the microphone in one hand, and in the other, his cane. He stands tall beside me, in a brand new trendy purple suit jacket, slick black dress pants, and a stylish tie knotted just right. He's a vision of grace, strength, and faith unshaken, even as his body betrays him.

The enticing aroma of trays of Greek gyros, tangy yogurt, and warm pita bread fills the space. The sizeable crowd peers back at us—all people who have become part of our fight.

We've made it—our one-year anniversary Haiti fundraiser on March 4. We all spent two months prepping for this night. Thirty minutes ago, Matt was melting into a table hunched over in pain, looking like a deflated pool float. Now, he's standing here before everyone, giving a full-on TED Talk. *Which angel injected him with Holy-Spirit espresso? Maybe the one that gave the prophet Elijah food?*

I stand beside him, my floor-length velvety purple dress draping over my frame. *I hope no one notices my waddling to ward off earthquakes from the ride. So embarrassing. Help me, Lord. Keep away all 10.0 episodes.*

Matt continues, smiling wide now. "Now, I'm usually not a fan of these fancy church fundraisin' banquets where we just feed ourselves fancy foods to raise money for ourselves." Aren giggles, sitting at the table to the left. *Theological bromance.*

"That's because Jesus said when you throw a banquet, don't invite the rich. Invite the poor, the crippled, those who can't pay you back."

He pauses to collect his breath. "But the people we're helpin' tonight are those who can't be here. Those who wake up every mornin' wonderin' if they'll eat, if they'll survive, if they'll have any hope. We're here to change that. To create real, lastin' change. The school we're buildin' in Haiti, the programs, the jobs—it's about givin' people a future where they don't have to fear. Christ called us to be His hands and feet in this hurtin' world."

When Matt closes, Winston jumps forward passionately, with fire in his eyes: "Please, if you feel led, give to Haiti. Matt's turning his test into a testimony, amen? God can do miracles, amen? But either way, we *will* see Matt again soon, amen? Glory!"

A few brave warriors in the crowd murmur cautious "amens"—because, well, we're Armenian evangelicals with strict church bylaws. Charisma isn't exactly our spiritual gift. We love Jesus, but we express it mostly through deeply suspicious nodding. Our closest version of "Pentecostal fire" is an intense debate over which grandma cooked the best dolma.

After Winston, Mitch, and Elisha share updates on their ongoing work in Haiti, they honor Matt with a touching tribute—a beautifully crafted plaque recognizing his unwavering dedication to advancing education and engineering initiatives in Haiti. While Matt's being crowned, I stand at his side, smiling with pride like any strategic First Lady. *You didn't buy this dress just to blend in with the floral arrangements, woman. Pose. Wave. Channel your inner Kate Middleton.*

As the applause fades, I take a breath and reach for the mic. My turn. *Just enjoy this. Keep waddling. Make 'em laugh.*

"Despite my losses, God has given me great joys—the greatest being marriage. This year has been a surprisingly artistic paradise of joy amidst grief. Who knew all it took for me to become a newbie painter was neurological pain? At this rate, if I break a leg, I might become the next Michelangelo." Chuckles ripple through the room.

"But all of my physical movement has really been a miracle of sustaining grace as I force myself to sit up every day. I haven't seen healing, but I have learned to rejoice in grief because God grants us gifts of joy and purpose in our valleys. But it gets better. My stylish hubby even made the Guinness Book of World Records this year for being the first engineering PhD featured in a VOGUE fashion show. Miracles happen, church. So, we might be in our jailhouse of pain—but we're still rocking. Hit it, Brian!"

The projector screen behind me lights up. A clip plays of Matt, dressed in full 1950s Grease-style attire, sunglasses perched on his bald head, singing *Jailhouse Rock* as a solo.

The room erupts into laughter. The youth group loses it, shouting out cheers.

A few minutes later, I close. "As I accept this Oscar for reaching my one-year anniversary, I'd like to thank the academy, my husband for being incredibly attractive, and my father-in-law for doing this—Brian, hit it!"

Stayin' Alive blares through the auditorium speakers, as a video of Joel grooving across the screen sends the crowd into hysterics, proving that disco never dies.

After the speeches, the hall hums with energy. Elisha and the team sell handcrafted Haitian goods. A slideshow of Matt's work in Haiti plays on a loop. Anna sneaks up behind Matt, kissing his cheek, then Mom plants one squarely on my left eye for good measure. Team member Tim slides up. "Power couple. The king of logic and the queen of creativity. Who knew Matt had Elvis in him?"

Matt barely touches the Greek food—he's still surviving on soft foods, and some liquids now. Joel circles, camera in hand, but his eyes betray a sense of deep sadness tonight. *His son can't even eat.*

An hour later, we crank up the magic again. Violin and flute in hand, Matt and I step onto the stage once more. The lights dim. A hush falls. Time for some special duets with Trouble.

The first notes of Céline Dion's *My Heart Will Go On* from the *Titanic* movie spill into the room. Then, *Can You Feel the Love Tonight*. Finally, *Can't Help Falling in Love*. All the classics.

As my bow glides across the strings, my chest feels two sizes too small for this moment. This is the most *us* anniversary imaginable. No Hawaii. No champagne. Just performance for me. Charity for Matt.

Two birds. One stone. Still used. Still purposed. Our *third* musical performance since we got married. Another rebellion of joy in grief. Only God could orchestrate such a night. Put that in your pipe and smoke it, Satan. The more joy we have despite our pain, the dumber you look.

Our decision to *live*, even now, is a testimony. If there's nothing more after this life, why would we even bother? Wouldn't the despair swallow us whole? But because there *is* more—because eternity is real—*this life* takes on a whole new meaning. *That's* what joy in grief is about.

Embracing *life* in all circumstances.

Sure, a few times throughout the night, it looks like either one of us might pass out. But we know we will lie flat on our backs all next week, so we push through. We always do, thanks to God's grace. *And now we're hosting fundraisers?* Philippians 4:13 really is true: "I can do all things through Christ who strengthens me"

(NKJV). God continues to showcase His glory by displaying *His* strength in our otherwise weak bodies. As Paul wrote about his own chronic affliction, "[God] said to me, 'My grace is sufficient for you, for my power is made perfect in weakness.'" 2 Corinthians 12:9.

I even pulled off my solo violin set earlier—fifteen songs, each note a little battle, each mistake a badge of honor, while my brain pirouetted like a malfunctioning ballerina.

Mistakes? Gasp! *Yes.* And guess what? I'm fine with it. *Character development? Maybe my worth is getting closer to being in Christ alone.* I've been clinging to a really liberating verse lately, where Paul writes, "I care very little if I am judged by you or by any human court; indeed, I do not even judge myself." 1 Corinthians 4:3. *Talk about good self-talk therapy. All perfectionists should try it.*

As the night winds down, Winston saunters over, clapping Matt on the shoulder. "Buddy, we raised $13,000. You're the man, the myth, the legend."

Elisha sidles up behind me, whispering, "Matt's outfit tonight? On point. The powers of Lara."

Winston adds, "Don't forget buddy. The best is yet to come, either way. Think wedding feast of the Lamb in Heaven." Isaiah 25:6 promises that in Heaven, God will "prepare a feast of rich food for all peoples, a banquet of aged wine—the best of meats and the finest of wines."

Then, a gentle tap on my shoulder—"Your dress is stunning, Lara!" my friend Miriam beams.

I turn, grinning. "Thanks! Purple's so regal, right? I even convinced Matt to match."

In this tender moment, I consider how our purple attire tonight symbolizes our future royal "inheritance" in God's "kingdom of light." Colossians 1:12. It's like God is whispering, *Forget hospital gowns—one day, you and Matt will wear royal robes as sons and daughters of the King, feasting at the wedding banquet of the Lamb.*

Bring on the celestial champagne.
And make it bottomless.

52

Normal

"You keep stroking his head, and it's gonna turn into the Shekinah glory."

Winston's charisma cuts through the tension, a feeble attempt to lighten the weight in our family room.

I jab back, "Well, if it works, I'm opening a healing ministry."

The Haiti team is visiting tonight, two days after the fundraiser. Matt's pain has been escalating the last hour, carving deep lines into his face, and he finally lets out a sharp exhale. "Okay. Need to go to the hospital. Feels like an obstruction again. Dad'll take me."

Matt has continued on the second chemo since December, even though it's not doing much to control the cancer. And now, even soft foods can't seem to pass through his system. The last two days he's been vomiting up the little amounts of soft food he tries to consume. Time for a pure liquid diet—permanently.

Winston furrows his brows, etched with concern. "A quick prayer session first." The team gathers around, offering raw, fervent prayers, hands stretched out, resting on Matt's frame. Then Matt's eyes glisten. "Can we sing *Because He Lives* one more time before I go?"

The house instantly swells with the anthem of hope ringing through the walls. Powerful hope. Then, Winston closes, his voice wavering with emotion. "Listen, buddy. Hang in there. Remember—test to testimony. And hey, I always tell you this. Either way, we'll see you soon. God is still good." *I don't like the sound of "either way."* He gives Matt's shoulder a firm squeeze, as if anchoring him to the faith they share.

Matt spends the next two weeks in the hospital. I hold my phone all day, twisting a strand of hair, debating whether to call. I don't want to wake his naps, or be a burden. I hate not being there, but the car ride would be impossibly far for my brain, especially doing a round trip back. So, I decide to send him a five-foot giant stuffed animal bear instead. Something larger-than-life just to bridge the space between us.

Joel wastes no time posting a Facebook photo of it towering over Matt's hospital bed, with the caption, "Lara just never does anything small. This thing is bigger than Matt. Hospital security actually spoke to me about whether this bear counted as an unauthorized guest."

I text Joel back, "You think this is big? I almost went with the life-size giraffe. But you know, restraint."

But the jokes are no use. Restlessness gnaws at me. Even with all our recent victories, I still just want us to be normal.

Normal.

What a nice word.

A normal couple.

A couple that doesn't measure time in hospital admissions and CAT scan results. *Is it wrong to want that, Lord?* Every night, Psalm 6:6-7 speaks to me—"I am worn out from my groaning. All night long I flood my bed with weeping and drench my couch with tears[.]"

One night, to empty my turbulent emotions, I write. I just pick up a notepad and the words pour out as I lie in bed. A poem—I title it: **NORMAL:**

Normal

So so tired of faking nice
Feels like every minute we're rolling dice
Can't bring myself to smile no more
All I want is to feel normal

The only thing I want is normalcy
Begging and begging, but it eludes me
Trying my best not to drown each day
Illness is a game I don't want to play

'Cause I ain't feeling normal
I'm missing that normal
I want that normal
I want to feel normal

It ain't so easy to forget the past
Times when you could breathe without a gasp
On top of the world, flying high
Now you just sit here wondering why

The bottom line is it ain't fair
All the injustice we just can't square
But God's got a point you have to trust
No matter how dark the pain cuts

You pray and you pray, asking Him to show
The reasons your pain has to cut so low
The truth is, sometimes we just can't see
What will be revealed in eternity

Where we'll feel normal
We'll get to be normal
I miss that normal
I want that normal

Reading it back, a melody unmistakably hums in the back of my mind. I go sit at our keyboard, press down some chords, and suddenly, it all makes sense. *This isn't a poem—it's a song.* The music flows from me, unbidden, like a caged bird finding its voice yet again. Before I know it, I'm steaming a pot of my favorite hibiscus tea and composing feverishly, driven by something I can't explain.

Three more songs follow the next week—*Heart Thief*, a pop song about Matt's love, and two more sophisticated jazz pieces. Songwriting becomes escape. Therapy. Never done it before. Another surprise gift from God.

I perform the songs in the music room. Record. Edit. Sculpt the sounds with a conviction I didn't know I had, all lying down.

Thank you Jesus for the gift of music. I feel like I've self-enrolled in arts school even though I'm chained at home away from Trouble. Music is the language our souls speak when words fail, isn't it? A sacred thread pulling us closer to our Creator, reminding us that even in our brokenness, we were made for something glorious. I mean, when you listen to Mozart's *Eine Kleine Nachtmusik*, it literally sends shivers down your spine, compelling you to recognize that beauty of this magnitude cannot be accidental—it must derive from something transcendent.

God.

Then, I send an email to our community: "Friends, I've decided to release a jazz/pop album of four songs I composed. The first is a minimalist, jazzy rap called '**NORMAL**.' It's about longing for normalcy. It expresses the weight of pain but ends on a note of eternal hope in Christ. Hope these songs bring you some joy today." *Maybe this will help someone else, too.*

But God doesn't just give me music for these hard days. He steps in with His quiet mercy. One night, weeping at 3 A.M. in my own physical pain, I beg God. *Yes, You've given me reasons for suffering, but then why do You choose to heal other Christians, but not us? It's not fair.*

The very next morning, I wake up to a Facebook message from an acquaintance who knows nothing about my prayer life. She attaches a clip from *The Chosen*, a television series about Jesus' life I had never seen before. The clip is titled, "Why Haven't You Healed Me?" *Are you serious?!*

In the clip, Jesus tells one of His disciples—who struggled with a chronic health condition—that Jesus had *entrusted* him to tell a different story. Jesus tells him there are many stories of supernatural healing, but not many about someone who stays faithful to God despite not being healed. Someone who is patient in suffering because he knows eternity with no suffering is on the horizon.

Wow. Lord, this must be from You. Even though this is not a real scene from the Bible—the directors have clearly taken creative liberties—I can imagine the real Jesus giving this message, because its spirit aligns with Scripture.

A few hours later, Sevan texts me, without knowing about the clip or *The Chosen*. "Lars, just something on my heart today. God has *entrusted* you. You and Matt are witnesses. What's more powerful for proving God exists? Someone preaching when they've got an amazing life or someone who still believes Jesus is good when they're literally in the fire?"

I cry instantaneously, out of *purpose*, out of an empowered *calling*. God is reminding me yet again that He allows some suffering in part to advance the gospel. *Test to testimony.*

Indeed, I recall how Helen Roseveare, a medical missionary to the Congo who was raped and imprisoned, testified that God shockingly asked her, "Can you thank me for *trusting* you with this even if you don't know why?" She said God's one question turned her entire perspective around, making her cling permanently the rest of her life to Philippians 1:29 (NLT)—"[Y]ou have been given...the privilege of suffering for [Christ]." *Imagine if all Christians believed suffering is a privilege. This is so counterintuitive, yet it's all over the Bible. Change me, Lord.*

𝄞

"What? You've got to be kidding me."

Matt's voice carries from his office, frustration tightening every syllable. His latest obstruction had cleared after two weeks, and for a few days with him at home, we'd dared to breathe again.

But now I find him hunched over his computer, jaw clenched, eyes glued to the screen. "Crescent Bay's Institutional Review Board finally denied me access to the Axelrodis drug."

His tone is flat, but anger simmers beneath. "They waited months just to waste my time."

My stomach knots. "What?"

His fingers twitch over the mouse, nestled on top of a "Kitten Support" mousepad. "They say they don't have the resources for just a one-person trial and can't deal with the paperwork. But they do compassionate use access exceptions all the time. Which, by definition, is treatment for one person. Doesn't make sense."

"Wait. They're rejecting you for 'compassionate use' because it requires too much compassion? No resources for *one* person? I hope no one asks them for a Band-Aid." *Lara, stop. Be strong for him.* I inhale a breath. "Oh, love."

An hour later, we're on the phone with Auntie Ann. She assures us her acquaintance will reach out to Axelrodis and Crescent Bay to try to push through the red tape. A thread of hope, thin but unbroken. *God must have a plan for this. Why would Auntie Ann randomly meet that woman at that conference over the holidays?*

The next day, Joel arrives unannounced at noon. "You two need a change of scenery. Let's go." Three blocks later, we're at the beach.

The waves roll in and we three musketeers sit in silence on a bench, watching the water swallow the horizon, pretending we don't know what's coming. Pretending we're *normal*.

At one point, Matt stands between me and Joel for a picture

with the ocean backdrop, leaning on his cane. The wind picks up, whipping past us, and suddenly, his precious Indiana Jones hat flies off his head, sailing over the edge of the overlook.

Without hesitation, Matt wobbles toward the cliff on his cane. *Does he think it landed on the rocky embankment a short way down the cliff? Or is it lost forever?*

"Matt, *stop*!" I yell, and Joel immediately lunges forward.

It's no use.

Matt is already stepping carefully down the uneven slope. It's not a sheer drop, but it's steep enough down towards the ocean to make our stomachs twist. Joel and I watch, breaths held, as Matt plants his cane down on the rocky embankment, steadying himself as he crouches down to grab the hat.

This is *still* Matt. An old-world hero tied to tradition and familiarity. The man who would risk everything to save what he loves—even a battered old hat.

Great. All we need right now is a dramatic side quest where my boy risks his life for that ridiculous piece of fabric. This is the dumbest possible way for this story to end. I should start carrying a "Reasons We Almost Died" journal: Entry No. 348.

We are literally reenacting the scene from *Raiders of the Lost Ark* where Indiana Jones risks his life to grab his hat as a stone door is about to close. I couldn't make this stuff up if I tried. Apparently, Trouble can.

Matt clutches his treasured hat, then takes a slow, careful step backward. A moment later, he's climbing back up toward us, breathing hard but grinning like a man who just conquered Everest. Joel and I exhale at the same time.

Joel snorts. "Do we cheer or tackle you before you try to duel a seagull next?"

Matt giggles. "I was gonna save that for the walk back."

We make it home, shaken but intact.

That night, Matt and I lie in bed, hands intertwined, watching *The Lord of the Rings* and *The Chronicles of Narnia* back-to-back.

Escaping into other worlds where good triumphs in *this* life, where adventure means hope. Nothing says "romantic night in" like watching fantasy movies where people constantly almost die. *Fitting.* Frodo is out there fighting for his life, and honestly? Relatable.

At the end of *Narnia*, Matt turns to me. "See, Aslan gets resurrected at the end. That will be our story too, Lara."

53

Hope

Matt stumbles out of Joel's car on our driveway, barely managing to stay upright. Two massive flower bouquets weigh his arms down, his body swaying as he leans against the car. My heart jumps as I watch him from the front house window—*is he going to fall?*

Matt was just in the hospital for another ten days. More obstructions. More astronomical pain. He can only have liquids, and his body is now rejecting even certain broths. He's lost an incredible amount of weight. Every sip, every swallow feels like Russian roulette between nourishment and agony.

But today—two days before Easter—I'm just grateful Matt's arriving home again. I dart to him on our front lawn, pressing kisses across his face as I pry the bouquets from his grip before they topple. Joel hands Matt his cane.

"Babe, these flowers are incredible! Thank you!"

"Always. Wanted to reenact that video you sent me. Had to pick flowers for my girl. Metaphorically."

Four days ago, while he was in the hospital, I texted Matt *Historia de un Amor*, a romantic Spanish love song about a man picking flowers for his señorita. He texted back minutes later—"Made me cry. Wishing for a day when we could be free from illness, when I could just walk through an orchard and pick you a flower. I'll be home soon, and we'll be together again."

I loop an arm around him as we shuffle inside, his cane tapping against the pavement. The delicate scent of the roses drifts between us. We sink immediately onto the couch in each other's arms, shocked that he made it out alive. One more time.

As I stroke his head feverishly, Matt's lips twitch. "This week was tough."

Tough is an understatement. They had to insert the dreaded NG tube down his nose again to try to drain fluids to keep his pain down.

"Isn't it time to take this down?" Joel says randomly, sipping from his celebrated coffee mug while eyeing a large piece of cardboard paper on the wall—the one we used in our *married life* film a year ago. It's titled **"House Rules,"** with my handwriting in bold letters:

1. **We praise our wife each day.**
2. **We adjudicate all disputes with a mediator Lara selects.**
3. **We give to our wives with a generous heart.**
4. **This is not a democracy. Lara gets two votes and Matt gets one vote. See Ephesians 5:25, stating men have to sacrifice for their wives.**

"Sarcasm stays up," I declare.

As Joel leaves, I spot the eagle pendant I had given Matt, still glistening around his neck. Lower, I catch sight of two new nephrostomy tubes circling his legs. My throat tightens. His kidneys are failing thanks to the pressure from the cancer, and the usual stents are no longer enough. They had to operate to insert these tubes yesterday. Another scar. Another battle wound. Another loss.

He catches me staring. "Lara," he hesitates, "You don't mind the tubes?" None of the tubes on his body ever affected Matt's confidence before. His identity is rooted in Christ, not this fragile temporary body. But he's exhausted.

"Silverman, you're sexy with or without tubes. Probably more so with them."

He laughs. "You know I look like a walking science experiment at this point."

"And yet, *still* the most attractive man alive. Oh, I missed you. I wonder if I can just sleep on a cot beside you in your hospital room, so I won't have to do a car ride back."

His face suddenly shifts, flickering something new, something important.

"I have some news." His lips press together. "The Review Board contacted me today. They reversed their decision. They're submittin' the paperwork to get me compassionate use access." *Did I just hear correctly?*

"Are you serious?!" Relief washes over me. He barely has time to nod before I smother him in kisses. *Lord, can this be true?*

"No way... See babe! I told you! God gave you Psalm 91 as a promise of rescue! We have to call Auntie Ann and thank her!"

But after a second, something dims in his expression. "Well, I'm not countin' my chickens yet. We still need approval from Doctor Kranter. Haven't heard back." A sadness flicks over his eyes.

"But now that we have board approval, he'll probably sign off, babe! Doesn't it feel like God's opening this door? If there's a time to have hope, wouldn't this be it?" My mind races. "Oh, you'll go to Haiti again, love. You will."

His eyes glisten with hope. I grab my phone, scroll fast, then hit play. His favorite anime song fills the room—one where the protagonist is just about to face his final battle with the villain. "This one's for you, Trouble."

Four hours later, Matt shuffles out of our bathroom, trailing fatigue but holding something behind his back as I lie in bed. He spreads an array of folded paper across the bed on top of me.

"Origami. Made these in the hospital to compete with your

Valentine's petals. Romantic escalation," he says, giggling. "And here's a stuffed Easter bunny for my little Kitten. Got it at the hospital gift shop."

"Aw, I love it! I can't believe we're making it to Easter babe. I still can't believe they approved the drug."

"I told the nurses while they were drainin' my stomach," he murmurs, half-laughing, "I don't care what happens, I have to be out for Easter Sunday."

𝄞

Matt and I stand in the pews, holding each other up.

Easter.

Matt, a shadow of the man he once was, leans on his blue cane. Yet his voice rises to Jesus, unwavering, as he sings none other than *How Great Thou Art*.

Around us, the congregation sings, and the stained-glass windows shimmer with morning light. I anchor myself in this moment—this breath, this miracle. I can't believe Matt is standing here, still next to me.

A true Easter resurrection.

Matt will live.

54

Hi, Doc?

"Hi, Doc?"

Matt steps into our master bedroom two days after Easter, gripping his phone and miming to me that it's Doctor Kranter on the line.

Matt taps the speaker as we both sit upright on our bed. Pounding rain drums against our bedroom window.

"I'm relieved you're calling Doctor Kranter," Matt says, his voice steady but edged. "Been waiting to hear from you. Now that the Axelrodis drug is approved, how do we move forward?"

A pause.

Too long.

Then, Doctor Kranter's voice filters through, flat and clinical.

"Unfortunately, I don't have any further treatment options for you."

The words land like bricks on concrete.

Another pause.

Even longer this time.

Matt stiffens, eyes darting between me and his phone, his brows knitting together. "Wait—the Board just reversed its decision.

They're letting me use Axelrodis under compassionate care and I thought you would sign—"

"Even so," Doctor Kranter interrupts, "it's not an option now given your overall condition. I spoke with Axelrodis' medical director this morning about your latest labs and situation. Your liver function, the countless obstructions, your weakened immune system. All of it makes this treatment way too risky. Your body won't tolerate it. He agreed."

Silence.

Then, with the precision of a guillotine: "Just one dose will probably kill you."

Matt's expression turns grave.

He doesn't move.

I do.

I grab his hand, cold and limp in mine.

Inside, I scream: *He's dying anyway, you idiot! What do we have to lose?*

"The drug isn't designed for small intestinal cancer," Kranter adds. "It was always a long shot. Even in the best-case scenario for its own indication, it only has a ten percent success rate. I don't feel comfortable approving it, and the Axelrodis medical doctor agreed, in light of your current status."

Deafening silence.

"I can only recommend hospice at this point."

Matt doesn't flinch, doesn't respond.

Kranter continues, voice even.

Detached.

Cold.

"It's been three years. We don't have anything else. The second chemo isn't helping you, even in the increased doses I've tried on you."

Ice water floods my veins. I understand oncologists probably build walls to avoid heartbreak from patients dying—it's survival. Prosecutors do it too, facing gore daily. *But can't this guy show just a shred of compassion? Just in his voice?*

After some pointless niceties that don't feel so nice, the call ends.

Matt just sits. Blinking. Breathing shallow.

And then—he breaks.

His whole body caves, shoulders shaking as sobs punch out of him, raw and helpless. He clutches his stomach like he's trying to hold himself together, but he's unraveling, coming apart right in front of me. He's never cried *like this*.

"It's over, isn't it?" he pleads, eyes wet with tears.

"Oh love," I say, holding him in my arms, rubbing his back with the palm of my hand.

I have no words. But inside I'm screaming—*we're never giving up*.

Outside, the storm rages on and wind rattles the windows. A mirage of our pain.

Then, Matt unravels from my arms and just sits. In silence. In contemplation. Tears streaming silently down his cheeks. Fifteen minutes pass as I wipe those silent tears. *Don't make the same mistake as last time. Grieve with him. Stay quiet and just be a loving presence.*

Finally, he speaks. "Maybe it's time... Maybe I should join hospice. Stop chemo. Why keep poisoning myself? It's not helping. You know I haven't been able to keep much broth down the last few days."

His face shifts, almost morphs now. The grief is still there, but a tint of something else appears, something I haven't seen before.

Acceptance.

His eyes communicate a new realization—he really *is* going to die. He can't fight anymore. He's at a dead end. A real one this time.

He continues, his face muted, looking down at the ground. "I'll just starve until I die."

Silence. Tears sting in my eyes. *I refuse to believe this is happening.*

"I had this gut sense all along. That the Axelrodis drug won't even help me given the obstructions. Didn't want to confront it."

I scramble for something, anything. "But babe, what about that Dumford trial you're waitlisted on—"

He shakes his head. "That trial's on hold and who knows when it will open up again? They said likely a year."

"But—"

"And...even if Kranter or another doctor approved Axelrodis, you heard him. Just one dose will kill me. Even the Axelrodis medical doctor apparently withdrew his approval. I'll have more time if I choose hospice rather than take that gamble."

He looks straight into my eyes. "Wanted to serve God. Missions. Teaching. Helping." His big brown eyes plead for hope, even as they search for comfort in resignation.

Tears stream down my face now, my voice breaking up. "You *did* serve. You *are* serving. You built up this youth group and have seen the fruit. You've made an impact—"

His eyes close. Exhaustion. Acceptance.

It doesn't seem to matter now.

I look outside the window. The storm howls on. *Lord, is this a cruel April Fools' joke?*

We waited so long, and the Review Board had just reversed its decision.

What about Psalm 91?

What about our Easter resurrection?

55

The "H" Word

The rain pours in thick sheets as I step out of Joel's car, my jacket and violin case soaked within seconds. *I've got to tell him. It's now or never.*

My eyes lock onto the hospital entrance, its fluorescent "Crescent Bay Medical" lights glowing. Joel and I walk in as the glass doors slide open with a mechanical hiss.

We hurry down the hall and soon, the elevator to the 14th floor feels like it's closing in on us. Too small. Too quiet. My heart races like a trapped animal as the walls of the elevator spin in wild circles, shaking violently due to the car ride. *Just hold onto Joel. Courage.*

All the while, Joel's words from yesterday haunt me. "I thought to myself," he'd said, eyes full of fire, "why should I be so selfish and ask Matt to suffer longer for us? His body is resisting. We've turned over every stone, Lara. Nothing left to try. If he wants to stop chemo and go into hospice, what can we do but support him?" Then, a tear slipped down his cheek.

Joel. The man who never flinches, even when the worst news lands like a sledgehammer. The man who's slept countless nights in the hospital, never leaving Matt's side and taking care of his needs. But even he believes it's time to let go, if that's what Matt wants.

The parents have been impressing upon me that I have to explicitly tell Matt I support his decision to enter hospice, if that is what *he* ultimately wants.

What an impossible situation for a wife. On the one hand, I want to fight for Matt's life and tell Matt to kick this "H word" out of his mind. On the other hand, am I dreaming? No options left. It's not my body, is it? I'm not the one being poisoned by chemo, am I? I'm not the one already starving on broth then vomiting it out, am I?

I took a vow a year ago that I would stand by Matt and honor him. That means I must tell him I support his ultimate decision, so he doesn't worry about my emotions on top of it all. *But can I actually do it?*

The elevator dings. I step out, and the hallway stretches before us—cold, sterile, endless. Joel and I waddle forward, my violin case in one hand, clinging to Joel with the other. Every step feels like wading through wet cement in a 12.0 earthquake. *Please Lord, calm my brain down. You brought me here.*

Finally, Joel stops outside one door. He nods. *This is it.*

I lift my hand, knocking gently as I sing aloud those timeless, beautiful lyrics from Elvis' *Can't Help Falling in Love*. I push the door open and step inside, smiling wide and stopping for a breath. "I'm still falling in love with you, Matt."

"Lara?"

Matt's eyes turn to me, widening in shock. His voice is weak but laced with surprise, and a genuine smile grows wide on his face.

"I'll give you two some privacy," Joel says, slipping out into the hall.

I drop my violin case on a table and rush to Matt, my hands finding his cheek, his jaw, his shoulder, his arm—anywhere I can anchor myself.

He's even thinner. Paler. He looks so fragile in a way that twists my stomach.

"You did such a long car ride?"

I stroke his head almost violently. "Oh babe, I just had to do it. I don't care. I can't stay away from you anymore."

Matt landed in the hospital again a few days after the Kranter call. Agonizing pain and obstructions. Cancer growing. Now, even a "simple liquid" diet has proven too much for his intestinal tract to handle. Every sip of any broth causes him extreme agony and vomiting. So, he's stopped eating entirely to prevent any future obstructions. His IV drips steadily beside his bed, pumping pain meds into his body around the clock to control his pain.

He lies here, reclined at a 45-degree angle on the bed, wrapped in a blue polka dot hospital gown, white sheets, and an almost ethereal peace that terrifies me. There's no fight in his eyes—only peace. Almost like he *knows* the fight's almost over.

Matt's faith has always been unshakable. He's always said, "God is a good Father. Even when we don't understand Him." That faith has animated his joy, his life, his ability to sit in the mysteries without lashing out. (Unlike yours truly.) But now, something's different. It's not just faith; it's absolute child-like abandonment to his Savior. *He doesn't even seem worried anymore that he might be "letting people down" by dying? Good... but...dying? Really, Lord?*

I press away from him, lift my violin from its case, stand at the edge of the bed, and waddle back and forth violently in an effort to ground myself against the earthquakes.

"Presenting a private concerto for Doctor Matthew Silverman," I say, shaking from nerves and pain. Matt's lips curve up into a gentle smile. "There's my girl."

As the room floats in circles, my fingers start gliding the bow over the strings. *Can't Help Falling In Love.*

Song after song, Matt claps softly, smiling angelically, his eyes soft, glistening with deep joy. It's as if he's transcended carnal reasoning entirely, as if he's already halfway to Heaven, leaving the rest of us behind. *This cannot be happening.*

When I'm spent, I go sit by his side. "Can I sing now, to relax you? It will distract me from the brain zaps. Or am I bothering you?"

"Of course. I love hearin' my girl sing."

The next few hours pass like a dream. Love ballads spill from my lips—each pulling us both further into our most potent love language left.

Music.

Matt drifts in and out of sleep, his breathing soft and steady, his pale white hand resting warmly in mine, lighter than it used to be.

Finally, I get to one of my favorites from *My Fair Lady*—*Wouldn't It Be Loverly*. I sing softly in a British accent, wistfully longing for a time when illness wasn't ravaging my husband's body. A tear slips down my cheek as I look at my husband's tired eyes, asleep now.

A nurse peeks in, her smile cautious, like she's stepping into something sacred. "This room feels different," she whispers. "We need more music like this around here." She steps closer to adjust Matt's IV. "Matt is the best patient we've ever had. He even encouraged the hospital chaplain yesterday." *Still testifying, even to chaplains. Oh, my sweet Trouble. Test to testimony, until the end.*

When the nurse leaves, Matt's eyes flutter open.

"Babe, mind if I lie down next to you?"

"Of course." I carefully climb onto his fragile hospital bed, somehow squeezing myself at his side, curling his hand in mine.

"My girl is here."

"I love you."

Silence. My chest falters against the heavy weight I've been carrying for two days. *Just say it.*

"Matt," I say, my voice wavering now. "I… I want you to know it's okay."

"What's okay?"

"It's okay if…you know. If you…"

I hesitate.

"What Lara?"

"If you ultimately decide you...want to go on hospice."

I did it. But the words feel foreign, like I've just betrayed every promise I made to fight for him.

𝄞

"Lara, I've finally decided to start hospice."

Five days later, my hands are trembling at home, pressing the phone to my ear.

Matt exhales through the phone from the hospital. "If God wants to do a miracle in hospice, He can. I trust Him either way. Been fightin' for you. For us. But it seems...maybe...it's just God's time? Thanks for assurin' me you'll walk with me, sweetheart."

Hospice.

The sound of it coils around my throat. My heart starts pounding, but I force out something that might sound like a response.

"Of course. I'm at your side no matter what." My fingers curl into my sweater, gripping the fabric like it might hold me together. The conversation blurs and minutes later, we've hung up.

Hospice.

The word sears into me now.

A year ago, Matt and I said our vows.

Now we're on the edge of "until death do us part."

I squeeze my eyes shut, but the memory punches through anyway.

Aunt Jackie's deathbed. Her hollowed-out face. The helplessness, the pain.

And now—it's happening again. *Lord, are You really going to take my husband? I trusted You. I came along for Your wild ride, trusting You would let me keep just one beautiful thing!*

Fifteen minutes later, my phone buzzes. I blink at the Facebook notification on my screen—Anna's Facebook post: "After three years of battling cancer, searching for treatments, and now unable to eat or drink anything, our son Matthew has made the courageous decision to enter hospice, without any further chemo or treatments."

I blink hard, then rush to open one of my daily devotional apps to get encouragement of any kind. *I can't do this.*

And there it is. The verse of the day, Psalm 23:4: "[T]hough I walk through the valley of the shadow of death, I will fear no evil; for You are with me; Your rod and Your staff, they comfort me" (NKJV). *You've got to be kidding me.*

The devotional states, "Are you facing a change you feel unprepared for? Perhaps the death of a loved one or friend? God will strengthen you and hold you up in His everlasting arms as you focus yourself on His promise of eternity." *Oh. My. Gosh.*

An hour later, my friend Liana's weekly Christian inspiration listserv email lands in my inbox, featuring the verse of the week—none other than Psalm 23.

Okay, Lord. Someone's about to die. Is it me? It can't be Matt! You gave us Psalm 91 for Matt! You do not lie… I am confused by these mixed signals again!

I'm standing at the edge of a cliff, and I can't feel the ground. My hands grasp for something—anything—to hold onto.

The violin. *I need music.*

Solution—*Go the Distance*, from the *Hercules* movie.

The first note wavers. I shake then push hard, dragging the bow across the strings as if the melody is escaping my chest. I sing the lyrics in my mind, visualizing how Matt has gone the distance these last three years. I picture him, like Hercules, pushing through every painful mile of this evil disease, holding onto the hope that there's a place of welcome and rest ahead.

I lower the violin and stop to think. Is Matt *actually* heading Home now? To that *eternal glory*? Is all of Heaven waiting to welcome him in?

The "H" Word

Psalm 23, Lord? Really?
No melody can save him.
My husband is going to die.

Act Four

"I consider that our present sufferings are not worth comparing with the glory that will be revealed in us."

— ROMANS 8:18

"Jesus said to her, 'I am the resurrection and the life. The one who believes in Me will live, even though they die[.]'"

— JOHN 11:25

"You intended to harm me, but God intended it for good to accomplish what is now being done, the saving of many lives."

— GENESIS 50:20

56

The Fruit of the Vine

First day of hospice

The moment I step into my in-laws' family room, my eyes lock onto Matt.

He's sitting on the couch in a **Camp Arev** shirt, a half-smile curling his lips, like none of this touches him.

The weight in my chest tightens. Ninety days prior on barely a liquid diet, and now four days without a single sip of water or food, and he still looks at me like that. Like he's fine. Like he's always fine.

We decided to do hospice at my in-laws' house—bigger space, more help, more family. I just made the trek down slowly with Mom. Matt came straight from the hospital with his brother Jeff.

"There's my girl," Matt chirps, his voice steady, bright. His arms open, expecting me to fall into them.

I do.

His grip is weak, but he pulls me in. His skin is almost paper-thin, his body sinking into itself given his tremendous weight loss. But his eyes—they shine like they know something I don't. *How is he not thrown at all?*

It's like he's floating on a tangible cloud of relief—perhaps because he finally knows the outcome? Uncertainty is one of the hardest parts of being human. His body language evidences a stark shift in his outlook compared to weeks before. I can almost touch his thoughts—*my suffering will end soon. Finally. I'm going to die. And I'm fine with it.* If a saint could somehow become even more Godly, Matt just got an upgrade. Ironically, when dying.

"How's my Kitten?" he asks, stroking my hand.

"I missed you so much. Should I sing you a song?"

"Anything but that Britney person."

Matt's casual demeanor today is but one thing—the personification of supernatural courage. In marriage, he's taught me how to go through this world fearlessly. Chemo after chemo, surgery after surgery, blood test, CAT scan, you name it, he's come back, laid down, smiled, and said the same thing every single time— "There's my girl."

No bitterness.

No fear.

Some frustration?

Yes.

But not more. He's faced every stage of his illness with grace. Not with misguided certainty that he would *definitely* heal. Yes, he's had hope throughout, but he's authentically grieved his losses with joy at the same time. And now in hospice, he's teaching me how to die. With integrity. With perspective. With courage. With joy.

But I'm not giving up yet. I don't care what Matt thinks. Sure, I had a momentary breakdown after Matt chose hospice, but I've since refocused myself on God's promise to Matt. *Psalm 91. God's going to pull a last-minute miracle. God delivers on His promises. Camera crews better be at the ready.* Psalm 91:3 says, "[God] will save you from...the deadly pestilence."

I must have been mistaken about that Psalm 23 coincidence. Sometimes Psalm 23 is just about God walking with us *through* a tough valley, and Matt *coming close* to dying right now certainly qualifies. Maybe God was just encouraging me that He will hold us until he saves Matt.

Ground rules for hospice: Matt and I sleep in the upstairs loft wearing emergency buzzer necklaces to call for medicine or help. Hospice nurses every other day. Joel and Matt's siblings camp downstairs, ready to run at a moment's notice. Auntie Ann and Cousin Joey visiting on and off (reinforcements).

On the third day of hospice, Matt's extended family floods in—Florida, LA, East Coast. They take turns sitting with him, whispering, crying. But Matt? He stays the same. Calm. Unshaken. He nods, listens, smiles. The incredible amount of weight he's lost doesn't touch the light of joy and strength in his eyes. They powerfully testify, "I do not fear death." His attitude reminds me of a quote by Emmanuel Ndikumana: "You Christian Americans have a strange attitude toward death. You act as if it is the end."

Not so for Matt. Matt is literally living out his favorite verse, Romans 8:38-39—"For I am convinced that neither death nor life, neither angels nor demons, neither the present nor the future, nor any powers, neither height nor depth, nor anything else in all creation, will be able to separate us from the love of God that is in Christ Jesus our Lord."

Nothing—not cancer, not death—will separate Matt from God. Meanwhile, I'm in the corner anxiety-Googling "hospice miracles" like it's an extreme sport. *Lord, please save my husband. You are good. I believe You will save.*

A week later, Matt shows no signs of stopping, inputting his final student grades for work. And today, true to form, he's filming his "goodbye devotional" for the youth group, called "The Fruit of the Vine." He sits on a chair, upright and professional, half the man he once was physically, but still here, still working. Smiling ear to ear in a blue and green checkered button down I just bought him.

"This will give me more of a 'last presidential address' feel," he joked earlier, as I helped him put it on. Now, I watch from the doorway as he starts talking into the camera:

> There are lots of things people chase in life. Wealth, fame, power, comfort. But people often get to a point when they realize the thing they were chasing just wasn't satisfying. As I get to the end of my own life now, I'm contemplating what kind of impact I'm leavin' behind. In John 15 verse 1, Jesus tells his disciples that if they want their work to matter, they must stay connected to Him: 'I am the True Vine and my Father is the gardener...Remain in Me, as I also remain in you. No branch can bear fruit by itself; it must remain in the vine.'
>
> If we want our lives to have meaningful and lasting fruit, we need to stay connected to Him. Read the Bible; don't just open it and recite a few verses. Meditate on it, chew it, digest it, take it to heart. You need to be so deep in the Bible that it's comin' out of you without even thinkin' about it. It's showin' up in the way you speak and the things you do such that people look at you and ask, where did that wisdom come from? And all you can say is: it's the Bible, not me.
>
> Pursue deep, meaningful relationships with other Christians. Check in with them, weekly. Jesus tells us we are brothers and sisters, not a social club. You don't see one grape on a vine by itself. Grapes grow in clusters. God's love pours into our hearts and we can't help but pour out that love into others. That's how we make a real impact on others' lives.

Matt's eyes portray a simple determination—*I'm not stopping until the end.* He was playing flute at our anniversary a month ago and Jesus is still giving Matt purposeful work. On a deathbed.

When he's done reciting his script, I notice this one doesn't end like all the others. *He no longer will be "just one phone call away."* My heart drops.

Three weeks pass.

No food, no water intake—just the occasional homemade water popsicle with one teaspoon of orange juice in it. But somehow, he's still sitting up, laughing, talking like none of this is happening. *God's miraculous sustaining. I've never seen anything like this.* Countless friends, adoring teachers, and students visit and lean in to catch his wise words as Christ's peace radiates off his body. There's still this sense that he's just "hanging out," almost like he's about to go on an extended vacation. *That* kind of peace. *Either my husband is a nut, or he really knows something we don't about dying.*

When Pastor Nerses and his wife visit, Matt asks about her bruised finger he heard about a month ago. She stares at him like she doesn't know whether to laugh or cry at the absurdity of him asking about *her* triviality in the middle of *his* hospice.

Every night, Matt tells me he's dying with grace and joy because "death is just a doorway to God. A final entrance into Jesus' everlasting Kingdom. No more suffering or pain. Just eternal glory." He reminds me that "to be away from the body [is to be] at home with the Lord." 2 Corinthians 5:8.

Inspired by his faith, I start wondering myself: What *is* life after death really like? I crack open theological books on Heaven to scope out our eternal real estate, debating it all with Matt and filming a mini YouTube series called "What Heaven is Like." *Don't invest in a rental.*

As I dive deeper, I'm struck by the richness of God's promises. Heaven isn't some boring, float-on-a-cloud place where we will be rolling our eyes thinking, "another day, another taco." No, the Bible paints a far more tangible, vibrant picture: in God's "new earth" (Revelation 21:1), we'll eat, drink, work, laugh, rest, worship, and play in glorified, resurrected bodies—just like Jesus' own body after He rose from the dead. Isaiah 65:17-25, Luke 22:30, Philippians 3:21, Romans 8:23—it's all there. God designed us to dwell with Him *physically* on earth, and that's exactly what we'll get in Heaven. (That whole "bodiless soul, bored on a cloud" myth? Satan's lie to make us dread eternity.)

Instead, Christians will enjoy fruitful work serving God and reigning over His new earth. Revelation 22:3; 2 Timothy 2:12. Christians will also savor full-on celestial feasts. When Jesus celebrated the Passover with His disciples, He referred to eating and drinking in the eternal kingdom. Mark 14:25. He even ate fish *after* His resurrection—John 21:9-13—a preview of our eternal culinary adventures. *Thank you, Lord. Eternal life without burritos and sour cream would be punishment to me.*

As I'm absorbing all this, God shines His spotlight on something specific. Tim from the Haiti team emails me one afternoon: "There is far better ahead in eternity, Lara." Hours later, my third devotional app pops up with the exact same phrase: "God's gifts in eternal life, whatever they will be, will be *far better* than any temporary gifts on this earth."

Wow, that's wild, Lord. Psalm 16:11 even explicitly says God has "eternal pleasures at [His] right hand." Why don't we all live with eternity as our prize then? Because we're simply not convinced that God's eternal treasures *are* superior.

But imagine, for a moment, God's boundless creativity before the dawn of time—dreaming up the very concept of flavor. He didn't just craft the essentials. He invented garlic powder and paprika, the very seasonings that transform ordinary French fries into something mouthwatering.

This is the same God who painted peacocks with iridescent splendor and designed mandarinfish to shimmer like tiny, living jewels beneath the sea. If He poured that much creativity into this temporary, fallen world, what "eternal pleasures" does He have waiting for us on the other side of glory? *Wow. If life in Heaven really is vastly superior to this life, that gives me so much hope amidst all this loss and pain. Lord, help me cling to this. Like Matt.*

Meanwhile, back on the earthly stage, despite our inner turmoil watching Matt suffer, Matt's joy ties the family together. As Billy Graham preached, "Courage is contagious. When a brave man takes a stand, the spines of others are often stiffened." In such an intense situation, you would expect conflicts breaking out left and right, but we've held each other up.

Except last week's squabble, when emotions were running high and another family member and I had a sharp disagreement about Matt's pain medicine protocol. We avoided each other at all costs for a few hours after. Apparently Matt, lying down, caught wind, and called us both up to the loft. "Love each other," he insisted, forcing our hands on top of one another. We both stared at him sheepishly, then burst out laughing. *Stupid spat*: over. Matt has been a consensus seeker in all his church ministries. His favorite Bible story, in fact, is Jacob and Esau's reconciliation.

Jesus is also weaving joy into the fabric of our days in surprising ways, helping us lean into life's simple pleasures. *Joy in grief.*

Every night, Matt settles into a cozy spot on the family room couch as Joel pops in his favorite classics—*The Exodus, Back to the Future, The Andy Griffith Show*. Matt watches them all, grinning like a kid, with a tasteless homemade grape juice popsicle in hand, savoring it like it's the most exquisite dessert on earth. I sit by his side stroking his bald head like I'm trying to unlock a genie.

Then, there are the video games. Matt and his two siblings lose themselves in the glow of the screen, fingers flying over controllers, shouting like they're seven again.

And, of course, the craps games. Bright emerald green felt, white dice, the clatter of chips, the electricity of a well-placed bet—all of it hums through our family room. Matt wins every other round, his brilliance and luck uncanny and his smile downright contagious.

Living in hospice feels a lot like standing on sacred ground. It reminds me of what Justin Martyr wrote in A.D. 150 about Christians: "You can kill us, but you cannot hurt us." Matt is here, fully alive in the moments that remain, refusing to let fear have the final say. His attitude shouts 1 Corinthians 15:55: "Where, O death, is your victory?"

𝄞

"We'll miss you Matt. We're planting mango trees in Haiti in honor of our new school." A Haitian boy speaks into his phone camera to Matt.

Winston and the Haiti team are visiting today in the loft. Matt sits upright in bed, FaceTiming with the Haiti kids he's mentored over the years, as a last goodbye.

"That's good to hear. I'm proud of you. I have faith you will eat of their fruit," Matt says, a tear slipping down his cheek.

The air, thick with a tangible heaviness, mixes with a radiating peace from the Holy Spirit.

"Speaking of fruit, Winston, can you please give the Haiti kids my last 'Fruit of the vine' devotional when you fly next week?"

"Matthew John Silverman," Winston replies, tears welling up in his eyes, "I'll take it around the world, even to Vietnam. People have been asking about you and your steadfast faith. You've really turned your test into a testimony, buddy."

Afterward, we all sing *Because He Lives* and the final lyrics linger in the silence, weaving through the air like a benediction.

Winston's passionate voice slices through the emotion. "Hey, buddy. This isn't goodbye. You know that. We'll see you again on the other side. And soon."

Matt's lips curve into a much needed smile. "I know it."

57

Don't Let Death Scare You

32 days without food

"Don't let things like death scare you or make you think God's abandoned you. For the Christian, death is our final reward, the moment when we cross the finish line and say, *We've done it*. 2 Timothy 4:7 says, 'I have fought the good fight, I have finished the race, I have kept the faith.'"

Matt sits on the family room couch next to me in his blue "Science Rocks" sweatshirt and checkered gray pajama bottoms, his gaze fixed on thirty young faces staring back at him, hanging onto his every word.

The youth group.

Some fidgeting, some wiping their sniffles—all shocked at the sight of Matt's scary thin face and frame now—but all locked in, silent, waiting. Even the Boldi kids are here today. Our fellow jazz musicians.

Four weeks into hospice, and Matt is still teaching, still leading. And we're still rejoicing. We surprised our moms with flowers for Mother's Day. We giggled as Joel unwrapped his birthday gift—an *I'm Not Old, I'm Classic* t-shirt. But today, the kids are here. This morning Matt said, "I think today's youth group lesson is why God's kept me alive. One final goodbye."

Matt takes a breath and continues. "We weren't meant to live on this earth for eternity. That would be pretty lousy. War, disease, pain, sickness. We're lookin' forward to a new Kingdom, a better Kingdom. And for the Christian, that's what our hope should always be in."

Matt's eyes fill now with unshed tears, and his voice wavers. Even so, a quiet, unshakable hope clings to him like a second skin. Hope is the most powerful thing a Christian has.

"If our hope is in the things of this world, we're gonna get disappointed time and time again. Here, the moths and vermin destroy, thieves break in and steal. Nothin' on this earth is gonna last but the promises we have in Heaven can't be taken away."

Matt's tears flow freely now, and the room thickens with emotion. "Remember that no mistake or sin you commit will cause God to give up on those who put their trust in Him. That's His promise to all who put their hope in Him."

Matt pauses to grab a tissue and blows his nose. Then, a beat later, he sits up straighter, a small spark returning to his eyes.

"We each have a different race to run. Some races are shorter or longer than others. My challenge to you is just to run your race well, stay the course, however long it's going to be. You want to hear 'Well done good and faithful servant' at the end. Christ's victory came through His humiliation. Our victory is to remain rich in spirit while poor in circumstance, and alive in hope even as our bodies waste away."

Matt pursued wisdom his entire life. When he moved up north ten years ago to grow this church's youth ministry, there were only three kids. Now, he's seeing the fruit of his labor—thirty adoring kids—growing in Christ with their eyes set on him as he pours out his wisdom. *Wow.* God is giving Matt this final gift of joy and purpose in his suffering. No one will leave this room unchanged.

Matt's approach to death is teaching his community countless things:

For the Christian, trials are just trials, not defeats.

We can't choose our circumstances, but we can choose our response.

All things really are possible with God.

Even facing death without a trace of fear.

We can have joy when facing death because Heaven *is* worth dying for.

We are in fact "more than conquerors through Him who loved us." Romans 8:37.

Charles Spurgeon even wrote, "It cannot be any serious loss to a saint to die...Death, if rightly viewed, is a blessing from the Lord's hand." *This is agonizing to read when the good die young.* But Scripture does present an interesting duality. While God grieves death because it was not part of His original plan, at the same time, the "death of His faithful servants" is "precious" to Him because Jesus died to purchase their presence and intimacy with Him in Heaven. Psalm 116:15.

When Matt's done, the kids embrace him one by one, whispering their goodbyes. As they leave, Matt and I stay put while some family members slip into the dining room behind the kitchen to eat the food the church ladies brought. We shield Matt from the sight of what he can no longer have. Food is a wound even for us now. Every bite is a reminder that Matt can't eat. *Unbearable.*

"Hmm," Matt considers. "I think I'd like to chew on that salmon I smelled yesterday." He hasn't chewed on anything in four weeks. Even gum will cause him acute pain by getting his digestive juices flowing. When Anna brings him salmon, Matt presses a tiny piece between his teeth a moment, as if testing the very idea of eating again. Then, he spits it out. *That's it.* Joel, Anna, and I look at each other, tense.

Minutes later, Matt's brother Jeff and Cousin Joey slowly hoist Matt onto their shoulders, and carefully carry him upstairs to the loft, inching along like a slow-moving parade, with Matt in the middle. He can't carry his weight anymore. No muscles, no fat. Just bones.

I immediately approach Auntie Ann, pleading for reassurance. "God's gonna do a miracle, right? God gave us Psalm 91 for Matt."

She sighs deeply, wrapping me in a warm embrace. "Oh Lara, I know how hard it is, honey. But we have to let God's will be done, whatever it is. We're praying nonstop, but maybe the miracle was Matt staying alive long enough to marry you."

Auntie Ann is incredibly wise. But the truth still stings. *Lord, is this how you view my marriage? An event? A moment? Isn't marriage a covenant for a lifetime, not just one year?* Matt has tried to drill into me that all of life—even the longest marriage—is just a blip. That our marriages are only a "foretaste" of the greater joys and pleasures to come with Jesus in Heaven. *But I want Matt too.*

Anna walks by. "We need to comfort Matt, Lara. Tell him you will be okay when he's gone, so it calms his fears. I'm doing the same, even if I don't believe it." *How are we going to be "okay" without Matt?*

I climb upstairs to find Matt, lying down, typing on his laptop. "Trouble," I mumble. "I still don't believe you're dying, okay? I know it sounds ridiculous. But look, I know your greatest fear was leaving behind a widow, like your grandpa. I don't want you to feel that way, okay? Even if you die, I'll be strong. I've got everyone to support me."

He smiles, some tension in his face easing. "Thanks, sweetheart. Yes, God will take care of you. He has good plans for you, Lara." *Has he finally given up that fear of letting me down? Letting others down?*

He turns his laptop toward me. "Want to read my life testimony? Sendin' it out tonight." I nod, and my eyes start scanning his precious words:

> I was twenty years old, my second year studying chemical engineering, when a few simple Bible verses changed my life. Up to this point, my education was my biggest focus. I was used to being the smart one, having all the answers, and life was pretty good. Even after going through non-Hodgkin's lymphoma as a teen, I had my life pretty

well together. A prestigious degree from a prestigious university. What more could someone ask for?

I had started going to church on Sundays with my cousins, not really out of a great interest in God as much as something to do to hang out. Yet I couldn't help but notice that the church people...they had something... something real...something I hadn't experienced before, something different from admiration and good grades. I got interested in studying the Bible on an intellectual level. There was wisdom and knowledge there I had never seen.

I decided to join some Bible study groups and ask questions, challenging the teachers, seeking answers. And, the more I asked, the more my curiosity grew. Was this Jesus person real? Did he really perform miracles? Did he really rise from the dead? Then came the opportunity. A weekend college getaway at **Camp Arev** where we could just focus on learning. No shallow, 4th-grade level answers.

That weekend transformed me. I'll never forget the theme of the weekend: the power of prayer. We looked at the Book of James and talked about what it meant to make a real prayer of faith: to pray and believe God was going to respond. I realized I didn't have that faith—but if I prayed for it, God would answer and give me the faith. I realized it wasn't my intellectual doubts getting in my way of true prayer, but my own pride. I wasn't interested in giving up my good life to follow some God who might send me half-way around the world to serve people I had never met before.

But as I read my Bible that night, I came across Romans

8:38-39, and I realized any plan God had for my life would be a better plan than anything I could come up with, and that this God was not only real, but in control. So in humility, I prayed a simple prayer: 'God, give me the faith to make a prayer of faith.'

In that moment, everything changed. It was like a wrecking ball crashed through some unseen wall in my heart, and the very next words I heard came from someone in the room behind me reading out loud those very same words in Romans 8:38-39. My life changed coming down from that mountain. My priorities were now about serving this God who died on a cross so that I would have eternal life. To top it off, I've found myself traveling to Haiti a dozen times, serving the poorest people in the western hemisphere. And I wouldn't change it for anything.

As I find myself now, alongside my beautiful wife, counting down my final days at the age of forty, I'm grateful God has blessed me with twenty years of fruitful ministry, countless relationships to encourage me, and most importantly, the knowledge that my salvation can never be taken away. No power of hell, no crafty scheme of any man, can ever take away the perfect gifts of God, and I go home now to a rest that is sweeter than the greatest treasures this world has to offer. I have Heaven, where there will be no more sickness, pain or death, and I can spend all my days with my God who loved me to the death.

- Matthew John Silverman, May 2024

58

Because He Lives

39 days without food

The familiar melody of *Do-Re-Mi* from *The Sound of Music* floats through the Silvermans' backyard garden, my vocal vibrato cutting through the crisp morning air and the scent of freshly cut grass.

Five weeks into hospice, and Matt is still upstairs sleeping. I came down minutes ago for breakfast, grabbed my two little nieces' hands, and started serenading them around Anna's pink rose bushes.

Goal: mold them into musical theater prodigies—and distract myself.

The girls' giggles ripple through the air, a sustaining splash of weightless joy these heavy days. Then, I see them.

Joel and Jeff, guiding Matt out into the garden inch by inch, his arms draped over their shoulders. Matt's legs underneath his gray pajamas can't hold him anymore. He winces as they ease him onto a yellow lawn chair, his hand drifting to his ostomy bag, an unspoken testament to everything he's endured.

In no time, Matt watches us—me, Anna, his sister's entire family, all waddling in the gigantic rectangular blue pool right in front of him. We call out to him every few seconds, trying to make him feel part of it all. The pool shimmers in the sunlight, a tangible gift of beauty in our otherwise heavy environment. A literal stream in our barren desert. I can't swim—I can't bend my head or ears forward or backward or go underwater—but I can walk slowly upright, letting the water lap gently against me.

Matt waves, his smile soft. My heart knots with guilt. *Are we being cruel? Enjoying this while he just...watches?*

After half an hour, we're out of the pool and circling Matt, as if proximity alone could hold him here longer. Mom and Pops arrive, and Mom wastes no time, slobbering a kiss on Matt's left eye.

Matt clears his throat. "Been thinkin'. There's a time for everythin' under the sun. Ecclesiastes." The eagle necklace I gave him months back protrudes from under his pajama shirt. "A time for grief, a time for laughter, a time for work, a time for rest." We should be comforting him. Instead, he's still carrying us.

Then, Matt's PhD brain verbally dissects his own dying process like it's just another research paper. "Because I'm dehydratin' and starvin', I'll probably start hallucinatin' soon. Thought it would have happened by now." He says it so casually, like a computer relaying information. *Is he hiding his fear or does he genuinely have courage to face this?*

Pops shifts uneasily in his lawn chair, his face twisted in frustration. He blurts, "Matt, why? Why you? Where is the Lord?"

Matt reaches for Pops' hand earnestly. "It's normal to ask these kinds of questions. We don't always get answers, but we know God brings good from it."

As I stare into Pops' sad eyes, a burst of emotion overwhelms me. *Am I supposed to grieve, yell, hope?* I need to clear my head. "Pops," I nod toward the front door of the house. "Let's go for a quick walk before I have to lie down."

We step out the front door into the quiet suburban street, lined with towering oak trees swaying gently in the breeze. After a block of walking silent side by side, Pops exhales, staring straight ahead. "Life's not fair."

"Yeah," I respond. "If it were fair, I would've won a Baskin Robbins scratch off by now." *Sarcasm always keeps pain away, doesn't it Lara? No.*

Seconds later, Pops adds, "Been thinking, Lars. Aunt Jackie didn't deserve to die young either. But look at Matt. It's almost like he knows something we don't. Like he's got the Wi-Fi password for Heaven."

I swallow hard. "Yeah. He does."

Is Matt changing Pops also? My family used to be "shove it down" people when it comes to grief. Is Pops handling this better than my own bipolar "deny it but study death and heaven anyway" method?

After a short two-block loop past neatly trimmed lawns, we're back at the house, only to find Jeff and Matt hunched over the family room table, cards in their hands, deep in conversation.

"I wanna buy four chickens, six sheep, and two acres of land," Matt declares, his voice laced with mischief as he lays down a blue card.

Jeff giggles, grabbing a red card. "Yes sir. And I'll plant corn this round, unless I go all in on fertilizer."

"What's this?" I ask.

"Remember those notes I scribbled last week?" Matt replies. "I created a board game and Jeff just made the cards. Tryin' it out. Here, look at this." He turns around his card and I read the inscription: "*Roots*."

"Roots?" I ask. "Brilliant title babe! What's the premise?"

"Grow crops, manage resources, earn points." *Only Matt could invent a board game in hospice.* With joy. Without eating. Without drinking.

Why not?

Nothing to fear.

Purpose until the very end.

A few hours later at 5 P.M., as he lies on the couch resting,

Matt's eyes dim for a moment then reignite with fire. "Who's up for Bible study again?"

His siblings, Joel, Anna, and I all gather around him, our Bibles open. His voice, though weaker, still carries authority. He teaches, weaving Scripture with personal insight, and it lights him up with strength in a way food no longer can. His family drinks it in, thirsty for every word, asking question after question.

Jesus, salvation, Old Testament, New Testament. Nothing's off limits. Questions from his siblings like "did Moses have GPS in the wilderness or just good instincts?" This might as well be a docu-series called *The Gospel According to Trouble*. Joel whispers to me, "I never thought I'd see my other two kids so into this Bible stuff. I saw the two of them actually reading and debating the Book of Matthew earlier."

There can be no doubt—God is answering one of Matt's lifelong prayers in his final days. The chance to share his faith in a tangible way with his family members, whose salvation he's spent countless years praying for. *Miracles.*

Hours later, I climb the stairs into the loft at 10 P.M. *Should I give it to him tonight?*

The dim glow from the television flickers against the walls, casting restless shadows across the dark room. *Because He Lives* hums softly through the speakers. *Joel must have left Matt's favorite Celtic worship band on repeat.*

Matt lies asleep, motionless on our bed, his body swallowed by blankets, a bare wisp of what he used to be.

Buzz. Buzz. His phone vibrates on the bedside table, and I flip it open to see if it's urgent. A text message from Matt's pastor friend Jason. But it's Matt's original text that makes my stomach drop—"Spent the first twenty years of my life focused on myself, and the second twenty years focused on God. Looking forward to glory." *Eternal glory. Might my Trouble be there soon? Is this really happening, Lord?*

Jason's reply flashes on the screen: "Amen. He is faithful. He's used you mightily for His glory—and perhaps He is calling you Home now."

Matt suddenly stirs, his eyelids fluttering open. "There's my girl."

"Ready for a shower, Trouble? Let's get you some comfort." He nods, eyes heavy with exhaustion.

In the silence, I turn on the light and waddle to and from the loft bathroom filling a large plastic basin with new warm water each round. In minutes, the scent of soap permeates the air. Without leaning backward or forward to prevent harder spinning in my brain, I carefully roll Matt onto his side and spread a waterproof blanket beneath him. My hands shake, my mind flashing back to when Mom did this for me—just three years ago. *Be the hands of Jesus, Lara. There's a reason you know how to do this. God is redeeming your past. Serve this man, your beloved.*

Matt lies flat as I gently stroke the soap all over his skin, the warm water splashing over him in slow, deliberate waves. I linger, memorizing every inch of his peaceful expression in the dim light. *I love this man.*

Fifteen minutes later, I help him dry and dress again, then rub lotion onto his feet. *This always relaxes him.* After one more bathroom trip, I return to find Matt half-upright in bed, relaxing, watching YouTube on his phone.

"Monkeys again?" I tease, throwing a towel into the laundry bin.

His eyes crinkle. "It's the ticket."

I sit beside him on the bed, and our fingers entwine as we flip through the *Musical Love Story* album Matt gifted me on Valentine's Day. Each page unfolds our beautiful, unexpected journey—a love story only God could have written in the midst of our respective fires. When we reach the last page, the air between us feels heavier, loaded with unspoken fears.

"Lara," Matt says cautiously. "Do you mind if I make some big donations? To the church, to Haiti—one last gift?"

I stroke his head. "Of course, love. I know the 'Matt Silverman donation principle'—squeeze your wallet until it's uncomfortable, then squeeze just a little more."

"Just one last squeeze," he murmurs, squeezing my hand. "Oh my brave girl. Willin' to marry a man with cancer. You made me a husband, you know. You gave me a foretaste of Heaven."

I smile through the ache rising in my chest. "Well, you were willing to marry me with all my physical and spiritual issues." My voice cracks. "Oh, you don't deserve to die, love."

My eyes swell with tears now. "We only had one year. I know I'm supposed to focus on eternity. But I'm just so sad we might not get both."

"A thousand years wouldn't be enough with you, Kitten." He hesitates, eyes somewhat distant, lost. "Thought we'd go to Haiti. Armenia. Together."

A wave of something—urgency, clarity, desperation—rushes over me. *It's time.* I reach for my backpack and pull out a small red box, my hands trembling. *Thank God for Auntie Arax and overnight shipping.*

I flip open the lid, and inside, a bold ring gleams under the soft lamp—an emerald set into a sturdy band of brushed steel. I hold it out to him, the weight of it solid in my hand.

"Matthew John Silverman," I whisper, the words trembling with everything I've held back. "I have an important question for you."

He looks at me with a tilted, curious smirk—his signature face that still weakens my knees.

"Will you be my best friend in Heaven?"

His eyes soften. He lets out a breath that's almost a laugh and says, "Of course."

A laugh bubbles out of me as I wipe a tear away. I slip the ring onto his finger, watching it settle on his fragile hand. "I still hate that we won't be married there. If we had twenty years here, maybe we'd be sick of each other. But I'm not ready to let you go."

"Just promise me you won't cross-examine me in Heaven, okay?" he says, chuckling. A beat later, he furrows his brow and his voice drops, steady and deep, rooted in a place only faith can reach. "Lara, listen to me. Because He lives, we'll be together again. That's all that matters. Rejoicing in Christ. Together forever. Here, let's pray."

I lie down beside him, grabbing his hand. As harder turbulent waves crash into my exhausted skull, Matt's voice immediately sends calm through my body.

"Dear Lord, we beg you for a miracle, if that's Your will. We're still askin' Lord. We want to spend our lives together. But if You have other plans, please grant us courage to face the future. Not our will, but Yours, be done. Amen."

After five minutes of quiet, I find the courage to speak. "Matt, are you…scared at all?"

He shakes his head slowly, his eyes still closed. "No. I've got my ticket punched."

"First-class to Heaven?"

"Hopefully with extra legroom."

Other couples binge-watch Netflix; we're still binge-planning our eternity.

And then, we sleep.

Hours later, at 2 A.M., Matt jerks upright, reaching for the vomit bag. "Buzz Jeff for another one—just in case."

59

Kingdom Economics: Sorrow In, Joy Out

53 days without food

"I can't breathe."

I jolt awake to find Matt gasping on the twin bed next to my bed, his frail hand reaching out. *Oh my gosh. This cannot be happening.*

Five days ago, Matt decided to lie in the loft bed permanently and stop moving downstairs. His body can't handle the movement anymore. It's now Holocaust thin. Shocking. Skeletal. A hospital bed arrived yesterday, a twin-sized symbol of a wedge between us now. No more queen bed. Reality creeps closer, but denial and hope wrap around me like armor. *Psalm 91.*

I press my call button immediately. Joel rushes upstairs, kneeling beside the bed to hook Matt up to the new breathing aid machine. A few seconds later, Matt whispers, "Okay. It's helping." *Thank God.*

I get up to find Anna at the top of the stairs. She whispers, "I want to have hope, but his body's shutting down." She walks into the bedroom and grips Matt's hand. She's living a mother's worst nightmare. A second time.

I watch from the corner of the room at a distance, my mind a whirl. *What a cruel, broken world. Lord, are You really trustworthy with all this pain? This is not how the world is supposed to be. The good die young. Evil men prosper.*

Matt smiles at Anna, slurring his words slightly. "Mom, you know I'll be okay in Heaven, right? Just have joy, knowing I'll be whole again."

As he is talking, Cousin Joey steps in. "Hospice nurse is here. And Pastor Calvin."

"Matt, mind if I step out for a bit?" I ask. "Be right back."

I grab my violin and slip outside the front of the house. I walk onto the quiet sidewalk right out front and lift my violin, pressing it against my shoulder.

I draw my bow and the notes spill out, shaky at first, then steady. *Because He Lives.* Matt's favorite worship song. I've practiced it for weeks, and now it escapes out of me. Cars pass, drivers stare. *Let them think I'm crazy.* Music is the only thing that makes sense right now.

As the melody rises, emotions tumble through me.

Hope.

Joy.

Despair.

Back to hope.

Stay strong, Lara. Strong. I cling to the truth Matt once pointed me to in 2 Corinthians 4:17: "For our light and momentary troubles are *achieving* for us an eternal glory that far outweighs them all." I recall hearing John Piper preach that this verse means that *none* of our suffering—not even the anguish in our final moments—is "meaningless…Every millisecond of your misery in the path of obedience to Christ is producing an eternal weight of glory you will get because of that."

As C.S. Lewis wrote, "They say of some temporal suffering,

'No future bliss can make up for it,' not knowing that Heaven, once attained, will work backwards and turn even that agony into a glory." God promises to one day right all wrongs.

But how will God actually accomplish that? No clue, but lately I've found countless Bible verses emphasizing that God does in fact delight to turn agony into joy, flipping evil around in that way. *E.g.*, Psalm 30:11 ("You turned my wailing into dancing; you removed my sackcloth and clothed me with joy."); John 16:20 ("You will grieve, but your grief will turn to joy."); Isaiah 61:3 (God promises "to bestow on them a crown of beauty instead of ashes, [and] the oil of joy instead of mourning"); Psalm 126:5-6. Kingdom Economics seems akin to: deposit sorrow, withdraw joy. With divine interest.

Even Jesus spoke of His impending death and suffering in John 12:23-24 as the *means* to His glorification. He endured the cross "[f]or the joy set before Him[.]" Hebrews 12:2. Romans 8:17 makes this astonishing promise for *us* too—"Now if we are children, then we are heirs—heirs of God and co-heirs with Christ, if indeed we share in his *sufferings* in order that we may also share in his *glory*." It seems, then, that the cross always leads to glory.

Oh Lord, this "grief to joy" principle is an immeasurable comfort, but so hard in the moment of pain. Why can't You just give us "joy to joy"? Why do we need to suffer to get joy? But this suggests we can paradoxically rejoice in loss because it's somehow leading to glory...

Whether we like it or not, that's the gospel pattern. Just like Jesus, our suffering Savior. First death, *then* resurrection. Why are we surprised? It's a pattern Jesus explicitly called us to—"Whoever wants to be my disciple must deny themselves and take up their cross and follow me." Matthew 16:24. We are called to take up our crosses—whatever they are—and follow Him not just for denial's sake, but to mysteriously participate in the gospel pattern itself. *Hmm.*

The good news is that Scripture repeatedly measures our

earthly suffering against the joys of Heaven, and Heaven always wins out. *E.g.*, Romans 8:18 ("[O]ur present sufferings are not worth comparing with the glory that will be revealed in us.") This means that leaving Heaven out of any analysis of suffering and death would be akin to leaving out the whole other side of the equation.

The winning side.

Matt always tells me that Christians who get the short stick in life—either who die young or suffer poor health or other tragedies—might be tempted to say, "I lost the lottery. This is all I get." But Matt says having an eternal perspective changes everything.

Along the same lines, God's been drawing my attention lately to the doctrine of "rewards," a theme echoed often in Scripture yet rarely taught from the pulpit. In Heaven, Jesus will reward each Christian according to their works. Matthew 16:27 ("[H]e will reward each person according to what they have done.") And because God knows humans can't endure pain without hope, He explicitly promises that perseverance in light of great suffering on earth will be "richly rewarded." Hebrews 10:35; 2 Chronicles 15:7.

James 1:12 even explicitly states, "Blessed is the one who perseveres under trial because, having stood the test, that person will receive the crown of life[.]" Jesus Himself preached, "Rejoice in [the day of persecution] and leap for joy, because great is your reward in Heaven." Luke 6:23. *Okay. Courage, Lara. This affliction is achieving glory and reward for Matt. Keep trusting. Suffering is just "training for reigning." Maybe Matt will be a Prime Minister in Heaven. Seriously. Only God knows what eternal rewards are in store...*

When I finish playing, I lower my violin and glance around. No applause obviously. Just a very confused squirrel glaring at me like it's witnessing a weird human ritual. (In the movies, playing an instrument outside is a poetic act. In reality, it's just me dodging the Silvermans' sprinkler every twenty seconds and trying not to pass out or sob between notes.)

I return to the loft and peek in, overhearing Matt chatting with Pastor Calvin, who's sitting next to Matt's bed.

"If I could just have a break from seein' everyone else's pain," Matt murmurs. "That's the thing that hurts the most." A weight drops in my heart.

I sneak in, putting my violin case down and lying down on the other bed. *I hate this separation from him.*

After a second, Matt adds, solemn, "I'm ready for this pain to end."

Silence hangs.

"I'm surprised I'm even here fifty days later," he adds. "This is a miracle. God always pushes me to the edge. I wasn't even supposed to survive this cancer past six months. But when will this end?"

Calvin pauses thoughtfully. "God's timing."

"Matt doesn't deserve this, Calvin," I blurt. "Why is this happening?"

Calvin exhales, hard and slow. "Do you know what happened at the end of the Book of Job?" *Yeah, I'm intimately familiar with that guy. Unfortunately.* "God finally showed up and talked to Job. But He never answered Job's *why* questions."

Calvin opens his Bible and reads God's response to Job in Job 38:2-4. "'Who is this that obscures my plans with words without knowledge? Brace yourself like a man; I will question you, and you shall answer me. Where were you when I laid the earth's foundation? Tell me, if you understand.'"

Calvin looks up. "Basically, God showed Job all the marvels of His creation, implying Job was wrong to question God's wisdom. Job couldn't have created the world himself, so he had no right to judge God's wisdom in running it. Job humbly repented in response, admitting he 'spoke of things [he] did not understand[.]' That's Job 42:3. God's usually accomplishing some good purpose far beyond anything we can understand, Lara. That's why He calls us to rest in His love, not the why's. Kids don't always understand their parents' decisions, but the parents always act in their best interest. Think of it that way."

Matt's sister knocks, announcing "Aren's here." Aren walks in, settling into a chair by Matt's bed, joining our quiet space. No one speaks. After a few uncomfortable seconds, I break the ice.

"But I still believe God's gonna pull a miracle. He does it in the Bible all the time. Red Sea. Lazarus. Last-minute saves everywhere."

Aren nods, his voice measured. "We're praying."

"But we trust His outcome," Calvin adds.

"Not to sound callous," Aren says, turning to Matt, "but even if this is your time, forty more years on this fallen earth is a blip in light of eternity, right?"

Matt's eyes brighten, and his voice shakes. "Yeah. Honestly, I just can't wait to taste the wedding feast of the Lamb. The food. The wine. Lara's Auntie Nanor sent us a devotional about the food and glories in Heaven this morning. Gave me hope."

Matt's got the smartest long-term investment strategy on the planet. If your treasure has always been in Heaven, dying means you are actually *getting* your treasure. As Matthew 6:19-20 states, "Do not store up for yourselves treasures on earth…But store up for yourselves treasures in Heaven[.]"

Aren leans in, with fervor now. "Amen. Just imagine Matt. You'll be in God's presence. What you'll be experiencing in glory is unfathomable." *Am I the only one on this sinking boat not wanting to surrender?*

"Yes," Matt says, smiling mischievously. "Imagine that I will *never* have to witness Armenians on a church banquet committee wage holy war over silverware table placement again. And how bad can Heaven really be? No sin equals no disputes equals no lawsuits equals no lawyers equals absolute societal bliss." He giggles then winks at me. "Look at this girl. Smiling through all this. That takes so much strength."

I feel like I'm a mess in the making. But Matt's encouragement gives me strength to push forward.

Aren laughs. "You know, we all thought you were too holy to even notice girls, Matt. Then Lara popped on the scene."

Matt chuckles. "What can I say? Cats have a certain seductive charm."

60

Glory

60 *days without food*

I push open the front door and race up to the loft. *Something feels off.*

This past week, every hour I can sit up, I sit beside Matt, holding his hand as he lies flat. He drifts in and out, his eyes barely cracking open when he speaks. He's still with us mentally, but he wafts in and out of a mental stupor and sleep.

The sharpness, the brilliance that once defined him, is slipping, and it guts me. He's still here, but fading—like sand slipping through our fingers.

A few hours ago, I asked Matt if it was okay for me to step out for a while with Mom for her birthday. "No matter what happens, Kitten, I love you," he said softly. I kissed him, his lips still warm, still present.

But now, I'm back in the loft and staring at Matt lying still, his eyes closed, mouth open. He seems awake, but unresponsive—starkly different than before. Jeff dabs a sponge to Matt's cracked lips.

"What's that?" I whisper to Joel.

"The hospice nurse said it'll help his thirst."

I swallow hard. Joel shifts uneasily, and looks me straight in the eyes. "He hasn't been reacting much the past hour, and…hasn't been able to recognize any of us."

My stomach drops, heavy and cold, like ten tons have been anchored on it. *What? No. How could this transition happen so fast?*

I walk up to Matt and caress his left arm. "Matt, it's me, love. It's me! Lara!"

After a few seconds, Matt's eyes slowly flutter open. He blinks, scanning the room, then locks onto me. "Lara?!" A broad, beaming smile spreads across his face.

Joel and Jeff exchange a glance—relief, disbelief.

I choke back a sob. "Yes, Matt. It's me! I'm here!"

Strong connections of joy create strong reactions in the brain. Neuroscience 101.

Seconds later, his eyelids droop, and he's asleep again. Just like that. *Oh, my sweet love. Will we never talk again?*

A young genius in a mental decline. The curse of this fallen world is only one thing. Unbearable.

An hour later, I retreat to the other wing of the house to Matt's childhood bedroom, lying flat on his childhood bed as tears soak my face. Above me, a sign stares back—"Be Brave." A scrap of metal from Haiti that Matt brought home eight years ago. *Why do I need courage, Lord? He's not going to die. You promised a miracle.*

A few days pass in slow torment for everyone.

June 10 arrives.

I wake up suffocating under the weight of dread. *I need relief, help, something, anything.* I flip open one of my devotional apps, and the verse of the day sears into me—Genesis 50:20. The same verse God gave Matt when he was first diagnosed. *What does this mean, Lord? Is Matt going to get a deliverance like Joseph today?*

But then, my eyes carefully pore over the devotional's words:

> It's hard to believe God is working for good when our challenges lead us not into life, but into death. But as Christians, we know Genesis 50:20 is just as true for those whom God doesn't rescue on this side of eternity as it was for Joseph, whom God did rescue. There is no greater comfort than to know that no matter how absurd or irrational circumstances seem, God is in control and uses everything for good. We must always trust Him.

The words knock the wind out of me. Tightness coils in my chest. *Oh my gosh. No. Is Matt really going to die? My baby! You lied, Lord! What about Psalm 91? Have we really been in the Psalm 23 valley of the shadow of death all this time?*

All day long, we all sit silently in the loft holding Matt's hand as Matt—now completely unconscious—draws increasingly infrequent breaths. Hours pass in a blur. Matt's breathing slows, each exhale fragile, like it just might be his last. Then, at 5 P.M., his sister, who is a vet, rushes to his side and bends down.

She leans in, listening, and her face twists. "He's not breathing."

A sharp wave of numbness immediately crashes over me. Her words float as if they are disconnected from reality. Anna collapses onto the ground, hovering over Matt's bed, sobbing uncontrollably.

I stand up from my chair and freeze.

I don't move.

Don't flinch.

Matt's siblings sit internalizing, processing. This family has been through agony. They went through this twenty years ago during Matt's first cancer.

This time, he's gone.

Gone.

I'm still frozen.

Suddenly, arms wrap around me from behind. I turn.

Joel.

We hug, then I push away. *Lara, do something. Go somewhere. This didn't just happen.*

"I have to be alone," I blurt. *Why am I not crying? Is this really happening?*

I stumble downstairs, phone clutched in my hand, retreating to the tiny laundry room. I slam the door shut behind me, sealing myself in.

My face finally begins to flush bright red and my chest burns. Reality slams into me.

I clench my fists and yell, "Oh, Matt...Matt...WHY GOD, why? WHY?"

The agony now pours out in shouts, sobs, whispers. My knees wobble and tears flow violently.

After a few minutes, I suddenly yelp out something new—part anguish, part indescribable joy. "If Matt went to Heaven...maybe I will be there soon too?" *God told me He's coming for me two and a half years ago! I still have no idea God's timing though... Lara, stop. You don't want to die! Ugh. What do I do Lord? Is this really happening?*

My phone suddenly buzzes—five missed calls from Winston. He's been calling nonstop the last week. I hit dial. Only thing that comes to mind.

"Winston, he's gone! He passed Winston!"

Silence.

After a few moments, Winston finally speaks, exhaling hard through the phone. "Oh, Lara. *Wow.* Matthew Silverman."

"He's in Heaven right, Winston? Right?" I plead with urgency.

"Yes, Lara. Listen. Listen. If I know one thing, it's that Matthew John Silverman is in Heaven. God will comfort you. Matt is in glory. Finally, glory."

61

Empty

I step through the front door of our "Silverman cottage" in Daly City, and it hits me like a punch to the gut.
Empty.
No *Silverman Theater* sign above the fireplace.
No Kitten's Kitchen apron flitting over the counter.
No framed picture of Matthew preaching in Vietnam.
No delicious smell of brownies wafting through the air.
No Victorian candles decorating the walls.
Just bare walls.
Bare wooden floors.
Empty.
The movers have stripped it down to its bones, leaving behind a few scraps of our life together. I'm here for one last look before I move back in with Mom and Pops permanently. They say I shouldn't be alone. Emotionally. Physically.
They're right.
I drift through each room in the house, feeling like I'm walking through a movie set long after the cameras have stopped rolling. Scenes replay in my head:
Cooking.

Teasing.
Sunsets.
Devotionals.
Science textbooks.
Violin and flute duets.
Matt, standing in the doorway, grinning, "There's my girl."
Gone.
Empty.

The only reminder that Matt Silverman ever lived here is his blue "Science Rocks" sweatshirt I'm wearing today so that I can bask myself in his sweet smell.

Since Matt died a month ago, I've felt God's surprisingly intense and supernatural peace and sustaining through my support system. Golden Girls, friends visiting. Pops making Joel fancy drip coffee at our house like old times. It feels like God whispers every time Joel walks through our front door—*Take this joy in grief and trust me. Matt's safe with Me.*

Pops and I even fired up our Bible study again. "Now that Matt's moved to Heaven, you're officially our new man of the Lord, Pops." While his eyes daily ask the unanswerable—*why Matt?*—Pops clings to Scripture with a steadiness I haven't seen before. Just last week, he concluded our resurrection bodies will be like "God's software update." Our theological debates dissect critical questions like whether Heaven will serve Armenian coffee and what kind of homes we'll be living in, with first-rate or third-rate accommodations.

My other coping mechanism? Music. *The musical love story isn't over.* I've buried myself in violin and piano tributes in Matt's honor. *Historia de un amor. Because You Loved Me. My Girl.* Anything to fill the void. I even learned the *Romeo and Juliet* theme. Too on the nose? Music helps me express what words can't.

But standing here today, in this stripped-down house, I see it now for what it all was—escapism wrapped in melody. *Or maybe just a desperate means to find joy in grief. I'm in the graduate course now apparently.*

Our old life here feels like a dream. This house—our "British" cottage filled with love and music—is just a shell now. Surreal doesn't quite capture it. In the kitchen, my eyes land on the counter where our wedding guestbook sits open, the ink of well-wishes ironically frozen in time:

May you live a long, prosperous life together!
God is good! He's giving you a life together!
Keep trusting the Lord. He has great plans for you two.
May you two find healing. We're praying!

My fingers grip the counter, my throat tightening. *Lord, I know Your peace is sustaining me in my grief moment to moment, but I must be honest with how I feel today... Was this all a cruel joke?*

Did you cast me as an actress in my own wedding, with the tragic role ending exactly one year and three months later? A one-year run with no encore, no cast party, no standing ovation? Just a curtain call with a morbid black curtain coming down? Did You pick me for this role because I could play it well? Is that it? How do I rate this experience? The character development is top-notch (is it?), but the plot could use a little more romance and a little less tragedy.

Yes, I knew what I was signing up for—marrying a man with cancer—but I also believed, deep down, that You were good. Didn't that mean You'd draw the line somewhere? Let me keep something—just once? You finally called me to date this amazing man after so many years of singleness. If You are all we need, why did You create Eve for Adam then?

I'm sorry, Lord. This is the naked truth. I know You've graciously given me multiple reasons for suffering the last few years, but I still don't have Job-like faith. Definitely not enough to say, "The Lord gave and the Lord has taken away; may the name of the Lord be praised." Job 1:21. *Please give me that kind of faith. Save me from myself. I thought I was growing spiritually. But now?*

As I wander into our master bedroom, the truth bites again like an unwelcome mosquito.

It's really over.

No KITTEN TERRITORY plaque.

No MEOW sign.

No dice scattered from Matt's *Dungeons & Dragons* nights.

No "Victorian" bookshelf.

Just an empty queen bed and four light blue walls staring back at me, asking, *You want something?*

God asks us to make Him our all, but is that really what we feel when our lover passes away? So much for the bag of basic blessings. The "perfect Armenian" life.

No law career.

No health.

No husband.

Wave after wave. Literally. Metaphorically. Every time I finally come to acceptance on one thing and take a breath above water, it feels like God pushes me right back down. You'd think that after experiencing so much suffering, I'd be desensitized and far more spiritually mature, less prone to lashing out.

But the truth is, my humanity resists—flinching at every fresh wound. I was in the boat *with Matt* before. Now, I'm rowing solo. Psalm 42:7 speaks to my soul—"Deep calls to deep in the roar of [God's] waterfalls; all [His] waves and breakers have swept over me."

At least I'm not alone in this experience. C.S. Lewis, one of the most influential voices in modern Christian thought, married his wife Joy when she was already dying of cancer too. He wrestled with anger and doubt even before she finally died, writing, "We are not necessarily doubting that God will do the best for us; we are wondering how painful the best will turn out to be."

I sit on our empty bed and questions plague my mind.

Isn't it strange to love a God who seems to be actively working against your happiness? I'm tired of mixing joy with grief. I want plain, simple, easy happiness.

What does a Christian do when everything is all cross but no Easter?

Why did God grant the "desire[] of my heart" (Psalm 37:4) only to take him away?

If God withholds "no good thing" (Psalm 84:11), can I put in a request for Matt back then?

How did Matt have the resolve and childlike trust *never* to ask why?

Why was James killed in Acts 12 while Peter was miraculously rescued? How is that fair?

I guess I can't deny God warned me and prepared me for this moment. When He first called me to date Matt, He gave me that devotional about the couple who, even as the wife succumbed to cancer, were encouraged by God to hold onto joy despite upcoming death. And, He gave me Psalm 23 right at the start of hospice. Turns out we were indeed walking through the valley of the shadow of death.

Then what does Psalm 91 mean? I genuinely thought God had explicitly promised to "save" Matt from the "deadly pestilence." Psalm 91:3. Even Charles Spurgeon recounted how, while walking home during a deadly cholera outbreak, he spotted a flyer in a shop bearing Psalm 91:10: "No harm will overtake you, no plague will come near your tent." In that moment, he felt God was promising him that he would be spared from the illness even as he continued ministering to the sick. God kept that promise. So why did God give Matt this verse too?

In hindsight, it appears God was promising Matt His protection, care, and comfort, and that He would "be with [Matt] in trouble." Psalm 91:15. And, as Matt always preached, the ultimate "save" from illness *is* in fact Heaven. In support of my hospice interpretation, Psalm 91:14 states, "With *long life* I will satisfy him and show him my salvation." I interpreted that phrase to mean God was promising to give Matt "long life" *on earth*. If he was heading into *eternal life*, that wouldn't just be *long*, it would be *eternal*.

On the other hand, "salvation" implies eternity. *Ugh.* I feel like a lawyer interpreting a legal statute, arguing both sides of the case. Matt warned that this is the precise danger in importing specific outcomes onto verses God speaks to us directly (or verses in general). But then how come Spurgeon could take the plain language at face value and place his hope in an earthly save, but Matt couldn't?

Sigh. Sadly, I *still* have no neat theological formula to determine when a verse God gives us is a personal promise of a specific outcome versus a general principle. I've experienced both. When God gave me the Jericho story during my jaw ordeal, and the rainbows in 2017 while I was single, He promised explicit deliverance in both instances—and He fulfilled both just as He said He would. But Psalm 91 turned out not to be an earthly save for Matt. All I can say is hearing the Shepherd's voice is the easy part. Defining His meaning in each instance is trickier.

Solution? *I know what Matt would say.* Regardless of convictions, we must have the humility to say, *"Your will be done, even if I misunderstood You."* That's what Matt did at the end of the day. Initially, it seemed God really encouraged Matt that healing would come on earth.

Matt wasn't one to fabricate emotional predictions or convictions, and six months after diagnosis, he even preached that he believed his "illness wouldn't end in death." In March 2022, he again wrote, "It's necessary for me to remain, so remain I shall." Shrinking cancer on scans, supernatural strength despite chemo, UCSD's initial approval, Auntie Ann's timely encounter just before hospice, the Review Board's reversal—all of these felt like "signs" pointing to earthly healing. C.S. Lewis wrote that he and his wife also experienced "false hopes" that encouraged them she would survive her cancer, ironically the "nearer Joy came to death." God's wild ride can be perplexing sometimes.

But Matt ultimately embraced the right posture, harboring no bitterness when his conviction turned out wrong in the end.

Looking back, I believe God intentionally gave Matt such strong hope in his spirit at the start because Matt *was* in fact going to have far more time to live, "remain," and serve than ever expected—three more years. So, quite literally, he did "remain" two years past March 2022. *Long enough to marry me.*

I stroll into the music room now, where we recorded faith discussions and music videos together.

No flute.

No violin.

No music stand.

No sheet music.

No tripod or camera.

Then, in Matt's old office, his sermon journal calls to me amid a pile of papers. I flip to the bookmarked page and find his familiar scrawl—*If just one more life is saved because of my suffering, I am happy to go through it again.*

His words tug at my heart, as if Matt himself is saying, "God has a purpose." *I know He does. God gave me Genesis 50:20 the morning of Matt's death. Hmm. Purpose.*

Matt took a risk when he preached that sermon in Haiti years ago, long before his second cancer. And it appears God took Matt at his word and entrusted him.

God found a servant willing to suffer to prove the beauty and truth of the gospel. So God made him a witness in the greatest legal case of all time—God's case to the world that He exists and loves humanity. That case was definitively won when Jesus died on the Cross, but He gave us the gospel message to carry to the world as witnesses. As Matt preached once, "part of partnering with God in advancing the gospel is suffering alongside him."

1 Peter 2:21 states, "Christ suffered for you, leaving you an example, that you should follow in His steps." The Apostle Paul put it this way—"For we...are always being given over to death for Jesus' sake, so that His life may also be revealed in our mortal body." 2 Corinthians 4:11.

This is precisely what I learned from Winston two years ago, and from my friend Steven's timely devotional thereafter—"Costly sacrifices and suffering for the sake of the gospel are required today." *Test to testimony.*

I can't deny it. How a Christian like Matt faces undeserved early death is probably the greatest witness to unbelievers that Jesus exists, and of His sustaining love and grace. Matt's testimony shouted with a megaphone, "Jesus is real. A good force is out there taking care of me in this evil world and is going to pull a good purpose out of this cancer. And to top it off, He has joys waiting for me after I die."

Maybe Matt's death really will save lives somehow? The death of the first Christian martyr, Stephen, led to major persecution against the early Christian community in Jerusalem, resulting in many believers fleeing into other regions where they "preached the word" to others. Acts 8:4. God turning evil on its head.

Matt even wrote right after his diagnosis, "Genesis 50:20 says God allowed Joseph's suffering for good, specifically 'the saving of many lives.' This means our suffering can play a role in others' salvation too. Jesus said in John 12:24 that 'unless a kernel of wheat falls to the ground and dies, it remains only a single seed. But if it dies, it produces many seeds.'" Maybe complete surrender to God's will really is the ultimate goal in Christianity, because we can trust that God will use all our individual sacrifices and tragedies for something greater? Even death?

I exhale hard.

I should have encouraged Matt by focusing on eternity, just like he did for me. It pains me that I hurt him by always insisting that God *would* heal him. My encouragement was well-meaning, but too tightly tethered to earthly outcomes.

I saunter to the living room. *At least the keyboard is still here.* One last thing to move.

I sit and quietly play. *My Funny Valentine.* The first song I sang for Matt on our first real date. The memory feels like a ghost.

Where is Matt right now…really?
Is he talking to Aunt Jackie about chemistry?
Debating astrophysics with the angels?
He's probably already started a theology podcast with Moses and Paul.

62

God Always Writes the Best Stories

"Matt Silverman once told me, 'God always writes the best stories.' I'd like to tell you one now. You see, I started praying for an Armenian Christian husband at age sixteen. And eighteen years later, on January 1, 2022, in the throes of my own serious illness, God sent me a five-foot ten, half Armenian half Jewish package named Matt Silverman."

I inhale a breath and tighten my grip on the edges of the podium. The podium where Matt and I stood together last Christmas testifying about *joy*. My knuckles pale. I choke back my tears. *I have to keep going. I want to do this.*

For Matt.

For God.

The CACC sanctuary is packed and silent—every chair filled, bodies pressed against the back wall, spilling into the aisles. A sea of solemn faces stares back at me. I swallow hard. Even when cancer gnawed at him, Matt had showed up to funerals of others he barely knew, offering comfort to families and grieving with strangers.

Today, we are at his.

To my left stand two breathtaking towers of white lilies on either side of the Cross symbol—where Matt and I knelt down together once—their delicate petals curling outward like open palms in prayer.

A strange stillness settles over me as I glance at the pages trembling in my hands. Yet underneath it, something deeper hums—peace. It's a joy I can't explain, not fully. Christians call it grace.

Last week, despite my disillusionment, the tribute I'm reading today poured out of me onto my laptop, as if the words had always been there.

Not mine—God's.

I clear my throat and force my gaze back to the crowd. "God's hand in orchestrating our love story was so evident that you could say Matt was personally signed, sealed, and delivered from God to my doorstep. After about six visits, we realized we were falling in love, hard. As Matt once said, 'We never dated did we? We just fell in love.' Falling in love amidst both our illnesses was a miracle in and of itself. But even after, Matt grounded us in Ephesians 5:16, which says we must "mak[e] the most of every opportunity, because the days are evil.' Indeed, they say that those who are not scared to die are not afraid to live.

"So we didn't waste time. We made Christian parodies, filmed a movie, started a theology and music YouTube channel, performed three musical concerts, gave Christian testimonies, and raised $13,000 for a new school in Haiti. I say this not to boast but to bear witness to the truth of 2 Corinthians 12:9, where God says, 'My grace is sufficient for you, for my power is made perfect in weakness.' Our productivity was a miracle because behind the scenes, we laid down holding hands half of every day of our marriage. But time and time again, I saw God give us strength, even in pain, to do the work He called us to do."

I pause and take a breath. *I can't believe I'm doing this without breaking down.*

"In hospice, Matt didn't eat a single crumb for eight weeks, and watched his body deteriorate without complaining once about dying young. And despite facing cancer twice, Matt praised God not only publicly but to me privately until his last breath—without a trace of bitterness. This is Matt Silverman. A model of Christlike submission to God's will. A living testimony of what he preached.

"His courageous outlook bears powerful witness to the reality that for the Christian, death is nothing but a doorway into Christ's presence forever. For this reason, I proclaim today—my husband is alive. Right now! Jesus said in John 11:25, 'I am the resurrection and the life. The one who believes in Me will live, even though they die[.]' *This* is the power of the gospel.

"I will not mince words. We begged God for a long life together. God answered *no*. But, Matt always told me, 'This life is a blip in light of eternity, so focus on eternal things.' 1 Corinthians 13:13 states, '[T]hese three remain: faith, hope and love. But the greatest of these is love.' Thus, ultimately God did not deny us more beautiful years of mutual love. Matt and I will have all of eternity to enjoy Heaven together in resurrected bodies. This gives me unshakeable hope amidst my unfathomable loss.

"And as I cry out to God *why?*, I will remember one of Matt's lasting legacies—his constant preaching that God has a sovereign and good purpose for all suffering, even if we cannot understand it now. Thus, our love story—as tragic as it is—has great meaning to God."

A murmur ripples through the room as my voice trembles. I can't believe what I'm saying, deriving wisdom only from what Matt taught me. I've gone from a person who believes marriage is only intended for a "forty year commitment with kebab barbecues" to proclaiming that even a one year marriage has strong purpose.

I press on. "Words cannot convey the transformative impact his compassion had on my personal faith. And let's not forget the beauty of Christianity—God's story never ends in ashes. Just look at Jesus hanging on the cross, then resurrecting. When Matt was first diagnosed, the church sermon series was on the story of

Joseph, and Matt drew great strength from that famous line in Genesis 50 that says God uses evil for good.

"Three years later, the same day Matt entered Heaven, my Christian devotional featured that same verse, emphasizing how God works all things for good, no matter how tragic. That's *not* a coincidence. It's an encouragement from God that there's a purpose to Matt's story and this is *not* its end. Perhaps the purpose is the saving of many lives, like it was for Joseph. And just as Joseph's sufferings led to his premiership, I believe God will richly reward Matt in Heaven for suffering so faithfully. In Christianity, the cross always leads to glory."

My speech ends and I waddle back to my front row pew in my black dress, my legs weak beneath me. One by one, other speakers take their place—Winston, Joel, Aren, Jason, Calvin, youth group kids. Their voices blend into the air, a chorus of tributes to Matt's countless ministries serving God.

Then, when Anna steps up, her words hit me like a rock—"Matthew means blessing."

My breath catches. *Yes. God blessed me with Matt's love.* He should have died six months after diagnosis, but God gave him three years so that we could be miraculous gifts to each other. I taught Matt how to live and enjoy life *right when* he needed to make the most of his remaining time, and Matt taught me how to die *right when* I needed to learn that it's okay to die.

The sanctuary soon swells with the sound of Matt's favorite worship songs. Voices rise, raw and trembling. And before I know it, we're at the climax—*Because He Lives*.

Being a Christian is both the strangest and most miraculous thing. As I stare death in the face—the ultimate sadness—joy from the Holy Spirit surges through me now, unexplainable, undeniable, lifting me up in a way that defies logic. A sense of peace washes over me—almost like a sacred embrace—as if God Himself draws near. It's not psychological or manufactured; it feels otherworldly, like Heaven brushing against my soul.

Tears finally spill over as I sing the lyrics, and I can't stop them. *Thank you, Lord. I am actually praising in this grief. Because Jesus lives, I will see Matt again.* As 1 Thessalonians 4:13 states, Christians "do not grieve like the rest of mankind, who have no hope." *The hope of our eternal reunion is really taking some of the sting out of this today.*

The service ends and I waddle out of the sanctuary into the annex on Mom's arm. Then, when I see them, a deeper realization slams into me.

Matt's hat collection and Eagle Scout uniform all hanging on display.

His **Camp Arev** t-shirts stacked neatly side by side, each one a badge of honor from twenty years of serving God, guiding young souls to Him.

The prototype of "*Roots*," the board game Matt invented in hospice.

A sob bursts from me, raw and unrelenting, and Mom draws me in for a tight embrace. Within seconds, solemn faces file past, offering condolences, shaking my hand in line. I nod, smile through tears, and note mentally, *Never wear mascara to a memorial unless you want to look like a raccoon.*

The faces marching past all seem etched with the same questions—*What have I done for God's Kingdom? What purpose does He have for me like He had for Matt? How can I give more of my life to God the way Matt did?*

Finally, Aren steps up. "God's using this. Matt's rejoicing in glory right now. Unbelievable to imagine. How fitting that the last time he came to church was Easter. Think about *that*. Resurrection Sunday. You know, Matt always had a way of preaching things that others couldn't. When pastors preach on controversial topics, people throw tomatoes. But Matt? He'd say the same thing, and everyone would go weak at the knees and say, 'Aw, that's Matt.'"

"Thanks, Aren," I say, a smile tugging at my lips.

When the crowd thins and the church empties, Joel, Mom,

and I decide to wander back into the sanctuary one last time. The silence is heavy, surreal.

"Joel, I want one more photo with you and Matt," I ask. "The three musketeers."

We stand side by side, smiling back tears and holding hands as Mom snaps the picture, Matt's framed photo behind us. We stand here awkwardly in silence, the weight of it all pressing down.

Then—Joel finally breaks the silence. "You two made every minute count. It may have been short, but it was full—blessings, joy. A lifetime packed into one year of marriage."

I nod, but the ache in my chest tightens. *Does that make up for forty years lost? Do I really believe what I proclaimed today?*

Joel catches the hesitation in my eyes. "Matt always trusted things would work out for him, and they did—because eternal life was always what mattered to him. This temporal life is just that—temporal."

His words settle in me like a seed.

Has Matt's faith changed Joel too?

63

The Email

"God can send signs that our loved ones still love us and are safe with Him in Heaven." Sevan's mother-in-law's voice beams with positivity through the phone.

"Really?" I ask, lying in my bed at 9 P.M. at my parents' house, watching the ceiling spin in slow, meaningless circles above me.

"Yes!" she chirps. "I was in the car upset one day, missing my dad, and I asked God to tell me he was okay in Heaven. And then, just like that, the song my dad used to play for me came on the radio. I cried instantly."

"Wow, that's so cool. Thanks for sharing, Auntie Sue."

When we hang up, I'm encouraged for a moment, then tears soak my face, hot and unrelenting.

My birthday is in three days. *Who cares about dumb birthdays? What is there to celebrate?*

Let me be honest—I'm ashamed.

I had proclaimed God's faithfulness from the pulpit at Matt's memorial. But now, here I am—reeling, unraveling. I know all of what I said was true, theologically speaking, but I still don't understand why our loving God couldn't have accomplished His purposes in another, less tragic way. *I'm too selfish for tragedy.*

I still experience the Holy Spirit's supernatural peace throughout the day, which is honestly a miraculous sensation I wasn't quite expecting. *Thank you, Lord. I never thought I would be keeping it together like this.* But that peace nonetheless mingles on and off with other extreme emotions—sadness, disillusionment—that surface and stick through the night. As C.S. Lewis wrote, "In grief, nothing stays put." Sometimes, I spiral deep into the darkness and don't even care to stop myself—bitter, angry, cynical.

Let's just say tonight is one of those "very, very cynical" nights. *Three full years strictly bedridden. Only one year and three months married.* Is this God's abundance? What kind of rainbow promise fades after one year? What is the point of receiving a gift if it's going to be ripped away? Does God love other Christians more than me? What's good for the goose is good for the gander, Lord—and last time I checked, I'm a pretty nice goose. So where's my divine VIP treatment? I refuse to take off my wedding ring. Ever. *Great. Now I've officially transformed into crazy Miss Havisham from Great Expectations, clinging to the past like a Dickensian ghost in lace and ashes.*

Apparently, even the greats like Martin Luther and Charles Spurgeon suffered from depression. *Does that even help me? Ugh. How I miss Matt.*

Psalm 88 has been a lifeline at least. Yeah, *that one*. The darkest Psalm in the Bible. The one no one puts on coffee mugs. Psalm 88:6 states, "You have put me in the lowest pit, in the darkest depths." I might just start an Etsy brand at this point—*Christian Lament Merch Because Let's Get Real: Life Stinks*. At least Scripture gets it. It records very real suffering without sugarcoating it. Disease, murder, racism, adultery, famine, war, death.

I pull the blanket over my head, willing the world to disappear. And then, in the darkness, I remember Auntie Sue's words on the phone and whisper—"Lord, if You are good, if You love me, please encourage me. Any shape, any form. Sometime this birthday week.

Just remind me that Matt is alive and still loves me, and that this suffering isn't for nothing. Please. I beg You."

𝄞

Buzz.

I jolt awake in the morning to my phone vibrating, and squint at the screen.

A text from Sevan—"Happy birthday, Lars. I love you and Matt loves you and I just have this feeling that Matt is CELEBRATING your birthday in Heaven right now!"

I roll my eyes, then crumble, tears spilling over. *Sure, Sevan. I love you and appreciate the gesture, but if God really wanted Matt celebrating my birthday, why didn't He just keep him here?*

After forcing myself to type a polite reply, I swipe over to my email tab and the first message in my inbox stops my breath cold.

MattSilverman3943xxxxxx@gmail.com.

The room tilts, figuratively and literally.

My pulse starts hammering.

I stare at the screen, frozen. I can hardly believe my eyes. *Check the timestamp. If this email says it was sent from "Eternity," I'm officially losing it.*

My hands tremble as I click the email open, and my eyes feast over the words:

> "Kitten, I don't know where you'll be in the world today, but I hope this message finds its way to you at the right timing. Play the attached video."

I rush to click the video file, and there's Matt, sitting there wrapped in his blue "Science Rocks" hospice sweatshirt, his eyes glowing. His deep voice sings into my eardrums:

"Kitten, happy birthday. I want you to know I love you and am celebrating you in Heaven right now. I know I'm not with you, but that doesn't mean I can't be celebrating too."

I hit pause. My heart pounds against my ribs. Wait… *Celebrating you in Heaven right now.* The exact same words Sevan just texted me: "Matt is CELEBRATING your birthday in Heaven right now!"

My hands clutch the phone tighter. Tears blur the screen. *God, did You actually just answer my prayer for a sign this week? On my birthday no less?*

I can't breathe, can't think. Only one thought crashes through instantly—*YES!* God literally just answered my prayer and told me through this insane coincidental timing that Matt *is* alive! Even *celebrating*!

What are the chances Sevan would say specifically *that* to me on my birthday *and* that Matt would prepare in advance to send me a birthday message that says the exact same thing? My entire body leaps with joy as I immediately sit upright, processing it all:

Matt is alive!
Heaven is real and Matt is there!
There is more to me than this dumb, sick, earthly body!
God must have a loving purpose for all this suffering if He loves me enough to send me a sign from Matt in Heaven on my birthday!

My thoughts race, from exhilaration to sheer shock. *Matt must have set up a scheduled email in advance or lined someone up to send the email today. Jeff? Joel?* It doesn't matter. There he is, staring at me through the screen, with that quiet strength I miss so much. I press play again, and Matt continues speaking:

"Jesus' resurrection means we'll be in Heaven together. For all eternity. We'll get to travel and cook together—all those things you wanted to do that we couldn't, we'll do. We're Christians. We'll only be separated for a little while."

I choke on a sob. He really believed it. And now, I think...*I finally do too.*

Wow. I tremble as the realization settles in deep. *For all eternity.* Everything I proclaimed at his memorial—it's not just words.

It's truth.

There *is* more to our existence than the bag of basic blessings this short life offers. All of this will be made up. I don't need to fear missing out on Matt's love anymore. Just last week, my pastor friend, Shant, even comforted me. "Heaven is the final state of glorification of all believers, in all its majesty. Glorification is the ultimate state of bliss, and if it does *not* include marriage, that means it must be even better than marriage. There's something about the love there that we just don't understand yet. But we know that the intimacy you will experience with Matt there will be far richer than your marriage here because it will be purified. Sinless. Elevated."

Wait, let me process this again. The minute Matt died, eternity wasn't theoretical anymore. Matt was either alive in this Heaven place or not. I know deep in my heart the Bible is true because it is the Word of God, but the Holy Spirit just graciously reassured me in a surprising, extra-Biblical way—*Matt's in Heaven! He's alive! He's even celebrating my birthday!*

While dying on the cross, Jesus told the thief dying next to him: "[T]oday you will be with Me in paradise." Luke 23:43. So... because paradise truly does await us, real joy and peace can only be found in surrendering to God's plan for our temporal lives, because we know our stories do not end in this life. *Right?!*

Right.

Life does *not* end with suffering or happiness on this fallen earth.

There *is* more to the story after death. *Eternal glory. And there's a reason the script is written this way. I just don't have access to the whole screenplay yet. The Author knows how the story ends—and it's not in ashes.*

I immediately call Sevan. "Sevan! I asked God for a sign of encouragement a few nights ago, and He just gave it to me. Matt is celebrating today!"

Sevan gasps when she hears about Matt's timely video message that mirrored her text. "So cool, Lars! I even asked God this morning to use me to encourage you somehow. I guess God made me collude with Matt, without us even knowing."

God's little winks keep coming the rest of the day.

Winston's wife Kimmy posts on my Facebook wall—"I know your birthday is hard with the grief, but please know that Matt is celebrating you in Heaven." *Wow.*

Miriam's birthday card reads, "May you feel wonderfully celebrated by all your loved ones today, especially Matt. I'm sure he is!"

A text arrives from my friend Rachel: "Lara, I know it must be hard today, but God is telling you the story isn't over." Forty minutes later, a text from Lisa—"I'm praying for you. Remember, your story isn't over. Heaven will reveal God's glory in all your grief."

Coincidence? *No.*

The story isn't over.

When I call Joel, he denies sending the email on Matt's behalf, but jokes, "Heaven's got an IT department now? Who's their service provider—Holy Spirit Broadband?"

Finally, around 4 P.M., Mom steps into my room holding an envelope. "A birthday card from Judge Santin." I tear it open, scanning the words. One line stands out—"Please consider writing a book on your journey."

I blink. *That's interesting.* Winston called last week to tell me the same thing. Didn't think much of it. *Could this be a direction from You, Lord?*

The next week, one of Auntie Ann's acquaintances randomly emails me. I don't know him, but he says he's been encouraged as a Christian by our journey. His last line? "Please consider writing a book."

Okay, Lord. You couldn't have made this job offer any clearer than if You gave me a burning bush with smoke inscribing, *Lara's Memoir Coming Soon.* But how can I give people hope when I don't have a happy ending with Matt, or healing myself?

After praying for guidance, the next few weeks I stumble upon Ephesians 2:10 three different times—"For we are God's handiwork, created in Christ Jesus to do good works, which God prepared in advance for us to do."

And just like that, I know.

If God is calling me to do a "good work" by sharing my journey and lessons learned, He'll use my suffering in ways I can't imagine. *Using evil for good.*

A light bulb clicks on in my soul.

There is a purpose to all this suffering. Just like God's been teaching me all along. Wow.

Maybe—just maybe—I *can* trust God is good, even in the losses. Even in the pain. Even without knowing the specific purpose for everything. And more importantly, maybe I can *love* Him again. Love Him, *for Him*, not for what He can do for me.

For the first time in a very long time, hope doesn't feel so far away.

I'll write the book, Lord. But could You also throw in a surprise book deal and a catchy title?

How about *Purring Through Sorrow: Kitten's Guide to Grief?*

64

The Story Is Not Over

I stand here, June 2025, eleven months after Matt's surprise birthday email, bow in hand, violin tucked under my chin. *My Heart Will Go On.*

Each note hums through my bones. Then, like a sudden tremor, an earthquake rattles the spinning room. My knees wobble, and I sink into a chair, gripping the cushion. A breath, then a smile.

Something shifted in me after Matt's email—*Matt is thriving in Heaven. The story is not over. Eternal glory. This pain is all temporary.*

Embracing joy, though, still felt like betraying Matt at first. One morning, I told Mom I felt guilty laughing without Matt here. Then, my friend Trina's Instagram story a few hours later—"Joyful perseverance means we can both grieve what's gone while savoring what's good." *Joy in grief. How could I forget so fast?* That night, while cracking an Armenian joke to Pops, it struck me. Why not turn my pain into comedy? Why not laugh a little again? *Why not?*

So I did. *The show must go on.* I grabbed my phone camera and tripod, and pretended to be a funny old Armenian grandma in a headscarf ranting about how young Armenians can't cook. Normal people process grief with therapy. I processed mine by yelling about dolma. Ninety skits later, I was an accidental comedian, making thousands of Armenians laugh on social media. I was an aching paradox—giving others joy but carrying tears at night.

But it was classic God, giving me joy through performance, yet again. I never imagined my life taking this turn. *Comedian by day. Sobbing 'Lord, this wasn't the plan' by night.* But hey, at least it's dramatic enough for a Netflix special: *From Courtroom to Comedy: The Career Pivot of the Century.* Apparently, I'm the spiritual love child of Job and Lucille Ball.

Through the laughter, God showed up in other ways. Three random Armenian Christian women who liked my skits contacted me and started walking with me in my grief. An acquaintance emailed me, telling me his non-Christian friends had found my skits, which sparked their interest in Matt's Christian devotionals. *God's still using our secular platform! Comedy, jazz...God uses it all.* Maybe I should rename our channel to "The Accidental Evangelists."

Continuing Matt's legacy also gave me profound purpose, including sharing our story on Christian blogs, selling "Why Not" hats for Matt's birthday to raise funds for Haiti, and publishing a paperback book containing Matt's prolific sermon collection on his birthday. The Haiti team dedicated a science classroom at their new school in Matt's memory, and Auntie Ann set up a campership at **Camp Arev** in his name, to provide financial aid to those in need.

And today, as I play the violin, I catch Pops standing at the kitchen door—eyeing me with pride—and my heart warms. *God's love comes full circle.* Once, Matt stood in Daly City, watching. Different eyes, same love. God's gifts of love and His presence, unwavering.

Indeed, the past year, God—who "comforts us in all our troubles" (2 Corinthians 1:3)—has continued to pursue my heart, whispering comfort at dozens of timely moments. A few examples:

One—While watering our garden one day, a single white

butterfly appeared before me. Strange, since I'd never seen butterflies there. It felt like comfort from God somehow, as I've read butterflies can represent new life. I'm careful not to believe in "new age/feel good spirituality," so I asked God to explicitly confirm this was the Holy Spirit's comfort. Two days later, a card arrived with three large white butterflies on it and a Biblical encouragement about grief over Matt. *Thank you, Lord!*

Two—The night before Matt's birthday, while crying, I opened my *Daily Streams* devotional: "The Lord is near to the brokenhearted. Remembering that an eternal Kingdom awaits God's children fills us with His peace in our present sufferings and grief over death."

Three—On March 4, my two year wedding anniversary, a package from my friend Evelina arrived in the mail—a flowery pink devotional book titled *A Hug from God*. Two hours later, another friend texted me, without knowing about the book: "God knows exactly when we need a hug Lara, doesn't He?" *Miracles. I couldn't make this stuff up.*

Four—On the one-year anniversary of Matt's death a week ago, I woke up to the *YouVersion* app daily verse, Revelation 21:4, which sets forth Heaven's healing promise: "He will wipe every tear from their eyes. There will be no more death or mourning or crying or pain, for the old order of things has passed away." Later that night, during our nightly Bible study, Pops landed on John 11:25: "I am the resurrection and the life. The one who believes in Me will live, even though they die." On a day heavy with longing, God gave me precisely the comforting verses I needed about how Matt is alive in Heaven.

Five—I'm deeply ashamed to admit my grief journey involved some serious backsliding again, especially last Thanksgiving seven months ago, when my average prayer was a cross between an overheated legal deposition and an unhinged Yelp review—"Dear God, one star. You disappointed me, isn't that correct?" One night I even bitterly prayed, "I'm done with You, Lord. I'm sad You are who You are."

Yet even then, God found me. Some hours later, a friend—unaware of my meltdown—ironically texted me Job 13:24, where Job, in his own grief, broke down and called God his "enemy."

Four days later, one of my devotionals featured the story of Job—"Do you feel God is cruelly picking on you in your suffering? When you bitterly resent His will, You wrongfully question His wisdom, just as Job did. Job's suffering was intended to showcase God's glory because Job would ultimately stay faithful to God despite his severe losses, but it also refined Job by cleansing him of pride. What about you? Has pride blinded you into doubting God's faithfulness? Repent and draw near to Him."

Chills. Half an hour later, I randomly opened my friend Edward's Instagram story only to read, "Have you turned away from Jesus? Come back to the Giver of life." *You never let me go, Lord.* I immediately repented and wept.

The next morning, God's forgiveness met me, swift and overwhelming. A curious phrase stirred in my spirit: *Dine with Me.* I blinked in confusion. *Dine, Lord?* But that night, during Pops' Bible reading, we came across Revelation 3:20, where Jesus, *after* rebuking a church for having lukewarm faith, followed up with a stunning invitation to return and feast with Him—"If anyone hears my voice and opens the door, I will come in and eat with that person, and they with me."

In that tender moment, I realized that *Dine with me* was the Holy Spirit's way of saying He had already welcomed me back to the table upon my repentance, no questions asked. I could be a solid defense witness for 2 Timothy 2:13—"If we are faithless, He remains faithful, for He cannot disown Himself." After all, isn't that what a good father does? He welcomes you back home, feeds you dinner, and yes, sometimes rebukes you when you're on the wrong path. Just read God's proclamation in Revelation 3:19: "Those *whom I love* I rebuke and discipline."

What is more, God used His rebuke of my pride to perform redemptive heart surgery on me, thus finally reshaping not just my attitude in grief, but my entire perspective on life. A few months ago, during a season of intentional fasting from certain foods as a means to draw closer to God (my first time trying it, *e.g.*, Acts 14:23, Daniel 9:3), I experienced some powerful spiritual breakthroughs. God finally opened my eyes to the root of my problem the last eight years: the prideful belief that God is not good because I have unfulfilled, good desires. Matt, good health, career, children. You name it.

Every believer wrestles with this at some point. As a mentor told me once, "Disappointment is a cancer eating up the heart of believers." I believe this is because, in Sunday School, they don't tell us our Christian calling involves suffering; that some of us will live with chronic pain; that the Bible never promises a spouse, a specific job or career, or good health. But the Bible is filled with countless examples of God saying "no" to good desires. *E.g.*, Paul and his painful "thorn," David's longing to build God's temple, Moses' yearning to enter the Promised Land.

Living with unfulfilled longings is thus completely *normal* in the life of faith. Even God's most faithful "were still living by faith when they died. They did not receive the things promised." Hebrews 11:13. Explain that, you "prosperity gospel" fraudsters! This means it's bad theology when Christians say, "If there's a Godly desire on your heart, God put it there and will grant it." Sure, it seems God does plant *some* desires in us so that He will fulfill them—but He definitely doesn't operate that way in all cases. Matt wanted to continue his missions work, and we both wanted to have a long, beautiful marriage with children. When Christians say "God is faithful," it does *not* mean He will grant all our good desires. "Many are the plans in a person's heart, but it is the Lord's purpose that prevails." Proverbs 19:21.

While considering this idea seriously, I finally realized I had completely missed the mark of what it even means to be a disciple of Christ—a *servant*. Colossians 3:24; Ephesians 6:6. Paul, James, and Peter all opened their epistles identifying themselves as "servant[s] of Jesus Christ." Jesus, too, "made Himself nothing," coming as a "servant" whose only desire was to do His Father's will. Philippians 2:7.

As Jesus' disciples, we are called to follow in His footsteps by desiring our Master's will over our own. That comes at a cost. Jesus did not sugarcoat it—"Whoever wants to be my disciple must deny themselves and take up their cross daily and follow me. For whoever wants to save their life will lose it, but whoever loses their life for me will save it." Luke 9:23-24. As His servants, our response must echo Galatians 2:20: "I have been crucified with Christ and I no longer live, but Christ lives in me."

Choosing to follow Christ, then, means choosing to die—to my personal rights, cherished interests, and self-will—so that His plans, His purposes, and His will prevail. Many Christians secretly fear God's will because (a) we know He allows suffering and says "no" to some earthly desires, but (b) *we* are first in our lives as our own masters. We don't want to die to self. Who does?

But are we willing to take Jesus' words seriously? To take up our cross and make the Lord first in our hearts, souls, and minds? To surrender our choices, lay even our good desires on the altar as Abraham did with Isaac, and obey without bargaining? Do we want to hear "Well done, good and faithful servant" at the end of our lives like Matt did? If I'm following His lead, my flesh and desires will be crucified. He gave up everything for me, so why shouldn't I?

Nor are we mere servants—we are simultaneously beloved "heirs" of a royal inheritance, welcomed into God's eternal Kingdom through His great love for us (Romans 8:17). Our service flows not from obligation but from devotion to our Father.

This concept of servanthood has permanently reframed my perspective on my entire purpose on earth. As Matt tried to instill in me, the Christian's aim is not obtaining blessings but fulfilling the specific good works God prepared for us to do to further His Kingdom. God is not sitting up there to fulfill our desires. Instead,

He has preordained the best assignment for each of us, a unique place where He needs each one of us to serve His specific *purpose*.

Sometimes that sacred purpose requires God to withhold even our good earthly desires. For some, that purpose may simply be declaring God's abiding goodness even in the face of great losses. It's a hard pill to swallow. But it's the way of the cross. As Pastor Joe Sweet preached once, "The American dream is not the gospel. It's an idol. Blessings come and go. ... We either quit, judge God, and walk away because we're not getting our way, or we submit in faith."

Make no mistake—in a world where babies die young and new parents are lost to cancer, God's definition of the "best assignment" often looks downright mysterious. But as Augustine wrote, "If you understand, it is not God you understand." Through countless tears, I've finally accepted that some things we won't get answers to until eternity. As Proverbs 3:5 says, "Trust in the Lord with all your heart and lean not on your own understanding[.]" His ways truly are "higher."

God has given me some answers, though. One day, while wrestling with Psalm 84:11 ("[N]o good thing does he withhold"), my devotional app spoke to my heart—"God doesn't withhold blessings because He loves the sufferer less. Nor does He grant desires because the recipients are more deserving or qualified. We are all the chief of sinners who are given undeserved grace." All we can say, as Elisabeth Elliot did, is that "[w]hen the answer is no, ... [f]ar greater things are at stake. There is another level, another kingdom, an invisible kingdom which you and I cannot see now but toward which we move and to which we belong."

Moreover, I've realized that the "good thing[s]" God promises not to withhold are *not* the earthly blessings we often long for. They refer to His presence, His peace. Christians live victoriously not because we get every physical *desire*, but because we have Him, the living water who satisfies our spiritual thirst, which is our greatest *need* (Psalm 107:9).

All of these heart transformations reflect God's patient,

persistent work of reshaping me into an entirely different person. Still, let's not romanticize it—my spiritual growth "arc" over the last eight years hasn't been a graceful ascent. Picture a cartoon pendulum on espresso—swinging wildly between weak faith, seething anger, and bursts of unshakable hope and faith. I've wrestled God like a raccoon attacking a dumpster—scrappy, stubborn, and absolutely convinced I deserved to win. I never truly feared losing my faith. Just sacrificing my will to His.

But turns out God doesn't microwave us into spiritual maturity. He slow-cooks us through sorrow, walking us inch by inch from defiance to surrender, from resignation to true acceptance. I'm now living proof—God can change a heart, even after years of wrestling. In some ways, I give myself compassion; it's hard to die to your own life dreams and accept a cup of suffering, isn't it? On the other hand, I feel sorrow for having wasted so many years being bitter. Now, I'm asking you: If God has promised to complete the good work He began in you (Philippians 1:6)—gently softening your heart to trust His purposes in the end—why not surrender sooner than I did?

I hope when you look at Matt's life, you see a man who trusted God through the fire—and you think, *that's the road I want to walk*. And when you look at mine, I hope you see someone who wanted God's gifts more than God, but nonetheless was *still* held by His grace through the fire—and you think, *if she could change in the end, maybe I can too*.

When all is said and done, my great "why" questions still remain. Why the genocides? Why does He prevent some tragedies but allow others to unfold?

But like Job—who repented after God's thunderous reply to his grievances—I've finally come to recognize my immature insistence that God's justice and timing mirror mine, and that divinity should operate within the logic of human fairness. It took me eight years, but I truly do believe now that He *is* working out good purposes far beyond what I can comprehend. Even then, God has graciously given me some answers (for why He allows suffering) to fuel my faith. These years have been a physical and emotional battlefield, yet they've taught me more about Christ and unseen spiritual realities than a lifetime of ease ever could.

But God's grace always has the final word, doesn't it? At the end of the Book of Job, God blesses Job with *double* what he lost, showcasing God's "grief to glory" redemptive pattern. Job 42:10. Matt and I certainly didn't get that kind of ending. But one night recently, I asked Jesus directly—*Do You promise restoration like Job's to those of us who don't see redemption on this side of Heaven?*

Three days later, Auntie Nanor texted me that she was praying Isaiah 61 over me. Hours later, my friend Liana's weekly Christian newsletter landed in my inbox, featuring Isaiah 61:7—"[Y]ou will inherit a *double* portion in your land, and everlasting joy will be yours." The message wrote, "You might not feel blessed now, but God promises to redeem your pain, now or in eternity. What a promise for those facing grave circumstances."

I immediately thanked God for reminding me that His rewards aren't limited to this life. Easter always follows the cross. Maybe that old Wrigley's Doublemint Gum jingle was on point—*Double your pleasure, double your fun.* Maybe even *double your redemption. The story isn't over.*

As far as redemption on earth, at least I've made surprising peace with my suffering. Not because it stopped. (No changes: still bedridden most of the day; getting in a car remains a once-a-month thrill.) No, it's because I've come to know *who* God is, as a person. Job said it best—"My ears had heard of You, but now my eyes have seen You." Job 42:5.

No, He's not the God I once imagined.

He doesn't always rescue and heal.

He doesn't always explain.

But He *is* the God who gave me joy in grief.

The One who gave me His nonstop presence, and drew near even when I pushed Him away.

The One who turned my lost dreams into streams in the desert.

The One who slipped surprises and resurrections into my dungeon.

The One who didn't erase my grief after His dream to me but conquered it with love—by gifting me the love of my life right when I needed Godly comfort the most.

The One who called me to bear a cross of debilitating weakness so that His strength would be displayed through my frail body.

The One who showed me that true joy lies not in the "perfect" Armenian life but in Him.

At the end of the day, I'm still a believer because God's "goodness and love" truly did "follow me all the days of my life." Psalm 23. If He didn't show up in my suffering, I wouldn't be writing this book—I would've given up long ago.

So God's presence got me this far, but what lies ahead?

What about that dream from God three and a half years ago now? When He said He was "coming to take [me] home." It still sits etched in my heart, and I've cried rivers asking God what good it did for me to know that in advance. But looking back now, I can see some glimpses of His mercy—hints, really, of a bigger picture I'll probably only fully understand in Heaven. I believe God gave me that dream—though my death wasn't strictly imminent—for these reasons:

To show me that His will was to heal me *there*, not *here*—and to push me toward final acceptance of the neurological pain, like Paul's "thorn in the flesh"—perhaps so I'd stop going mad chasing cures, bewildered at why He wasn't blessing my efforts.

To focus my eyes on eternity, so I'd be ready whenever my time comes.

To comfort me that He wouldn't let me suffer this debilitating pain for a lifetime, which, sadly, is also why I've believed and grieved that my death will come sooner rather than later.

To encourage me not to give up by living fully and making my work on earth count in my remaining time, despite the severe pain.

To prepare me to love and marry a man with cancer. The dream reshaped my entire view of death—and Matt's illness. Most people wouldn't risk loving someone with cancer. Maybe the dream prepared my heart for the kind of faith and perspective that love would require, helping me choose joy in the time we had.

Some of these reasons might be right. Some might be wrong. One thing is abundantly clear—*God is preparing me for a new season now.*

A month ago, my friend Kelly sent me a sermon clip about the disciples caught in the storm. The pastor declared, "If God is coming soon to take you Home, He's saying: Do not fear—I am with you." The next morning, two of my devotional apps featured that exact same storm story. I blinked at my phone screen. *Is this a message from You, Lord? Is it finally time?*

Then came the flood. The next few days, Joshua 1:9 showed up everywhere I turned—"Be strong and courageous. Do not be afraid; do not be discouraged, for the Lord your God will be with you wherever you go." The following week, Isaiah 41:13 echoed loud and clear, three separate times—"I am the Lord your God who takes hold of your right hand, and says to you, 'Do not fear; I will help you.'"

Even Sara, who hadn't texted me in a year, sent Isaiah 43:2 out of the blue—"I feel like God wants you to have this verse for this season: 'When you pass through the waters, I will be with you... when you walk through the fire, you will not be burned.'" Later that night, my third devotional stated, "Could God be preparing you to face a terrifying valley? No matter what difficult circumstances come your way, remember the battle is the Lord's. He will protect you and see you through." *Okay, now I know a storm's about to break. Lord, You're preparing me to be brave.*

I immediately cried as I prayed—*Are You finally about to take me Home?* The next morning, I opened my devotional and there it was—Psalm 23:4: "[T]hough I walk through the valley of the shadow of death, I will fear no evil; for You are with me; Your rod and Your staff, they comfort me" (NKJV). Coincidence? I doubt it. After all, God gave me Psalm 23 just two months before Matt died.

So here I am today. Violin in hand, spirit braced, convinced that God is declaring—*I'm finally about to deliver on My promise to take you Home.*

Whether that turns out right or wrong in the near future, I don't know.

Here's what I *do* know.

No matter when Christ comes for me in this life, I have a quiet, inner joy I never expected to find in such grief. Why?

Because it's finally anchored in eternity.

Funny, right? The girl who once thought healing was the only happy ending now finds victory in just remaining a Christian in this fire. Turns out, *that's* what makes the God of the universe proud. Not the high-powered career, not the courtroom wins.

Just faith that refuses to crack.

Faith that, though tested, emerges refined, like gold through fire.

Faith that knows this life is just a trailer for the real thing.

Because Christians die, only to live. And we victoriously live, even while we're dying. We're not escapist loonies with unwarranted optimism. We're realists with eternal insurance. There's a big difference.

So knowing that God—and Matt—is joyfully waiting to welcome me into eternity some day, why can't I be joyful even as I grieve today? Jesus said, "Blessed are you who weep now, for you will laugh" (Luke 6:21). C.S. Lewis wrote, "Joy is the serious business of Heaven."

And here's the kicker—if I can still crack a joke after eight years of suffering, doesn't that say something about a good God who always prevails?

That Satan bimbo came at me with countless plays—career loss, mystery diagnoses, chronic pain, three years of strict isolation, grief, the loss of my husband and all my dreams—and still, here I am.

Acting as a comedian.

Laughing.

Writing a memoir, literally on a bed lying down with my head spinning.

I mean, is this really the best Satan's band of half-witted demons can do?

What's more, when Jesus really *does* come to take me Home someday, Jesus said I'll just land straight in "paradise." Think Hawaii on steroids, people. Does that sound like something to fear? As theologian Dietrich Bonhoeffer said, standing on the brink of literal death: "This is the end—for me, the beginning of life." That's why I plan to sing off stage with a smile, whenever that time comes.

This is what it means to be more than conquerors in Christ.

This is getting excited about what awaits me beyond the veil of this earth.

This is fighting to live here, but trusting God's will at the end of the day.

This is clinging to what Job said—"Though He slay me, yet will I hope in Him" (Job 13:15). *I kind of like that Job guy now. What great faith.*

Alas, I still don't know why God diverged me from law, but hey, God hasn't "wasted" my brain. Here I am, pouring it onto these pages, for a reason only He knows.

But I have a feeling it's a good one.

And while I didn't get to be a prosecutor or a judge, suffering doesn't get the last line in this script. Not when God's the playwright.

So who knows? Maybe God's saving me for the big leagues. Maybe one day I will judge fallen angels. Check out 1 Corinthians 6:3, baby. Wouldn't that be just God's style? Redeeming everything? How's that for a comeback career?

The Story Is Not Over

Maybe someday I'll stand in the courts of Heaven before the throne of the most famous Judge in the universe—God—and state: "Good morning, Your Honor. My name is Lara Silverman, and I represent the Everlasting Kingdom of Jesus Christ."

Now *that* is a performance I wouldn't mind giving.

For now, I close my eyes, violin bow resting in my hands, and whisper, "Not my will, but Thine, be done. Give me life. Give me joy."

It's like Shakespeare said, isn't it? *All's well that ends well.*

But Christians sing a deeper truth still—*All's well, even when it ends in ashes.*

Because we know the Composer.

Because we trust His final movement.

Because even in the blaze, there's a redemptive melody no flame can silence.

A melody we can sing through the fire.

Bottom line?

God didn't hold up His end of the deal.

But there was never a deal to begin with.

Matt is in Heaven, waiting to continue the story with me—whenever I get there.

And finally, I think I can forgive God for the last eight years.

Even for taking Aunt Jackie.

Because the story isn't over.

Not even close.

Epilogue

The curtain falls. The lights dim. But the story, of course, goes on. Not just mine, but yours. The Author is still at work, writing beyond what we can see. I leave you here with quiet echoes of the themes I've tried to convey:

One—God wants His people to experience joy in their grief.

Two—Living for eternity allows us to experience true joy and live more fully in this life, because we won't be paralyzed by idolizing temporary blessings here.

Three—Our time in this world is fleeting. Take risks and make the most of every opportunity to serve God. Whether living or dying, live to the fullest today and have a "why not" attitude.

Four—Grief is not the end of the story for the believer. We can persevere despite our losses because life does not end with suffering or happiness on this fallen earth.

Five—Suffering, though often unexplainable, is never wasted. God has a mysterious good purpose for allowing all suffering, including testing and proving the genuineness of our faith, furthering the gospel, showcasing His glory, refining our character, allowing us to experience deeper intimacy with Him, preparing us for eternal roles in Heaven, and creating our eternal glory.

Six—Nothing will stop God's will. Even in the most miserable pit, God can do resurrections and miracles, if it is His will.

Seven—God does not dole out earthly blessings based on differing measures of His love.

Eight—God walks intimately beside us in our sorrow and never lets go, even when we want to walk away.

Nine—Our worth and joy is not found in earthly accomplishments or blessings, but in Christ.

Ten—Sometimes we hear from God, but misunderstand what

He means. We must take our convictions seriously, but never put our ultimate hope in a given outcome.

If you follow Jesus, I look forward to meeting you in Heaven, where the final Act is one of eternal joy! If you do not, consider inviting Him into your life. Why not? You just might be surprised. He loves you, and the best part of the story is yet to come.

Appendix One
Pictures

Matt and Lara Silverman One-Year Anniversary Haiti Fundraiser, March 2024

Matt in Alaska on "Make a Wish" Trip in 1999 after his first cancer went into remission, age 16

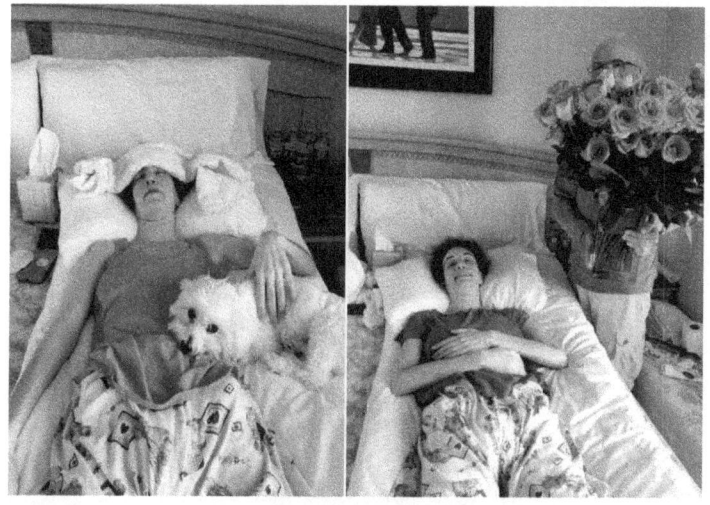

Lara at 90 pounds, bedridden but smiling, with father Vayel holding 50 roses a friend sent just in time, without knowing it was Lara's birthday

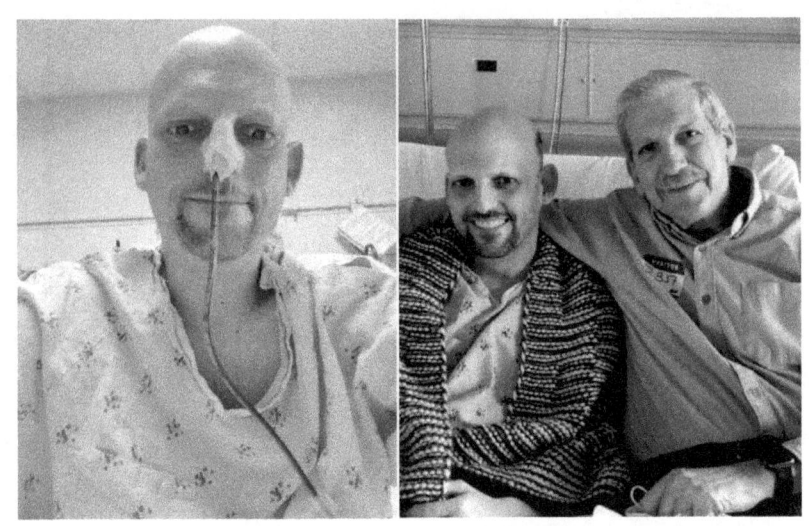

Matt almost dying, still smiling, in February 2023 with father Joel

Lara singing jazz for the first time again, standing upright after three years bedridden, still 100 pounds

Lara's first walk outside, away from her home, after four years

Engagement on Lara's 35th birthday

Matt and Lara performing a skit at Family Engagement Party

Lara and her sister Sevan

Lara's Bachelorette Party with balloons

First real date at a restaurant, Valentine's Day church dinner

Lara's first time back at her church, CACC, after five years

Bible Verse Inscription on Pulgas Water Temple: Isaiah 43:20

Matt and Lara's Wedding, March 4, 2023

Matt and Lara singing "Miracle of Miracles" from Fiddler on the Roof

Joel and Lara, and Matt and Pops at "Armenian pizza" night

Marie Antoinette & Louis XVI

Golden Girl No. 1 Arax Aunty, Pops, Mom, Anna, and Joel as pack of M&M's

Matt and Lara in 1940s gear, and Matt trying on fancy new wardrobe wearing his beloved Indiana Jones hat

"The Silverman Theater" sign, "Silverman Cottage" sign, and "Kitten Territory" sign

Matt playing Hamlet in "The Love Story Goes Marital" film

Matt and Lara singing jazz and oldies on "The Silverman Show"

Lara's debut pop/jazz album and violin performances

Winston's Haiti team at one-year anniversary Haiti Fundraiser

Joel, Auntie Ann, Sevan, Matt, Lara, Mom, Pops, and Anna at one-year anniversary Haiti Fundraiser

Matt, Anna, and Cooper sitting with giant bear stuffed animal from Lara

Lara and Joel dancing to "Stayin' Alive" by the Bee Gees

Matt's Youth Group visits Matt in hospice, May 2024

Matt winning craps game in hospice, with brother Jeff and Auntie Ann

Matt's creation of "Roots" board game in hospice

"A Musical Love Story" album Matt gave to Lara

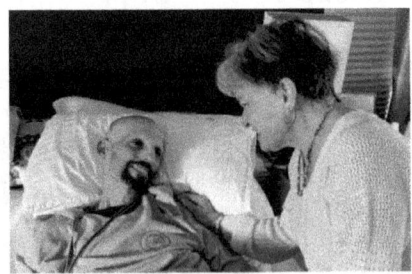

Matt's infectious smile in hospice, with Golden Girl Astrid

Joel and Lara with Matt's picture at Matt's memorial, July 2024

Lara's Armenian comedy channel after Matt's death

Matt doing chemical experiments for church youth, 2015

Matt in Fond Doux Haiti, 2010

Matt preaching in Vietnam, 2019

Appendix Two
Sermon Collections

1. **Resting in the Refiner's Fire: Matthew John Silverman's Reflections on Christian Courage and Perseverance In Pain and Suffering**

   E-book and Physical Paperback for purchase on Amazon:
   https://a.co/d/1VoF491

2. **Remaining on the Vine: Matthew John Silverman's Reflections on Christian Character, Growth, and Maturity**

   E-book for purchase on Amazon:
   https://a.co/d/4OZov1c

3. **Courageous Faith: Matthew John Silverman's Reflections on Standing Strong in Society**

   E-book for purchase on Amazon:
   https://a.co/d/3GmgHvg

To read blog articles and testimonies:
https://medium.com/@matthewjsilverman47
https://medium.com/@larapalanjian

Acknowledgments

I thank my Lord Jesus Christ for loving me, dying for my sins, sustaining my faith and strength, and carrying me every single step.

To my dear friends, extended family, and church community—thank you for loving me on this wild journey. Your intimate prayers, encouragement, and unseen sacrifices stitched strength into the fabric of these pages. You know who you are. I couldn't have survived without you.

To Joel and Anna Silverman—thank you for raising the love of my life and loving me as your own. Sharing in the ecstatic wonder of my love story with you was a true gift from God.

To my mother, father, sister, and Matthew—there are no words deep enough. Thank you for your unwavering and tender love through this storm of physical and emotional pain. For sitting compassionately beside me in the dark, hand in hand, hour after hour. For never once saying no when I asked you to read the Bible or theological books aloud to me. For showing up in the front row of every play, every musical, and every dream. I love you with all of my heart.

And to you, dear reader—thank you so much for giving me your precious time. If this memoir has touched you, it would mean the world if you would leave a review on Amazon here:

About the Author

Lara Silverman is a Christian author, lawyer, jazz singer, actress, and host of the *Singing Through Fire* podcast. She has played leading roles with professional music and theater companies around the San Francisco Bay Area, including Cinnabar Theater, Golden Thread Productions, Novato Theater Company, and the Sixteenth Street Players.

Lara holds a J.D. from Stanford Law School and a B.A. in both Economics and Political Science from UC Berkeley, where she was one of six finalists for the *University Medal*, Berkeley's highest academic distinction. Before falling seriously ill in 2018, Lara worked for two federal judges and practiced high stakes litigation for three years at *Arnold & Porter Kaye Scholer LLP*, where she specialized in intellectual property, antitrust, and contract cases of all kinds. She is a John Marshall Fellow and a Blackstone Legal Fellow.

In 2023, Lara co-founded *The Silverman Show*—a multifaceted comedy, music, and theology show—and released her debut jazz/pop album as her own music producer in February 2024. In September 2024, she debuted as *Mrs. Serious* in her solo Armenian comedy show online, amassing upwards of 300,000 views on individual videos on social media.

Lara's writing has been featured in various respected Christian blogs, where her reflections on faith, suffering, and grace have encouraged readers across diverse audiences. Even as she remains mostly bedridden today, she anchors her unwavering hope in God.

To connect and watch Lara's music, comedy, and Christian content on social media:

The Silverman Show YouTube channel:

https://youtube.com/@thesilvermanshow?si=z3Z3Zavikp4YwIci

Facebook page:
www.facebook.com/Lara.palanjian.silverman

Instagram handle: @larapalanjian

www.ingramcontent.com/pod-product-compliance
Lightning Source LLC
Chambersburg PA
CBHW031417150426
43191CB00006B/311